# LEADING FOR EQUITY AND SOCIAL JUSTICE

## Systemic Transformation in Canadian Education

Educational institutions, and in particular educational leaders, play critical roles in identifying and rectifying the many inequities that oppress, marginalize, and exclude individual students, educational actors, and some minoritized groups in Canadian education.

*Leading for Equity and Social Justice* provides a deep look at some of these inequities and injustices and offers transformative leadership as one way for leaders to stimulate, support, and foster equitable and socially just practices in educational institutions. This collection emphasizes the systemic nature of inequality and supports the necessity of systemic change to target not only individuals but also structures, policies, and far-reaching practices. Focusing on various marginalized groups – including the Indigenous community, LGBTQ2S+ peoples, refugees, newcomers, and specific groups of teachers – chapters explore transformative leadership in practice and how to achieve inclusion, respect, and excellence in schools.

Arguing that leadership involves much more than simply putting policy into practice, *Leading for Equity and Social Justice* promotes the need for leaders to recognize their role as advocates and activists.

ANDRÉANNE GÉLINAS-PROULX is a professor of educational administration at Université du Québec en Outaouais.

CAROLYN M. SHIELDS is a professor of educational leadership at Wayne State University.

# Leading for Equity and Social Justice

*Systemic Transformation in Canadian Education*

Edited by
Andréanne Gélinas-Proulx
and Carolyn M. Shields

UNIVERSITY OF TORONTO PRESS
Toronto  Buffalo  London

ISBN 978-1-4875-4250-4 (cloth)      ISBN 978-1-4875-4252-8 (EPUB)
ISBN 978-1-4875-4251-1 (paper)      ISBN 978-1-4875-4253-5 (PDF)

**Library and Archives Canada Cataloguing in Publication**
Title: Leading for equity and social justice : systemic transformation in Canadian
    education / edited by Andréanne Gélinas-Proulx and Carolyn M. Shields.
Names: Gélinas-Proulx, Andréanne, editor. | Shields, Carolyn M., editor.
Description: Includes bibliographical references and index.
Identifiers: Canadiana (print) 20220165408 | Canadiana (ebook) 20220165424 |
    ISBN 9781487542504 (hardcover) | ISBN 9781487542511 (softcover) |
    ISBN 9781487542528 (EPUB) | ISBN 9781487542535 (PDF)
Subjects: LCSH: Educational equalization – Canada. | LCSH: Social justice and
    education – Canada. | LCSH: Transformational leadership – Canada. | LCSH:
    Educational leadership – Canada. | LCSH: Minorities – Education – Canada.
Classification: LCC LC213.3.C3 L43 2022 | DDC 379.2/60971–dc23

This book has been published with the help of a grant from the Federation for the
Humanities and Social Sciences, through the Awards to Scholarly Publications
Program, using funds provided by the Social Sciences and Humanities Research
Council of Canada.

We wish to acknowledge the land on which the University of Toronto Press
operates. This land is the traditional territory of the Wendat, the Anishnaabeg, the
Haudenosaunee, the Métis, and the Mississaugas of the Credit First Nation.

University of Toronto Press acknowledges the financial support of the Government of
Canada, the Canada Council for the Arts, and the Ontario Arts Council, an agency of
the Government of Ontario, for its publishing activities.

Canada Council    Conseil des Arts
for the Arts      du Canada

ONTARIO ARTS COUNCIL
CONSEIL DES ARTS DE L'ONTARIO

an Ontario government agency
un organisme du gouvernement de l'Ontario

Funded by the    Financé par le
Government       gouvernement
of Canada        du Canada

Canadä

# Contents

**Part III: Decentring Discrimination**

# Foreword: Leadership as an Equitable Mission in Canadian Educational Institutions

Several weeks have passed since the chapters in this volume were written, and since then a number of potentially landscape-changing events have occurred. These events have the potential to influence the course of equitable leadership in Canadian educational institutions. One was the murder conviction of Derek Chauvin, the white police officer who pinned George Floyd, an African American man, to the ground for over nine minutes until he died. The entire event was captured on video, contradicting the erroneous initial police version that he died from medical complications (McDonnell, del Rio, Eligon, & Hassan, 2021). The incident and subsequent video prompted outrage in the United States and around the world and was accompanied by demonstrations against racism generally and racist policing and judicial systems in particular (McDonnell et al., 2021; Trinh, 2021). For some, the guilty verdict in the case of Derek Chauvin represented a change in the trajectory of judicial decisions on police actions against racialized groups. Up until this time, the actions of law enforcement personnel in encounters such as this had, for the most part, been endorsed by judicial systems; there have been few convictions of police officers who have injured or killed racialized individuals. The most notorious of these not guilty verdicts was for the beating of Rodney King in the 1990s by members of the Los Angeles police, which was also captured in vivid detail on video.

The US has not been the only country immersed in issues of race and racism. Contrary to a common belief, Canada also has racism issues (Boutilier, Gillis, & Hasham, 2021; Bresge, 2021; Joy, 2021a); it has seen its share of incidents over the years, and in particular, in the past few months. One of these incidents involved the shocking murder of a Muslim family that was out for an evening walk in London, Ontario. Reports indicate that the accused, a twenty-two-year-old white male, drove his truck up onto the sidewalk, intentionally running down the family, killing four of them and seriously injuring the fifth, a nine-year-old boy (Casey, 2021). This was not the only tragic racially motivated event in recent years, however. There have been a number of incidents including the

Quebec City mosque massacre in 2017, where a gunman killed six worshippers and wounded five others, the 2020 murder of a man at a mosque in Rexdale, Ontario, the recent harassment of Black Muslim women in Edmonton (Mosleh, 2021), and increased harassment of people of Asian heritage as the COVID-19 pandemic has continued beyond 2021 (Karamali, 2021; Zhang et al., 2020).

One other significant event, or series of events, to emerge in Canada has been the discovery of children's remains near the grounds of former residential schools for First Nations children. Employing ground-penetrating radar technology, investigators uncovered the remains of 215 children at the site of the former Kamloops Indian Residential School in southern British Columbia. Other discoveries quickly followed, one revealing 715 graves near the former Marieval Indian Residential School in Saskatchewan, and another 182 graves uncovered near the former St. Eugene's Mission School in British Columbia. Tragically, these discoveries undoubtedly represent the tip of a much larger iceberg. More of these discoveries are certain to emerge. The Truth and Reconciliation Commission of Canada (2015) indicates that there may be as many as 6,000 of these unmarked graves on the grounds of what were once 130 residential schools across Canada. These revelations highlight Canada's shameful racist history, wherein First Nations children were forcibly removed from their families and communities and placed in these often-distant institutions in the mistaken belief that they would provide the children with a better education than they could receive in their own communities. Instead, children emerged from these government-sponsored religious institutions traumatized; that is, if they managed to survive their residential ordeals at all, which many did not.

So what does this mean for our institutions and communities? And what does it mean for the future of educational leadership and equity in Canada and elsewhere? On the surface, it would appear that these recent events might prompt the privileged among us to take seriously issues of not just race but also gender, sexual orientation, class, religion, language, culture, and ability, among others, and to do something meaningful about them. These shocking events have spurred, at least in the short term, some of those who are not marginalized on a daily basis to acknowledge the presence of racism – and perhaps other forms of oppression – in their communities. Indeed, there has been no shortage of condemnations of historical and contemporary racism in the media and from politicians as of late (Connolly, 2021). Some reactions have even moved beyond mere rhetoric. In 2021, thousands of people – both Indigenous and non-Indigenous – took part in marches on Canada Day to mourn the thousands of children who perished in residential schools. Canada also appointed its first Inuit governor general in 2021, Mary Simon, from Kuujjuaq in northeastern Quebec. And in the US, as we have seen, the judicial system convicted and sentenced Derek Chauvin to twenty-two and a half years for the murder of

George Floyd. The trajectory of attitudes towards, and actions on, equity issues, then, would seem to be changing, at least on a superficial level.

Despite this apparent promise for equity issues, marginalized groups continue to be cynical, or at best, cautious, about the future (Bowden, 2021; Francis, Kwong, Vega, & Osman; Mester & Spillman, 2021; New York Times Opinion, 2021). They have seen opportunities come and go, without any real changes in their day-to-day lives. Rhetoric around improvements fade after whatever crisis of the time has passed and the status quo endures. For some, though, recent events and these latest revelations and actions represent a "sliver of hope" (Mester & Spillman, 2021). Most acknowledge, however, that if this hope is to be realized changes need to be systemic (Joy, 2021b). Agents of change need to acknowledge that racism, and inequities generally, are systemic in nature – not the product of the actions of a "few bad apples," but of enduring patterns built into the very fabric of our institutions and communities. The systemic or structural nature of racism and inequity is not a straightforward matter, however. It is complicated by the relationship between the lives of individual people and the institutional arrangements that shapes these lives. Shohat and Stam's (1994) view of the nature of systemic racism still applies today. For them, racism is

> both individual and systemic, interwoven into the fabric both of the psyche and of the social system, at once grindingly quotidian and maddeningly abstract. It is not merely an attitudinal issue, but a historically contingent institutional and discursive apparatus linked to the drastically unequal distribution of resources and opportunities, the unfair apportioning of justice, wealth, pleasure and pain. It is less an error in logic, less about "attitudes" than about the deferring of hopes and the destruction of lives. (p. 23)

Systemic change requires nothing less than the development of a new social order – something that many authors refer to in their chapters in this volume. Ideally, this new order would bring with it institutional patterns and individual psyches that promote equity. In this enterprise, people's behaviour and institutional norms, policies, and practices would be aligned with equity.

Educational institutions and, in particular, the leaders who guide them have an important role to play in promoting equity at this crucial juncture of history, and the chapters in this uniquely Canadian volume are valuable tools in this endeavour. In many respects, the chapters that follow provide us with a useful set of guidelines for this important undertaking. Employing Shields's (2003, 2010) idea of transformative leadership, this volume lays out a way forward for educational leadership to stimulate, support, and foster equitable practices in educational institutions and beyond. Among other things, the chapters emphasize the systemic nature of (in)equity, the importance of critique and advocacy, and the necessity of operationalizing leadership as a collective endeavour.

Following Shields (2003, 2010), the chapters in this volume emphasize the systemic nature of inequity and the necessity of generating system-wide change. The authors acknowledge that inequity cannot be reduced to poorly behaving individuals, so-called "bad actors." Instead, inequity extends beyond these individuals – a part of wider patterns that are woven into institutional and community norms, policies, and practices. Changes to equitable patterns, then, in the transformational view that measures reach "deep and wide," requires targeting not just individual people but also the structures, policies, and far-reaching practices that give rise to the actions of these individuals. In this volume, Atleo provides a way of understanding these sorts of transformations. She relates a 4,500-year-old story of the establishment of a new social order: A young *hawith* ("chief"), discouraged by a rapidly diminishing seal population – the main source of nourishment for his household and the wider community – finds a way to lay conventional wisdom and practice aside and establish a completely new way of "being, seeing, and doing." In doing so, he is instrumental in establishing a new social order – one that was capable of sustaining his and other households in the community, allowing many to participate on an equitable footing in a new resource economy. The lesson for the equity-minded here is that equitable institutions and communities can only be realized with the advent of a new social order.

The chapters in this volume also emphasize the importance of a critical understanding of the institutions and communities in which people work and live. Establishing systemic changes and instituting a new social order requires the development of a critical consciousness in all members of the school and school community. Reflecting critically on the circumstances in which they find themselves, including the sometimes difficult-to-identify inequities, allows members of the school community to recognize unstated, implicit, and subtle points of view and the often taken-for-granted conditions that provide the basis for such views and practices. Reflections of this sort can occur when administrators and teachers engage others in critical conversations, sponsor activities that are specifically designed to facilitate such conversations, foster conditions where people feel safe having these sometimes difficult conversations (Ryan, 2016), and ask pointed questions like: "What is happening here?" "Who says this is the way things should be?" "What other purposes are being served?" "Whose voices are being excluded and silenced?" "What action can we take?" and "Who can we enlist to support us?" (Smyth, 1996).

The chapters also highlight the importance of the advocacy component of leadership. Those who act in leadership positions – formal or informal – are not the moral ciphers leadership scholars once thought they were, or at least thought they should be (Greenfield, 1978). Leadership involves much more than simply putting policy into practice. More than this, though, not all policies are equitable, life in schools is a lot more complicated than pre-established frameworks often assume, and equity-minded educators often encounter resistance to their initiatives. The consequence is that those who work in leadership positions need to actively promote equity in their schools and communities; they need to become activists. Among other things, they need to actively attempt to persuade people to embrace equity, provide them with helpful information and resources on equity-related issues, use appropriate language in these efforts, and do their best to avoid preaching at others (Ryan, 2016). Given the fluid power relationships that do not always favour the equity-minded, leaders will need to be strategic in their actions. This means that they will need to position themselves appropriately, work to understand organizational politics, and judiciously choose courses of action that will help them achieve their equity goals.

Some of the chapters also hint at approaching leadership from a collective orientation. This is different than the way in which the general population, organizations, and scholars have often conceptualized leadership. The generally accepted view of leadership sees it as an individual enterprise – as something that resides in individuals (Ryan, 2006). A collective orientation towards leadership does not try to suggest that individuals do not exercise leadership or are not involved in what some would consider leadership activities. Leadership obviously relies on the actions of individuals, and it is in the interest of everyone that particular people exercise the (leadership) skills that they possess. But centring leadership on individuals is problematic for two reasons. First, endowing particular individuals with power over others is inherently exclusive, and ultimately inequitable. Equitable organizations and communities become possible when power is distributed and everyone has the opportunity to influence actions that will have an impact on them. The other reason that individual leadership will not advance equity is that organizations will have to start over when a dominant leader moves on, even if that person was a promoter of equity. For equity to sustain itself, it has to be built into leadership structures rather than rest with a single individual or select group of individuals, so that when individuals in formal (or informal) leadership positions depart, little will change when new members join the organization. This equitable power distribution should ideally extend to the communities that schools serve, making it possible for community members to be part of the leadership structure.

If politicians, policymakers, educators, parents, and community members in Canada and elsewhere are to usher in more equitable schools, institutions, and communities, then they need to take seriously the leadership insights of the authors of the chapters of this volume. Now is the time to push for equitable change. This window of opportunity might not last. We need to take advantage of this moment and make the changes that will make our schools and communities more equitable – and better – places.

James Ryan

# REFERENCES

Boutilier, A., Gillis, W., & Hasham, A. (2021, June 12). "White supremacy is as old as Canada": How a history of hate set the stage for the London attack. *Toronto Star.* https://www.thestar.com/news/canada/2021/06/12/how-southwestern-ontarios -history-with-white-supremacists-set-the-stage-for-the-london-attack.html

Bowden, O. (2021, July 2). "Another political extravaganza?" Muslim academics, community members skeptical about what might be achieved at Islamophobia summit. *Toronto Star.* https://www.thestar.com/news/gta/2021/07/02/another -political-extravaganza-muslim-academics-community-members-skeptical -about-what-might-be-achieved-at-islamophobia-summit.html

Bresge, A. (2021, May 21). About 70 per cent of Black Canadians have experienced racism on a regular or occasional basis, according to study. *Globe and Mail.* https://www.theglobeandmail.com/canada/article-70-of-black-canadians-have -experienced-racism-on-a-regular-or/

Casey, L. (2021, June 7). "Dark day": Police say five pedestrians run down in London, Ont., targeted as Muslims. *Toronto Star.* https://www.thestar.com/politics/2021 /06/07/dark-day-police-say-five-pedestrians-run-down-in-london-ont-targeted -as-muslims.html?li_source=LI&li_medium=thestar_recommended_for_you

Connolly, A. (2021, April 3). Canadians must stand up against "unacceptable" rise in anti-Asian racism: Minister. *Global News.* https://globalnews.ca/news/7734109 /anti-asian-racism-canada-what-to-do/

Francis, A., Kwong, E., Vega, M., & Osman, L. (2021, May 23). 19 Black Canadians on what has changed one year since George Floyd's murder. And what next steps we need to take. *Toronto Star.* https://www.thestar.com/news/gta/2021/05/23 /19-black-canadians-on-what-has-changed-one-year-since-george-floyds-murder -and-what-next-steps-we-need-to-take.html

Greenfield, T.B. (1978). Reflections on organization theory and the truths of Irreconcilable realities: Perspective. *Educational Administration Quarterly, 14*(2), 1–23. doi: 10.1177/0013161X7801400203

Joy, A. (2021a, April 10). We're smug about violent racism in the U.S., but there's blood on Canadian hands, too. *CBC News.* https://www.cbc.ca/news/opinion /opinion-racism-canada-1.5979488

Joy, A. (2021b, April 24). Why the verdict in George Floyd's murder is only a bittersweet glimpse of justice. *CBC News.* https://www.cbc.ca/news/opinion /opinion-derek-chauvin-trial-george-floyd-police-1.5995218

Karamali, K. (2021, March 23). Anti-Asian racism in Canada more "frequent" as report tallies hundreds of attacks during pandemic. *Global News.* https:// globalnews.ca/news/7715260/anti-asian-racism-report-pandemic/

McDonnell, G., del Rio, N., Eligon, J., & Hassan, A. (2021, May 25). A timeline of what has happened in the year since George Floyd's death. *New York Times.* https://www.nytimes.com/2021/05/25/us/george-floyd-protests-unrest-events -timeline.html?action=click&module=Spotlight&pgtype=Homepage

Mester, M., & Spillman, E. (2021, April 21). "Sliver of hope": Relief, caution felt across nation as George Floyd verdict absorbed. *Associated Press*. https://ktla.com/news/nationworld/sliver-of-hope-relief-caution-felt-across-nation-as-george-floyd-verdict-absorbed/

Mosleh, O. (2021, July 4). As Muslim women are attacked in Alberta, a community asks: Can Canada face its Islamophobia problem? *Toronto Star*. https://www.thestar.com/news/canada/2021/07/04/they-only-call-it-a-hate-crime-after-you-get-killed-as-muslim-women-are-attacked-in-alberta-a-community-asks-can-canada-face-its-islamophobia-problem.html

New York Times Opinion. (2021, May 21). "We still aren't safe": 6 Young Americans on George Floyd's Death. *New York Times*. https://www.nytimes.com/2021/05/21/opinion/young-americans-race-blm.html?action=click&module=Opinion&pgtype=Homepage

Ryan, J. (2006). *Inclusive leadership*. San Francisco, CA: Jossey-Bass.

Ryan, J. (2016). Promoting inclusion in Ontario: Principals' work in diverse settings. *International Studies in Educational Administration, 44*(2), 79–93.

Shields, C.M. (2003). *Good intentions are not enough: Transformative leadership for communities of difference*. Lanham, MD: Scarecrow Press.

Shields, C.M. (2010). Transformative leadership: Working for equity in diverse contexts. *Educational Administration Quarterly, 46*(4), 558–89. doi: 10.1177/0013161X10375609

Shohat, E., & Stam, R. (1994). *Unthinking Eurocentrism: Multiculturalism and the media*. New York, NY: Routledge.

Smyth, J. (1996). The socially just alternative to the self-managing school. In K. Leithwood, J. Chapman, D. Corson, P. Hallinger, & A. Hart (Eds.), *International handbook of leadership and administration* (pp. 1097–1131). Dordrecht, Netherlands: Kluwer.

Trinh, J. (2021, May 26). Black activists continue fight for racial justice 1 year after George Floyd's death. *CBC News*. https://www.cbc.ca/news/canada/ottawa/ottawa-activists-racial-justice-fight-1.6040162

Truth and Reconciliation Commission of Canada. (2015). *Honouring the truth, reconciling for the future: Summary of the final report of the Truth and Reconciliation Commission of Canada*. Ottawa, ON: Truth and Reconciliation Commission of Canada. https://publications.gc.ca/collections/collection_2015/trc/IR4-7-2015-eng.pdf

Zhang, W., Chai, L., Fan, J. Wang, P., Wei, X., & Yang, L. (2020). COVID-19, racial discrimination, and psychological distress. *Annals of Epidemiology, 52*, 106. doi: 10.1016/j.annepidem.2020.08.032

# Acknowledgments

This book has been under preparation for several years and owes a debt of thanks to many people whom we will identify below. First, however, we want to acknowledge that much has changed in the world and in Canada since we began the preparation of this volume. Sensitivities have changed due to the murder of George Floyd on 25 May 2020 and the global awareness of the Black Lives Matter movement. In addition, the simultaneously devastating impact of the COVID-19 pandemic; the uncovering of the graves of Indigenous children on and near the properties of former residential schools; the burning heat and raging floods in British Columbia, Oregon, Australia, and Turkey; and ongoing earthquakes in Haiti have all raised awareness of inequity, injustice, and racism the world over. The need for action regarding justice and equity is now even more relevant. Were we just beginning work on this book today, our calls for advocacy and action may have been more pressing and our critique of the status quo more acerbic. Indeed, we may have included chapters addressing different issues entirely. Nevertheless, this volume stands as an appeal, at a point in time, for making education at all levels more inclusive, dialogic, and equitable. Moreover, educators must play an important role in promoting understanding of inequity, including awareness of how the relatively privileged majority benefits from, and is complicit in, the suffering of others. Thus, although we recognize the need for much more work, we hope that the present volume will provide a basis for many useful conversations and for transformative action.

As the editors of this volume, we find it is important to acknowledge the help and the work of all those who supported us during this publication adventure begun in 2019. First of all, we would like to thank our publisher, the University of Toronto Press, and more specifically Meg Patterson, Acquisitions Editor, for her precious advice and trust.

Also, this collective work could not have been realized without the great collaboration of all its authors. We are thankful for their perseverance and hard work to make this project come to fruition. Furthermore, this team work could not have happened without our common Association. We want to recognize the important role of the Canadian Association for the Studies of Educational Administration/Association Canadienne pour l'Étude de l'Administration Scolaire (CASEA-ACÉAS). Its past president, Shelleyann Scott, supported the creation of an equity committee of which this book is one of the results.

We are also truly pleased and grateful that James Ryan, professor at the Ontario Institute for Studies in Education (OISE) at the University of Toronto, accepted our invitation to write the preface of this book. He is one of the few Canadian pioneers who has dedicated his career to inclusive leadership and has blazed a path for more equitable schools in Canada.

On a more personal note, we would like to thank our families for their encouragement, support, and love. Merci infiniment!

Finally, we acknowledge that this book has been published with the help of a grant from the Federation for the Humanities and Social Sciences, through the Awards to Scholarly Publications Program, using funds provided by the Social Sciences and Humanities Research Council of Canada.

We are grateful to all those we have mentioned by name, but also to the hundreds of educators and students who have provided the impetus for these chapters, and whose work for equity, inclusion, and social justice is the foundation for a stronger, more deeply democratic future for Canada.

Carolyn M. Shields and Andréanne Gélinas-Proulx

# LEADING FOR EQUITY AND SOCIAL JUSTICE

# Introduction: Leading for Systemic Educational Transformation in Canada

CAROLYN M. SHIELDS AND ANDRÉANNE GÉLINAS-PROULX

*Canada is the most multicultural country in the world.* (as cited in Park, 2018)
*Young refugees face racism in schools, mostly from teachers.* (CBC, 2018)
*LGBTQ2+ students ... report feeling less safe at school.* (Kosciw, Greytak, Zongrone, Clark, & Truong, 2018)
*Canada has repeatedly chosen to normalize inequality rather than fix the problem.* (Blackstock, 2019)
*Canadians are reluctant to talk about race.* (Robson, 2018)

Students from minoritized[1] backgrounds worldwide face various kinds of discrimination and marginalization in public schools, and as the opening quotations indicate, Canada is not immune. Indeed, racism, homophobia, xenophobia, and various other "-isms" and "-obias" perpetuate both unsafe and uncomfortable conditions for many students in Canada including, but not limited to, those of non-European descent, non-Christians, Indigenous populations, refugees, LGBTQ2+ students, those with disabilities or accents, students who speak a language other than that of instruction, and so forth.

It is important at the outset to acknowledge that in Canada, as in most developed countries, schooling takes place within a wider national historic context of colonialism, domination, and white supremacy. Hence, although there is much that school leaders can do within the context of their organizations to create more equitable and socially just learning environments for all students, it is also important for leaders who consider themselves transformative to both teach about and fight for wider societal reform. Structural racism, implicit bias, and discrimination permeate Canadian life as evidenced by racist graffiti, by racial slurs expressed by prominent politicians and media personnel, by the continued presence of nooses found in various sites,[2] by disproportionate police action against individuals from visible minority groups, and more. The dispossession of Indigenous lands and cultures and the resulting continued unequal educational outcomes are but two more examples of the ways in which, historically, Canadian culture has shaped the conduct of educational institutions. As Lynam, Browne, Kirkham, and Anderson (2007) point out, the position of French theorist Pierre Bourdieu "assumes a link between experience and broader policy and associated ideological structures" (p. 28). Bourdieu introduces the concept of *habitus*, explaining that it represents all of the particular structuring assumptions of a given culture and provides guidance about what is acceptable and what is not permitted within a given field, such as education. We acknowledge that without widespread systemic change in beliefs, values, policies, and practices, education will continue to operate within a system of hegemony and oppression.

This book is intended to highlight some of the ways in which educational institutions marginalize and oppress those from non-dominant cultures, and to suggest ways in which educational leaders may begin to lead for systemic transformation with visions of education that are inclusive, equitable, excellent, and socially just for all students. Before proceeding, we acknowledge that although in many of the chapters leaders are seen as synonymous with the formally appointed school principal, we understand that informal influential leaders exist, and must exist, throughout any organization. Our goal is therefore to address anyone in a position to exercise influence to create schools that are more inclusive, equitable, excellent, and socially just for all.

We acknowledge that our vision requires recognition of the historic, colonial, and hegemonic foundations of the present Canadian educational systems. Hence, the current systemic inequities must be deconstructed and replaced with new and more equitable ideologies, policies, practices, pedagogies, and curricula. In other words, in a time of conflict, crisis, and public unrest, we argue for a complete rethinking and reconstruction of Canadian education. Moreover, given the increasing public awareness of systemic racism and inequity fuelled by the death of George Floyd in the United States in the summer of 2020, the inequitable racial outcomes of the ongoing COVID-19 pandemic, and increasing awareness of racism in Canadian institutions such as the Royal Canadian Mounted Police, Canadian schools and universities, and society as a whole, the time to address inequity is now. The need for this kind of rethinking is also reflected in the recent recommendations of the Advisory Committee on Equity, Diversity, Inclusion, and Decolonization (AC-EDID) of the Federation for the Humanities and Social Science released in April 2021, *Igniting Change*.

To be clear, we start by explaining what we mean by several terms that are often contested, shifting signifiers. We start with the premise that schools should be *inclusive* places, in which everyone is fully accepted and respected without regard to socio-economic status, ability or disability, ethnicity, religion, gender identity, or place of origin. In other words, public schools must embrace everyone regardless of circumstance and welcome multiple perspectives. But we maintain that educational institutions must do more than simply include everyone; they must also create working conditions and learning opportunities that are equitable, in which all may *participate* fully.

Here we define "equitable" in opposition to the commonly used term "equality," which suggests that to be fair, people should be treated the same way. Because each individual is unique, however, with differing strengths, needs, and circumstances, equity is not simply a matter of providing *equal access* to everyone, but of providing differential resources and supports as necessary to ensure equitable achievement and results; equitable treatment thus provides each person with the support and resources necessary to achieve fair, reasonable, and similar *outcomes*. A socially just institution or society would, therefore, strive to ensure equitable distribution of opportunity and outcomes for all.

We also advocate a comprehensive concept of *excellence* that is measured in terms of both individual achievement and public good. Hence, we aim to promote achievement of individual fulfilment and growth not confined to desired academic standards or test scores, but achievement that can also be assessed in terms of socio-emotional and cultural learning. In addition, excellence requires development in terms of civic participation and the creation of a society of mutual responsibility and benefit.

Finally, "social justice," as we conceptualize it, requires acknowledging and striving to overcome injustice wherever it may be found, including the inequitable distribution of power, hegemony, implicit bias, and systemic discrimination including racism, homophobia, xenophobia, and so on. It requires advocacy, activism, and actions to redress policies and practices that marginalize, exclude, or oppress others.

## The Context: An Overview

Despite the questionable BBC claim given above and the common perception that Canada is extremely diverse, it is important to note that the visible diversity experienced by people living in Canada in the twenty-first century is a relatively new phenomenon. As of the 2016 census, Statistics Canada reports that 22.3 per cent of the Canadian population is categorized as "visible minority."[3] This represents a considerable increase from 1960, when visible minorities represented only 2 per cent of the population. By the turn of the century (in 2001), the visible minority population in Canada had increased to 12.9 per cent (Cardozo & Pendakur, 2008, p. 13). Hence, it is likely not an exaggeration to assert that many educators today were educated and prepared for their careers in a time when the need to address diversity and resultant disparities and inequities was not as fully recognized as it is now. But lack of knowledge or inadequate preparation are no longer acceptable excuses.

Educators must also acknowledge that racism is not new in Canada. From the presence of the Ku Klux Klan in British Columbia, Saskatchewan, and Quebec during the 1920s to the denial of landing rights to immigrants arriving on the SS *Komagata Maru* in 1914, the Chinese Exclusion Act of 1923, or the Japanese internment during the Second World War, Canada has a long history of racism. In fact, after listing several efforts to combat racism in the country,[4] *A Canada for All: Canada's Action Plan against Racism* (Department of Canadian Heritage, 2005) asserted that "in spite of these domestic and international efforts, public opinion research suggests that racism remains a serious problem" (p. 4). Moreover, as clearly indicated in numerous reports, most recently the Truth and Reconciliation report released in 2015, the original founding First Nations peoples were not, and have never been, treated as equal partners in Confederation. The report describes numerous instances of physical, biological, and cultural genocide, and states that "in its dealing with Aboriginal people, Canada did all these things" (Truth and Reconciliation Commission of Canada, 2015, p. 1).

Almost half a century ago, in recognition of changed immigration patterns and increasing diversity, Prime Minister Pierre Trudeau announced that Canada would adopt a multicultural policy within an official bilingual framework of two official languages. The policy, officially affirmed in the 1988 Canadian Multiculturalism Act, "provides that every individual is equal before and under the law and has the right to the equal protection and benefit of the law without discrimination and that everyone has the freedom of conscience, religion, thought, belief, opinion, expression, peaceful assembly and association and guarantees those rights and freedoms equally to male and female persons" (Preamble, para. 1). However, simply proclaiming something by this Act does not automatically solve the problem, and numerous asymmetries resulting in social, cultural, economic, and educational disparities have existed and still exist barely under the surface of Canadian life. Robson (2018) found that there is a "common misconception that racism is something that occurs in the U.S. and not in Canada." In fact, the belief is so widespread that in a recent email from an American tour guide offering a trip to Underground Railroad sites in Canada, the following comment was used to entice travellers: "Talk to strangers feeling a sense of NO RACISM HERE!!" (personal communication, emphasis in original).

Obviously, the tour guide's comment was not true. In 2017, Muslim worshippers at a downtown Toronto mosque were confronted by protesters carrying signs that read "No to Islam," and "Muslims Are Terrorists" (Kestler-D'Amours, 2017). In February 2020, during the COVID-19 pandemic, Chinese-Canadians reported an uptake of xenophobia including online comments like, "Stop immigration from China because they carry this disease" (Kestler-D'Amours, 2020). In Winnipeg, Indigenous people make up only 10.6 per cent of the population but more than 60 per cent of people who have died as a result of police encounters; elsewhere reports have surfaced of other police mistreatment including the high-profile case of Chief Adam's beating following a stop for an expired license in Fort McMurray, Alberta (Keller & Kirkup, 2020). Multiple other incidents could also be cited.

In education, despite Canada's reputation for excellence, equity, and high levels of achievement, including high achievement by immigrant students (as reported by the analysis of PISA scores), there are also continued, well-known disparities in student outcomes including drop-out rates, disciplinary incidents, and academic achievement overall (Kerr, Mandzuk, & Raptis, 2011). Moreover, these disparities relate not only to issues of race, but also to socioeconomic status, citizenship, home language, sexual orientation, and so forth (Caro, McDonald, & Willms, 2009). As one of the opening quotations indicates, LGBTQ2+ students still too often experience prejudice and discrimination in schools. A 2014 report, for example, found that "70% of students reported hearing 'That's so gay' every day in school," and "40% reported hearing words like 'faggot' or 'dyke' every day" (Canadian Civil Liberties Association, 2014). Hence, discussion of race and racism must be extended to include other kinds of discrimination and marginalization for minoritized and non-dominant students.

To address the inequities in Canadian education, we start with the assumption that educational leaders can be (and even should be) change agents. Nevertheless, this has not always been considered a central, or even an appropriate, role for educators. Moreover, as Weiner (2003) reminds us, leaders wanting to implement significant change "must have one foot in the dominant structures of power and authority" (p. 89) in order to be able to exercise influence within the organization.

## From Educational Administration to Educational Leadership: A Brief Overview

In 1906, Eben Mumford, a scholar at the University of Chicago, wrote an article entitled *The Origins of Leadership*, in which he started with the premise that

> leadership is a function common to all the different stages of the social process, from its simplest and most primitive to its most complex and highly developed manifestations; [and] second, that it is a function in the expression of all kinds of social interests, whether the interactions be inter-individual, inter-groupal, or infra-groupal. (p. 218)

### Emphasizing Administration

The foregoing quotation demonstrates that use of the term "leadership" is nothing new. Nevertheless, as educational leadership strove to become a credible academic discipline, the preferred term for at least half a century was "administration," or sometimes "management." This is evident in early books with titles like *Administrative Behavior in Education* (Campbell & Gregg, 1957), *The Use of Theory in Educational Administration* (Coladarci & Getzels, 1955), and *Human Relations in School Administration* (Griffiths, 1956), as well as in such journal names, still in use, as *Journal of Education Administration* or *Educational Administration Quarterly*. The use of the term "administration" reflected the influence of early management theorists like Max Weber, Frederick W. Taylor, and Henri Fayol, whose hierarchical and "scientific" approaches to organizations still influence educational leadership today. The knowledge base of early studies and teaching of educational administration around the turn of the twentieth century was described as consisting of "school management, teacher supervision and practical field based experiences, 'war stories' for students to emulate from former school administrators" (Hoyle, 1991, as cited in Papa, 2009, p. 5). At a historic meeting of the National Council of Professors of Educational Administration (NCPEA) in Denver in 1954, Halpin (1970) pointed out that what was then being funded in the name of research was "distinctly a-theoretical in character and sloppy in quality" (as cited in Papa, 2009, p. 7).

In part to overcome this trend and to enhance the credibility of educational administration as a discipline, a group of prominent educational leaders gathered together in Chicago in 1957. The "Chicago School," as the group came to be known, has strongly influenced the norms of what we now prefer to call educational leadership in North America. Emphasizing the need for a theory-based approach to educational administration, the group posited, among other beliefs, that "ought" questions had no place in science, and hence lay outside the study and practice of educational administration. They argued, for example, that "generalizations prescribing courses of action or specifying what administrators or organizations should do are beyond the purview of researchers and the capacity of science" (Culbertson, 1981, p. 27). Indeed, Culbertson continues:

> The available literature on educational administration in 1957, seminar scholars agreed, was largely hortatory in character. Theory oriented research could remedy this situation, they believed, by making a sharp distinction between what is and what ought to be. Theory and research needed, in other words, to concentrate only on the former. (p. 27)

This emphasis led to decades of research focused on such aspects of educational leadership practice as accountability measures advocated by management theorists or such practices as decision-making or problem-solving. In fact, logical positivism, in which inquiry is limited to "phenomena about which facts or sense data can be gathered in order to classify phenomena and to discover laws" (Culbertson, 1981, p. 30), became the epistemological gold standard. Decades later, this concept was emphasized once again, with Hoy and Miskel (1991) stating, "The road to generalized knowledge can lie only in tough minded empirical research, not introspection and subjective experience" (p. 25).

One important implication of this movement was that ethical issues and ethical discussions came to be excluded from thinking about educational administration and leadership. Culbertson (1981) explains: "By concluding that meaningful generalizations cannot be developed about ethical matters, logical positivists laid the base for the is-ought distinction which assumed prominence in the theory movement and which was highlighted at the 1957 seminar" (p. 31). The wholehearted acceptance by the theory movement of these positivist presuppositions has led to what Culbertson (1981) described as "unrealistic expectations and undesirable excesses" (p. 43). This emphasis helps to explain why educational leadership is still too often conceptualized in rigid positivistic or scientific terms comprising a series of prescriptive interventions.

It is the foregoing undue emphasis on rational-technical approaches to educational leadership and the quest for generalized knowledge that will improve practice that this book hopes to address through its emphasis on more critical approaches to leadership. This, too, is not a new preoccupation, although the need for courageous critique is perhaps more salient than ever.

## Moving towards Leadership

During the 1970s, the paradigm wars between those who argued for rigorous objective and scientific leadership approaches and those who posited the need for more subjective approaches heated up, with Greenfield (1980) arguing that "the root problems of organization thus dissolve into questions about what people do, why they do it, and whether what they do is right" (p. 27). And a quarter of a century later, Oakes and Rogers (2006) asserted that

> merely documenting inequality will not, in and of itself, lead to more adequate and equitable schooling. Straightforward and obvious claims of injustice can be transformed, in the hands of lawyers, researchers, and policymakers, into highly technical disputes about statistical methods or esoteric debates about motivational theories. Scientific and technical arguments have a limited capacity to resolve matters that reach so deeply into cultural values and political contention. (p. 13)

Hence, although the concern for equity and ethics is not new in scholarly discussions of leadership, it has still not become fully integrated into many theoretical approaches, leadership frameworks, or actual practice. Here, we argue for a more holistic set of principles that, as Greenfield (1980) argued some forty years ago, recognizes that moral decisions are part of the everyday life of educational leaders and therefore that the "*is* and *ought* are intimately joined in human interaction" (p. 32). In fact, we further posit that only this juncture of the *is* and the *ought* can lead to the transformation of existing disparities and create learning environments that are equitable, excellent, inclusive, and socially just. Only a theory of leadership that is both critical and comprehensive will help educators to successfully address the needs and concerns of minoritized or non-dominant children, youth, families, and members of the wider community.

It is our firm belief that, despite their utility to guide some aspects of practice, too many of the dominant frameworks that influence leadership preparation and practice in Canada rely on leaders' actions without paying adequate attention to underlying belief systems and values that shape the ontologies and epistemologies that determine the desired action. Two examples are the well-known 2006 Ontario Leadership Framework (OLF) (revised in 2012 and currently under revision again) and the very similar British Columbia Education Leadership Development Framework. The OLF, for example, relies heavily on the research of Kenneth Leithwood and his colleagues, who have articulated the theory of transformational leadership focused primarily on four domains of practices: setting directions; building relationships and developing people; developing the organization to support desired practices; and improving the instructional program (Leithwood, Patten, & Jantzi, 2010) – to which the framework adds "securing accountability" (Leithwood, 2012). The 2017 British Columbia framework is similar to that of the OLF and identifies the same five key areas (albeit in a different order) of setting strategic directions, leading the organization, ensuring accountability, developing people, and building relationships (British Columbia Ministry of Education, 2017).

In the OLF, for example, there is reference to "priority placed by the Ontario government on social justice in the province's public schools," (Leithwood, 2012, p. 13) but no other mention of social justice in the document. There is also recognition that schools serve "highly diverse communities" and of the "province's commitment to inclusive education" (p. 13), but no discussion of what this means for leaders who want to address the needs of the most vulnerable. The BC framework asserts that the strength of the BC system is due to "the cadre of dedicated teachers and high levels of social equity in our education system" (British Columbia Ministry of Education, 2017, p. 6), although this is the only mention of "equity" in the document, which is also silent with respect to "social justice" or "diversity."

In fact, the processes called for in these frameworks – such as establishing organizational vision, building trust, collaborating with families, and building shared leadership or creating and enforcing "consistent, school-wide discipline policies" (Leithwood, 2012, p. 29) – all reflect what Hodgkinson (1978) called the "depths of ambiguity." The frameworks are silent on criteria to help leaders determine what might comprise a desirable vision, how to build trust, and so forth. They are silent about how one makes choices among many desirable goals or policies available, or how to make decisions related to appropriate expenditure of resources – or even what hiring "highly qualified teachers" might mean. In fact, it might well be argued that they have co-opted the ideas of social justice and diversity in the hegemonic interest of the status quo rather than adopt a leadership approach that challenges inequity and systemic bias. Although there is little doubt that having a shared vision about "student learning and well-being" (Leithwood, 2012, p. 33) is critically important, both the Ontario and the British Columbia leadership frameworks are silent about what might comprise such a vision. Further, educators focused on equity and socially just approaches would take exception to an emphasis on "consistent, school-wide discipline policies" that do not take a child's individual circumstances into consideration and that, therefore, treat all children alike, more like widgets than unique human beings located in specific webs of meaning.

## Becoming Agents of Change

As editors and authors of this volume focused on leading for systemic educational transformation in Canada, we strongly reject the tendency, identified by Riehl (2000), of educational leaders of diverse schools to take an assimilation approach. Riehl asserted that "assimilation has been the dominant approach to diversity in the public schools, and equality of opportunity through homogenization has been the goal" (p. 56). In her review of research on educational leadership she found that "succeeding generations of administrators have espoused treating teachers and students equally, regardless of their social class, race, or ethnicity" (p. 56).

Riehl also found a persistent pessimism about the ability of principals to be agents of change, in large part because "administrators are steeped in a structural-functionalist perspective that tends to view the existing social order as legitimate, that espouses the values of democracy and meritocracy, and that adopts a managerial orientation instead of a socially transformative one" (p. 59). We concur that if educational leaders remain frozen within a structural-functionalist perspective, educational transformation will not occur. However, we also agree with Riehl's optimism that principals can be agents of change who frame new beliefs about diversity and new meanings of inclusion and equity, and hence, have the potential to "engage in inclusive, transformative practice" (p. 71).

We begin by acknowledging that, as many other researchers have found, although the effects of leadership on student learning are mainly indirect, that "school leaders are capable of having significant positive effects on student learning and other important outcomes" (Leithwood, Patten, & Jantzi, 2010). To do so, we posit, requires that educational leaders explicitly ground their work in conceptions of equity and justice. Here we recognize, with March (1972), that "like truth and beauty, justice is an ideal rather than a state of existence. We do not achieve it; we pursue it" (as cited in Greenfield, 1980, p. 38).

Although we may never fully "arrive," our argument is that educators and educational leaders must forcefully and relentlessly pursue justice. They must strive to create organizations in which all participants – students, staff, parents, and community members – are included, welcomed, and respected. They must become advocates and even activists if our educational organizations are to fulfil the promise of helping all students reach their full potential, and of developing a strong and viable civil society.

This notion of striving, but of never arriving, is important. It suggests that a focus on social justice is never binary but rather exists along a continuum. There is no sense in which we believe that one is either socially just (good), or socially unjust (bad), or in which one is wholly oppressed or oppressor. Instead, we recognize that both can reside in one human being. For example, a Black school principal may develop incredible programs to empower Black girls, but tend to ignore other non-dominant groups, believing that there will be a spillover effect. As seen some years ago in a California referendum, an immigrant population that has suffered incredible discrimination may still vote against LGBTQ2+ rights, failing to understand the lack of civil rights offered to the second group. Similarly, a member of the LGBTQ2+ community may fail to acknowledge how the historic religious oppression of Sikh or Muslim populations also reflects the historic discrimination faced by many minoritized groups.

Thus, to equitably address the needs of all children, Foster (1986) argued that leadership should be "critically educative" – that it should not "only look at the conditions in which we live" but decide how to change them (p. 185). The emphasis on examining the conditions in which students, teachers, and other members of the school community live is an essential component of our advocated approach to leadership. It is for that reason that you will find in this volume chapters relating to the educational conditions of Indigenous, refugee, visible minority, LGBTQ2+, and other students who are often marginalized in school settings. It is essential to understand their unique experiences and needs in order to successfully include all students in the life and work of schools.

Numerous Canadian and non-Canadian scholars have addressed this need for leadership that is grounded in equity and that emphasizes more critical awareness. For example, Langlois and Lapointe (2010), drawing on the work of Starratt (1991), have long addressed the need for an ethical approach to leadership. Likewise, the work of Ryan (2006, 2010, 2014) on inclusive leadership, Shields (2010, 2016, 2020) on transformative leadership, Portelli on leadership for equity (Portelli, & Campbell-Stephens, 2009; Portelli, Shields, & Vibert, 2007), and Armstrong on social justice leadership (Armstrong & McMahon, 2014; Armstrong, Tuters, & Carrier, 2013) aligns with that of numerous American and British scholars who call for an emphasis on cultural awareness (Ladson-Billings, 2014), culturally responsive leadership (Khalifa, Gooden, & Davis, 2016), socially just leadership (Jean-Marie, 2008; Jean-Marie, Normore, &

Brooks, 2009; Theoharis, 2007, 2009), and critically focused spirituality (Dantley, 2005). Some francophone Canadian scholars also ground their work in intercultural competency (Gélinas-Proulx, Labelle, & Jacquin, 2017), competency related to equity and diversity (Larochelle-Audet, Magnan, Potvin, Doré, 2018), and diverse students living in poverty (Archambault & Richer, 2014). This book stands on the shoulders of many as the authors of the twelve chapters presented here draw on many earlier theoretical contributions to present this compilation of research-based visions of equitable and socially just educational leadership.

## Overview of the Book

All of the authors of the following chapters advocate a critical, activist, and transformative approach to educational leadership. All also acknowledge the need for justice within education to extend from pre-K to higher education and to all members of the community, including the educators themselves, as well as the families and community members who surround and support the school community. In this volume, however, the focus is on students – the students populating schools, colleges, and universities in Canada who are marginalized, minoritized, and sometimes oppressed. Moreover, it is important to acknowledge that despite common underlying assumptions, each author is solely responsible for the information and opinions contained within each chapter.

This book is divided into three main sections. Throughout, we emphasize that all educators are also leaders and hence, that as leaders, we must not only understand the conditions in which our students live, but our own "conditions" – our implicit biases, our power, the privilege we have as scholars and leaders, and the ways in which we are complicit in perpetuating inequity as well as how we can influence change. In other words, although some write as members of oppressed groups, they do not generalize or essentialize their experience. Through their educational attainment, they also recognize the privilege of their positions and their responsibility to be part of the solution.

Part I, Transformative Leadership in Practice, comprises three chapters that explicitly ground their visions of systemic change in the theory of transformative leadership. In this first chapter, Shields presents transformative leadership theory (TLT) and clarifies the distinctions between it and the perhaps more widely known theory of transformational leadership. In chapter 2, Gélinas-Proulx and Villella argue that transformative leadership could help school leaders in French minoritized contexts to fulfil their mission of providing equitable and excellent education that simultaneously promotes the viability of the French language in Canada. In chapter 3, Roache and Marshall explore more fully the application of TLT to redress the marginalization of some of Canada's vulnerable populations.

Part II, Equitable and Socially Just Approaches to Leadership, presents four conceptual chapters that examine other ways of thinking about leadership that have the potential to transform schools into places of inclusion, equity, justice, and excellence for all. Kowalchuk starts by addressing the need for leaders' acts of subversion, political savvy, and resilience in her discussion of leadership for social justice and equity. In chapter 5, Campbell and Watson emphasize the critical importance of understanding and rejecting deficit thinking by using culturally relevant and responsive pedagogy. Kirk and Osiname then present, in chapter 6, a way of reflecting critically on one's own social justice leadership through a process they call duo-ethnography. Finally, Shah and Tuters extend our thinking in chapter 7 by describing ways to resist the alt-right neo-liberalism of higher education and decentre whiteness specifically among education faculty.

In part III, Decentring Discrimination, we present five chapters that focus specifically on groups of students and teachers who are traditionally marginalized, whose experiences are often negative, and whose academic outcomes suffer concomitantly. Using Indigenous epistemology, Atleo provides an overview in chapter 8 of the oppressive and colonizing conditions under which First Nations people still live, work, and learn. In chapter 9, Zook describes the often dangerous situation of LGBTQ2+ students, with an emphasis on the discrimination faced by transgender students. Ebied then describes the challenges faced by refugee students and concludes chapter 10 by describing one hopeful way forward. In chapter 11, Hamm draws on his experiences as a principal to examine the need for opportunities for student leadership, including for newcomers. Finally, in chapter 12, as a reminder that discrimination and racism are faced by educators as well as students and that the need for socially just leaders is endless, Howard critiques Quebec's Bill 21 that prohibits teachers and school principals from wearing religious symbols in educational organizations.

In general, the authors of the chapters in this volume unite in a call for criteria related to justice for all students to replace an almost singular emphasis on functions, technique, and performance. We believe it is time to reclaim the language of equity, social justice, and transformation for critical approaches to leadership that clearly acknowledge and address implicit bias, racism, coloniality, and the multiple ways in which current educational systems continue to marginalize and oppress students.

Some may call our ideas "revolutionary" or "radical," and perhaps in some ways they are, given the call for re-examining and often challenging everything we think and do. Others may feel the ideas presented here are quite mundane and do not necessarily represent a complete rethinking of social justice in education. Obviously that will depend on the perspective of the reader, their prior experience, and the context within which they work. The concepts presented here do not necessarily require new funding paradigms, demolishing schools, or eliminating teachers. They do, however, require courageously addressing discrimination and implicit bias head-on. They require reflection, conscientization, difficult conversations, bold action, and transformation of the ways in which we relate to and work with others. They require rethinking and then redressing inequities related to power, policies, practices, and pedagogies.

We acknowledge that addressing inequity is often risky as it requires challenging powerful forces and voices that support and perpetuate the status quo. But it is time to take up the responsibility that accompanies the privilege of holding positions of authority. It is time to act with clarity, conviction, and moral courage, and to stand for systemic change. It is time for Canadian education to provide caring and equitable learning environments in which all are included, respected, and valued. It is our hope that this volume will prompt the sort of reflection and action that will enable equitable and socially just systemic transformation.

## NOTES

1  We use the term "minoritized" rather than the common word "minority" to indicate that it is not simply a matter of numbers or percentages. Populations that are in the vast majority, such as Indigenous students in on-reserve schools, can still be marginalized due to powerful voices making policy or establishing curriculum, for example, that continues to exclude culturally relevant materials and that excludes the voices and desires of the population being "served." Hence, the term minoritized implies a kind of hegemony of power that perpetuates inequity.
2  In recent years, and particularly in construction sites across Ontario, workers have discovered nooses, either painted on their lockers (Rodriguez, 2021) or draped across elements of the worksite (Hayes, 2021).
3  The term is defined by Statistics Canada (2017) as "persons, other than Aboriginal persons, who are non-Caucasian in race or non-white in color." Thus, the definition excludes those who are Middle Eastern, for example, as well as many who speak a language other than one of the two official languages of Canada.
4  Mentioned were the Canadian Human Rights Act, the Canadian Bill of Rights, the Employment Equity Act, the Official Languages Act, the Canadian Multiculturalism Act, the Immigration and Refugee Protection Act, and the Citizenship Act (Department of Canadian Heritage, 2005, p. 3).

## REFERENCES

Advisory Committee on Equity, Diversity, Inclusion, and Decolonization (AC-EDID). (2021). Igniting change: Final report and recommendations. Federation for the Humanities and Social Science. http://www.ideas-idees.ca/sites/default/files/sites/default/uploads/congress/igniting-change-final-report-and-recommendations-en.pdf

Archambault, J., & Richer, C. (2014). Leadership for social justice throughout fifteen years of intervention in a disadvantaged and multicultural Canadian urban area: *The Supporting Montréal Schools Program*. In I. Bogotch & C.M. Shields (Eds.), *International handbook of educational leadership and social (in)justice* (pp. 1023–45). Dordrecht, Netherlands: Springer.

Armstrong, D., & McMahon, B. (2014). Developing socially just leaders: Integrative antiracist approaches in a transformational paradigm. In A. Normore & N. Erbe (Eds.), *Collective efficacy: Interdisciplinary perspectives on international leadership* (pp. 23–39). London, UK: Emerald.

Armstrong, D., Tuters, S., & Carrier, N. (2013). Micropolitics and social justice leadership: Bridging beliefs and behaviours. *Journal of Educational Administration and Foundations, 23*(2), 35–53.

Blackstock, C. (2019, December 9). Canada must stop normalizing inequality for Indigenous people. *Macleans*. https://www.macleans.ca/opinion/canada-must -stop-normalizing-inequality-for-indigenous-people/

British Columbia Ministry of Education. (2017). *Leadership development in the B.C. education sector: Provincial leadership development framework*. Government of British Columbia. https://www2.gov.bc.ca/assets/gov/education/administration /kindergarten-to-grade-12/leadership/bc-leadership-development-framework.pdf

Campbell, R.F., & Gregg, R.T. (Eds.). (1957). *Administrative behavior in education*. New York, NY: Harper.

Canadian Civil Liberties Association. (2014). *LGBTQ rights in schools: Information guide July 2014*. https://ccla.org/cclanewsite/wp-content/uploads/2015/02/LGBTQ -Rights-in-Schools-CCLA-and-CCLET-FINAL.pdf.pdf

Cardozo, A., & Pendakur, R. (2008). *Canada's visible minority population: 1967–2017*. Vancouver, BC: Centre of Excellence for Research on Immigration and Diversity.

Caro, D.H., McDonald, J.T., & Willms, J.D. (2009). Socio-economic status and academic achievement trajectories from childhood to adolescence. *Canadian Journal of Education/Revue Canadienne de l'Éducation, 32*(3), 558–90. https:// www.jstor.org/stable/canajeducrevucan.32.3.558

CBC News. (2018, October 15). Young refugees face racism in schools, mostly from teachers. *CBC News*. https://www.cbc.ca/news/canada/new-brunswick/refugees -face-school-racism-1.4863418

Coladarci, A.P., & Getzels, J.W. (1955). *The use of theory in educational administration*. Stanford, CA: Stanford University Press.

Culbertson, J.A. (1981). Perspective: Antecedents of the theory movement. *Educational Administration Quarterly, 17*(1), 25–47. doi: 10.1177/0013161X810 1700103

Dantley, M.E. (2005). African American spirituality and Cornel West's notions of prophetic pragmatism: Restructuring educational leadership in American urban schools. *Educational Administration Quarterly, 41*(4), 651–74. doi: 10.1177/0013161 X04274274

Department of Canadian Heritage. (2005). *A Canada for all: Canada's action plan against racism.* Minister of Public Works and Government Services Canada. https://publications.gc.ca/collections/Collection/CH34-7-2005E.pdf

Foster, W. (1986). *Paradigms and promises.* Amherst, NY: Prometheus.

Gélinas-Proulx, A., Labelle, J., & Jacquin, P. (2017). Compétence interculturelle: Adaptation d'un Modèle initial pour les directions d'établissement scolaire de langue française du Québec et du Nouveau-Brunswick. *Revue des Sciences de l'Éducation, 43*(2), 119–52. doi: 10.7202/1043028ar

Greenfield, T.B. (1980). The man who comes back through the door in the wall: Discovering truth, discovering self, discovering organizations. *Educational Administration Quarterly, 16*(3), 26–59. doi: 10.1177/0013161X8001600305

Griffiths, D. (1956). *Human relations in school administration.* New York, NY: Appleton-Century-Crofts.

Hayes, M. (2021). Construction industry faces reckoning over racism on job sites. *Globe and Mail.* https://www.theglobeandmail.com/canada/article-construction -industry-faces-reckoning-over-racism-on-job-sites/

Hodgkinson, C. (1978). *Towards a philosophy of administration.* Oxford, UK: Basil Blackwell.

Hoy, W., & Miskel, C. (1991). *Educational administration* (4th ed.). New York, NY: McGraw-Hill.

Jean-Marie, G. (2008). Leadership for social justice: An agenda for 21st century schools. *The Educational Forum, 72,* 340–54. doi: 10.1080/00131720802362058

Jean-Marie, G., Normore, A.H., & Brooks, J.S. (2009). Leadership for social justice: Preparing 21st century school leaders for a new social order. *Journal of Research on Leadership Education, 4*(1), 1–31. doi: 10.1177/194277510900400102

Keller, J., & Kirkup, K. (2020, June 24). Charges dropped against First Nations Chief Allan Adams after violent arrest. *Globe and Mail.* https://www.theglobeandmail .com/canada/article-charges-dropped-against-first-nations-chief-allan-adam -after-violent/

Kerr, D., Mandzuk, D., & Raptis, H. (2011). The role of the social foundations of education in programs of teacher preparation in Canada. *Canadian Journal of Education/Revue Canadienne de l'Éducation, 34*(4), 118–34. https://journals.sfu .ca/cje/index.php/cje-rce/article/view/674

Kestler-D'Amours, J. (2017, February 25). Canadians fear rising xenophobia, hate crimes in wake of mosque attack. *Deutsche Welle.* https://p.dw.com/p/2YDk0

Kestler-D'Amours, J. (2020, February 2). Chinese Canadians denounce rising xenophobia tied to coronavirus. *Al Jazeera.* https://www.aljazeera.com/news/2020 /02/chinese-canadians-denounce-rising-xenophobia-tied-coronavirus-20020219 1216923.html

Khalifa, M.A., Gooden, M.A., & Davis, J.E. (2016). Culturally responsive school leadership: A synthesis of the literature. *Review of Educational Research, 86*(4), 1272–1311. doi: 10.3102/0034654316630383

Kosciw, J.G., Greytak, E.A., Zongrone, A.D., Clark, C.M., & Truong, N.L. (2018). *The 2017 national school climate survey: The experiences of lesbian, gay, bisexual, transgender, and queer youth in our nation's schools*. New York, NY: GLSEN. https://www.glsen.org/sites/default/files/2019-10/GLSEN-2017-National-School -Climate-Survey-NSCS-Full-Report.pdf

Ladson-Billings, G. (2014). Culturally relevant pedagogy 2.0: A.k.a the remix. *Harvard Educational Review, 84*(1), 74–84. doi: 10.17763/haer.84.1.p2rj1314 85484751

Langlois, L., & Lapointe, C. (2010). Can ethics be learned? Results from a three-year action-research project. *Journal of Educational Administration, 48*(2), 147–63. doi: 10.1108/09578231011027824

Larochelle-Audet, J. Magnan, M.-O., Potvin, M., & Doré, E. (2018). *Les compétences des directions en matière d'équité et de diversité: Pistes pour les cadres de référence et la formation*. Rapport du groupe de travail sur les compétences et la formation des directions en matière d'équité et de diversité. Montréal, QC: OFDE. http:// ofde.ca/wp-content/uploads/2018/03/Groupe-directions_rapport_fev2018 .compressed.pdf

Leithwood, K. (2012). *The Ontario leadership framework 2012 with a discussion of research foundations*. Ontario Institute for Education Leadership. https://www .education-leadership-ontario.ca/application/files/2514/9452/5287/The _Ontario_Leadership_Framework_2012_-_with_a_Discussion_of_the _Research_Foundations.pdf

Leithwood, K., Patten, S., & Jantzi, D. (2010). Testing a conception of how school leadership influences student learning. *Educational Administration Quarterly, 46*(5), 671–706. doi: 10.1177/0013161X10377347

Lynam, M.J., Browne, A.J., Kirkham, S.R., & Anderson, J.M. (2007). Re-thinking the complexities of "culture": What might we learn from Bourdieu? *Nursing Inquiry, 14*(1), 23–34. doi: 10.1111/j.1440-1800.2007.00348.x

March, J.G. (1972). Model bias in social action. *Review of Educational Research, 42*(4), 413–29. doi: 10.3102/00346543042004413

Mumford, E. (1906). The origins of leadership. *American Journal of Sociology, 12*(2), 216–40. https://www.jstor.org/stable/2762385

Oakes, J., & Rogers, J. (2006). *Learning power*. New York, NY: Teachers College Press.

Papa, R. (2009). *The discipline of education administration: Crediting the past*. https:// cnx.org/resources/f57361be94dde10d8391b18a7207144c45dd7804/4papasmall.pdf

Park, V. (2018, November 4). "Canada is the most multicultural country in the world." *BBC News*. https://www.bbc.com/news/world-us-canada-46086919

Portelli, J.P. & Campbell-Stephens, R. (2009). *Leading for equity: The investing in diversity approach*. Toronto, ON: Edphil Books.

Portelli, J.P., Shields, C.M., & Vibert, A.B. (2007). *Toward an equitable education: Poverty, diversity, and students at risk*. Toronto, ON: OISE/CLD.

Riehl, C. J. (2000). The principal's role in creating inclusive schools for diverse students: A review of normative, empirical, and critical literature on the practice of educational administration. *Review of Educational Research, 70*(1), 55–81. doi: 10.3102/00346543070001055

Robson, K. (2018, December 28). Why won't Canada collect data on race and student success? *Vancouver Sun.* https://vancouversun.com/opinion/op-ed/karen-robson -why-wont-canada-collect-data-on-race-and-student-success

Rodriguez, J. (2021). "I do not feel safe at work": Black man says noose drawn on his office locker. *CTV News.* https://www.ctvnews.ca/canada/i-do-not-feel-safe-at -work-black-man-says-noose-drawn-on-his-office-locker-1.5502205

Ryan, J. (2006). *Inclusive leadership.* San Francisco, CA: Jossey-Bass.

Ryan, J. (2010). Promoting social justice in schools: Principals' political strategies. *International Journal Leadership in Education, 13*(4), 357–76. doi: 10.1080/1360 3124.2010.503281

Ryan, J. (2014). Promoting inclusive leadership in diverse schools. In I. Bogotch & C.M. Shields (Eds.), *International handbook of educational leadership and social (in)justice* (pp. 359–80). Dordrecht, Netherlands: Springer.

Shields, C.M. (2010). Transformative leadership: Working for equity in diverse contexts. *Educational Administration Quarterly, 46*(4), 558–89. doi: 10.1177 /0013161X10375609

Shields, C.M. (2016). *Transformative leadership in education: Equitable change in an uncertain and complex world* (2nd ed.). New York, NY: Routledge.

Shields, C.M. (2020). *Becoming a transformative leader.* New York, NY: Routledge.

Starratt, J. (1991). Building an ethical school: A theory for practice in educational leadership. *Educational Administration Quarterly, 27*(2), 185–202. doi: 10.1177 /0013161X91027002005

Statistics Canada. (2017). *Visible minority and population group reference guide, census of population, 2016.* https://www12.statcan.gc.ca/census-recensement/2016 /ref/guides/006/98-500-x2016006-eng.cfm.

Theoharis, G. (2007). Social justice educational leaders and resistance: Toward a theory of social justice leadership. *Educational Administration Quarterly, 43*(2), 221–58. doi: 10.1177/0013161X06293717

Theoharis, G. (2009). *The school leaders our children deserve: Seven keys to equity, social justice, and school reform.* New York, NY: Teachers College Press.

Truth and Reconciliation Commission of Canada. (2015). *Honouring the truth, reconciling for the future: Summary of the final report of the Truth and Reconciliation Commission of Canada.* Ottawa, ON: Truth and Reconciliation Commission of Canada. https://publications.gc.ca/collections/collection_2015 /trc/IR4-7-2015-eng.pdf

Weiner, E.J. (2003). Secretary Paulo Freire and the democratization of power: Toward a theory of transformative leadership. *Educational Philosophy and Theory, 35*(1), 89–106. doi: 10.1111/1469-5812.00007

# PART I

# Transformative Leadership in Practice

# 1 Transformative Leadership Theory: A Comprehensive Approach to Equity, Inclusion, Excellence, and Social Justice

CAROLYN M. SHIELDS

Canada's original founding document, the British North America Act of 1867, stated that one of the goals of the union of Canada was to "promote the interests of the British Empire." Since that time, Canadian law has moved slowly towards a human rights approach to individual rights and freedoms, as evidenced, among other steps, by signing on to the Universal Declaration of Human Rights, the creation of Canada's own Charter of Rights and Freedoms, and recognition in the Truth and Reconciliation report released in 2015 of the inequitable treatment of Indigenous and First Nations peoples. Despite this formal legislation intended, one might argue, to ensure the equity of rights and freedoms, the reality is that Canadian culture is fraught with the persistence of discriminatory attitudes, policies, and practices resulting from our history of colonialism and domination focused on the good of the British Empire. As expressed in the Introduction to this book, structural racism, implicit bias, and discrimination permeate Canadian life, and our education systems and institutions are not immune.

French sociologist Pierre Bourdieu introduced the concept of *habitus* to explain the link between the underlying ideology of a culture and its accepted policies and practices. He defines *habitus* as a "system of durable, transposable dispositions [that] function as structuring structures" of a given culture and that provide implicit guidance about what is acceptable and what is not permitted within a given field, like education (as cited in Swingewood, 1998, p. 95). Thus, because they pervade the wider Canadian culture, we also find certain beliefs, values, policies, and practices in Canadian education that continue to either oppress and marginalize or privilege some students and groups of students to the disadvantage of others.

Although there is much that school leaders can do within the context of their organizations to create more equitable and socially just learning environments for all students, it is also important for leaders who consider themselves transformative to both teach about and fight for wider societal reform. Here I posit that one of the ways educators may begin to address persistent inequities and injustices is by adopting a critical and comprehensive theory of leadership that works to redress the oppression and marginalization exercised on minoritized populations within Canada and many other developed countries.

In 2003, Weiner described transformative leadership theory (TLT) as an "exercise of power and authority that begins with questions of justice, democracy, and the dialectic between individual accountability and social responsibility" (p. 89). He argued that

> transformative leadership, to be transformative, must confront more than just what is, and work toward creating an alternative political and social imagination that does not rest solely on the rule of capital or the hollow moralism of neoconservatives, but is rooted in radical democratic struggle. (p. 97)

With Weiner and others, I describe transformative leadership theory (TLT) as a comprehensive, distinct, and promising theoretical approach to educational leadership in that it "begins with questions of justice and democracy; it critiques inequitable practices and offers the promise not only of greater individual achievement but of a better life lived in common with others" (Shields, 2010, p. 1).

In 1991, Quantz, Rogers, and Dantley, discussing the confused state of American schooling, the public scepticism about the efficacy and legitimacy of schools, and the need for change, stated that "of the commonly discussed theories, only the concept of transformative leadership appears to provide an appropriate direction" (p. 96). They went on to assert the need for a clear vision of how the theory might act as a guide for "understanding the present political and moral issues" (p. 96) and for transforming schools. Yet, later in their article, Quantz et al. fail to clearly distinguish between transformative and transformational leadership and, at one point, use the terms synonymously in the same paragraph. They are not the only scholars to confuse the terms – transforming, transformational, and transformative – all of which derive from the same etymological roots and are often used interchangeably in common parlance.

Transformational and transformative come from the old French verb *transformer* and the Latin *transformare*, both meaning to change the form of something. Although often used as synonyms, there are slight but significant differences between the two. WikiDiff (n.d.) indicates that transformative "causes" transformation while transformational is "of, pertaining to or leading to transformation." Transformative, the site states, is "anything that has the power to transform/modify/alter something into something else." Hence, the subtle difference implies that transformative is indicative of agency, action, and even activism, while transformational describes the new outcomes of such activity.

In recent years, scholars have attempted to clarify the distinctions among theories that raise important considerations for equitable and socially just education. As such, in this chapter, I will discuss the origins of TLT, distinguish it from transformational leadership, and identify its principles and tenets. Finally, by presenting an extended vignette of a transformed school, I will demonstrate its potential as "an appropriate direction" for educational leaders wanting to create equitable, inclusive, excellent and socially just learning environments in which to work and learn.[1]

First, however, I want to reiterate some of the concerns expressed almost half a century ago by Thomas Greenfield (1980) about the nature of his work. Clearly identified with what was then a new subjectivist movement (described in the Introduction to this volume) and with the ensuing paradigm wars, he stated:

> [It] is a matter of record. What others have said I have tried to acknowledge in my writings. Readers of this paper will see how heavily the ideas I expound are dependent upon others and upon a long-standing tradition of scholarship and philosophy ... It is not my school. It is not my theory ... I have been speaking for the better part of a decade on behalf of other voices and will do so now again. They are voices – some contemporary, some historic, and some ancient – of those who are the foundational thinkers. (p. 27)

I adopt Greenfield's statement as my own: Transformative leadership theory is not my theory. I have been speaking for my whole career, for the better part of four decades, on behalf of other voices as well as my own. Transformative leadership theory is not new. However, I have worked assiduously to articulate it and to advocate for it as one comprehensive and critical approach to leadership that may help to balance the current heavy reliance on more technical, process-oriented theories like transformational leadership theory.

## The Origins of Transformative Leadership

Both transformative and transformational leadership theory trace their origins to the work of James McGregor Burns, who identified transactional leadership as the dominant approach in 1978 and argued for what he named a new and more radical concept of transforming leadership. In turn, transforming leadership has given rise to both the theory of transformational leadership and that of transformative leadership.

Transforming leadership, as conceived by Burns (1978), occurs when a leader "recognizes and exploits an existing need or demand of a potential follower ... looks for potential motives in followers, seeks to satisfy higher needs, and engages the full person of the follower" (p. 4). To be a leader, according to Burns, is to induce "followers to act for certain goals that represent the values and the motivations – the wants and needs, the aspirations and expectations – *of both leaders and followers*" (p. 19, emphasis in original). Van Oord (2013) nuanced Burns' perspective by stating that "transformational leadership remains embedded in organizational management" in that the "leader is always the person with the top job in an institution" and "the leader remains the leader just as the followers remain followers" (p. 421).

Identifying the roots of transformational leadership as being attributed to Burns, and drawing on his own fifteen years of studying transformational leadership in education, Leithwood (2010) stated, "The model has four major dimensions – setting directions, developing people, redesigning the organization, and managing the instructional program – each of which includes three or four more specific sets of practices" (p. 158). These are the dimensions and practices, with slight modifications in wording from time to time, that still define transformational leadership today.

Burns (1978), however, called for a leadership revolution, saying that "revolution is a complete and pervasive transformation of an entire social system" (p. 202). He then emphasized the need for "*real change* – that is, a transformation to the marked degree in the attitudes, norms, institutions, and behaviors that structure our daily lives" (p. 414, emphasis in original). In 2003, Burns also called for leadership that would constitute a revolution that requires complete and pervasive transformation of the conditions that leave "billions of the world's people in the direst want" (p. 2). These calls for revolution, for a theory that includes attitudes and norms and not simply practices, and for an emphasis on redressing the conditions of those in the direst want all suggest that his notion of transforming leadership is closer to that of transformative leadership than to transformational leadership.

Although transformative leadership's roots are also attributed to Burns, other influences figure prominently in its articulation. Weiner (2003) argues that Antonio Gramsci's "ideas concerning the link between leadership and hegemony provide an important theoretical referent for developing a theory of transformative leadership" (p. 89). Weiner and others (see, for example, Jackson, 2007; Miller, Brown, & Hopson, 2011) also advocate consideration of the work and career of Brazilian Paulo Freire "when developing a theory of transformative leadership" in that it "offers a geography of leadership within the terrain of democratic struggle" (Weiner, 2003, p. 91). More recently, Bolivian scholars Anello, Hernandez, and Khadem (2014) articulated a form of transformative leadership that they claim helps leaders fulfil the admonition of Mahatma Gandhi "to be the change you wish to see in the world." Their model of transformative leadership calls for both personal and social transformation (see pp. 91–124).

Hence, we see that although some of the influences are similar, the two leadership theories have developed quite differently as articulated here in the statements of Blackmore (2011), Starratt (2011), van Oord (2013), and Hewitt, Davis, and Lashley (2014). In 2011, Blackmore argued that

> [w]hile seductive, this transformational leadership discourse appropriates critical perspectives while depoliticizing their social-justice intent, as the notion of transformational leadership has been framed narrowly within the school effectiveness-improvement paradigms … In contrast, *transformative leadership* discourses derive from a critical tradition, promoting emancipatory pedagogies that arise from political and social movements, feminist perspectives, and critical pedagogy. (p. 21)

In the same volume, *Transformative Leadership: A Reader*, Starratt (2011) began his chapter by positing that "the distinction between transformational and transformative leadership is an important one, not only for the field of education, but also for leadership theory and research in other fields" (p. 131).

By 2013, van Oord could summarize the situation, stating of transformative leadership that

> the term is not new; for many years the concepts of transformational and transformative leadership were used as synonyms. Recognizing this conceptual murkiness, scholars such as [Carolyn] Shields … have in recent years successfully endeavored to define and theorize transformative leadership as distinctively separate from the transformational approach. Transformative leadership is characterized by its activist agenda and its overriding commitment to social justice, equality and a democratic society. (pp. 421–2)

The next year, Hewitt et al. (2014) asserted that

> leadership preparation programs must cultivate leaders who can navigate schools as they are to improve their effectiveness while also fundamentally rethinking and reworking education toward what it might be – socially just, equitable, and democratic. The former – efforts to reform and improve schools by making them more effective – is embodied in the concept of transformational leadership … while the latter – efforts to problematize how we do school and to effect profound, equitable change – is embodied in the concept of transformative leadership. (pp. 225–6)

These comments emphasize, first, that transformative leadership, as I articulate it below, is grounded in the work of numerous critical scholars, and second, that it is important to distinguish between transformational and transformative leadership because each suggests a different path to reforming or transforming education today.

## Clarifying the Distinctions between Transformational and Transformative Leadership

In social science, a theory is a group of ideas, guiding principles, or hypotheses intended to explain, predict, or help to understand something. It is intended to establish a general relationship between or among what are often called "variables." A theory is based on certain assumptions that can be tested to provide support for, or to challenge, the theory. According to the University of California, Berkley, a theory is "a broad, natural explanation for a wide range of phenomena. Theories are concise, coherent, systematic, predictive, and broadly applicable, often integrating and generalizing many hypotheses" (Bradford, 2017).

For transformative leadership, I previously identified two general principles (or hypotheses) and eight specific tenets, or variables (Shields, 2016). The first principle, proposition, or hypothesis (to use the language of quantitative research), is that when a person feels respected, included, and valued, it is easier to concentrate on their assigned task and the work will be more successfully completed. This principle applies to adults in any workplace as well as to students in educational settings. If a student has to worry about whether he will be teased or bullied upon leaving the classroom, or whether their family will have food or shelter, or if she should hide facts about her family (e.g., socioeconomic status, gender identity, religious beliefs) it is more difficult to concentrate on the learning activity at hand. However, when students feel that the learning environment is safe and respectful, and that they and their perspectives are valued, they are more able to concentrate on the specified activity and, concomitantly, their academic performance (sometimes assessed solely by test scores) will improve. Obviously, this proposition can be tested empirically.

The second principle (or hypothesis) is that when the good of individual achievement is balanced with the value of public good and civic engagement, then society as a whole (i.e., our democracy) is strengthened. In education, therefore, when a focus on individual academic achievement is balanced with a focus on collective civic engagement, social responsibility, and deep democracy, students learn about the importance of collective action and support for one another.

These two principles are supported by the following eight tenets drawn from the work of multiple scholars of transformative leadership including Foster (1986), Quantz et al. (1991), Weiner (2003), and many others:

1. A mandate to effect deep and equitable change.
2. A need to deconstruct knowledge frameworks that perpetuate inequity and injustice and to reconstruct them in more equitable ways.
3. A need to address the inequitable distribution of power.
4. An emphasis on both private and public (individual and collective) good.

5. A focus on emancipation, democracy, equity, and justice.
6. An emphasis on interdependence, interconnectedness, and global awareness.
7. The necessity of balancing critique with promise.
8. A call to exhibit moral courage. (Shields, 2016, pp. 20–1)

These tenets have been extensively elaborated elsewhere (Shields, 2016, 2020), and so I refrain from repeating their details here. Nevertheless, it is worth emphasizing that TLT is a critical theory, focused on the need for equity and the full inclusion and participation of those who are often the most marginalized or excluded in society. TLT is what one could call a normative theory, in that it is embedded in explicit values of equity and justice that provide a standard for evaluating the present state of an organization and implying a clear direction for action. It is also important to note that though these tenets have been numbered here for ease of reference, they are holistic and interactive. All are necessary; none can be missed; but where you start depends on your circumstances.

In contrast, transformational leadership, as described by Leithwood (2010), emphasizes the four processes that he calls dimensions or practices: setting directions, developing people, redesigning the organization, and managing the instructional program (p. 158). Here, however, there is no specific direction indicated; there is no clear sense of which direction to set, which criteria could be used for redesigning the organization, or how to organize the instructional program. Instead, transformational leadership leaves notions of efficiency and effectiveness to individual interpretation.

Thus, one can differentiate between the theories of transformative leadership and transformational leadership in terms of their underlying goals, stated values, epistemologies, and ontologies. To clarify the differences, I previously developed the following chart (Shields, 2016, p. 22), reproduced here as table 1.1. Leithwood's dimensions of transformational leadership are on the left, and my own articulation of the tenets of TLT is on the right.

A close examination of the left-hand column reveals that two of the dominant leadership frameworks used in Canada, the Ontario Leadership Framework (OLF) and the British Columbia Leadership Development Framework (BCLDF),[2] are solidly embedded in transformational leadership theory, despite the stated intent of both provinces to create equitable and excellent experiences for students. The OLF document, for example, advocates "setting directions, building relationships and developing people, developing the organization to support desired practices, and improving the instructional program" – to which the framework adds "securing accountability" (Leithwood, 2012, p. 6). As Leithwood explains, "each of these domains includes a handful of more specific practices" (p. 7). The BCLDF likewise identifies "areas of professional practice … [that] lay the foundation for a shared vocabulary, alignment of development

Table 1.1. Comparing leadership theories

| Transformational leadership | Transformative leadership |
|---|---|
| *Setting directions* | **Need for deep and equitable change** (Examines the context for specific inequities; suggests an explicit direction for change: equity, inclusion, and social justice.) |
| *Redesigning the organization* Build a cohesive school culture. | **Deconstruct knowledge frameworks that perpetuate inequity and reconstruct more equitable knowledge frameworks** (Specific cultural change.) |
| (Power – empowering change and people.) | **Address the inequitable distribution of power** (More specific change.) |
| (Not addressed explicitly – focus on whole school improvement.) | **Schooling as both a public and private good** |
| *Improving the instructional program* | **Focus on emancipation, democracy, equity, and justice** (That is, build a cohesive school culture around some disputed but specifically democratic values.) |
| *Developing people* | **Emphasis on interdependence, interconnectedness, and global awareness** (This suggests an explicit curricular focus on inclusion and understanding of multiple perspectives.) |
| Evaluate practices, refine, increase effectiveness. | **Engage in both critique and promise** (Actions that promote equity, inclusion, and social justice.) |
| Not addressed. | **The need for moral courage** (The disruption of power, privilege, and underlying assumptions may cause discomfort and resistance.) |

programs and communication of priorities" (British Columbia Ministry of Education, 2017, p. 17). The areas are (1) setting strategic directions, (2) leading the organization, (3) ensuring accountabilities, and (4) developing people – the same domains identified by the OLF. In comparison, the practices described in the right-hand column, while still undoubtedly comprising outcomes that help to determine the success or failure of an organization, are ultimately determined by an underlying moral and ethical compass that helps leaders make the difficult choices required to "level the playing field" so that all may succeed. In this case, the specifics remain unspecified, although the goals and values are explicit.

It is clear, however, that the values embedded in the tenets of TLT (on the right) suggest not only practices, but directions for these practices. For example, under transformational leadership, one might determine that the desirable goal or direction of a school in a given year is to recruit new students, to achieve an athletic championship, or to have the highest test scores in the region. In transformative leadership, the underlying goal is always to develop an equitable, inclusive, and socially just organization – one which might well achieve one of the other goals as well.

When one examines the details of the OLF, there is reference to "priority placed by the Ontario government on social justice in the province's public schools" (Leithwood, 2012, p. 11), but no other mention of social justice in the document. There is continued recognition that schools serve "highly diverse communities" and of the "province's commitment to inclusive education" (p. 13), but no discussion of what this means for leaders who want to address the needs of the most vulnerable. Similarly, the only mention of equity in the BCLDF is that it is a given: "Teaching excellence, effective leadership and social equity have made British Columbia's education system one of the strongest in the world" (British Columbia Ministry of Education, 2017, p. 3). There is no mention in either document of equity as a goal or as a value that might drive leadership considerations. In fact, in both documents, the processes called for (such as establishing organizational vision, building trust, collaborating with families, and building shared leadership) all reflect what Hodgkinson (1978) called the "depths of ambiguity."

One way transformative leadership addresses this critique is by being solidly grounded in the specific values of excellence, equity, inclusion, and social justice. Other theories, including transformational leadership, leave the specific values up to the organization and the leader. Thus, there is no normative or value-guided direction related to the desired practices. There is no focus on the need for the values of equity or inclusion to drive decision-making. As a further example, one could determine that, because test scores are often an indication of an "improved instructional program," it would be useful to adopt, as some schools have done, a direct instruction approach to pedagogy, which mandates that all teachers move through the curriculum at the same time and pace, use the same materials and writing prompts, and require students who fail to reach desired standards to attend after-school or Saturday classes. In contrast, an equitable, value-based approach would ask teachers to develop pedagogies that connect with their specific group of students, identifying their interests and challenges and modifying instruction accordingly. As we will see in the vignette presented in the next section, adopting a transformative leadership approach could help to address the disconnect between these frameworks and a desire to create an equitable system.

Another key distinction between TLT and many other more positivist theories is its strong emphasis on the underlying beliefs and assumptions that determine what is valued. Again, a lack of belief statements, or general hypotheses, in other frameworks helps to explain the dissonance that often occurs between stated goals and advocated practices. In contrast, TLT explicitly responds to Johnson's (2008) finding that "what separates successful leaders from unsuccessful ones is their mental models or meaning structures, not their knowledge, information, training, or experience per se" (p. 85).

This explicit emphasis on beliefs and mindsets is also central to the ways in which Anello et al. (2014) conceptualize transformative leadership. They posit that "critical to the process of transformative learning is becoming aware of our own and others' tacit assumptions and expectations" (p. 5). Once we submit our own implicit beliefs, tacit assumptions, and mental models to critical scrutiny against the values of equity, inclusion, and social justice, we may find that changes are needed. Moreover, these changes will not simply pertain to our own thinking, but to the structures and functions of the organizations within which we work. As Quantz et al. (1991) argued, "To adopt transformative leadership requires understanding how its adoption would affect the historically bureaucratic structure of schools and the traditional functionalist discourse used to describe them" (p. 98).

## Transformative Leadership in Action

In contrast to the frameworks selected by Ontario and British Columbia, some other jurisdictions have adopted frameworks that specifically focus on equity. In New Zealand, for example, the principles of several federally funded professional development programs, including Te Kotahitanga (TKI) and Kia Eke Panuku (KEP), have been widely adopted. The latter was explicitly based on the "need to dismantle what is not working, and learn new theories, discourses, and practices," in part by developing transformative leaders (KEP, n.d., para. 1), while Te Kotahitanga was guided by "the need to explicitly reject deficit theorising as a means of explaining Māori students' educational achievement levels," and by encouraging teachers to take an "agentic position in theorising about their practice" (TKI, n.d., para. 2). Here, to provide an illustration of what TLT can look like on the ground, I provide an extended description of transformative leadership in action, drawn from a visit I made to a New Zealand school in 2018. I conducted an extended interview with "Marie," the principal of "Royal College" (both pseudonyms). This brief overview of a transformed, national award-winning school is illustrative of how TLT can provide practical guidance for school leaders wanting to create equitable, inclusive, excellent, and socially just learning environments and experiences for all students.[3]

*Our co-ed high school is a decile 1 school[4] with only about 320 students, about 65 per cent Māori and Pacifica, and approximately 35 per cent Pakeja (white). When I arrived eight years ago it was down to 260, with our senior school achievement rates ranging from 3–30 per cent. Thirty years ago there had been a lot of white flight, and more recently there had been news reports of gangs and violence and a lot of deficit thinking. We had more people out of classes than in class, a lot of people just hanging around the school, with visible gangs, high violence, high suspension and drop-out rates. You could come in and just feel this heavy blanket of despair, a feeling there was no future.*

*There was a lot of deficit thinking and the talk about the young people was "All these brown kids – what can you do with them?" The evidence from the Education Review Office was very damning. Finances were in deficit. Leadership was very traditional and top-down, and quite transactional. Everything needed attention – the quality of teaching and learning, the culture of the school, the behaviour. It was so big that we needed to focus on what was going to make a difference. The government told me I had one semester before they closed us down, although I didn't tell the staff because they were under enough pressure.*

*We all realized there was sense of urgency and a need to engage everyone here. We had to take ownership of the failure and turn things around. As leader, I took responsibility. "The buck stops with me." We went out and apologized to the iwi (the community) for not serving the young people. It was clear that we had to rebuild trust because the message from the parents was that they wanted the very best education for the young people.*

*I deconstructed what was here and looked at the legacy of failure. We needed a relational approach within a cultural response of teaching and relational pedagogy. We read a lot about equity and opportunity. We co-constructed a new approach from the evidence. Our school motto is "Student success is the only option." But we don't just focus on academics; we listen to student, parent, and community voices and try to make everyone feel valued and connected and part of the culture here.*

*The first year, the achievement results doubled from thirty at best to sixty, which isn't much, because they were originally so bad, but we stayed open. Attendance went from 50 to 80 per cent. Part of it was transforming the curriculum to align with the students' interests, strengths, aspirations, future pathways. We have a very broad and rich curriculum. We've been able to bring in a service academy. We have a teenage parent unit here with early childhood education attached. We also have a dance program, apprenticeships and trades, and university pathways. Students feel valued and connected and part of the culture here. They feel that we believe in them and that because of what we're offering, they can be successful and achieve.*

*There was a new sense of hope and optimism. We shifted away from blaming our students, our parents, our community. We felt we had agency, and were not deficit theorizing about the teachers but were affirming. Some teachers left because the new approach didn't fit with their personality.*

*I tried to be authentic and open and to connect with the community. So in my view, the leadership approach here is very much transformative. We're open and honest. It's all based on evidence and about equity. We try to distribute leadership, build capacity, and sustain it.*

*We start each school year by meeting on one of the local maraes and listening to their goals. For example, one year, the marae council expressed concern about cleaning up and protecting the surrounding waterways and so we planned a thematic unit across the curriculum and engaged students to help with the project.*

*About a third of the staff have been trained in restorative practices. It's culturally appropriate in terms of the way that we are restoring harm and wrong-doing. But it also aligns with that relational approach. Everyone is involved in whatever's happened. Before it was punitive: "We'll kick you out, and if you're not here you can't learn."*

*Every Monday, as a staff, we have an hour of professional learning around what our evidence shows about the areas that we need to move forward and develop. Every Friday morning, we meet in inquiry groups again around accelerating progress to ensure equity for our young people. So, we're looking at deliberate excellent instruction. The groups discuss what we have been doing to support our learners and what shifts we have seen. We try to learn from our collaboration to make bigger shifts. Then the groups present and share to the wider staff. We've got an equity team that meets as well, where we look at a range of data about every student from years seven to thirteen. We have a breakfast program. Our PTA room has food for young people, and teachers also have food. We also have raised money to ensure that all students could go to camp and participate in sports, regardless of whether they could buy the sports gear and the shoes.*

*We're now the school of choice for transgender students. There's a very inclusive culture. We have the majority of transgender students from a neighbouring community; they're coming here to feel included and part of the culture.*

*But we have a long way to go. It's heartbreaking. We still have a high suicide rate in the community, so I am on call 24/7 and, as part of it, we have a procedure to monitor Facebook pages and if I'm contacted, I contact the family right away.*

*Discrimination is really embedded within our political and educational systems, and across our society. Privilege is there, and if we think about our [Māori] young people, they're way behind the starting line. I even heard it in a recent meeting with people from the Ministry who thought we needed to learn to use restraints because of our population. Really? I challenged them. You need to have those difficult conversations; in terms of leadership, that discomfort is there, but it needs to happen.*

*We need to challenge discrimination and deficit thinking when we see them creeping back into our assumptions and beliefs and keep pushing forward for our young people, because it's all about them. We need to have every child on a confident pathway to their dreams and aspirations.*

In the foregoing vignette, we see evidence of the practical application of the hypotheses and tenets of transformative leadership. Although this is simply a cursory overview of the thought processes, belief systems, and discussions that led to the transformation of this school, it demonstrates clearly the power of adopting an approach guided by transformative leadership theory. Here, we can see the tenets of TLT in practice.

The principal, who described her own leadership approach as *transformative*, began by accepting the *mandate for deep and equitable change*, even to the point of taking responsibility for failures prior to her arrival at Royal College. Moreover, she communicated this mandate in such a way that the staff collectively accepted the need for evidence-based and equitable change, and widely distributing leadership responsibilities. Adopting this mandate requires knowing yourself and your non-negotiables, as well as your community and your organization.

The need to *deconstruct knowledge frameworks that perpetuate inequity and reconstruct them in equitable ways* is clearly at the front and centre of Marie's desire to continue to deconstruct (a word she actually used) deficit thinking, to emphasize the agency of all (both students and teachers), and to introduce both restorative practices and culturally relevant pedagogy. Confronting inequity wherever it is found and working to ensure the success of students who are traditionally marginalized is at the centre of TLT. As seen here, some educators will embrace the opportunity, while a few may choose to leave the organization instead of adapting to new frameworks.

*Re-distribution of inequitable instances of power* is also evident in the change from a top-down leadership approach to one in which all participate in ensuring collaborative professional learning, and in decision-making more generally. Here, we see how a change from the previous transactional leadership approach to one in which teachers and the whole community are valued and involved in offering high-quality education to all students has changed the culture, the tone, and the morale of the whole community.

*Balancing private and public good* is evident throughout the interview with Marie. There was definitely concern about the students gaining a credential and being able to go on to university, but also concern for their sense of belonging to the school community – their connections to one another and to the school as a whole. This tenet recognizes the importance of individual achievement and increasing competency and self-confidence, but also of engaging in activities that build a sense of collective efficacy and community.

*A focus on emancipation, democracy, equity, and justice* was evident throughout. As Marie stated, the vision is grounded in equity. The professional development readings and conversations focus on equity, and every change made, including a new emphasis on restorative practices rather than punishment, is embedded in democracy and equity. This tenet also involves moving from general principles related to transforming underlying structures and school-wide policies to a focus on curriculum and pedagogy as well.

*Emphasizing interdependence, interconnectedness, and global awareness* extends the previous tenet in ways that help students become global citizens, taking responsibility for the welfare of others and recognizing how what happens in one part of the world affects what happens elsewhere. At Royal College, educators began by responding to the marae's concern for the surrounding waterways and created a whole school initiative to engage students in sharing responsibility for the wider community.

*Balancing critique and promise* is evident throughout. Not only did Marie critique the practices she found upon her arrival at Royal College, but she also worked to change them to provide the promise of increased and equitable opportunities for all students. Moreover, she engaged in critique of the systemic inequities without assigning blame to individual students, families, or teachers, thus overcoming the common tendency to locate responsibility for lack of success in the students' circumstances rather than in the school's approach. Here we clearly see that identifying the challenges was not enough, and had Marie not taken courageous action, the school would have been closed.

The whole endeavour required *moral courage*. Marie actually mentions the new sense of urgency and moral purpose throughout the school and even the community. She took risks apologizing for a situation for which she was not responsible to parents and the community. Knowing her job was on the line, Marie took the burden of knowing the school might close on her shoulders in order to permit the rest of the staff breathing room to make the required changes. Moreover, she also stood up to personnel from the Ministry during a professional development session when they expressed deficit perspectives about her students. This kind of courage is what is required to transform schools. Moreover, what we have seen is true transformation as defined by Burns (2003); that is, "a metamorphosis in form or structure, a change in the very condition or nature of a thing ... a radical change ... as when a frog is transformed into a prince or a carriage maker into an auto factory" (p. 24). It is not simply tinkering; true transformation involves deep-seated and systemic change.

Transformation of this nature changed what might have been called "Hopeless High School" into a place called Royal College, in which students became agents of their own learning and citizens of the community. From a place beset with drugs and violence, Royal College became a school in which achievement, attendance, and confidence rose to such a point that transgender students from the whole vicinity found safety, acceptance, and belonging. These changes clearly support the first principle of transformative leadership theory that *when a person feels respected, included, and valued, it is easier to concentrate on their assigned task and the work will be more successfully completed*. In the case of Royal College, the learning environment was transformed for both students and teachers, and, by every marker, success followed.

Similarly, the second proposition of transformative leadership was fulfilled, as *the whole community was strengthened when individual achievement was balanced with the value of public good and civic engagement*. Not only did teachers all participate in the professional learning of the staff, but, as Marie noted during the interview, you can now "feel that this is a happy, optimistic place." The growth in enrolment and the community's increased support through extensive donations to support the participation of the most needy children are further evidence of strengthened civil society.

## Concluding Thoughts

The transformation of Royal College clearly illustrates the potential and possibilities inherent in a critical and comprehensive approach such as TLT. The actions taken to transform Royal College were specific to its situation and population. Similarly, the ways in which transformative leadership could transform Canadian schools would depend on their location and population.

For example, a principal and staff in rural Saskatchewan might begin by finding data to update the report of the Saskatoon School Board from 2007, which stated that in 2001 almost one quarter of the province's students were First Nations and Métis, but that less than 57 per cent had graduated from Grade 12 (Thompson, 2007, p. 18). Educational leaders might then examine the joint statement of the Ministry of Education and the Federation of Sovereign Indigenous Nations (FSIN), which asserted that the Ministry

> recognizes that when it comes to First Nation education that the provincial school
> system is not the sole expert in how to educate First Nation students. In the spirit of
> building a truly collaborative partnership and reciprocal relationship between the
> education systems in our province, the provincial education system will be looking
> to First Nation education organizations for their expert opinion when it comes to
> educating First Nation students and that by working together in a respectful part-
> nership, we will improve the outcomes for all students in Saskatchewan. (Ministry
> of Education of Saskatchewan, 2018, p. 3)

To improve outcomes for all students, school leaders might ask which First Nations organizations, elders, and traditional knowledge keepers would be willing to partner with them and advise them; they could reach out to faculty from the First Nations University of Canada and ensure they were offering culturally and linguistically relevant and relational pedagogy for all students.

In an inner-city school in Vancouver, the process might be quite different. After examining their data and their processes, educators might identify which students and groups of students were not progressing well in terms of academics, who was disproportionately disciplined or suspended, or which students were participating in which extra-curricular activities. They might engage in a process, such as one of the starting points of Te Kotahitanga, to ask teachers to brainstorm reasons why these students were "failing." Upon discovering that the predominant reasons that were given blamed the students themselves or their family circumstances, or that teachers expressed fear of some of the older "Brown students" (see Sayani, 2010), the principal might introduce a number of activities intended to overcome deficit thinking and change the knowledge frameworks about students in order to help them identify and fulfil their dreams. After recognizing, with Wagstaff and Fusarelli (1999), that the principal's explicit rejection of deficit thinking was the single most important factor in the academic achievement of minoritized students, educators would be ready to implement more comprehensive high-quality opportunities for all students.

In a French-language school in Quebec or in a minority linguistic context in the rest of Canada, in addition to "educating" all students, one of the goals would clearly be to ensure the preservation of the French language. Here, the staff might begin by wrestling with the question of how to respect newcomers' need to sometimes communicate in their home language, while at the same time promoting the use and advancement of French.

In Toronto, which is often considered to be Canada's most multicultural city, staff might first develop a profile of the school in which the students' ethnic origins, religious adherence, home languages, sexual orientations, and gender identities were highlighted. Having carefully and ethically documented the student demographics, it would be possible to analyse which students were most and least successful and in which ways, who participated in which classes or activities, and where there seemed to be the least equity in opportunities or outcomes. Using the school profile as a baseline, transformative leaders could then re-examine policies and practices to ensure they benefited all students.

We could go on to discuss the need for data and understanding of the unique characteristics of each school and each region in Canada. Educators could begin by identifying inequitable outcomes such as high school graduation rates, disciplinary incidents, the segregation of English-language learners, the lack of opportunity for Muslim girls to participate in extra-curricular activities, drop-out rates of LGBTQ2+ students, student needs to work part time to support impoverished families, disproportionate failure and stigmatism of children in care,[5] the lack of support and discriminatory policies and practices for children and youth experiencing homelessness, and many other ways in which neither the playing field nor the outcomes of education are equitable.

What is important is that any plans to reform schools begin with the goal of achieving inclusive, equitable, excellent, and socially just education for all. Once this mandate has been understood and accepted, educators must engage in careful and continuous examination of their own – and their community's – underlying beliefs, values, and assumptions. They will need to identify knowledge frameworks that perpetuate inequity and ascertain how to challenge and change them. Determining where there is inequitable use of power, and where there is a need to change the emphasis to balance public and private good goals, will also precede decisions about new approaches or new programs.

It is critically important not to jump too quickly to adopt a new program or curriculum before ensuring that the prevailing implicit beliefs will support the safe, respectful, and inclusive environment needed to achieve the desired transformation. However, it is also necessary to ensure that the curriculum is respectful of and responsive to student needs and perspectives, and that all are included and feel welcome. Moreover, helping each member of the school community understand their place in the larger global community, and how interconnected and interdependent the world is, is also an essential task.[6]

**Needed: A Systemic Approach**

Clearly, identifying inequities and critiquing current educational policies and practices is only a beginning. It is, moreover, the easy part of transformation. Taking action to transform schools in more equitable ways requires adopting an activist stance of both critique and promise. And this kind of action, as Marie clearly exemplified, requires moral courage. There are risks, as the case of Royal College demonstrated, including the risk Marie accepted of having the school close and losing her job. Nevertheless, the potential for transformative leaders to make a meaningful difference in the lives of teachers, students, and the wider community is implicit in the vignette.

There is no doubt that societal transformation is a much larger and longer-term project, but we must start where we are and do what we can. Providing students with safe learning environments in which they are valued and respected and in which they learn to understand their place in the wider community is an important step forward. Educators who acknowledge their own privilege and responsibility, speak out in the face of prejudice or discrimination, listen respectfully to all perspectives, challenge unjust policies and practices, acknowledge the intrinsic worth of all human beings, and take action to redress wrongs exemplify the courageous stance needed for visions of a better future to become reality.

It is my hope that this chapter will provide the incentive for educators across Canada to adopt a form of leadership focused on equity, inclusion, and social justice. In fact, based on thirty years of research about transformative leaders and their efforts to transform schools, I am convinced that it is this approach that will not only further equity, but also excellence for all students. Only when we take steps to offer both excellent and socially just education to all students will we be able to echo the words of Nelson Mandela, who claimed that "education is the most powerful weapon we have to change the world."

## NOTES

1  Here I use the terms equity, equitable, inclusive, excellent, and socially just consistent with the descriptions and meanings identified in the Introduction to this book.
2  Note that this is different from the Leadership Standards produced by the BC Principals' & Vice Principals' Association (BCPVPA).
3  The extended vignette is compiled from data presented in a lengthy interview with the school's principal. In the interest of brevity, I have extrapolated her comments, but as much as possible I have used her own words. To maintain confidentiality, I have also removed identifying details and have used pseudonyms for people and places throughout.
4  In New Zealand, schools are categorized by pre-dominant socio-economic status from decile 1 to decile 10, with 1 being the lowest (i.e., with the highest possible poverty and deprivation population).
5  The term "in care" is commonly used to refer to students in foster care, governmental group homes, hospitals, and so forth.
6  The global COVID-19 pandemic in 2020–2 is certainly illustrative of the pressing need for global understanding and awareness, although there are many other possible examples.

## REFERENCES

Anello, E., Hernandez, J., & Khadem, M. (2014). *Transformative leadership: Developing the hidden dimension.* Houston, TX: Harmony Equity Press.
Blackmore, J. (2011). Leadership in pursuit of purpose: Social, economic and political transformation. In C.M. Shields (Ed.), *Transformative leadership: A reader* (pp. 21–36). New York, NY: Peter Lang.
Bradford, A. (2017, July 28). What is a scientific theory? *LiveScience.* https://www .livescience.com/21491-what-is-a-scientific-theory-definition-of-theory.html
British Columbia Ministry of Education. (2017). *Leadership development in the B.C. education sector: Provincial leadership development framework.* Government of British Columbia. https://www2.gov.bc.ca/assets/gov/education/administration /kindergarten-to-grade-12/leadership/bc-leadership-development-framework.pdf
Burns, J.M. (1978). *Leadership.* New York, NY: Harper & Row.
Burns, J.M. (2003). *Transforming leadership.* New York, NY: Grove Press.
Foster, W. (1986). *Paradigms and promises.* Amherst, NY: Prometheus Books.
Greenfield, T.B. (1980). The man who comes back through the door in the wall: Discovering truth, discovering self, discovering organizations. *Educational Administration Quarterly, 16*(3), 26–59. doi: 10.1177/0013161X8001600305
Hewitt, K.K., Davis, A.W., & Lashley, C. (2014). Transformational and transformative leadership in a research-informed leadership preparation program. *Journal of Research on Leadership Education, 9*(3) 225–53. doi: 10.1177/1942775114552329

Hodgkinson, C. (1978). *Towards a philosophy of administration*. New York, NY: Palgrave Macmillan.

Jackson, S. (2007). Freire re-viewed. *Educational Theory, 57*(2), 199–213. doi: 10.1111/j.1741-5446.2007.00252.x

Johnson, H.H. (2008). Mental models and transformative learning: The key to leadership development? *Human Resource Development Quarterly, 19*(1), 85–9. doi: 10.1002/hrdq.1227

Kia Eke Panuku (KEP). (n.d.). *About Kia Eke Panuku: The response*. New Zealand Ministry of Education. Retrieved 1 May 2020 from https://kep.org.nz/about

Leithwood, K. (2010). Transformational school leadership. In E. Baker, B. McGaw, & P. Peterson (Eds.), *International encyclopedia of education* (3rd ed.). Oxford, UK: Elsevier.

Leithwood, K. (2012). *The Ontario leadership framework 2012 with a discussion of research foundations*. Ontario Institute for Education Leadership. https://www.education-leadership-ontario.ca/application/files/2514/9452/5287/The_Ontario_Leadership_Framework_2012_-_with_a_Discussion_of_the_Research_Foundations.pdf

Miller, P.M., Brown, T., & Hopson, R. (2011). Centering love, hope, and trust in the community: Transformative urban leadership informed by Paulo Freire. *Urban Education, 46*(5), 1078–99. doi: 10.1177/0042085910395951

Ministry of Education of Saskatchewan. (2018). *Inspiring success: First Nations and Métis PreK–12 education policy framework*. Government of Saskatchewan. https://pubsaskdev.blob.core.windows.net/pubsask-prod/107115/107115-Inspiring_Success_Policy_Framework.pdf

Quantz, R.A., Rogers, J., & Dantley, M. (1991). Rethinking transformative leadership: Toward democratic reform of schools. *Journal of Education, 173*(3), 96–118. doi: 10.1177/002205749117300307

Sayani, A. (2010). *Pathologies and complicities: High school and the identities of disaffected South Asian "Brown boys"* (Unpublished doctoral dissertation). University of British Columbia, Vancouver, BC.

Shields, C.M. (2010). Transformative leadership. In E. Baker, B. McGaw, & P. Peterson (Eds.), *International encyclopedia of education* (3rd ed.). Oxford, UK: Elsevier.

Shields, C.M. (2016). *Transformative leadership: Primer*. New York, NY: Peter Lang.

Shields, C.M. (2020). *Becoming a transformative leader: A guide to creating equitable schools*. New York, NY: Routledge.

Starratt, R.J. (2011). Preparing transformative educators for the work of leading schools in a multicultural, diverse, and democratic society. In C.M. Shields (Ed.), *Transformative leadership: A reader* (pp. 131–6). New York, NY: Peter Lang.

Swingewood, A. (1998). *Cultural theory and the problem of modernity*. New York, NY: St. Martin's Press..

Te Kete Ipurangi (TKI). (n.d.). *The development of Te Kotahitanga*. New Zealand Ministry of Education. Retrieved 1 May 2020 from https://tekotahitanga.tki.org.nz/About/The-Development-of-Te-Kotahitanga

Thompson, L. (2007). *First Nations and Métis education: An advisory for school boards*. Saskatchewan School Boards Association. https://saskschoolboards.ca/wp-content/uploads/2015/08/Module_11_FNM_Education.pdf

van Oord, L. (2013). Towards transformative leadership in education. *International Journal of Leadership in Education: Theory and Practice, 16*(4), 419–34. doi: 10.1080/13603124.2013.776116

Wagstaff, L., & Fusarelli, L. (1999). Establishing collaborative governance and leadership. In P. Reyes, J. Scribner, & A. Scribner (Eds.), *Lessons from high-performing Hispanic schools: Creating learning communities* (pp. 19–35). New York, NY: Teachers College Press.

Weiner, E.J. (2003). Secretary Paulo Freire and the democratization of power: Toward a theory of transformative leadership. *Educational Philosophy and Theory, 35*(1), 89–106. doi: 10.1111/1469-5812.00007

WikiDiff. (n.d.). Transformative or transformational – What's the difference? Retrieved 1 May 2020 from https://wikidiff.com/transformational/transformative

## 2 Transformative Leadership: Leading French-Language Schools in Canadian Anglo-dominant Contexts[1]

ANDRÉANNE GÉLINAS-PROULX AND MÉLISSA VILLELLA

*Non! S'engager pour la langue française n'est pas un combat d'arrière-garde! C'est au contraire une cause juste et moderne qui ne sera définitivement perdue que lorsque tous ceux qui doivent la défendre l'auront abandonnée. Alors agissons!*

– Dominique Hoppe[2]

*Les humains doivent se reconnaître dans leur humanité commune, en même temps que reconnaître leur diversité tant individuelle que culturelle.*

– Edgar Morin[3]

French-language schools in Canada's public education systems are led by principals who demonstrate, or should demonstrate, a leadership style that considers their specific Anglo-dominant or "minoritized" contexts[4] in order to better foster equity, inclusion, excellence, and social justice among students, staff, and the local and broader community of the school. This chapter will therefore begin with an overview of the surrounding contexts where French-language school principals operate. It will then show how these principals would benefit from referring to transformative leadership theory (TLT) and its eight tenets (Shields, 2013, 2014, 2016).

In the spirit of transparency, some background information on the authors will be presented before diving into the heart of this chapter. Andréanne Gélinas-Proulx is Canadian; her language of origin is French, and English is her second language. Mélissa Villella is also Canadian; her languages of origin are French and English, while Italian is a second language. Before becoming a professor of school administration at Université du Québec en Outaouais, Andréanne taught in French-language schools in Quebec, in the Republic of Togo, and in Prince Edward Island, where she was also a school principal. Mélissa is currently a professor of school administration at Université du Québec en Abitibi-Témiscamingue; she has also been a part-time professor at the

University of Ottawa, a teacher in Ontario and Quebec, as well as the principal of Franco-Ontarian schools and the director of programs and services of one of Canada's largest French-language minority community centres. Andréanne's research focuses on leadership and the intercultural competence of school principals. As for Mélissa, her doctoral thesis and associated work focus on the intercultural and anti-racist competency of school leaders.

## Francophone Minoritized Contexts in Canada: Legislation

Officially, Canada is considered a bilingual and multicultural country. These two characteristics are protected by legislation, as we will see in the following sections. Nevertheless, as we will also see, principals of French-language schools in Canadian minoritized contexts experience particular challenges as they strive to both maintain their language and provide excellent and equitable education for their students.

On one hand, the country's bilingual status was formalized in 1867 in the Constitution Act and in 1969 with the adoption of the first Official Languages Act (Office of the Commissioner of Official Languages, n.d.). Moreover, the country's bilingual status is embedded in the 1982 Canadian Charter of Rights and Freedoms (hereafter referred to as the Charter). Section 16 (1) of the Charter states: "English and French are the official languages of Canada and have equality of status and equal rights and privileges as to their use in all institutions of the Parliament and government of Canada." This section states that only the English and French linguistic communities are recognized as official language communities. However, even though both official languages have equal status at the federal government level, French is considered the minority language in all provinces and territories of Canada except Quebec, where English is considered the minority language. As a result, French is more often the language of the minority in Canada, and its speakers are more often members of the country's official language minority community. Demographically, the 2016 census indicates that 21.1 per cent of the Canadian population speaks French most often at home (Statistics Canada, 2017b).[5] According to the same census, in the province of Quebec, the majority of the population (82.4 per cent) speaks French most often at home. In comparison, in other Canadian provinces and territories, French is spoken most often at home by only 2.5 per cent of the population (Statistics Canada, 2017b).

On the other hand, Canada adopted a Canadian multiculturalism policy in 1971, and section 27 of the 1982 Charter states that "[t]his Charter shall be interpreted in a manner consistent with the preservation and enhancement of the multicultural heritage of Canadians." In addition, the Canadian Multiculturalism Act came into effect in 1988 (Brosseau & Dewing, 2018). However, the multicultural status of the country precludes official recognition of languages other than English and French, despite the fact that immigrants have contributed – and are contributing – to the country's growth. Any speaker of a language other than English or French can therefore be considered a member of a non-official language community (NOLC). Moreover, even if citizens or permanent residents have a non-official Canadian language of origin, or if they do not speak official languages at home, they are nonetheless asked during the Canadian census to specify if they know enough of the official languages to converse in them (Statistics Canada, 2017b).

It is also important to note that official bilingual and multicultural statuses are only a part of the country's history, since Canada also has Indigenous communities, also known as First Nations, Métis, and Inuit (FNMI). In this regard, section 25 of the Charter grants the following rights and freedoms to Indigenous people:

> The guarantee in this Charter of certain rights and freedoms shall not be construed so as to abrogate or derogate from any aboriginal, treaty or other rights or freedoms that pertain to the aboriginal peoples of Canada including (*a*) any rights or freedoms that have been recognized by the Royal Proclamation of October 7, 1763; and (*b*) any rights or freedoms that now exist by way of land claims agreements or may be so acquired.

From this section of the Charter, it can be concluded that Canada recognizes the cultural and heritage status of FNMI, but that FNMI (like NOLC) do not have any of their languages acknowledged in the Charter. Thus, from this analysis of the Charter, not all historic linguistic and cultural communities in Canada benefit from the same status, rights, or freedoms. Such differences are also the case in education, as we will see shortly.

With the exception of the federally funded school system for FNMI, school decentralization exists in Canada (Dalley & Villella, 2013). In this sense, the education systems in Canada (i.e., one per province and territory) also embody the country's bilingualism. In fact, in order to ensure both majority and minority language education, minority language education rights have been included in section 23 of the Charter:

(1) Citizens of Canada
   (a) whose first language learned and still understood is that of the English or French linguistic minority population of the province in which they reside, or
   (b) who have received their primary school instruction in Canada in English or French and reside in a province where the language in which they received that instruction is the language of the English or French linguistic minority population of the province,

> have the right to have their children receive primary and secondary
> school instruction in that language in that province.
> (2) Citizens of Canada of whom any child has received or is receiving
> primary or secondary school instruction in English or French in Canada,
> have the right to have all their children receive primary and secondary
> school instruction in the same language.
> (3) The right of citizens of Canada under subsections (1) and (2) to have
> their children receive primary and secondary school instruction in the
> language of the English or French linguistic minority population of a
> province
>> (a) applies wherever in the province the number of children of citizens
>> who have such a right is sufficient to warrant the provision to them
>> out of public funds of minority language instruction; and
>> (b) includes, where the number of those children so warrants, the right to
>> have them receive that instruction in minority language educational
>> facilities provided out of public funds.

Thus, in Anglo-dominant Canadian contexts, parents of children to which section 23 of the Charter applies have the right to be educated in a minority language (i.e., completely in French). This means that the official language of both schooling and communication is French, and not that of a French-language immersion program within an English school system. Moreover, publicly funded French-language schools in these contexts ensure the vitality and sustainability of the French language (Landry, Allard, & Deveau, 2010). In 2016–17, the Association canadienne d'éducation de langue française (ACELF) counted 699 francophone schools in these contexts (ACELF, n.d.). While these schools have an educational mission, they also help to build identity, promote francophone pride, and cultivate students' sense of belonging to francophone and Acadian communities (e.g., Ontario Ministry of Education, 2011).

## French-Language Schools in Canadian Minoritized Contexts

Principals of French-language schools in Canadian minoritized contexts are guided by a foundational threefold mission: the transmission of knowledge, socialization in terms of societal values, and the (re)production of the French language (Gérin-Lajoie, 2002). This school mission obviously complicates the tasks of school principals (Bouchamma, 2004). On this topic, Racine (2007) presents some challenges such as "linguistic assimilation, the decline of the French language in Canada, exogamy, the attraction of Anglo-Saxon culture, or general acculturation to the majority language and culture" (translation, p. 245).[6] In Canada, the meaning of the word exogamy is based on an anthropological definition that carries with it the notion that language refers to a culture (Daveluy, 2007; Taylor, 2002). In more concrete terms, it refers to marriages or common-law unions between members of different linguistic or cultural groups (Landry et al., 2010).[7] Among other things, the language(s) spoken at home is/are used to determine the effects of language exogamy in Canadian homes. According to the most recent census, 65.6 per cent of people with French as their language of origin speak another language at home when they live in a minoritized context; in 64.5 per cent of these cases, the other language is English (Statistics Canada, 2017a). Furthermore, Landry and Gélinas-Proulx (2018) specify what is meant by "attraction to Anglo-Saxon culture and generalized acculturation" by showing their effects:

> [G]reater prestige is given to the majority language, [and] media use in the majority language, interpersonal communications in the majority language to a large extent, and less political capital in the minority language are also factors that contribute to subtractive bilingualism [i.e., learning one language at the expense of another] and cause the loss of the minority language (Landry et al., 2010). As a result, identity tensions are felt among students attending Francophone schools in FMC [Francophone minority context] because of this power relationship between Anglophone and Francophone cultures, thereby complicating the construction of their identity (Cormier, 2005; Landry, 2015; Landry et al., 2013; Pilote & Magnan, 2008). (translation, p. 103)

To these challenges should be added those of recruiting and retaining students that chose, or could choose, English-language schools and even French immersion schools and programs (Government of Ontario, 2004). However, competition for recruitment also takes place among French-language schools in a "school market" context. For example, in some regions of provinces such as Ontario and Alberta, there may be competition between government funded French-language public and Catholic schools to recruit the same francophone student. "The school market is understood in terms of the effects of interdependence and competitiveness generated between schools in the same local arena" (translation, Delvaux & Van Zanten, 2006; Maroy & Van Zanten, 2007, as cited in Bélanger, Dalley, Dionne, & Beaulieu, 2011, p. 376). However, there is a substantial risk that some schools will be marginalized by parents who find them less attractive, as Bélanger et al. (2011) show. Moreover, another possible issue comes from the fact that "various promotional strategies [implemented by schools] are used to recruit or retain the best students, thus excluding students who do not fit the definition of a good student" (translation, Bagley, Woods, & Glatter, 2001, as cited in Bélanger et al., 2011, p. 380). In addition, some Franco-Ontarian schools use the *Programme d'appui pour les nouveaux arrivants* (PANA) as a strategy for recruiting immigrant students. Although the intention of PANA is to better include immigrant students, some report feeling that they spent more time than necessary in classes offering this program, and consequently, they perceive this experience as discriminatory and stigmatizing (Veronis & Huot, 2017).

In minoritized contexts, the work of French-language school principals is certainly complicated by the fact that students in their schools seem to struggle academically more than students in English-language schools, at least on certain standardized assessments, in certain subjects, and even on certain concepts (Brochu, Deussing, Houme, & Chuy, 2012; O'Grady & Houme, 2014; Shipley, 2011). The 2018 Programme for International Student Assessment (PISA) clearly indicates, in reading and in science, that results of French-language school students in minoritized contexts are lower than those of English-language school students (O'Grady et al., 2018).

School principals also face challenges in terms of resources. Following a questionnaire surveying 672 teachers in minoritized contexts across Canada, the 2004 report of Gilbert, Letouzé, Thériault, and Landry shows that one of the main challenges in French-language schools is the lack of "resources, whether financial, material, pedagogical, human or technological" (translation, p. 20). As for pedagogical resources, the report states that they are not adapted for French-language schools in a minoritized context. With respect to material resources, Gilbert et al. (2004) state that some students in French-language schools have been educated in the last decade, or are still being educated, in facilities deemed unacceptable. After a ten-year battle, a Supreme Court of Canada appeal judgment, handed down in June 2020, decided that British Columbia does not provide equivalent facilities and transportation for francophone students compared to anglophone students, and that the former do not benefit from a comparable educational experience (Supreme Court of Canada, 2020). The judgement specified the following:

> The trial judge's order concerning school transportation is restored: the respondents are required to pay $6 million in *Charter* damages to the CSF [Conseil scolaire francophone de la Colombie-Britannique] over a period of 10 years in respect of the inadequate funding of school transportation from 2002–3 to 2011–12. The respondents are also required to pay $1.1 million in damages to the CSF to compensate it for the amount it was denied in respect of the Annual Facilities Grant Rural Factor. (Supreme Court of Canada, 2020)

Thus, in an attempt to counter such injustices, court cases have also taken place, or are taking place, in British Columbia, Saskatchewan, Yukon, and the Northwest Territories (Fédération nationale des conseils scolaires francophones, n.d.). For example, a five-year negotiation period between the territorial government and the Commission scolaire francophone du Yukon finally ended on 12 March 2020. After a lawsuit filed in 2009, certain issues remained in dispute, and negotiations had been underway since 2015. The agreement reached in 2020 includes, among other things, the construction of a French-language high school and measures to address the lack of learning spaces in one of the territory's French-language schools (Government of Yukon, 2020). With regard to human resources, the lack of qualified staff is a major challenge encountered by these schools and causes significant stress for school principals, who must by any and all means fill vacant positions and provide temporary replacements. For example, Adam (2019) points out that French-language elementary and secondary schools in Ontario are currently facing a serious shortage of qualified teachers. This is a persistent problem; for example, in 2006, the Ontario College of Teachers reported a similar shortage. However, this problem is not unique to Ontario. An attempt to solve the problem across the country was put into action in 2019 as part of the federal government's Action Plan for Official Languages (Government of Canada, 2018). Thus, a program was created: the Teacher Recruitment and Retention Strategy in Minority French-Language Schools (Department of Canadian Heritage, 2020).

Moreover, francophone students and school staff experience individual situations of inequity, injustice, and discrimination related to their linguistic identity that principals must be attuned to and address. Several scholars have identified examples of situations of injustice and exclusion within the scope of their work. For example, in her doctoral thesis on French-language schools in New Brunswick, Dalley (2000) shows "how the school institution and teachers marginalize the Acadian language, which is a marker of identity. They thus produce and reproduce the hegemony of standard French and the Acadian linguistic insecurity [felt by students]" (translation, p. 142). In addition, Dalley and Cotnam-Kappel (2013) report a situation in which a student was pressured by her peers to express herself in French: "A girl explained to Mr. Leduc that she and some friends refused to use English with another girl; the former thus forced the latter to switch to French" (translation, pp. 4–5). Finally, Lamoureux and Cotnam (2012), in their collection of several narratives on identity, explain how their participants struggled to establish their French identity in Ontario:

> [A]ll of these authors have something in common: they each claim to live moments where they need to carve out a place for themselves within the Franco-Ontarian community. They show that being "attracted" by the *Francophonie* is unfortunately an insufficient criterion to facilitate their "rootedness" in certain Francophone communities, despite the vision of a "diverse Francophone community"... and give us food for thought about the identification markers that we recognize as legitimate or not and the welcome we give to those who present themselves with different identification markers. (translation, p. 16)

In addition, in French-language schools in minoritized contexts, there are also other minoritized sub-groups based on race, ethnic origin, sexual orientation, gender identity, socio-economic status, language(s) of origin, parental language(s), physical and intellectual capacity, and so on. These sub-groups are doubly or even triply minoritized (Gérin-Lajoie & Jacquet, 2008), and these levels of minorization can add up when an individual has several social marginalization markers. Furthermore, it seems that this multiple minorization of certain individuals can lead to more pronounced discrimination and power relationships against them (Jacquet, Sabatier, & Masinda, 2008). For example, a white French-language school principal from London, Ontario, was removed from his position in 2021 two years after he not only paraded around a school gym wearing a Black student's hair as a wig during a fundraiser for another student who had cancer, but also after wearing the same hair as a wig again six months later for Halloween in 2019 (CBC News, 2021).

Black, immigrant, and francophone individuals living in minoritized contexts may belong to a racialized group, a cultural group, and an ethnic group, or all three at the same time. For some, there is a "white–Black issue" that may constitute a greater challenge to integration at the systemic level (Veronis & Huot, 2017, p. 38). This challenge continues to emerge in the literature based on the lived experience of Black and immigrant[8] children and adults in minoritized francophone school systems (Carr, 2006; Dalley, 2020; Ibrahim, 2014, 2016; Jabouin, 2018; Schroeter & James, 2015). For example, some Black and immigrant students in a French-language secondary school in Ontario had less access to Black pedagogy, didactics, curriculum, and identity models than some Black students in an English-language school in the same province (Ibrahim, 2014). In another French-language high school in Alberta, some Black refugee students perceived that white school staff, including the white principal, had lower educational or career aspirations for them than for white refugee students enrolled in the same newcomer program (Schroeter & James, 2015). Similarly, an immigrant researcher who is also a former French-language school student in Northern Ontario highlights the challenges he experienced in high school due to systemic racisms and how he survived some of these racist situations (Ng-A-Fook, 2016).

For others, the challenge in terms of integration is a language issue. Many Black and immigrant students enrolled in French-language schools already have language skills and accents in French that are different from the skills and accents of other students in minoritized contexts (Ibrahim, 2016); the former are more likely to come from countries that are – or were – under French colonial administration (Schroeter & James, 2015). However, these students are discriminated against not only because francophone immigrants do not speak the same variety of French, but also because they do not necessarily use English as a language of communication among peers as do many students in French-language schools (Ibrahim, 2014, 2016). This discrimination is not limited to students, however; some researchers point out that Black, immigrant, and francophone student-teachers or new teachers find it more difficult to integrate into certain French-language school systems in minoritized contexts than their white counterparts born or educated in Canada (Dalley, 2020; Duchesne, Gravelle, & Gagnon, 2019; Jabouin, 2018; Mujawamariya, 2002; Mujawamariya & Moldeauveanu, 2006). The former seem to have less access to teaching placements, permanent positions, or long-term substitute teaching contracts in some French-language schools compared to Canadian-born white student-teachers and teachers (Dalley, 2020; Jabouin, 2018). Not all Black teachers feel supported by their union either (MacDonald-Dupuis, 2020). In some cases, school leaders, such as associate teachers and principals, attribute this difficulty of integration into French-language school systems to a lack of teaching skills among Black and immigrant student-teachers, when in fact it is more a matter of cross-comprehension of French or French accents (Dalley, 2020; Mujawamariya & Moldeaveanu, 2006).

In short, taking into account the diversity that characterizes French-language schools, the contexts in which principals exercise their leadership is proving to be increasingly complex (Gélinas Proulx, IsaBelle, & Meunier, 2014; Landry & Gélinas-Proulx, 2018).

Overall, researchers maintain that it would be desirable for principals to adopt a leadership style that transcends their current socio-cultural reality in order for French-language schools to meet the needs of their students in minoritized contexts, to provide them with a learning experience free of discrimination, and to ensure the well-being of all school staff (Boudreau, 2014; Godin, Lapointe, Langlois, & St-Germain, 2004; Lapointe, 2002; Leurebourg, 2013; Racine, 2007; Weatherall, 2011). To this end, we suggest Shields's (2010, 2013, 2016, 2020) transformative leadership theory.

## Benefits of Transformative Leadership

Shields (2010) notes that transformative leadership inextricably links education, educational leadership, and the social contexts in which they are included. Thus, in their article published in the *Canadian Journal of Education* in 2016, Gélinas-Proulx and Shields demonstrate this through a literature review on educational leadership in minoritized francophone contexts (Boudreau, 2014; Godin et al., 2004; Lapointe, 2002; Lapointe, Langlois, & Godin, 2005; Leurebourg, 2013; Ontario Ministry of Education, 2011; Racine, 2007; Table nationale sur l'éducation, 2012; Weatherall, 2011). According to them, transformative leadership theory (TLT), through its eight tenets (see chapter 1 in this volume), ties in with the components of leadership identified for these contexts in the literature and thus forms a coherent whole to guide leaders of these schools. Since then, another publication has made the link between transformative leadership and leading in increasingly diverse ethnocultural, linguistic, and religious minoritized francophone contexts (Landry & Gélinas-Proulx, 2018). Therefore, after a brief description of TLT, we will in this section provide a reminder of the eight tenets of transformative leadership by showing in concrete terms how they apply to principals of French-language schools in minority language contexts in Canada.

Based on empirical research, Shields (2010) states that at the root of transformative leadership are justice and democracy, which contribute to citizenship. It is a matter of, on the one hand, critiquing inequitable practices and, on the other hand, proposing solutions, arguing that it is possible to achieve both a greater individual good and a public good. Thus, principals apply TLT to ensure that their organization is inclusive, equitable, and socially just (Shields & Sayani, 2005). Shields (2016) has also formulated two general principles that undergird the theory of transformative leadership. The first principle is based on the respect, inclusion, and value that people (students or employees) can feel that will help them to concentrate on their tasks and, thus, complete their work more easily and with success. The second principle is to find the balance between individual good and public good. As a result, civic engagement, democracy, and society as a whole are strengthened.

According to Shields (2016, 2020), there are eight tenets that define transformative leadership. The first two tenets must be met before moving on to any of the rest. However, the order in which the remaining six tenets are met does not matter, as they are part of a whole (i.e., they are interconnected and interrelated). In short, these tenets can be used to guide French-language principals in minoritized contexts to elaborate an action plan leading to equity and, thus, more inclusive education.

### First Tenet: The Mandate to Effect Deep and Equitable Change

School leaders accept, or give themselves, the mandate to make profound and equitable change. Thus, leaders in minoritized contexts who perceive inequities such as those mentioned above have an obligation to make changes and to not tolerate the status quo because they have analysed their own contexts (self, organization, and community) and the issues related to them.

The first tenet should be activated in order to improve the success and wellbeing of students in French-language schools in minoritized contexts. Some French-language school students have more difficulty than English-language school students on certain assessments and in certain subject areas. This gap requires that principals make the various players in the education system aware of the injustices, prejudices, and discrimination experienced by students and school staff. For example, since the importance of human and pedagogical resources adapted to minoritized contexts are not recognized as a legitimate need within the funding formula used to meet the needs of the school community, students of minoritized French-language schools are not being offered the same educational services received by anglophone students. Similarly, the school facilities are not of the same quality as those enjoyed by anglophone students. A concrete example is a minoritized French-language school in Prince Edward Island. This school previously housed students from kindergarten to Grade 12 in former Fisheries and Oceans Canada buildings. It was not until 2018 that the students were moved to a school building equivalent to those enjoyed by anglophone students, and only after years of advocacy on the part of the community and the school principal (Smith, 2018).

Moreover, this same tenet should be operationalized when certain sub-groups in the school, such as visible minority students, experience various forms of discrimination such as racism. In short, a thorough analysis and understanding of one's environment enables school principals to envision and undertake profound equitable and inclusive changes, not only in relation to the English-speaking majority, but also in relation to both privileged and oppressed groups within their own schools.

### Second Tenet: The Need to Deconstruct and Reconstruct Knowledge Frameworks That Perpetuate Inequity and Injustice

Leaders examine their frames of reference as well as biases and deconstruct the very frames of reference (beliefs and practices) that perpetuate the status quo or deficit thinking after recognizing the need for systemic change. Thus, first with themselves and then with school stakeholders, leaders will seek to modify the knowledge, beliefs, and (in)actions that generate inequities and injustices in order to reconstruct them from an equity and inclusive education perspective. To do this, courageous conversations are needed at multiple levels including among parents, community members, and with other leaders in the school system. If this tenet is not respected, it will be almost impossible to achieve equitable and inclusive change. It is important to undertake the second tenet in conjunction with the first, because principals who move too quickly to take action without having sought to deconstruct their own inequitable conceptual frameworks, and those of the various education stakeholders around them, may fail in their efforts to achieve lasting change. However, they can be helped by systemic allies and supervisors to change mindsets and beliefs in order to achieve sustainable changes.

With respect to the second tenet, principals of French-language schools in minoritized contexts may have to deconstruct conceptual frameworks or practices among school staff, parents, and students that run counter to the promotion of French. For example, they may have to encourage all members of the school community to value multiple accents rather than just valuing standard or local French accents (Dalley, 2000). As a former president of the Fédération de la jeunesse franco-ontarienne (FESFO) points out, "Outside the classroom, [students] sometimes use English formulations or prepositions at the end of

sentences. Teachers or other students can rephrase and correct us for the quality of our French ... When we are corrected four or five times in a conversation
for our French, it's bullying ... Everyone has an accent, and all French is good"
(translation, Pierroz, 2015). Principals may also need to explain to people why
the use of systems that punish students who do not express themselves in French
(e.g., forcing students to do push-ups, copy the dictionary) creates linguistic
insecurity among them as well as an aversion to the language (FESFO, 2014,
p. 14). Also, some teachers speak to students in English (FESFO, 2014; Pierroz,
2015), so the principals should have conversations about this with them as well.

Finally, it may also be relevant for school principals to have courageous conversations with the whole school community about anti-Black and anti-Indigenous racism, Islamophobia, homophobia and transphobia, and other forms
of discrimination that may be experienced by certain sub-groups of schools in
minoritized francophone contexts. Even if a discriminatory phenomenon is not
present in the school, these conversations should still happen in order to better
prepare students to integrate into society as a whole.

### Third Tenet: The Need to Address the Inequitable Distribution of Power

Leaders try to abolish the inequitable distribution of power within the school
by gradually reducing it. Thus, individuals and groups should not have privileges that others do not have in terms of power or resources because dominant
group privileges oppress dominated groups.

With the third tenet in mind, it is legitimate for principals to ask themselves whether some French-Canadian or white students and staff members
have more privileges than new Canadians or visible minority students and
staff members in their French-language schools in minoritized contexts, especially when learning and teaching are only evaluated from a single perspective. In fact, do their schools recognize fully all cultures, languages of origin,
and colonization experiences, or do they advocate only for a fixed folkloric or
nationalist French culture using a single language to the detriment of others?
For example, reflecting on his intercultural competence, one Franco-Ontarian
school principal who was part of Gélinas-Proulx's research (2014) asked, "How
can we make room for everyone without affecting somebody else? Maybe it's
because we've been saying 'go franco go' for 47 years, but I think ... I mean 'go
franco go,' then I'll say 'go Haiti go,' then all the other countries. How does that
work in practice?" (translation, p. 178).

Moreover, principals of publicly funded Catholic schools could take steps
to correct inequities in their school community, such as the refusal to admit a
Muslim child (Seebruch, 2020), even though section 93 of the 1867 Constitution Act has allowed certain provinces to give rights or privileges to denomi-
national schools since the time of Confedertion. Indeed, currently in Ontario,

French-language public schools receive a disproportionate number of students from immigrant backgrounds (Lanthier, 2017) compared to French-language Catholic public schools, which can refuse them at the elementary level on the basis of belonging to a religion not recognized by Rome (e.g., admission policy of the Conseil scolaire catholique MonAvenir).

For this same tenet, principals should also be able to question certain policies and practices developed and imposed on them by English-speaking groups in power and holding privileges (e.g., Ministries of Education), or by their employer (e.g., school board). For example, the principal of a French-language school in a minoritized context could question their supervisor about why the school board chose to place entirely English-only advertisements to recruit students in local newspapers instead of placing bilingual or French-only ones (St-Pierre, 2019). They might even suggest advertisements in other languages in line with their school context, such as Haitian Creole.

### Fourth Tenet: An Emphasis on Both Private and Public (Individual and Collective) Good

Leaders emphasize both the success and well-being of each individual (private good: e.g., being educated to have a job, a good salary) and the success and well-being of all (public good: e.g., an educated population is healthier, less criminalized).

In terms of private good, the fourth tenet can, among other things, be translated into the promotion of the French-language school as an institution that can enable students to be bi/plurilingual and bi/pluricultural. In terms of individual assets, principals of French-language schools in minoritized contexts who are aware of the difficulties students face in certain school subjects could deploy resources to ensure the success of each and every student. At the same time, they must ensure that these programs and services are provided in the classroom in order to promote the inclusion of all students in French-language schools (Villella, 2014).

In terms of public good, French-language schools are institutions that should promote the vitality of the world's francophone communities. Thus, from a public good perspective, principals could invite the families of students who are entitled to French-language instruction, or those who are not entitled under the Charter, to attend a French-language school in order to ensure not only the sustainability of the francophone community, but also its diversity. The public good argument should be made to school staff, the parents' council, and the employer about the importance of welcoming all children and their families to the French-language school. Moreover, moving beyond the school to Canadian society at large, learning how to live together is a desirable outcome in terms of unity for the public good of all. Thus, principals could invest in relationships with both the anglophone and francophone communities (St-Germain, 2011). To build these bridges, they could invite English-language schools to partici-pate in the activities of their French-language schools in order to foster the cross-comprehension necessary for living together in Canadian society.

*Fifth Tenet: A Focus on Emancipation, Democracy, Equity, and Justice*

Leaders need to prioritize emancipation, democracy, equity, inclusion, and social justice. In fact, leaders must give importance to these concepts, because if this is not done systematically, leaders will let other concerns dominate their agendas.

  According to the fifth tenet, one of the priorities of French-language school principals in minoritized contexts is the protection and enhancement of the French language for the emancipation of the community. This can be translated into the requirement that school communications and those with parents or guardians be in French. However, to achieve this, it is in principals' best interest to take charge of enhancing the value of the French language within the school community (i.e., offering French classes) so that all community members can feel included. For example, principals can encourage staff to work on the lin-guistic security of parents and guardians who speak little or no French (i.e., the language of their child's schooling) (McPhee, 2018). The notion of linguistic "security" here refers to the creation of a sense of confidence in expressing one-self in French, both orally and in writing (Desabrais, 2013). A plethora of other examples of practices to protect and enhance the French language are presented on the website of the École communautaire citoyenne (ecc-canada.ca). These examples are based on the conceptualization of collective and unifying projects within minoritized francophone school contexts that focus on long-term com-mitment: "The goals underlying the École communautaire citoyenne propose not only to focus on the overall success of students, but also attempt to include all groups of stakeholders, as learners, throughout their lives" (translation, Mar-tineau Vachon, 2018, p. 91). In addition, it is desirable that principals priori-tize teaching, learning, and assessment practices that value variations of French language and cultures, additive bilingualism,[9] pluralism, and the relationships between school, family, and community. They should also find equitable ways to include other majority and minority languages and cultures as well as all ethnic groups and visible minorities present in the surrounding contexts of the schools in order to value the multiple identities of all members of the school community.

*Sixth Tenet: An Emphasis on Interdependence, Interconnectedness, and Global Awareness*

Leaders demonstrate the interdependence and interconnection between human beings and raise awareness among peers about global phenomena (e.g., climate change, political conflicts, inequitable distribution of resources) from a citizenship education perspective.

In connection with the sixth tenet, French-language schools in minoritized contexts have been – or can be – inward-looking in order to protect themselves, primarily against any form of assimilation of the Francophonie and francophone citizens (ACELF, 2008; Dalley, 2014, 2020). In fact, the sixth tenet forces principals of French-language schools in minoritized contexts to take measures to ensure their schools decentre themselves and open up to the world around them. To do so, they could encourage and support equitable and inclusive school practices and projects from a global citizenship education perspective (see, for example, projetinclusioncrefo.ca; Guo, 2013; Tawil, 2013). Projects should extend beyond charity initiatives to raise awareness among school staff and students about the connections between local, national, and international issues (Guo, 2013). For example, students and staff could be made aware of the minoritized language contexts of other communities around the world (e.g., Indigenous peoples in Canada and elsewhere, Catalans in Spain, Corsicans in France) as well as all the languages that are at risk of extinction. The goal could be to learn from these groups and to forge ties with these communities in order to share "ethnolinguistic vitalization practices" (Weatherall, 2011). Principals of French-language schools in minoritized contexts (with the approval of their supervisors) could also encourage students and staff to participate safely in local, national, and international citizen advocacy movements when the cause is in line with the values promoted by the school, while encouraging them to express their perspectives in French. A recent example is the students in Manitoba and British Columbia who participated in the march for climate change influenced by the arrival in Canada of Greta Thunberg (Radio-Canada, 2019).

### Seventh Tenet: The Necessity of Balancing Critique with Promise

Leaders are to question inequitable practices and, in return, propose solutions that bring hope to all members of the school community. In fact, leaders should propose practical and just solutions following a critical analysis of inequitable practices.

The seventh tenet allows leaders to find local and systemic solutions to the problems identified in their French-language schools in minoritized contexts. In the first part of the chapter, we identified several issues specific to these contexts (e.g., attraction of the English language, linguistic assimilation, recruitment and competition related to school markets, gaps in academic achievement, lack of resources, inequities, discrimination, racism). Thus, as critical thinkers, principals should identify these and other problems and then try, with the help of their school community, to find solutions to them.

More concretely, principals should recognize the existence of systemic racism in both majority and minoritized contexts, such as in disturbing cases of anti-Black racism in some Ontario schools in recent years:

> [S]everal cases of young Black children physically restrained or handcuffed at school have made headlines, particularly in the Region of Peel. In 2014, the Human Rights Tribunal of Ontario recommended that an investigation be launched after it was shown that Black students at another school in Durham Region ... were nearly eight times more likely to face discipline than white students. (translation, MacDonald-Dupuis, 2019)

Second, the principals' critical analysis of the situation could lead them to perceive discrimination in terms of behaviour management actions and follow-up in their school. However, since principals should not remain passive in the face of such observations, they should act proactively to implement behaviour management strategies that are respectful of all students in collaboration with parents and the school staff. In fact, they should not blame the child nor the family, nor reinforce stereotypes, as one Franco-Ontarian principal did, according to the report of a Black mother: "The principal told me that my six-year-old son showed the characteristics of a criminal. I couldn't believe my ears" (translation, MacDonald-Dupuis, 2019).

## Eighth Tenet: The Call to Exhibit Moral Courage

Leaders show moral courage and activism, especially towards those who want to maintain the status quo, their privileges, and their power. Thus, in the face of resistance, leaders must know themselves well, believe strongly in equity, and act courageously. To do so will also require a sense of self-efficacy.

The eighth tenet requires principals of French-language schools in minoritized contexts to demonstrate moral courage in the face of adversity or resistance, whether it is within their own schools or at the systemic level. It is in the principals' interest to be aware of the avenues for advocating equity, inclusion, and social justice. They should know the mechanisms for contacting child protection authorities, and for accessing resources on political and human rights, as well as French-language legal aid when they, students, parents, or guardians encounter resistance. In addition, they should be able to rely on their professional association for support.

As an example of activism, Franco-Ontarian school principals in support of their students participated in demonstrations in 2018 for the opening of the Université de l'Ontario français, among other things, so that their high school students could obtain post-secondary education in French in their region: "[The principal] attended the demonstration with other staff members. She said she was proud of her students and to see the importance of the Francophonie in their approach" (translation, Radio-Canada, 2018). Since the Ford provincial government had cancelled the creation of the first French-language University in Ontario, these demonstrations showed the premier of Ontario the resistance of francophone communities (Ramlakhan, 2018). In similar fashion, Franco-Albertan school principals, backed by their counterparts in other provinces, could support initiatives by young Albertan francophone to maintain the Campus Saint-Jean (francophone campus) of the University of Alberta, which has been chronically underfunded for years (Vachet, 2020).

On the whole, it seems necessary to develop transformative leadership (Shields, 2010, 2013, 2016, 2020) among French-language school principals in minoritized contexts so that they can defend all of their students, staff, and school community members against injustices, inequities, and discrimination, both within the school itself and in relation to the anglophone majority. In this chapter, we argue that with the help of the eight tenets put forward by TLT, principals in minoritized francophone contexts will be better equipped to promote the sustainability of the Canadian Francophonie and social justice for all students and all adults in their school community, regardless of their race, ethnic origin, language of origin, religion, financial situation, or sexual orientation.

## Conclusion

In conclusion, Canadian francophone minoritized contexts bring their share of challenges to school principals. To meet these challenges, we suggest that principals would benefit from adopting transformative leadership in their practice. Through its two principles and eight tenets, transformative leadership provides school principals with theoretical tools to ensure greater social justice for youth and adults in Canada's French-language schools in minoritized contexts.

As such, transformative leadership should be developed not only by principals in francophone minoritized communities, but also by other leaders in the school system, both horizontally and vertically, such as superintendents, elected school officials, non-teaching staff, educators, and decision-makers in the various ministries of education. The goal is to make profound, equitable, and inclusive changes that promote the educational success, well-being, and agency of all students and adults in minoritized contexts, and such changes need to be initiated and supported at all levels. To this end, let us not forget that francophone students are to be considered transformative school leaders of today, and not just of tomorrow (Le Gal, 2019; Martineau Vachon, 2018).

Furthermore, transformative principals should be consulted by their superiors so that systemic decisions also meet the needs of their schools and its members. A principal should not be reduced to the role of technician, implementer, or auditor. In other words, principals should be seen as credible agents of change by their supervisors when they are dealing with issues in their schools.

The theory of transformative leadership for Canada's French-language schools in minoritized contexts suggested in this chapter will have to be demonstrated through empirical research with the education stakeholders concerned. However, it could be a useful tool for the initial training of future school leaders and for the ongoing training of current school leaders, as well as a relevant tool for principals to fulfil their role in minoritized contexts, whether rural or pluralistic, since equity, social justice, and the inclusion of all forms of diversity must be promoted in all settings.

We reiterate that transformative leadership (Shields, 2010, 2013, 2016, 2020) seems to be a relevant theory to guide French-language school principals in minoritized contexts in Canada in meeting the needs of all their students and staff members. Transformative leadership focuses primarily on social justice, as well as issues of equity, democracy, and inclusion. Transformative leadership is therefore an area that cannot be ignored in future study. The goal of transformative leadership in francophone minoritized contexts is, after all, the achievement of equality of opportunity for minoritized francophone compared to the anglophone majority, as well as equality of opportunity among francophone children and the francophone adults who should serve as role models for them.

Finally, we recognize that the task of principals in francophone minoritized contexts may seem to be an onerous one at first glance. However, like the task of teaching in minoritized francophone contexts, it is not an impossible one (Gilbert et al., 2004). On the contrary, transformative principals can draw on ideas – by, for, and with – all members of their community to ensure a highly inclusive francophone minoritized school environment.

## NOTES

1  This chapter is based on Gélinas-Proulx and Shields (2016).
2  "No! Committing to the French language is not a rearguard fight! On the contrary, it is a just and modern cause that will not be definitively lost until all those who have to defend it have abandoned it. So let's act!" (translation by authors of Dominique Hoppe).
3  "Humans must recognize themselves in their common humanity, as well as recognize their diversity, both individual and cultural" (translation by authors of Edgar Morin).
4  The expression "official language minority community" is frequently used in scientific literature, by political and educational institutions, as well as by educational associations. "In Canada, the term 'official language minority communities' refers to English-speaking communities in Quebec and French-speaking communities in the rest of Canada. More than two million Canadians belong to an official language

minority community" (TERMIUM Plus®, n.d.). However, Shields (2013) suggests the term "minoritized context." Based on her research, the author argues that the power possessed by "white middle class" people often marginalizes and excludes those who are not part of this group, whether they are numerically a minority or a majority. Thus, French-language schools in Canada outside of Quebec are in minoritized contexts, because the power that anglophones appear to hold tends to marginalize francophones, even though francophones are found in the majority in some communities. Moreover, the situation is even more complex because within those minoritized contexts there are minoritized sub-groups.

5  This percentage includes those who speak more then one language (including French) most often at home.

6  All French to English translations are by the authors of this chapter, unless otherwise noted.

7  More often, the phenomenon of exogamy in Canada has been discussed in terms of marriage or unions between anglophones and francophones (Bernard, 1998; Castonguay, 1999; Dalley, 2006), or between a francophone partner and a non-francophone partner (Rocque, 2006; Rocque & Taylor, 2011).

8  It is important to note that not all Black students are newcomers to Canada; according to the last census, more than four out of ten Black students were born in Canada (Statistics Canada, 2019). In fact, the presence of Black people in Canada dates back to the 1600s (Johnston, 2001).

9  Additive bilingualism happens when the learning of a second language does not harm the acquisition of the first language (Landry, Deveau, & Allard, 2006).

## REFERENCES

Adam, J. (2019, May 15). Pénurie d'enseignants francophones en Ontario: L'Université cherche des solutions. *uOttawa Gazette*. https://www.uottawa.ca/gazette/fr/nouvelles/penurie-denseignants-francophones-ontario-luniversite-cherche-solutions#

Association canadienne d'éducation de langue française (ACELF). (n.d.). *Voyage en francophonie canadienne: Écoles francophones du Canada*. Retrieved 19 October 2021 from https://vfc.acelf.ca/pdfs/carte-des-ecoles-francophones-2021.pdf

Association canadienne d'éducation de langue française (ACELF). (2008). *Réflexion sur la diversité culturelle au sein des écoles francophones du Canada*. Quebec City, QC: ACELF.

Bélanger, N., Dalley, P., Dionne, L., & Beaulieu, G. (2011). Les partenariats école-communauté et le marché scolaire de langue française en Ontario. *Revue des Sciences de l'Éducation, 37*(2), 375–402. doi: 10.7202/1008991ar

Bernard, R. (1998). *Le Canada français: Entre mythe et utopie*. Ottawa, ON: Le Nordir.

Bouchamma, Y. (2004). Gestion de l'éducation et construction identitaire sur le plan professionnel des directeurs et des directrices d'établissements scolaires.

*Éducation et Francophonie, 32*(2), 62–78. https://revue.acelf.ca/pdf/Gestiondel
education.pdf

Boudreau, L.C. (2014). *Comprendre le leadership des directions d'écoles en milieu
francophone minoritaire: Leadership, formation et créativité* (Unpublished doctoral
dissertation). Université de Moncton, NB.

Brochu, P., Deussing, M.-A., Houme, K., & Chuy, M. (2012). *À la hauteur: Résultats
canadiens de l'étude PISA de l'OCDE.* Conseil des ministres de l'Éducation
(Canada). http://cmec.ca/Publications/Lists/Publications/Attachments/318
/PISA2012_CanadianReport_FR_Web.pdf

Brosseau, L., & Dewing, M. (2018). *Canadian multiculturalism.* Ottawa, ON: Library
of Parliament. https://lop.parl.ca/staticfiles/PublicWebsite/Home/Research
Publications/BackgroundPapers/PDF/2009-20-e.pdf

*Canadian Charter of Rights and Freedoms,* s 7, Part 1 of the *Constitution Act,* 1982,
being Schedule B to the *Canada Act* 1982 (UK), 1982, c 11. https://laws-lois.justice
.gc.ca/eng/Const/page-12.html

Carr, P.R. (2006). Social justice and whiteness in education: Color-blind
policymaking and racism. *Journal for Critical Education Policy Studies, 4*(2),
297–329. http://www.jceps.com/wp-content/uploads/PDFs/04-2-13.pdf

Castonguay, C. (1999). Évolution démographique des Franco-Ontariens entre 1971
et 1991. In G. Forlot & N. Labrie (Eds.), *L'enjeu de la langue en Ontario français*
(pp. 15–32). Sudbury, ON: Prise de parole.

CBC News. (2021, May 29). Ontario principal removed after twice wearing hair of
Black student like a wig. *CBC News.* https://www.cbc.ca/news/canada/london
/ontario-principal-removed-hair-black-student-1.6045755

Dalley, P. (2000). *L'enseignante, agente de développement en Acadie du Nouveau-
Brunswick* (Doctoral dissertation, University of Toronto, ON). https://hdl.handle
.net/1807/13998

Dalley, P. (2006). Héritiers des mariages mixtes: Possibilités identitaires. *Éducation et
francophonie, 34*(1), 82–94. https://revue.acelf.ca/pdf/XXXIV_1_082.pdf

Dalley, P. (2014). Assimilation, intégration, inclusion: Quelle vision pour l'éducation
de langue française en contexte minoritaire? In L. Carlson Berg (Ed.), *La
francophonie canadienne dans toutes ses couleurs et le défi de l'inclusion scolaire*
(pp. 13–31). Quebec, QC: Presses de l'Université Laval.

Dalley, P. (2020). From Africa to teacher education in Ontario. In A. Phelan,
N. Ng-A-Fook, & R. Kane (Eds.), *Reconceptualizing teacher education worldwide:
A Canadian contribution to a global challenge* (pp. 141–68). Ottawa, ON: Presses
de l'Université d'Ottawa.

Dalley, P., & Cotnam-Kappel, M. (2013). Vers une pédagogie des droits et de la
citoyenneté mondiaux de l'enfant en Ontario français. *Revue d'Éducation, 3*(2),
4–5. https://education.uottawa.ca/sites/education.uottawa.ca/files/revue_edu_fr
_automne_2013.pdf

Dalley, P., & Villella, M. (2013). Review of *La direction d'école et le leadership pédagogique en milieu francophone minoritaire*, Rocques, J. (dir.) (2011). *Minorités Linguistiques et Société*, 3, 186–9. doi: 10.7202/1023806ar

Daveluy, M. (2007). L'exogamie langagière en Amazonie et au Canada. *Anthropologie et Sociétés*, *31*(1), 55–73. doi: 10.7202/015982ar

Department of Canadian Heritage. (2020). *Teacher recruitment and retention strategy in minority French-language schools*. Government of Canada. https://www.canada.ca/en/canadian-heritage/services/funding/official-languages/teacher-recruitment-minority-schools.html

Desabrais, T. (2013). *Les mots pour le dire...L'influence de l'(in)sécurité linguistique sur l'expérience d'étudiantes de milieux francophones minoritaires canadiens inscrites aux études supérieures* (Doctoral dissertation, Université d'Ottawa, ON). http://hdl.handle.net/10393/26263

Duchesne, C., Gravelle, F., & Gagnon, N. (2019). Des nouveaux·elles enseignant·e·s issus·e·s de l'immigration négocient leur place dans la culture enseignante de leur école. *Revue des Sciences de l'Éducation*, *45*(1), 187–214. doi: 10.7202/1064611ar

Fédération de la jeunesse franco-ontarienne (FESFO). (2014). *Pour s'exprimer dans notre langue: Consultation sur l'insécurité linguistique et la jeunesse franco-ontarienne: Rapport final*. Ottawa, ON: FESFO. https://fesfo.ca/wp-content/uploads/2017/01/RPT_PourSexprimerDansNotreLangue_Consultation2014.pdf

Fédération nationale des conseils scolaires francophones. (n.d.). *Causes actuelles*. Retrieved 19 October 2021 from http://fncsf.ca/education-en-langue-francaise-elf/droits-de-gestion-scolaire/causes-actuelles/

Gélinas-Proulx, A. (2014). *Modèles hypothétiques de la compétence et d'une formation interculturelles pour des directions et futures directions d'écoles de langue française au Canada* (Doctoral dissertation, Université d'Ottawa, ON). http://hdl.handle.net/10393/30655

Gélinas Proulx, A., IsaBelle, C., & Meunier, H. (2014). Compétence des nouvelles directions d'école de langue française au Canada pour la gestion inclusive de la diversité ethnoculturelle, linguistique et religieuse. *Alterstice*, *4*(1), 73–87. doi: 10.7202/1077483

Gélinas-Proulx, A., & Shields, C. (2016). Le leadership transformatif: Maintenir la langue française vivante au Canada. *Revue Canadienne de l'Éducation*, *39*(1), 1–24. https://journals.sfu.ca/cje/index.php/cje-rce/article/view/2017

Gérin-Lajoie, D. (2002). Le rôle du personnel enseignant dans le processus de reproduction linguistique et culturelle en milieu scolaire francophone en Ontario. *Revue des Sciences de l'Éducation*, *28*(1), 125–46. doi: 10.7202/007152ar

Gérin-Lajoie, D., & Jacquet, M. (2008). Regards croisés sur l'inclusion des minorités en contexte scolaire francophone minoritaire au Canada. *Éducation et Francophonie*, *36*(1), 25–43. doi: 10.7202/018088ar

Gilbert, A., Letouzé, S., Thériault, J.Y., & Landry, R. (2004). *Le personnel enseignant face aux défis de l'enseignement en milieu minoritaire francophone: Rapport final de la recherche*. Ottawa, ON: Centre interdisciplinaire de recherche sur la citoyenneté et les minorités, Université d'Ottawa, Institut canadien de recherche sur les minorités linguistiques, et Fédération canadienne des enseignantes et des enseignants.

Godin, J., Lapointe, C., Langlois, L., & St-Germain, M. (2004). Le leadership éducationnel en milieu francophone minoritaire: Un regard inédit sur une réalité méconnue. *Francophonies d'Amérique, 18*, 63–76. doi: 10.1353/fda.2005.0010

Government of Canada. (2018). *Investing in our future 2018–2023: Action plan for official languages*. Her Majesty the Queen in Right of Canada. https://www.canada.ca/content/dam/pch/documents/services/official-languages-bilingualism/official-languages-action-plan/action-plan.pdf

Government of Ontario. (2004). *L'aménagement linguistique: Une politique au service des écoles et de la communauté de langue française de l'Ontario*. Imprimeur de la Reine pour l'Ontario. http://www.edu.gov.on.ca/fre/document/policy/linguistique/policyguidef.pdf

Government of Yukon. (2020, April 3). *Conclusion d'une entente de règlement entre le gouvernement et la Commission scolaire francophone du Yukon* [Press release]. https://yukon.ca/fr/news/conclusion-dune-entente-de-reglement-entre-le-gouvernement-et-la-commission-scolaire

Guo, L. (2013). L'éducation à la citoyenneté mondiale traduite en actions pédagogiques en salle de classe. *Revue d'Éducation, 3*(2), 8–9. https://education.uottawa.ca/sites/education.uottawa.ca/files/revue_edu_fr_automne_2013.pdf

Ibrahim, A. (2014). *The rhizome of Blackness: A critical ethnography of hip-hop culture, language, identity and the politics of becoming*. New York, NY: Peter Lang.

Ibrahim, A. (2016). Who owns my language? African Canadian youth, postcoloniality, and the symbolic violence of language in a French language high school in Ontario. In A.A. Abdi & A. Ibrahim, (Eds.), *The education of African-Canadian children* (pp.146–63). Montreal, QC: McGill-Queen's University Press.

Jabouin, S. (2018). *Trajectoires d'insertion professionnelle des nouveaux enseignants originaires des Caraïbes et d'Afrique subsaharienne (NEOCAS) dans les écoles francophones de l'est de l'Ontario* (Doctoral dissertation, Université d'Ottawa, ON). https://ruor.uottawa.ca/handle/10393/38176

Jacquet, M., Moore, D., Sabatier, C., & Masinda, M. (2008). *L'intégration des jeunes immigrants francophones africains dans les écoles francophones en Colombie-Britannique* (Working Paper). Vancouver Research on Immigration and Integration in the Metropolis. http://community.smu.ca/atlantic/documents/Riim-Jacquet_Moore_Sabatier_Masinda2008_001.pdf

Johnston, J. (2001). Research Note: Mathieu Da Costa along the coasts of Nova Scotia: Some possibilities. *Journal of the Royal Nova Scotia Historical Society, 4*,

152–90. https://search.proquest.com/openview/ed79ee75682a35d1b2f968aae59cb 213/1?pq-origsite=gscholar&cbl=446300

Lamoureux, S.A., & Cotnam, M. (2012). *Prendre sa place. Parcours et trajectoires identitaires en Ontario français.* Ottawa, ON: Éditions David.

Landry, J.-S., & Gélinas-Proulx, A. (2018). Conciliation du leadership des directions d'école en contexte francophone minoritaire et en contexte de diversité ethnoculturelle, linguistique et religieuse. *Éducation et Francophonie, 46*(1), 98–121. doi: 10.7202/1047138ar

Landry, R., Allard, R., & Deveau, K. (2010). *École et autonomie culturelle: Enquête pancanadienne en milieu scolaire francophone minoritaire.* Ottawa, ON: Patrimoine canadien. https://publications.gc.ca/collections/collection_2011 /pc-ch/CH3-2-13-2010-fra.pdf

Landry, R., Deveau, K., & Allard, R. (2006). Vitalité ethnolinguistique et construction identitaire: Le cas de l'identité bilingue. *Éducation et Francophonie, 34*(1), 54–81. https://revue.acelf.ca/pdf/XXXIV_1_054.pdf

Lanthier, C. (2017, February 21). Immigration dans les écoles catholiques et publiques: Un double système encore pertinent en Ontario? *Radio-Canada.* https://ici.radio-canada.ca/nouvelle/1017970/immigration-enfants-ontario -ecoles-catholiques-publiques-financement

Lapointe, C. (2002). Diriger l'école en milieu linguistique et culturel minoritaire. In L. Langlois & C. Lapointe (Eds.), *Le leadership en éducation: Plusieurs regards, une même passion* (pp. 37–48). Montreal, QC: Chenelière/McGraw-Hill.

Lapointe, C., Langlois, L., & Godin, J. (2005). The leadership of heritage: Searching for a meaningful theory in official-language minority settings. *Journal of School Leadership, 15*(2), 143–58. doi: 10.1177/105268460501500203

Le Gal, J. (2019). *Les droits de l'enfant à l'école: Pour une éducation à la citoyenneté participative.* Espace Mendès-France. https://www.icem-pedagogie-freinet.org /sites/default/files/jean_le_gal_les_droits_de_lenfant_.pdf

Leurebourg, R. (2013). Rôles des directions d'école de langue française en situation minoritaire. *Revue Canadienne de l'Éducation, 36*(3), 272–97. https://www.jstor .org/stable/canajeducrevucan.36.3.272

Macdonald-Dupuis, N. (2019, June 28). "Plaqué au sol" à 6 ans: Un conseil scolaire nie avoir discriminé un élève noir. *Radio-Canada.* https://ici.radio-canada.ca /nouvelle/1202131/viamonde-conseil-scolaire-ecole-francophone-racisme -violence-scolaire

Macdonald-Dupuis, N. (2020, January 27). Des plaintes pour discrimination contre le syndicat des enseignants franco-ontariens. *Radio-Canada.* https://ici.radio -canada.ca/nouvelle/1489265/aefo-discrimination-enseignants-diversite-noirs -immigrants-syndicat

Martineau Vachon, H. (2018). L'École communautaire citoyenne. In C. IsaBelle (Ed.), *Système scolaire franco-ontarien: D'hier à aujourd'hui pour le plein potentiel des élèves* (pp. 71–95). Quebec City, QC: Presses de l'Université du Québec.

McPhee, M. (2018). *The experience of non-francophone parents with children in minority-language French schools in Prince Edward Island: A mixed methods study* (Doctoral dissertation, University of Prince Edward Island, Charlottetown, PE). https://islandscholar.ca/islandora/object/ir:22514/datastream/PDF/download/citation.pdf

Mujawamariya, D. (2002). Ce sont nos écoles aussi: Propos de minorités visibles et ethnoculturelles aspirant à la profession enseignante en Ontario français. *Éducation Canada*, 42(3), 21–35. https://www.edcan.ca/wp-content/uploads/EdCan-2002-v42-n3-Mujawamariya.pdf

Mujawamariya, D., & Moldeauveanu, M. (2006). Introduction. In D. Mujawamariya (Ed.), *L'éducation multiculturelle dans la formation des enseignants au Canada: Dilemmes et défis* (pp. 1–14). New York, NY: Peter Lang.

Ng-A-Fook, N. (2016). Becoming inter-national: Autobiography, curriculum, and hyph-e-nated subjectivities. In M.A. Doll (Ed.), *The reconceptualization of curriculum studies: A festschrift in honor of William F. Pinar* (pp. 121–9). London, UK: Routledge.

Office of the Commissioner of Official Languages. (n.d.). *Understanding your language rights*. Retrieved 19 October 2021 from https://www.clo-ocol.gc.ca/en/language_rights/act

O'Grady, K., Deussing, M.-A., Scerbina, T., Tao, Y., Fung, K., Elez, V., & Monk, J. (2018). *Measuring up: Canadian results of the OECD PISA 2018 study: The performance of Canadian 15-year-olds in reading, mathematics, and science*. Council of Ministers of Education, Canada. https://www.cmec.ca/Publications/Lists/Publications/Attachments/396/PISA2018_PublicReport_EN.pdf

O'Grady, K., & Houme, K. (2014). *Programme pancanadien d'évaluation: PPCE de 2013*. Conseil des ministres de l'Éducation (Canada). http://fr.scribd.com/doc/242165437/PCAP-2013-Public-Report-FR-pdf

Ontario College of Teachers. (2006, November 27). *La pénurie d'enseignants francophones persiste* [Press release]. https://oeeo.ca/public/media/press-releases/2006/20061127

Ontario Ministry of Education. (2011). *Un personnel qui se distingue! Profil d'enseignement et de leadership pour le personnel des écoles de langue française de l'Ontario: Guide d'utilisation*. Imprimeur de la Reine pour l'Ontario. http://www.edu.gov.on.ca/fre/amenagement/GuideProfilEnseignement.pdf

Pierroz, S. (2015, December 3). Insécurité linguistique des élèves francophones inquiets. *ONFR+*. https://onfr.tfo.org/intimidation-linguistique-des-eleves-francophones-inquiets/

Racine, I. (2007). *Prédispositions, pratiques et finalités du leadership éducatif des directions d'école de langue française de l'Ontario* (Doctoral dissertation, Université d'Ottawa, ON). http://hdl.handle.net/10393/29689

Radio-Canada. (2018, November 27). Manifestations d'élèves contre l'annulation du projet d'Université de l'Ontario français. *Radio-Canada*. https://ici.radio-canada

.ca/nouvelle/1138314/manifestations-eleves-annulation-projet-universite-ontario
-francais

Radio-Canada. (2019, September 25). Les écoles de la DSFM resteront ouvertes lors de la grève pour le climat. *Radio-Canada*. https://ici.radio-canada.ca/nouvelle /1316357/dsfm-ecole-greve-marche-climat-greta-thunberg-manitoba-winnipeg

Ramlakhan, K. (2018, December 1). "Proud of my culture": Thousands protest French-language service cuts. *CBC News*. https://www.cbc.ca/news/canada /ottawa/franco-ontarian-protest-ottawa-1.4928973

Rocque, J. (2006). Vers l'élaboration d'une politique de l'exogamie dans le cadre de la gestion scolaire francophone en milieu minoritaire. *Revue de la Common Law en français*, *8*, 121–53. https://ustboniface.ca/julesrocquevieux/file/8-I-03-Rocque.pdf

Rocque, J., & Taylor, G. (2011). La participation des couples mixtes à la gestion scolaire francophone. In J. Rocque (Ed.). *La direction d'école et le leadership pédagogique en milieu francophone minoritaire* (pp. 191–218). Winnipeg, MB: Presses de l'Université de St-Boniface.

Schroeter, S., & James, C. (2015). "We're here because we're Black": The schooling experiences of French-speaking African-Canadian students with refugee backgrounds. *Race, Ethnicity and Education*, *18*(1), 20–39. doi: 10.1080/13613324 .2014.885419

Seebruch, N. (2020, 28 January). Cornwall French Catholic elementary school denies admission for Muslim student. *Seaway News*. https://www.cornwallseawaynews .com/2020/01/28/cornwall-french-catholic-elementary-school-denies-admission -for-muslim-student/

Shields, C.M. (2010). Transformative leadership: Working for equity in diverse contexts. *Educational Administration Quarterly*, *46*(4), 558–89. doi: 10.1177 /0013161X10375609

Shields, C.M. (2013). *Transformative leadership in education: Equitable change in an uncertain and complex world*. New York, NY: Routledge.

Shields, C.M. (2014). Leadership for social justice education: A critical transformative approach. In I. Bogotch & C.M. Shields (Eds.), *International handbook of educational leadership and social (in)justice* (pp. 323–39). Dordrecht, Netherlands: Springer.

Shields, C.M. (2016). *Transformative leadership: Prime*. New York, NY: Peter Lang.

Shields, C.M. (2020). *Becoming a transformative leader: A guide to creating equitable schools*. New York, NY: Routledge.

Shields, C.M., & Sayani, A. (2005). Leading in the midst of diversity: The challenge of our times. In F.W. English (Ed.), *The SAGE handbook of educational leadership: Advances in theory, research, and practice* (pp. 380–406). Thousand Oaks, CA: SAGE Publications.

Shipley, L. (2011). *Profil des élèves et des écoles des groupes linguistiques minoritaires au Canada: Résultats du Programme international pour le suivi des acquis des élèves (PISA), 2009* (Statistique Canada – N° 81-595-M n° 092 au catalogue).

Ministre de l'Industrie. https://www150.statcan.gc.ca/n1/pub/81-595-m/81-595
-m2011092-fra.pdf

Smith, K. (2018, May 25). New French school, École La-Belle-Cloche, opens in Rollo
Bay. *The Guardian*. https://www.theguardian.pe.ca/news/local/new-french-school
-ecole-la-belle-cloche-opens-in-rollo-bay-213256/

Statistics Canada. (2017a). *Diversité linguistique et plurilinguisme au sein des foyers
canadiens: Recensement de la population, 2016*. Ministre de l'Industrie. https://
www12.statcan.gc.ca/census-recensement/2016/as-sa/98-200-x/2016010/98-200
-x2016010-fra.pdf

Statistics Canada. (2017b). *Mise à jour des données du Recensement de 2016 sur la
langue*. https://www12.statcan.gc.ca/census-recensement/2016/ref/lang/lang-note
-fra.cfm

Statistics Canada. (2019). *La population noire au Canada: Éducation, travail et
résilience*. Sa Majesté la Reine du chef du Canada. https://www150.statcan.gc.ca
/n1/fr/pub/89-657-x/89-657-x2020002-fra.pdf?st=5IdRXPPn

St-Germain, M. (2011). Le leadership et la gestion du temps. In J. Rocque (Ed.), *La
direction d'école et le leadership en milieu minoritaire* (pp. 219–56). Winnipeg,
MB: Presses de l'Université de St-Boniface.

St-Pierre, R. (2019, June 20). De l'argent pour une contestation contre "l'anglicisation
des écoles françaises." *Radio-Canada*. https://ici.radio-canada.ca/nouvelle
/1191883/basil-dorion-poursuite-conseil-scolaire-francophone-financement
-programme-contestation-judiciaire

Supreme Court of Canada. (2020, June 12). *Judgment in appeal* [Press release].
https://decisions.scc-csc.ca/scc-csc/news/en/item/6883/index.do

Table nationale sur l'éducation. (2012). *École communautaire citoyenne: Cadre
de référence pour l'émergence de l'École communautaire citoyenne au sein des
communautés francophones et acadiennes du Canada*. Centre franco-ontarien de
ressources pédagogiques. http://fncsf.ca/wp-content/uploads/2014/05/ECC
_cadre_reference_final1.pdf

Tawil, S. (2013). Le concept de "citoyenneté mondiale": Un apport potentiel pour
l'éducation multiculturelle? *Revue internationale d'éducation de Sèvres*, 63,
133–44. doi: 10.4000/ries.3501

Taylor, G. (2002). *I'm with you! Exogamous families' guide to the world of francophone
education*. Edmonton, AB: Fédération des parents francophones de l'Alberta.

TERMIUM Plus®. (n.d.). *Communauté de langue officielle en situation minoritaire*.
Public Works and Government Services Canada. Retrieved 19 October 2021 from
https://www.btb.termiumplus.gc.ca/tpv2alpha/alpha-eng.html?lang=eng
&srchtxt=Communaut%C3%A9de%20langue%20officielle%20en%20
situation%20minoritaire&i=1&index=frt&sg_kp_wet=1890972&fchrcrdnm=1

Vachet, B. (2020, May 21). Les étudiants du Campus Saint-Jean sont inquiets.
*ONFR+*. https://onfr.tfo.org/les-etudiants-du-campus-saint-jean-sont-inquiets/

Veronis, L., & Huot, S. (2017). *Les espaces de rencontres: Les expériences d'intégration
sociale et culturelle des immigrants et réfugiés francophones dans les communautés*

*francophones en situation minoritaire. Voies vers la prospérité, promotion des communautés accueillantes au Canada*. Immigration, Réfugiés et Citoyenneté Canada. http://p2pcanada.ca/wp-content/blogs.dir/1/files/2017/06/Espaces-de -Rencontres-Rapport-Francais.pdf

Villella, M. (2014). L'intégration avant tout! L'éducation bi/plurilingue et interculturelle. *Éducation Canada, 54*(1). https://www.edcan.ca/articles /lintegration-avant-tout/?lang=fr

Weatherall, L. (2011). *Le leadership en milieu minoritaire franco-canadien: L'apport du dispositif VelTIC* (Master's thesis, Université d'Ottawa, ON). http://hdl.handle .net/10393/20187

# 3 Transformative Educational Leadership: Leading for Equity and Social Justice in the Twenty-First Century

DARCIA ROACHE AND JASON MARSHALL

Until we transform our educational system into one that is more equitable, inclusive, and socially just ... unrest will continue to challenge the well-being of our democratic society.
– Dr. Carolyn Shields, Professor of Educational Leadership

## Perspectives of Leadership

Leadership as a concept has evolved over the last few decades, both in how it is defined and how it is practised. For us to have a comprehensive understanding of the concept and evolution of transformative leadership, it is imperative to examine, in detail, more traditional views of leadership to assist in contextualizing how transformative leadership differs from other popular leadership approaches. This will also enable us to explore its applicability to the educational context within the frameworks of social justice and equity. What follows, therefore, is a brief history of various perspectives of leadership, which acts as a segue into our discussion on transformative leadership in general and also within the context of education.

The word "lead" in leadership comes from the Old English *laedan*, corresponding to the Old Saxon *ledian* and Old High German *leiten*, which means "take with one" to "show the way" (Hoad, 1998). Leadership is associated with change, influence, respect, and loyalty. A plethora of information exists on the definition of leadership. Scholars and practitioners for centuries have defined leadership in various ways as influenced by several factors and challenges such as politics, organizational behaviour, and academics.

The evolution of leadership definitions spans from the 1900s to the twenty-first century after "decades of dissonance" (Northouse, 2013). Between 1900 and 1929, leadership was defined as "the ability to impress the will of the leader on those led and induce obedience, respect, loyalty, and cooperation" (Moore, 1927, p. 124; see also Northouse, 2013). From the 1930s to the 1950s, definitions of leadership focused more on the traits and behaviours of those individuals directing the activities of groups (Hemphill, 1949; Northouse, 2013). Then, from the 1960s to the 1980s, leaders were defined as "persons who influence other persons in a shared direction" (Seeman, 1960, p. 53), and leadership was defined as a reciprocal process involving people with diverse motives and shared values to achieve the goals of the leaders and followers (Burns, 1978).

As this brief literature review demonstrates, several different definitions of leadership have held prominence at various times throughout the modern era. Understanding how the concept of leadership has evolved is important for setting the context of our discussion on transformative leadership. Transformative leadership has brought an innovative and adaptive theory to leadership within the context of social justice and education. It provides a framework and understanding of leadership in education that has been absent from the literature until relatively recently.

Throughout this chapter, emphasis will be placed on transformative leadership in education, and how educational leaders are leading for equity and social justice in the twenty-first century. Reference will be made, in particular, to education in the Canadian context. The importance of transformative leadership in education, especially with reference to social justice, is emphasized by Shields (2015), who asserted that "transformative leadership breaks with tradition, focus[ing] on those who are most neglected and marginalized within existing structures" (p. 9). Shields's explanation provides us with clarity on the importance of this type of leadership in a world that is, for many, socially unjust. It is therefore critical to explore transformative leadership in more detail regarding its applicability to the educational context.

**Transformative Leadership**

Transformative leadership is not a wholly new construct in educational organizations. Shields (2011), for example, stated that "transformative leadership begins, not with commitment to organizational goals, but with questions of justice and democracy; it critiques inequitable practices and inextricably links education and educational leadership to the wider social context within which it is embedded" (p. 9). Regarding the individual and collective nature of transformative leadership, Shields referenced Weiner's (2003) definition of transformative leadership as "an exercise of power and authority that begins with questions of justice, democracy, and the dialectic between individual accountability and social responsibility" (p. 89). Furthermore, Foster (1989) stated that transformative leaders "both inspire and transform individual followers so that they too develop a new level of concern about their human condition and, sometimes, the condition of humanity at large" (p. 41).

Transformative leadership calls for a change in how things are done in educational organizations to achieve goals and for educational leaders to create educational environments that are based on inclusivity, equity, and justice.

According to Burns (1978), the notion of transforming leadership calls for revolution – "a complete and pervasive transformation of an entire social system" (p. 202) and "*real change* – that is, a transformation to the marked degree in the attitudes, norms, institutions, and behaviours that structure our daily lives" (p. 414, emphasis in original; see also Shields, 2015). Given the foregoing, we must recognize the value of transformative leadership as an approach for socially just and equitable education. As Shields (2018) puts it, transformative leaders have the ability to provide learning environments that are academically excellent, equitable, inclusive, and socially just, even in the face of the volatile, uncertain, complex, and ambiguous world of education today.

## Transformative Leadership Theory (TLT) for Social Justice and Equity in Education

Shields (2015) postulated that "in education, transformative ideals owe much to the work of Freire (1970, 1998), who used the terms transform, transformation, and transformative to describe the changes that may occur as a result of education" (p. 6). The term transformative is associated with adult learning (Mezirow, 1991, 1996; Shields 2015), health care, social service areas (Duncan, Alperstein, Mayers, Olckers, & Gibbs, 2006; Shields, 2015; Watkins, 2000), and educational leadership (Quantz, Rogers, & Dantley, 1991; Shields, 2003, 2015; Weiner, 2003). When we speak of transformative leadership theory (TLT), we are referring to a type of leadership theory that addresses issues related to social justice and inequity in education.

TLT has the potential to bring about meaningful change by promoting social justice and equity in education. Transformative educational leaders, with their collaborative approach and lack of tolerance for inequities, take account of the ways in which the inequities of the outside world affect the outcomes of what occurs in educational organizations (Shields, 2015). Education is not exempt from societal realities. Unfortunately, issues of race, discrimination, prejudice, and inequity are an inherent part of the myriad educational issues that educational leaders face in the twenty-first century.

### The Educational Experiences of Historically Marginalized Groups in Canada

In multicultural societies such as Canada, many of the everyday occurrences of inequity, racism, and homophobia permeate the education system. These unwanted experiences of individuals from historically marginalized groups such as Black Canadians, South Asians, and Indigenous peoples, should not go unnoticed or unaddressed. In education, it is important for leaders to be cognisant of the diversity that exists within the student body and to put measures in place to enhance the experiences of minority groups. For example, First Nation leaders have been very vocal about the disparity between reserve and off-reserve education (Assembly of First Nations, 2011; Bains, 2014; Porter, 2016a, 2016b). As Donnelly (2010) noted:

> Equity is a complex and complicated issue. Creating equity does not mean treating everyone equally. Creating equity would appear to suggest providing all students with the resources necessary for an education of equal quality to any other education program in the Canadian system. The reality is that we do not now create equity in Canadian schools; indeed, the circumstances of schools vary widely in major ways. (p. 1)

The education for First Nations students is chronically underfunded. While funding may be regarded as a policy issue, transformative leaders put systems in place within their educational institutions to promote equal access. Some First Nation leaders go as far as claiming it is a planned process of assimilation into white culture (Porter, 2016b). Many, including Atleo (2008), argue that the racist stereotypes of First Nations people still exist and influence education. Evan Taypotat, chief of the Kahkewistahaw First Nation, observes the following:

> A lot of people in this country we call Canada, are racist towards First Nations people. They say all these mean things online, but they don't even know our kids aren't given a fair chance. They haven't even stepped on a reserve. Let's give our kids a fair chance, just like farmer Joe's kids in Broadview. If we can do that, I promise you, the social differences, the "drunk Indian," the "you get free houses," those type of stereotypes will disappear, because our kids will get that proper education so that they can succeed at the post-secondary level. (as cited in Dart, 2019, para. 11)

Arresting or minimizing these issues (within the educational system) requires educational leaders who are able to efficiently navigate and address the complex dynamics and nuances of a diverse educational world characterized by uncertainty and ambiguity; education needs transformative leadership. This type of leadership is not leader-centred, as is often the case in many other traditional models of leadership, particularly within the business world, but rather is dependent on collaboration with other educational stakeholders.

First Nations students are not the only group to be subjected to negative educational experiences in Canada, however. Issues of racism and discrimination are also prevalent towards Black Canadians, Asians, Sikhs, members of the LGBTQ+ community, and other minority groups. For example, in Alberta, one report suggested that "Black youth continue to be disproportionately streamed into lower education tracks because of both individual prejudice and systemic factors. It was further suggested that instructors continue to hold racial stereotypes that affect their interactions with Black youth" (Maynard, 2020, para. 6). To use the words of one Black Alberta student, "they [teachers] don't care about Black students; they don't care if you are here or not" (as cited in Maynard, 2020, para. 7).

Unfortunately, these types of experiences are not restricted to Black students; students of South Asian descent are also subjected to racial indignities in Canada's education systems. For instance, Samuel and Burney (2003) reported that South Asian students at a predominantly white Canadian university claimed to have had experiences of what they interpreted as racism with faculty members who were unsympathetic and unwilling to give them support and encouragement. In the study, one of the participants – a South Asian medical student – shared that she felt she had been picked on and grilled with more questions than white students and professed that she felt humiliated and "tortured" by the procedure (p. 19).

These few examples illustrate that minoritized groups may not only be subject to overt discrimination in Canadian schools, but that this prejudice may also manifest in the form of microaggressions that are more subtle in nature. This suggests that the experiences of these groups in Canada may be based on a systemic structure of racism and "silent" prejudice. This needs to be addressed and corrected, and TLT provides insights into practical solutions.

## Using TLT to Promote Social Justice in Education

Education is not a business, at least not in the traditional sense. It is designed to facilitate the empowerment of people through their acquisition of knowledge (Marshall, Fayombo, & Marshall, 2015). When authors speak about leadership in education, a business-like approach is often proffered (Hardy, Bham, & Hobbs, 2020). Many of these models of leadership (e.g., transactional, transformational, autocratic) do not consider the unique nature of the educational sector when compared to other traditional institutions/organizations. Education is not inherently designed to provide opportunities for social and economic advancement to those who are disempowered and lack political capital (Haeffele & Storr, 2019), but it can be (and perhaps should be) a vehicle for social mobility. Historically marginalized groups and visible minorities (e.g., Indigenous peoples, Black Canadians, South Asians) in Canada who struggle economically and socially use education as an avenue to empower themselves. Therefore, it is imperative that educational leaders adopt an approach to leadership that aims to promote inclusion, justice, and equity so that these groups have fair and equitable access to educational resources and opportunities.

Social justice underpins several issues (e.g., discrimination, inequity, exclusion) reflected in society, many of which will have to be resolved at the government policy level. The process of bringing about educational change from the government may be extremely bureaucratic. The time for change is now, but the question is, Are we ready? The difficulty posed by this process is that it will require a complete overhaul of how things are done. It will mean addressing and preventing less visible practices of racism and discrimination at an institutional and policy level. Given education's role as an avenue to provide equal opportunity and to redistribute power, educational leaders cannot afford to wait for systemic change. The change has to start at an institutional level through institutional policy and, more importantly, institutional leadership. Put differently, educational leaders must lead for social justice and equity (Jean-Marie, Normore, & Brooks, 2009).

Transformative educational leadership, which promotes educational empowerment, social justice, and equity, is one way to bring about meaningful education reform and change. This theory of leadership in education is extremely important for those persons who are members of underserved communities. This is not to suggest that transformative leadership is the panacea for all educational issues. However, it does provide a useful framework of leadership practice for effectively addressing some of the major difficulties with which educational leaders are faced, especially in Western, cosmopolitan democracies like Canada.

When we speak about social justice, we are referring to the equitable and fair redistribution of wealth and power to every person. In education, as it stands, all students are equal, but, to borrow a phrase from George Orwell's famous *Animal Farm*, "some are more equal than others." Ironically, education provides a unique opportunity to "level" the playing field and ensure that each person has access and opportunity to enhance themselves. Unfortunately, however, the playing field in education is not level; all potential students are not equal. There are still myriad concerns in education that reflect issues pertaining to social justice. For example, persons who are economically advantaged are more likely to have access to higher education when compared to those who do not have financial stability (Gale & Tranter, 2011; Machin & Vignoles, 2004). Apart from this, issues of inequity are also pervasive.

According to Donnelly (2010), (in)equity in Canadian education has been a prominent issue for many decades. He cites, for example, the 1986 address of Norm Goble, then secretary general of the World Conference of Organizations of the Teaching Profession, on the state of equity in Canadian education delivered at the Ontario Institute of Studies in Education (OISE) in Toronto:

> Ministers of Education of the OECD countries, meeting 1978, adopted the radical vocabulary, declaring jointly that it was the mission of the public school "to give power to the underserved groups in society" ... [W]e are witnessing in many of the industrialized countries, an attempt to modify or moderate the socio-economic effects of education, and to control the socio-political role of the schools. (as cited in Donnelly, 2010, p. 1)

As Donnelly (2010) notes, Goble labelled what was happening in education reform as a challenge against equity (p. 1). Educational leaders who are transformative in their approach to leadership should look for instances of injustice and inequity, call it out, and take steps to eradicate it. Shields (2011, 2013, 2014) has articulated eight specific tenets of transformative leadership, demonstrating its critical foundations and social justice orientation. The tenets are:

1. A mandate for deep and equitable change.
2. A need to deconstruct frameworks that perpetuate inequity and injustice and to reconstruct them in more equitable ways.
3. A need to address the inequitable distribution of power.
4. An emphasis on both private and public (individual and collective) good.
5. A focus on emancipation, democracy, equity, and justice.
6. An emphasis on interdependence, interconnectedness, and global awareness.
7. The necessity of balancing critique with promise.
8. A call to exhibit moral courage. (see also chapter 1 in this volume)

The eight tenets identified above highlight the importance of the connection between transformative leadership, social justice, and equity. More specifically, they emphasize the fact that educational leaders who are serious about bringing about transformative change must have issues of justice and equity at the forefront of their agendas.

## Conclusion

According to Shields (2015), transformative leadership has the potential to create just and inclusive learning environments. Moreover, it represents "an alternative approach to leadership for deep and equitable change" (Shields, 2012, p. 1). Such change – which will aid in the creation of just and inclusive learning environments and improve student learning and academic performance – requires strong educational leadership in order to be successful in transforming the future of Canadian schooling. Transformative educational leaders have to drive the change they want to see in their schools.

There is a need for transformative leadership to enrich educational leaders in Canadian schools with visionary approaches and strategies to guide the change that learners require. Waite and Bogotch (2017) suggest that "Canadian educational leadership in the 21st century has been influenced by significant visionaries within and beyond Canada's boundaries. These visionaries have helped to establish an infrastructure for a distinctly varied school experience" (p. 6). Examples of these approaches are seen in the curricula that has been developed in recent years in response to students' needs (Waite & Bogotch, 2017), and emerging technologies, increasing diversity among students, and burgeoning expectations of employers are now commonplace in the twenty-first century (Thomas & Gordon-Brydson, 2019). Transformative leaders create stability for educational leaders to work with faculty to identify and execute change and create positive working environments for all (Shields, 2013, 2018).

While Canadian schools have a strong tradition of inclusion and social justice in the work of educational leaders and learners, there is still a lot of ground to be covered. For example, the "history of education for Indigenous peoples in Canada has structural and societal roots mired in marginalization and subjugation" (Toulouse, 2016, p. 1). Furthermore, the experiences of Black Canadians, South Asians, and Indigenous people within the Canadian education system has been a contentious one. As Toulouse (2016) notes, "the focus from the outset of imposed, colonial-based education has centred on assimilation and/or segregation of Indigenous peoples from their communities and worldviews" (p. 1). She continues: "Today, the improved state of education for Indigenous peoples has its foundations in the resilience of Indigenous communities and social justice movements advocating for inclusion and change" (p. 1). The power of this movement is also being seen among Black and South Asian communities, as each of these groups continue to fight for equity and equality in their educational experiences.

Transformative educational leaders are needed to influence and transform education and facilitate social change in the twenty-first century. Santamaria (2013) claimed that "educational leadership for social justice and equity is the primary leadership response to an inclusive and equitable education" (p. 347). A social justice approach assists educational leaders build multicultural education that explores other alternatives to mainstream leadership practice. TLT goes beyond merely advocating for multicultural education; it calls for action, equity, justice, and equality in the treatment of minority groups.

The need for social justice is no longer on the horizon – it is here. Incorporating the principles of social justice into education will require shifts in policy and practice. For example, in Canada, where certain groups have been historically marginalized, it is important to approach social justice in education systemically. That is, concerted efforts at the policy level should be made to bring redress to marginalized groups by providing fair opportunities in education (Turnbull, 2014). Educational resources should be of the same high-quality standard for *all* persons, regardless of race, class, or ethnicity. Ensuring that there is a level playing field necessitates the ratification and implementation of policies that facilitate such practices. For example, despite the growing number of people from minority groups (e.g., Black Canadians, South Asians, Indigenous peoples) who are attaining post-secondary degrees, particularly women, Reading and Wein (2013) rightly observe that "inadequate educational opportunities for most adults manifest as a lack of capacity to promote education among their children" (p. 15). These unequal opportunities point to the need for change in education to bring about social justice.

Transformative leadership is important for bringing about educational change in Canada. In Canada, we pride ourselves as an inclusive, multicultural society (Barton & Armstrong, 2007; Dion, 2018), yet we see the old lines rising between Canadian anglophones and francophones, between white and Indigenous peoples, between non-immigrants and immigrants, and even between people of different genders (Chung, 2010; Gaudreault, 2019). These divisions are not new but seem to be gathering strength in recent years. As a result, the role of social justice in the education system from primary to tertiary is that of a prescription that can help cure an illness. But it needs to be applied with due diligence by the leaders of educational organizations. As Lewis (2016) intones, leaders must move to promote "a justice of recognition and agency," which means they must recognize their own failings and biases that hinder the application of social justice. Social justice is about change. Transformative educational leadership, driven by the principles of social justice and equity, is the catalyst for meaningful educational change in the twenty-first century. The time for that change is now.

## REFERENCES

Assembly of First Nations. (2011). *Assembly of First Nations annual report 2010–11.*
    https://www.afn.ca/uploads/files/afn_annual_report_2010-11_en_web.pdf

Atleo, M.R. (2008). Watching to see until it becomes clear to you: Metaphorical
    mapping – A method for emergence. *International Journal of Qualitative in
    Education, 21*(3), 221–33. doi: 10.1080/09518390801998338

Bains, R. (2014). *Myths and realities of First Nations education.* Fraser Institute.
    https://www.fraserinstitute.org/sites/default/files/myths-and-realities-of-first
    -nations-education.pdf

Barton, L., & Armstrong, F. (Eds.) (2007). *Policy, experience and change: Cross-
    cultural reflections on inclusive education.* London, UK: Springer.

Burns, J.M. (1978). *Leadership.* New York, NY: Harper & Row.

Chung, M.M. (2010). *The relationships between racialized immigrants and Indigenous
    peoples in Canada: A literature review* (Unpublished master's thesis). Ryerson
    University, Toronto, ON.

Dart, C. (2019, August 3). First Nations schools are chronically underfunded.
    *CBC Docs POV.* https://www.cbc.ca/cbcdocspov/m_features/
    first-nations-schools-are-chronically-underfunded

Dion, S. (2018). *Inclusion and multicultural societies – Experiences from Canada*
    [Speech transcript]. Government of Canada. https://www.international.gc.ca
    /country_news-pays_nouvelles/2018-03-06-germany-allemagne.aspx
    ?lang=eng

Donnelly, M.L. (2010, October). *The state of equity in Canadian education*. Paper prepared for the Canada-United States Colloquium on Achieving Equity through Innovation, Toronto, ON. https://edpolicy.stanford.edu/sites/default/files /publications/state-equity-canadian-education.pdf

Duncan, M., Alperstein, M., Mayers, P., Olckers, L., & Gibbs, T. (2006). Not just another multi-professional course! Part 1. Rationale for a transformative curriculum. *Medical Teacher, 28*(1), 59–63. doi: 10.1080/01421590500312888

Foster, W. (1989). Towards a critical perspective of leadership. In J. Smyth (Ed.), *Critical perspectives on educational leadership* (pp. 39-62). London, UK: Falmer Press.

Freire, P. (1970). *Pedagogy of the oppressed*. New York, NY: Herder & Herder.

Freire, P. (1998). *Pedagogy of freedom: Ethics, democracy, and civic courage*. Lanham, MD: Rowman & Littlefield.

Gale, T., & Tranter, D. (2011). Social justice in Australian higher education policy: An historical and conceptual account of student participation. *Critical Studies in Education, 52*(1), 29–46. doi: 10.1080/17508487.2011.536511

Gaudreault, C. (2019). The impact of immigration on local ethnic groups' demographic representativeness: The case study of ethnic French Canadians in Quebec. *Nations and Nationalism, 26*(4), 923–42. doi: 10.1111/nana.12568

Haeffele, S., & Storr, V.H. (2019). Is social justice a mirage? *The Independent Review, 24*(1), 145–54.

Hardy, J., Bham, M., & Hobbs, C. (2020). *Leadership for educational psychologists: Principles & practicalities*. Hoboken, NJ: Wiley-Blackwell

Hemphill, J.K. (1949). *Situational factors in leadership*. Columbus, OH: Ohio State University.

Hoad, T.E. (1998). *The concise Oxford dictionary of English etymology*. Oxford, UK: Oxford University Press.

Jean-Marie, G., Normore, A.H., & Brooks, J.S. (2009). Leadership for social justice: Preparing 21st century school leaders for a new social order. *Journal of Research on Leadership Education, 4*(1), 1–31. doi: 10.1177/194277510900400102

Lewis, K. (2016). Social justice leadership and inclusion: A genealogy. *Journal of Educational Administration and History, 48*(4), 324–41. doi: 10.1080/00220620 .2016.1210589

Machin, S., & Vignoles, A. (2004). Educational inequality: The widening socio-economic gap. *Fiscal Studies, 25*(2), 107–28. doi: 10.1111/j.1475-5890.2004 .tb00099.x

Marshall, J.E., Fayombo, G., & Marshall, R. (2015). I paid for it, so I deserve it! Examining psycho-educational variables and student consumerist attitudes to higher education. *International Journal of Higher Education, 4*(4), 1–8. doi: 10.5430/ijhe.v4n4p73

Maynard, R. (2020, June 10). Canadian education is steeped in anti-Black racism. *The Walrus*. https://thewalrus.ca/canadian-education-is-steeped-in-anti-black-racism/

Mezirow, J. (1991). *Transformative dimensions of adult learning*. San Francisco, CA: Jossey-Bass.

Mezirow, J. (1996). Contemporary paradigms of learning. *Adult Education Quarterly*, *46*(3), 158–72. doi: 10.1177/074171369604600303

Moore, B.V. (1927). The May conference on leadership. *Personnel Journal*, 6, 124–8.

Northouse, P.G. (2013). *Leadership: Theory and practice* (6th ed.). Thousand Oaks, CA: SAGE Publications.

Porter, J. (2016a, March 14). First Nations students get 30 per cent less funding than other children, economist says. *CBC News*. https://www.cbc.ca/news/canada /thunder-bay/first-nations-education-funding-gap-1.3487822

Porter, J. (2016b, October 8). First Nations education: Are we still getting it wrong? *CBC News*. https://www.cbc.ca/news/canada/thunder-bay/first-nations-education -getting-it-wrong-1.3795927

Quantz, R.A., Rogers, J., & Dantley, M. (1991). Rethinking transformative leadership: Toward democratic reform of schools. *Journal of Education*, *173*(3), 96–118. doi: 10.1177/002205749117300307

Reading, C., & Wien, F. (2013). *Health inequalities and social determinants of Aboriginal peoples' health*. Prince George, BC: National Collaborating Centre for Aboriginal Health. https://www.nccih.ca/docs/determinants/RPT-Health Inequalities-Reading-Wien-EN.pdf

Samuel, E., & Burney, S. (2003). Racism, eh? Interactions of South Asian students with mainstream faculty in a predominantly white Canadian university. *Canadian Journal of Higher Education*, *33*(2), 81–114. doi: 10.47678/cjhe.v33i2.183433

Santamaria, L.J. (2013). Critical change for the greater good: Multicultural perceptions in educational leadership toward social justice and equity. *Educational Administration Quarterly*, *50*(3), 347–91. doi: 10.1177/0013161X13505287

Seeman, M. (1960). *Social status and leadership: The case of the school executive*. Columbus, OH: Ohio State University.

Shields, C.M. (2003). *Good intentions are not enough: Transformative leadership for communities of difference*. Lanham, MD: Scarecrow Press.

Shields, C.M. (2011). *Transformative leadership: A reader*. New York, NY: Peter Lang.

Shields, C.M. (2012). *Transformative leadership in education: Equitable and socially just change in an uncertain and complex world*. New York, NY: Routledge.

Shields, C.M. (2013). *Transformative leadership in education: Equitable change in an uncertain and complex world*. New York, NY: Routledge.

Shields, C.M. (2014). Ethical leadership: A critical transformative approach. In C.M. Branson and S.J. Gross (Eds.), *Handbook of ethical educational leadership* (pp. 24–42). New York, NY: Routledge.

Shields, C.M. (2015). From paradigm wars to transformative leadership: Can educational administration foster socially just schools? *SoJo Journal*, *1*(1), 1–22. https://eric.ed.gov/?id=EJ1247446

Shields, C.M. (2018). *Transformative leadership in education: Equitable and socially just change in an uncertain and complex world* (2nd ed.). New York: Routledge.

Thomas, A., & Gordon-Brydson, L.C. (2019). Meeting 21st century needs in higher education: Creating a model teaching and learning unit for institutions. *Journal of Arts Science & Technology, 12*(1), 3–16.

Toulouse, P. (2016). *What matters in Indigenous education: Implementing a vision committed to holism, diversity and engagement.* Measuring What Matters, People for Education. https://peopleforeducation.ca/report/what-matters-in-indigenous -education/

Turnbull, M. (2014). Education policy and social justice: The experience of South African school principals. *International Studies in Educational Administration, 42*(2), 97–109.

Waite, D., & Bogotch, I. (2017). *The Wiley international handbook of educational leadership.* Hoboken, NJ: Wiley-Blackwell.

Watkins, J. (2000). Leading via caring-healing: The fourfold way toward transformative leadership. *Nursing Administration Quarterly, 25*(1), 1–6. doi: 10.1097/00006216-200010000-00009

Weiner, E.J. (2003). Secretary Paulo Freire and the democratization of power: Toward a theory of transformative leadership. *Educational Philosophy and Theory, 35*(1), 89–106. doi: 10.1111/1469-5812.00007

# PART II

# Equitable and Socially Just Approaches to Leadership

# 4 Challenges and Choices: Sustaining Social Justice Leadership in Ontario Schools

DONNA KOWALCHUK

Is that the hill I'm prepared to die on? – Principal Florence

Major critical pedagogue Paulo Freire argues very convincingly that neutrality in education is impossible. This observation provides the context within which educational leaders and policy makers must examine the theoretical and political landscape in which educational policy and leadership are constructed. Along with Freire, critical scholars of education administration (Connell, 1993; Foster, 1986; Furman, 2012; Furman & Shields, 2005; Griffiths, 2013; Portelli, Shields, & Vibert, 2007; Portelli & Solomon, 2001; Ryan, 2006, 2012; Shields, 2010) and those of educational policy (Hursh & Martina, 2003; Joshee, 2008; Young & Diem, 2017) draw our attention to neoliberalism, or what can be referred to as the social and economic ideologies of the (globalized) market (Ball, 1998). Giroux (2007, 2018), a major writer on neoliberalism, claims that it is the most dangerous ideology of our time because it threatens democracy and functions either to ignore or to cancel out social injustice. With its roots in liberalism (McMahon & Portelli, 2012), neoliberalism has been at work in schools in capitalist societies since at least the 1980s (Davies & Bansel, 2007). According to McMahon and Portelli (2012), neoliberalism is not a term generally used by those associated with its thinking and policies. Basically, these researchers claim that the two liberal rights of individual rights and freedom have been taken to the extreme, becoming "a narrow and rigid form of individualism, which, in turn, led to excessive competition" (McMahon & Portelli, 2012, p. 2), and wherein freedom simply means any form of choice. Consequently, neoliberal ideals have informed educational goals and schooling, which, in the process, have silenced questions about power, privilege, and the relevance of cultural knowledge (McMahon & Portelli, 2012).

For decades, many newcomers to Canada, including refugees, have found new homes in Ontario, one of Canada's most populous provinces. The 2016 census highlights this diversity, reporting that almost 4 million people – nearly one third of Ontarians – identify as members of a visible minority (Statistics Canada, 2018). Accordingly, issues such as race, class, gender, language, disability, and sexual orientation set the circumstances for amplified marginalization of students and families accessing public education in Ontario. In response to the challenges of an increasingly diverse population in the province's schools, the Ontario Ministry of Education released *Realizing the Promise of Diversity: Ontario's Equity and Inclusive Education Strategy* (2009). It is designed to "promote fundamental human rights as described in the Ontario Human Rights Code and the Canadian Charter of Rights and Freedoms" (p. 13).

Earlier, in 2005, the Ministry developed and released its educational leadership strategy to strengthen school leadership across the province – part of its commitment to improving student achievement. A significant aspect of the strategy was utilizing the research on successful school leadership by Leithwood, Day, Sammons, Harris, and Hopkins (2006) to develop the Ontario Leadership Framework (Institute for Education Leadership, 2013). While not a policy per se, it has the de facto status of a government policy. Its aim is to be a practical guide for educational leaders in addressing the achievement needs of all students, as well as being the foundation of the Principal Performance Appraisal (PPA) policy. Examination of the research that supports the Ontario Leadership Framework (OLF) strongly suggests it is most closely aligned with transformational leadership theory (Leithwood, Jantzi, & Steinbah, 1999; Leithwood, Tomlinson, & Genge, 1996). Briefly, Leithwood and Riehl (2003) describe transformational leadership theory as an interactive hierarchical relationship between leaders – in a position of power to set a direction or purpose – and followers. While not overtly identified, neoliberal ideology has had a strong influence on this most dominant and traditional theory of educational leadership.

Counter to how leadership is conceived of in the neoliberal tradition, the efforts of social justice–minded school leaders most closely align theoretically with a conception of educational leadership viewed through a critical lens, as found in the research of Connell (1993), Foster (1986), Freire (1998), Portelli and Solomon (2001), Furman and Shields (2005), Portelli, Shields, and Vibert (2007), Ryan (2006, 2012), Shields (2010, 2016, 2019), Furman (2012), Griffiths (2013), and Kowalchuk (2017). From a critical approach, leading for social justice is at the service of learning and is underpinned by democracy, collaboration, and agency (Furman & Shields, 2005). Over twenty years ago, Connell (1993) argued that social justice matters for everyone connected with the education system, because education is a major public asset that "shapes the kind of society that is coming into being" (p. 14). In the study from which this chapter is drawn (Kowalchuk, 2017), one school administrator voices that social justice in schools is important because

[e]very human being out there needs to have the opportunity to better their life, irrespective of who they are, what race they are, what gender … This will allow you to better yourself – to become a better human being … to improve your quality of life. (Principal Jaabir)[1]

My purpose in writing this chapter is to generate some much-needed discussion on who speaks for "just" leadership for education reform. Macbeath (2015) claims that "leadership is a subversive activity … concerned with challenging inert ideas, asking hard, uncomfortable, and uninvited questions, [and] refusing to accept the status quo" (p. 27). In this way, I hope, this chapter is *subversive.*

To that end, I employ here a critical qualitative case study of fourteen principals and vice-principals from Ontario, Canada. Each of the school leaders studied through semi-structured interviews self-identified as having social justice at the centre of their practice. Recruitment of participants focused on inclusion from the broad spectrum of local contexts within Ontario (including urban and rural regions, elementary and secondary schools, and public and Catholic jurisdictions) and included principals and vice-principals who work in English-speaking environments and who self-identify as racialized or non-racialized people. One significant question the study examined was, "What strategies or practices do principals engage in to sustain their social justice work in schools?" Along with specifically focusing on the Ontario context, a significant aspect of the study and this chapter is that it gives voice to school leaders who have examined and reflected on their leadership and can offer their insights into social justice leadership at the crossroads of an *Equity and Inclusive Education Strategy* policy and an education leadership framework, the Ontario Leadership Framework, situated in neoliberal ideology. These principals argue that the claims in the OLF do not support them in their pursuit of a socially just school. Principal Collins voices this claim: "No, honestly, it [the OLF] doesn't help me at all in my social justice work … The framework or expectations are, you know, the standards of practice for principals; they're broad expectations." In fact, many principals assert that the OLF hinders their social justice leadership. If, as scholars claim, neoliberalism has influenced schools and by association the policies that underpin them, then few school leaders understand how to make social justice central to their leadership practice. And those who do face resistance.

As a result of the school leaders' social justice leadership efforts lying at the intersection of education policy and education leadership theory, tension, conflict, and challenges emerge. When school leaders use leadership to lever social justice – to respond to injustice, to challenge the status quo, and to keep student achievement the core business of schools – they confront resistance from staff, parents, and the community, from other principals and the principalship itself, from supervisors and the organization, and, ultimately, from exhaustion (Kowalchuk, 2017). Social justice leaders in the Ontario schools in this study understand that privilege and power are inherent in leadership and in the principal's role (Kowalchuk, 2017). If the OLF does not support social justice leadership, finding a way to continue to choose social justice over organizational demands and accountabilities is indispensable in sustaining social justice leadership.

Shields (2010) describes this resistance as keeping "one foot within the dominant structures of power and authority" (p. 570) while exercising oppositional power, taking risks, and forming strategic alliances to become an activist and a voice for change. Theoharis (2004) describes three ways in which resistance can be framed:

(a) *The resistance principals enact* against historic marginalization of particular students, (b) *the resistance the principals face* as a result of their social justice agenda, and (c) the *resistance or resilience these principals develop* as a result of facing constraints in their work. (p. 4)

Choice is a factor in all three of these aspects of resistance, as the principals in this study demonstrate in their efforts to engage with the OLF to enact social justice leadership. Grounded in Theoharis's (2007) idea of the resistance or resilience that principals develop, through voice and agency, in facing constraints to their work, this chapter not only examines how social justice–minded school leaders choose to sustain their work, but also how they choose to sustain themselves through acts of subversion, political savvy, and, ultimately, resilience. The following examines each of these choices followed by a critical analysis and discussion of each respectively.

## Subversion

Speaking the truth that the OLF does not support social justice leadership when school leaders are required by policy to ensure equity and inclusion in their schools is, by definition, a *subversive* activity; so too are the actions of school leaders using leadership to respond to injustice and to confront resistance. Consequently, principals argue that subversion is a necessary tool in navigating towards social justice in Ontario schools.

As Principal Idella explains, "The job [of principal] holds a lot of power … the institution holds so much power." Principal Florence adds, "Sometimes you have to work subversively … You have to understand the culture within which you're working and how best to leverage it in order to accomplish what you're hoping to." As such, subversion becomes a form of resistance. As a subversive activity, school leaders claim that social justice leadership requires both creativity and the appearance of compliance. School leaders view subversion as a "creative choice" that allows principals to exercise their power. Principal Florence explains her creativity with respect to subversion in this way: "You have to be very, um, creative in how you access resources to forward your [social justice] agenda ... and in working with the [administrative] team ... They might not see the need in the same way." The real need for creativity is not simply accessing an equitable distribution of resources, however; it is accessing an equitable distribution of resources within the hierarchy of relationships present in the education system. In discussing creativity in leadership choices, Principal Anderson notes that in order to ensure students get what they need, "it depends on how you spin it."

Creativity also allows school leaders to find ways to appear compliant. Principal Hadley attests that she and other principals have found ways to locate social justice within the external goals and expectations of their respective institutions. She gives the example of the STEM (science, technology, engineering, and mathematics) initiative: "If you look at the STEM fields in university, we do not have marginalized people represented ... minority populations are underrepresented." In Principal Hadley's case, boosting the capacity of marginalized students to succeed in STEM fields appears to be compliant, but it is also subversive, as it attempts to address the imbalance in these fields. Principal Gray also explains how subversion is creative while appearing compliant:

> Sometimes I guess people go underground. I'm sneaky ... Well, I do what I need to get done to make sure everything is done on time ... It allows me freedom and time to go deeper in those subjects. It's kind of like staying in the weeds ... And while you've got extra time, keep infusing social justice efforts and actions into the brew.

Principal Norman similarly describes subversion as justifiable scheming: "I think I am devious ... I need to be to survive and I need to advocate for social justice." That is not to say, however, that when school leaders subvert power through "creative compliance" (De Angelis et al., 2007) they are not leading authentically. Besides the deviousness required for enacting social justice, Principal Norman says that a principal should

> [a]lways be a model worthy of following ... Enact authentically the actions that relate to the words that I've spoken ... When I look at how I lead, it's by mutual respect and, again, putting into action those things that I believe are fundamental.

There are other examples of principal actions that are subversive. Many principals focused on building capacity in their schools through collaborative relationships to challenge the status quo on deficit thinking with staff. Other principals systematically dismantled the traditional hierarchical model of leadership in their schools, empowering them to strategically hold staff accountable for perpetuating practices that marginalize. The very fact that the principals in this study developed strategies to sustain their work against the many forces of resistance demonstrates yet another example of social justice leadership as a subversive action.

## Critical Analysis and Discussion of Subversion

Theoharis (2007) and MacBeath (2007) claim that social justice leadership is, by its very nature, centred on the idea of disrupting and subverting arrangements that promote marginalization and exclusionary processes. MacBeath (2007) suggests that "subversion" should not conjure up visions of radical disobedience but rather a much quieter intellectual, moral, and political revolution. "Subversion," says MacBeath,

> is intolerant, not in a bullish or confrontative sense, neither personalized nor necessarily even direct, but implicit in the fostering of a climate in which critical inquiry is simply the way we do things around here ... Intellectual and moral subversion go hand in hand. Responsibility is a moral commitment and one that is consciously and rigorously applied. It believes in accountability but one that derives from a strongly held value position rather than mandated targets. (pp. 245–6)

This dilemma surrounding subversion is a topic of dialogue in "Talking about Social Justice and Leadership in a Context of Accountability" (De Angelis et al., 2007). In a discussion about how social justice looks within the context of accountability in standardized testing, the participating principals were practical in their approaches to this dilemma:

> Among other things, they were reluctant to pursue courses of action that would leave them without their jobs. But at the same time, they also wanted to be true to their commitment to social justice. This requires that they engage in practices that simultaneously satisfy the powers-that-be and work in the interests of the marginalized ... Eventually, though, the practitioners came to more-or-less agree that their respective approaches could be described as "creative compliance." (De Angelis et al., 2007, p. 26)

The term "creative compliance" aptly describes how, in practice, the principals attempted to ameliorate the tension between institutional accountabilities and their own professional and personal accountability to social justice.

The school leaders represented in Kowalchuk (2017) subvert or creatively comply with resistance every day. While most principals openly discussed subversion, others, in true subversive style, did not. They became uneasy when asked how they sustain their leadership. Subversion does conjure up negative connotations because it suggests non-compliance. Some were conscious of the need for discretion; some were even fearful that, in some way, their responses and identities could be revealed. Because of these reasons, the school leaders were very reticent to provide concrete examples of what their creative choices were to subvert power and resist the historic marginalization of particular students.

School leaders claim that creativity and the appearance of compliance are always strategic. The principals interviewed in Kowalchuk (2007) are highly aware that their leadership is accountable to individuals within the hierarchy of public education and to public education itself. "Some of these maverick things that we are doing, we're going to be accountable to our bosses – our superintendent, our executive superintendents for equity and for student success … even the Ministry of Education" (Principal Jaabir). Still, there are those principals who, contrary to the opinions given here, may see their role and their educational institutions as power neutral. For Freire (1998), however, educational processes are never power neutral. He cautions that neutrality does not exist in educational institutions and suggests that "subversion" acknowledges the existence of power relations within the organization and within the individuals who subscribe to the organization. He contends that "subversion" is needed to navigate between opposing ideologies, essentially meaning that principals need to develop forms of resistance in order to lead for social justice. Subversion is one form of the resistance or resilience these principals develop as a result of facing constraints to their work. Political savvy is another.

## Political Savvy: Power, People, and Politics in the Workplace

School leaders claim that political savvy is strategic resistance. It involves power, people, and politics in the workplace, and is a critical skill for principals who want to enact social justice and simultaneously hold on to their jobs and self-respect.

> It's picking the right times to engage in those conversations about what people are or are not seeing or being mindful of [with respect to social justice] … You have to be diplomatic … and you have to be very strategic … We're immersed in a battle and there are many little fights along the way … If I didn't speak at the moment to correct a mindset, it doesn't mean I didn't hear it … It means I will strategize around how I am going to have influence over that person, that situation, that policy … strategically. I haven't deviated from what I believe – I am just savvy enough to know that I'm not going to gain any ground if I push back at that ignorant individual at this moment in time. (Principal Norman)

Principals claim that political savvy involves three steps: (1) knowing the power dynamics and the people in the hierarchical organization or institution; (2) strategically navigating the politics to honour dispositions of social justice;

and (3) choosing whether or not to juggle one's core personal values with those of the organization and its representatives.

The first step of political savvy is acknowledging the power that exists in a hierarchical institution, such as in schools and the education system as a whole. "Leadership is often about acquiring power … Once you take power out of [leadership], then it becomes collaboration" (Principal Florence). Power is dynamic and appears in various levels of the administrative hierarchy. With staff, power reveals itself when "the conversation stops when we [principals] walk into the staff room; teaching changes when we walk into a classroom; students change their behaviour when they see us" (Principal Anderson). It is also present in the relationships with staff.

> Through experience, I've learned where those [staff] boundaries are … If I can maintain those relationships with people, they will keep me going … I'll have a totally different conversation with three different people … and I'll shape my interaction with them [for a positive outcome]. (Principal Anderson)

Power is also present in the relationships with supervisors and those further up the hierarchy, including the organization itself. Principal Jaabir's quote is worth repeating: "Some of these maverick things that we are doing, we're going to be accountable to our bosses – our superintendent, our executive superintendents for equity and for student success … even the Ministry of Education, who has given us additional funding" (Principal Jaabir). For some school leaders, recognizing and understanding the existence of power and how it is both produced and subverted is empowering to them, and they embrace it. "I like living between a rock and a hard place. I always have. Because between the rock and the hard place is where the challenges occur" (Principal Evans).

Principals claim that strategically navigating the hierarchy of people and politics in the workplace to honour their social justice dispositions is the second step. "Ensuring that you have the perspective of others … I get the fragility of humanity and that lesson came from my family" (Principal Norman). Principals committed to social justice – whether they themselves are marginalized or whether they understand how their privilege inhibits their actions towards social justice – understand that they are responsible for enacting social justice in their schools. As a result of this responsibility, they place marginalized students and families at the top of the school's social and political hierarchy because they are the ones who need assistance in operating not only in schools, but in a society that views difference, such as language or culture, as a deficit. For everyone else in the organization, however, people who are marginalized are often not the priority and, consequently, hold the bottom positions in the power hierarchy. Ensuring that the people who are marginalized remain the focus of social justice leadership requires political savvy. As Principal Collins explains, people within the school – the staff – hold considerable power in the workplace:

At this school I was astute enough to know that there was an expectation that that's what I was going to come in with [social justice] and they [staff] already pre-planned how they were going to respond ... Some people were here for fifteen years, so they've been sort of part of the problem ... I had to be really politically astute and careful in how I framed it, so as to not offend people. It took me two months to figure out where I could get their buy-in ... It was the environment ... I'm coming at them through the back door and they still haven't figured that out! I am going to be patient ... In time, I'll come clean and put the five-year [social justice] vision on the table ... and [then] we could actually talk about Black people.

While one participant spoke about her lack of positional power as a vice-principal in a secondary school, most of the principals who were interviewed revealed that their superintendents (who hold even more positional power) were supportive of them. "I've been fortunate to have a great boss," says Principal Gray. Principal Idella explains the power dynamic between her and her supervisor in more detail:

She doesn't agree with [my politics] always, but she allows it and she really creates that environment that I feel completely safe telling her what I feel, what I think ... She's got the political savvies ... and that's how I get my voice and the principals' voice at the table ... Learning from her, by really watching and listening, so that I can understand the political landscape ... She said, "I'm going to take care of the politics and you're going to watch, and you're going to learn."

School leaders often feel caught within the hierarchy, in a workplace that feels like a culture of isolation, striving to serve the marginalized while, at the same time, navigating their staff and trying to build a positive relationship with their supervisor(s). In order to survive, principals seek alliances from trusted colleagues to sustain their leadership and themselves. "When you surround yourself with other social justice advocates or social justice leaders ... it stops being about power! That has helped sustain me, because it stops becoming about who holds more power, because we all want the same thing" (Principal Florence). Similarly, Principal Mackenzie advises, "Seek out who is open to thinking differently and, then, who will have to lead those conversations. Building capacity and allies is really critical to doing social justice work."

The third step of politically savvy is choosing whether or when to juggle one's core personal values with those of the organization and its representatives, which Principal Florence describes here:

We [social justice leaders] are a cautious group ... Do you work outside or inside [the system]? I believe you have more of a chance of having an impact if you work within the system ... Theoretically you're outside of the system but, in practice, you're inside the system.

Principal Gray agrees: "At the end of the day, we have to work within the system ... You have to be very strategic unless you are cornered." To clarify, when Principal Gray uses the phrase "within the system," she implies the system of complex historic principles and doctrines of a neoliberalism characterized by economic and political ideologies of a globalized market.

The politics within the system, so often resistant to social justice, is exactly where most principals gain their strength. "I inherently weave social justice throughout my job as a leader" (Principal Burgess). While Principal Evans feels productive when he is caught "living between a rock and a hard place," other principals find the politics somewhat overwhelming. For example, Principal Norman reveals, "I need to very carefully monitor my emotions." But these principals gain their strength by seeing the results of their social justice work – "When you see the impact of the work that you do, you celebrate those victories" (Principal Florence) – and by finding the silver lining in their occasional slip-ups – "I gain a kind of fortitude from being okay with my ignorance ... learning by virtue of my mistakes ... and I never take myself too seriously" (Principal Norman).

In practice, principal leadership is about decision-making, and decision-making is about management and administration. On a daily basis, principals in schools make dozens of decisions. Choice, however, is different from decision-making. Choice, here, is about leadership.

## Critical Analysis and Discussion of Political Savvy

Winton and Pollock (2012) cite much research literature in their study, "Preparing Politically Savvy Principals in Ontario, Canada," which claims that "how principals act politically impacts teaching, learning, change efforts, school governance, relationships, and democracy in education" (p. 3; see also Blase & Anderson, 1995; Blase & Blase, 2002; Malen & Cochran, 2008; Malen & Ogawa, 1988; Ryan, 2010). While principals' political actions impact the multiple variables present in the pursuit of social justice outcomes for students in schools and education, unfortunately, most acquire their political skills on the job, often through mistakes (Crow & Weindling, 2009).

Ryan (2010) cites research by Anderson (1991), Marshall and Scribner (1991), Lindle (1994), and McGinn (2005) that claims political savvy is part of the successful pursuit of social justice. He goes on to say that "a key element in this political action is political acumen" (p. 360), which he defines as "(1) understanding political environments, (2) applying the knowledge [principals] have acquired in the strategies that they employ, and (3) strategically monitoring their own actions – as they pursue their social justice goals" (p. 368). To reiterate the importance of political acumen for challenging injustice in schools and education, Ryan (2010) contests ultimately that those school leaders who are committed to equity and social justice do not have a choice:

If principals are to succeed in their social justice endeavours, then they have little choice but to play the political game, that is, to acknowledge the political realities of their organizations, hone their political skills and put these skills into play. Failure to do so will not bode well for the future of equity and social justice. (p. 374)

As is made clear in the research literature, choice influences decision-making. Choice is about having the power to select a course of action based on what is the right, best, or most appropriate choice. That choice is also influenced by which values have the most power in any given leadership situation. Choice, in contrast to decision-making, embodies our values. Social justice leadership is subject to choice simply because choosing social justice leadership requires a choice between personal agency – the leadership power within, based on values gained from direct or indirect lived experiences with marginalization – and organizational and societal power.

Power and choice are close relatives. Choice comprises both the act of choosing and the power to choose. Choosing social justice leadership for the principals interviewed here was easy. Having the power to choose is what is challenging. Principal Florence's quote, "Is that the hill I'm prepared to die on?" at the beginning of this chapter sets the context of the value/power/politics dilemma that school leaders are immersed in and at the brink of. For principals, the "hill" encapsulates the power dynamics within and from the various forms of resistance they experience. Principals must choose between their own values and accountabilities and those held by the organization of which they are a part; they must decide which will guide their practice and which will be compromised in order to enact and sustain their social justice work. Choice, then, becomes an act of resistance that principals can employ to attain the resilience they need in order to sustain their social justice leadership.

## Reframing Resistance: Resilience

A central finding of Kowalchuk's (2017) study was that the Ontario Leadership Framework, which is strongly influenced by neoliberal ideology, hinders principals in their pursuit of a socially just school. However, as Principal Gray succinctly notes, capturing the sentiments of the principals in this study, "At the end of the day, we have to work within the system." Principals understand that they work for social justice within a socially and historically constructed hierarchical education system. As such, principals need to be resilient. Here, Principal Anderson describes what it means to be resilient: "I burned myself twice; [and] I'm still here!" Principals say that resilience is needed in order to navigate and ameliorate the tension and conflict between institutional accountabilities and one's own professional/personal accountability to social justice.

Resilience can be represented by the act of choice because resilience refers to the capacity of adapting well in the face of a challenge or choice; it is not only required to sustain social justice leadership, but also to sustain oneself. When it comes to choice, there are, of course, limitations. Sustaining a focus on social justice is a challenging enterprise both professionally and personally; or, as Theoharis (2007) puts it, resilience, like choice, is a form of *"resistance principals develop* to sustain their social justice agenda in the face of resistance" (p. 248, emphasis added). According to Principal Florence, if resilience is the act of choice, then "it's [choice] about weighing it out ... Where are you going to invest your social justice capital in order to have the greatest impact in your sphere of influence?"

The principals claim that self-knowledge is where social justice leadership begins. If this is the case, then resilience is how social justice leadership is sustained. Resilience is a combination of both disposition and political savvy. Resilience is also a merger of moral courage, reflection, and perseverance. Principals draw upon these qualities as needed. Finally, resilience can be a fusion of subversion (exercising oppositional power and taking risks) and political savvy (forming strategic alliances to become champions and voices for change), both of which help principals to contest the resistance they face. In turn, these dispositions and strategies, or resilience, have their foundation in the principals' personal lived experiences of disability, race, gender, language, and their realization of privilege.

## Critical Analysis and Discussion of Resilience

In *Man's Search for Meaning*, Viktor Frankl (1959), who suffered a multitude of torments, explains resilience:

> Everything can be taken from a man but one thing: the last of the human freedoms – to choose one's attitude in any given set of circumstances, to choose one's own way. And there were always choices to make ... It is not freedom from conditions, but it *is* freedom to take a stand toward the conditions. (pp. 86, 153, emphasis in original)

Frankl argues that choosing one's way is one of the last of the human freedoms. He also makes clear that our choices are not without conditions, but he encourages us to take a stand towards those conditions. Choosing social justice leadership is a choice between personal agency – the leadership power within, based on values gained from direct or indirect lived experiences with marginalization – and organizational and societal power. Resilience lies in between our challenges and our choices.

More recently, Patterson and Kelleher (2005) have argued that resilience cannot be defined without considering its three dimensions: "the interpretation of current adversity and future possibility, the resilience capacity to tackle adversity, and the actions needed to become more resilient in the face of the adversity" (p. 3). In the first dimension, Patterson and Kelleher claim that "interpretation" falls between stimulus and response: "This filter is the most powerful factor in predicting your resilience level" (p. 3). The second dimension is comprised of three ways to compete with adversity: "personal values, personal efficacy and personal energy" (p. 6). The third dimension moves from interpretation and resilience capacity into action. They claim that "resilience strength is the sum of the dynamic interactions among the dimensions of resilience: interpretation, capacity and action" (p. 11).

The principals' actions in the study (Kowalchuk, 2017) align with this theory. Principals draw on their resilience capacity (second dimension) in what Patterson and Kelleher refer to as "the master filter" to interpret (first dimension) and then act or respond (third dimension) to the multiple forms of resistance, including the resistance inherent in the OLF.

Choice is a key aspect of resilience, navigating the OLF, and social justice. As such, it involves the repositioning of power. Foster (1986) argues that scholars and practitioners need to recognize that "at its heart, leadership – the search for democratic and rational participation in social events – is political" (p. 187). Consequently, it may be reasoned that at their core, leadership, resilience, and the repositioning of power are individual values that ultimately influence the choices principals and other educational leaders make: "Because a significant portion of the practice in educational administration requires rejecting some courses of action in favour of a preferred one, values are generally acknowledged to be central to the field" (Willower, 1992, as cited in Begley, 1999, p. 51). Hodgkinson (1991) claims that to be a leader and to cope with the pressures of organization life the administrator must know two things: "where their values are and where the power lies" (p. 6). This attestation about power reinforces Frankl's claim that one of the last of human freedoms is the power to choose – that "power ... is above all else the ability to impose one's will" (Hodgkinson, 1999, p. 6). Choice and true resilience are achievable when principals choose their personal values over those imposed by the organization. From a critical theoretical stance, doing so is the moral use of power.

**Conclusion**

Freire (1988) claimed that "thinking critically about practice, of today or yesterday, makes possible the improvement of tomorrow's practice" (p. 44). Jaramillo and Carreon (2014) caution that "neoliberal capitalism patterns the way we think, communicate, and relate to one another and our environment" (p. 394). Ultimately, those associated with schools and education must understand what is meant by "critical" in order not to reproduce neoliberalized conceptions of schools, of education policy, and of leadership. "Critical," in the context of this writing, asks how power is constructed and how it shapes individual consciousness and ways of seeing (Kincheloe, 2005). It encourages us to question the foundations of particular knowledges and concepts of neutrality and objectivity, meritocracy, and difference. It is centred on ideas of disrupting and subverting arrangements that promote marginalization and exclusionary processes.

Returning to the purpose of this chapter – to generate discussion about who speaks for "just" leadership reform – raises the question of whether other leadership frameworks in Canada are similarly conceived of within the same dominant neoliberal stance. At the beginning of the chapter we were reminded by Freire that neutrality in education is impossible. Consequently, consumers of education leadership frameworks (school leaders) and those who develop the frameworks (policymakers) need to ask, "In whose political interest is this theory of leadership?" and, alternately, "Whose political or social interests are being silenced or marginalized?" Posing these questions of leadership frameworks fulfils the purpose of this chapter – not only to generate a discussion, but also to stand subversively as a subtle mechanism to challenge inert ideas, ask hard, uncomfortable, and uninvited questions, and refuse to accept the status quo (MacBeath, 2015).

Through principal voice and agency, this chapter examined how school leaders who hold to "a strong core value system" (Principal Florence) find a way to continue to choose social justice by engaging in subversion, political savvy, and resilience to sustain not only their work but also themselves. Further, at the centre of this core value system, school leaders maintain, is "knowing thyself" through critical reflection. Through self-knowledge, school leaders claim they understand what they stand for. They realize that social justice, as Principal Idella explains, is just who they are: "Social justice for me, it's who I am, it's not something – an extra layer of my leadership or another layer as an educator – it's who I am." Through self-reflection, principals assert that they can test and check their assumptions and beliefs: "It's about ... knowing yourself, challenging yourself and actually being valued and heard" (Principal D'Andre).

Once comfortable with their self-knowledge, they are able to take a stand on social justice and recognize that knowledge continues to be constructed through dialogue and interaction, particularly with those who are marginalized: "I state my own feelings on things, plus my own ineptitude or my own lack of knowing" (Principal Gray). School leaders can then also draw on the power of self in leadership situations. When they interact with others to engage in social justice leadership, they are highly aware that neutrality does not exist in any exchange or dialogue. This awareness guides their interactions: "It is important to keep in mind at all times, to inform the work you do, how you interact with others in a supportive way and how you engage them in collaborative ways to do social justice work and to address societal inequities" (Principal Hadley).

Hodgkinson (1999) claims that "introspection ... is assumed to lead to an inner understanding which is accompanied by increased awareness or consciousness of one's being and of one's actions" (p. 16). He claims that, if knowledge is power, then self-reflection – to know thyself – becomes the source of leadership practice: "know thyself may be called the ultimate leadership imperative" (p. 17). The "onus is for the leader to acquire self-knowledge and self-mastery" (p. 18).

Knowing thyself in Freirean terms is "critical consciousness" and critical thinking. Freire (1998) asserts that this is the ability to critique truth and knowledge – "a disposition of critical self-consciousness" (p. 14) rooted in humility, faith, hope, critical thinking, and solidarity. Freire describes connecting to one's critical consciousness as *reflexivity*, a practice that guides leaders to question the dominant discourses of equality, difference, and freedom; to critique their ethics, values, personal prejudices, and biases; and then to embrace responsibility for their own liberation and the empowerment of others.

Who in our schools is our leadership serving? This is an important question for school leaders to continue to reflect upon. Principals claim that critical self-knowledge is where their social justice leadership begins and ends. In spite of the fact that principal practice in Ontario is led and supervised through the Ontario Leadership Framework, from this vantage point, principals claim they possess moral courage – the "courage to do the right thing for students" (Principal Hadley). Freire's philosophy claims that critical reflection is recursive and guides our actions; more than simply understanding the present, it is about thinking beyond the restrictions of our experiences and imagining a future filled with hope and possibility. As a school leader, it is about choosing the hill on which you are prepared to die. Or, as Paulo Freire (1998) put it, "the more I acknowledge my own process and attitudes and perceive the reasons behind these, the more I am capable of changing and advancing from the state of ingenuous curiosity to epistemological curiosity" (p. 44).

NOTE

1 Pseudonyms have been used for all interviewed participants quoted in this chapter.

REFERENCES

Anderson, G. (1991). Cognitive politics of principals and teachers: Ideological control in an elementary school. In J. Blase (Ed.), *The politics of life in schools* (pp. 120–38). London: SAGE Publications.

Ball, S.J. (1998). Big policies/small world: An introduction to international perspectives in education policy. *Comparative Education, 34*(2), 119–30. doi: 10.1080/03050069828225

Begley, P.T. (1999). Academic and practitioner perspectives on values. In P.T. Begley and P.E. Leonard (Eds.), *The values of educational administration* (pp. 51–69). London, UK: Falmer Press.

Blase, J., & Anderson, G.L. (1995). *The micropolitics of educational leadership: From control to empowerment*. New York, NY: Teachers College Press.

Blase, J., & Blase, J. (2002). The micropolitics of instructional supervision: A call for research. *Educational Administration Quarterly, 38*(1), 6–44. doi: 10.1177/0013161 X02381002

Connell, R.W. (1993). *Schools and social justice*. Philadelphia, PA: Temple University Press.

Crow, G.M., & Weindling, D. (2009). Learning to be political: New English headteachers' roles. *Educational Policy, 24*(1), 137–58. doi: 10.1177/089590480 9354495

Davies, B., & Bansel, P. (2007). Neoliberalism and education. *International Journal of Qualitative Studies in Education, 20*(3), 247–59. doi: 10.1080/09518390701281751

De Angelis, M., Griffiths, D., Joshee, R., Portelli, J., Ryan, J., & Zaretsky, L. (2007). Talking about social justice and leadership in a context of accountability. *Journal of Educational Administration and Foundations, 18*(1/2), 24–51.

Foster, W. (1986). *Paradigms and promises: New approaches to educational administration*. Buffalo, NY: Prometheus Books.

Frankl, V.E. (1959). *Man's search for meaning* (Revised and updated). Boston, MA: Beacon Press.

Freire, P. (1998). *Pedagogy of freedom: Ethics, democracy, and civic courage*. Lanham, MD: Rowman & Littlefield.

Furman, G.C. (2012). Social justice leadership as praxis: Developing capacities through preparation programs. *Educational Administration Quarterly, 48*(2), 191–229. doi: 10.1177/0013161X11427394

Furman, G.C., & Shields, C.M. (2005). How can educational leaders promote and support social justice and democratic community in schools? In W.A. Firestone & C. Riehl (Eds.), *A new agenda for research in educational leadership* (pp. 119–37). New York, NY: Teachers College Press.

Giroux, H.A. (2007). Introduction: Democracy, education, and the politics of critical pedagogy. In P. McLaren & J. Kincheloe (Eds.), *Critical pedagogy: Where are we now?* (pp. 1–5). New York, NY: Peter Lang.

Giroux, H.A. (2018). *Terror of neoliberalism: Authoritarianism and the eclipse of democracy*. New York, NY: Routledge.

Griffiths, D. (2013). *Principals of inclusion: Practical strategies to grow inclusion in urban schools*. Burlington, ON: Word & Deed Publishing.

Hodgkinson, C. (1991). *Educational leadership: The moral art*. Albany, NY: State University of New York Press.

Hodgkinson, C. (1999). The triumph of the will: An exploration of certain fundamental problematics in administrative philosophy. In P. Begley &

P.E. Leonard (Eds.), *The values of educational administration* (pp. 6–21). London: Falmer Press.

Hursh, D., & Martina, C.A. (2003). Neoliberalism and schooling in the US: How state and federal government education policies perpetuate inequality. *Journal for Critical Education Policy Studies*, *1*(2), 30–52.

Institute for Education Leadership. (2013). *The Ontario leadership framework: A school and system leader's guide to putting Ontario's leadership framework into action*. https://www.education-leadership-ontario.ca/application/files/8814/9452/4183/Ontario_Leadership_Framework_OLF.pdf

Jaramillo, N., & Carreon, M. (2014). Pedagogies of resistance and solidarity: Towards revolutionary and decolonial praxis. *Interface*, *6*(1), 392–411.

Joshee, R. (2008), Neoliberalism versus social justice: A view from Canada. In R.K. Hopson, C.C. Yeakey, & F.M. Boakari (Eds.), *Power, voice and the public good: Schooling and education in global societies* (pp. 31–53). Bingley, UK: Emerald Group Publishing. doi: 10.1016/S1479-358X(08)06002-6

Kincheloe, J.L. (2005). *Critical constructivism primer*. New York, NY: Peter Lang.

Kowalchuk, D.L. (2017). *Principals' engagement with the Ontario leadership framework to enact social justice leadership: Reflection, resistance and resilience* (Unpublished doctoral dissertation). University of Toronto, ON.

Leithwood, K., Day, C., Sammons, P., Harris, A., & Hopkins, D. (2006). *Seven strong claims about successful school leadership: Executive summary*. National College for School Leadership. https://dera.ioe.ac.uk/6967/1/download%3Fid=17387&filename=seven-claims-about-successful-school-leadership.pdf

Leithwood, K., Jantzi, D., & Steinbach, R. (1999). *Changing leadership for changing times*. Buckingham, UK: Open University Press.

Leithwood, K., & Riehl, C. (2003, April). *What do we already know about successful school leadership?* Paper presented at the annual meeting of the American Educational Research Association, Chicago, IL.

Leithwood, K., Tomlinson, D., & Genge, M. (1996). Transformational school leadership. In K. Leithwood, J. Chapman, D. Corson, P. Hallinger, & A. Hart (Eds.), *Second international handbook of educational leadership and administration* (pp. 798–814). Dordrecht, Netherlands: Kluwer Academic.

Lindle, J.C. (1994). *Surviving school micropolitics politics: Strategies for administrators*. Lancaster, PA: Technomic Publishing.

MacBeath, J. (2007). Leadership as a subversive activity. *Journal of Educational Administration*, *45*(3), 242–54. doi: 10.1108/09578230710747794

MacBeath, J. (2015). What are seven important questions about leadership? In D. Griffiths & J. Portelli (Eds.), *Key Questions for Educational Leaders* (pp. 23–9). Burlington, ON: Word & Deed Publishing.

Malen, B., & Cochran, M.V. (2008). Beyond pluralistic patterns of power: Research on the micropolitics of schools. In B.S. Cooper, J.G. Cibulka, & L.D. Fusarelli (Eds.), *Handbook of education politics and policy* (pp. 148–78). New York, NY: Routledge.

Malen, B., & Ogawa, R.T. (1988). Professional-patron influence on site-based governance councils: A confounding case study. *Educational Evaluation and Policy Analysis, 10*(4), 251–70. doi: 10.3102/01623737010004251

Marshall, C., & Scribner, J. (1991). "It's all political": Inquiry into the micropolitics of education. *Education and Urban Society, 23*(4), 347–55. doi: 10.1177/00131245910 23004001

McGinn, A. (2005). The story of 10 principals whose exercise of social and political acumen contributes to their success. *International Electronic Journal for Leadership in Learning, 9*(5). https://eric.ed.gov/?id=EJ985389

McMahon, B., & Portelli, J. (2012). The challenges of neoliberalism in education. In B. McMahon & J. Portelli (Eds.), *Student engagement in urban schools: Beyond neoliberal discourses* (pp. 1–10). Charlotte, NC: Information Age Publishing.

Ontario Ministry of Education (2009). *Realizing the promise of diversity: Ontario's equity and inclusive education strategy.* Queen's Printer for Ontario. http://www .edu.gov.on.ca/eng/policyfunding/equity.pdf

Patterson, J.L., & Kelleher, P. (2005). *Resilient school leaders: Strategies for turning adversity into achievement.* Alexandria, VA: Association for Supervision and Curriculum Development.

Portelli, J.P., Shields, C.M., & Vibert, A.B. (2007). *Toward an equitable education: Poverty, diversity and students at risk: The national report.* Ontario Institute for Studies in Education/Centre for Leadership and Diversity. https://www.oise .utoronto.ca/cld/UserFiles/File/Toward_an_Equitable_Education.pdf

Portelli, J.P., & Solomon, R. (2001). *The erosion of democracy in education: From critique to possibilities.* Calgary, AB: Detselig.

Ryan, J. (2006). *Inclusive leadership.* San Francisco, CA: Jossey-Bass.

Ryan, J. (2010). Promoting social justice in schools: Principals' political strategies. *International Journal Leadership in Education, 13*(4), 357–76. doi: 10.1080/13603124 .2010.503281

Ryan, J. (2012). *Struggling for inclusion: Educational leadership in a neoliberal world.* Charlotte, NC: Information Age Publishing.

Shields, C.M. (2010). Transformative leadership: Working for equity in diverse contexts. *Educational Administration Quarterly, 46*(4), 558–89. doi: 10.1177/0013 161X10375609

Shields, C.M. (2016). *Transformative leadership.* New York, NY: Peter Lang.

Shields, C.M. (2019). Tenet seven: Balancing critique and promise. In *Becoming a transformative leader: A guide to creating equitable schools* (pp. 141–63). New York, NY: Routledge.

Statistics Canada. (2018). *Canada at a glance 2018: Population.* https://www150 .statcan.gc.ca/n1/pub/12-581-x/2018000/pop-eng.htm

Theoharis, G. (2004, November). Toward a theory of social justice educational leadership. Paper prepared for *The Changing Face(s) of Educational Leadership: UCEA at the Crossroads,* Kansas City, KS.

Theoharis, G. (2007). Social justice educational leaders and resistance: Toward a theory of social justice leadership. *Educational Administration Quarterly, 43*(2), 221–58. doi: 10.1177/0013161X06293717

Winton, S., & Pollock, K. (2012). Preparing politically savvy principals in Ontario, Canada. *Journal of Educational Administration, 51*(1), 40–54. doi: 10.1108 /09578231311291422

Young, M., & Diem, S. (Eds.) (2017). *Critical approaches to education policy analysis: Moving beyond tradition.* Cham, Switzerland: Springer International Publishing.

# 5 Disrupting and Dismantling Deficit Thinking in Schools through Culturally Relevant and Responsive Pedagogy

ANDREW B. CAMPBELL AND KASCHKA WATSON

With its current population close to 37.5 million people, Canada is a large and diverse country committed to multi-culturalism (Statistics Canada, 2021). The country takes great pride in valuing diversity and promoting educational outcomes that are seen as being equitable (Campbell, 2020). Canada is known around the world as a "cultural mosaic," where immigrants integrate into Canadian society and where their diversity, cultures, identities, ethnicities, histories, and experiences are valued. Although all school-age children residing in Canada have access to free, publicly funded education in English and/or French language, there are long-standing and emerging inequities in the education system across the ten provinces and three territories (Campbell, 2020).

In Ontario, the most recent publication of the province's *Education Equity Action Plan* (Ministry of Education, 2017) outlines a set of best practices aimed at identifying and addressing discriminatory biases and systemic barriers in the education system. The equity action plan was developed to support the achievement and well-being of all students in Ontario's publicly funded schools. The equity action plan also shows that Ontario continues to be the province of choice for new immigrants to live, work, and pursue an education for their families and themselves. In fact, "over the past thirty years, Canada's population has become increasingly diverse ethnically and racially" (Henry et al., 2017, p. 5). Despite this diversity, many educational leaders – teachers and school administrators – are still lagging in inclusive practices. For example, many educational leaders lament that they do not have the necessary tools, while others who do, refuse to engage in inclusive practices and pedagogy. Others continue to demonstrate an attitude of bias and prejudice that place them at the lower end of the cultural competence continuum. In a study conducted by Ryan (2003) on leading for diversity, one respondent noted that "most of us [school administrators] don't have a background to give us a criteria to deal with this. You know, a teacher who started teaching in Ontario didn't have Chinese students, didn't have any Black kids, [and] would have one or two Indian kids in their class, maybe. And that's about it. Most of us who were born in Canada, many of us in small towns, have no experience dealing with those issues. So, we don't have the tools, and it's very hard to develop them" (p. 152).

In 2017, Dr. Campbell presented at a workshop where he invited educational leaders to complete the Cultural Competence Receptivity Scale[1] as a means of self-reflection and to act as an entry point into their conversations on issues surrounding equity, diversity and inclusion, and the need for educational leaders to develop cultural competence. It was quite revealing to see the disparities within the responses and a significant lack of authentic openness and willingness to grow as culturally responsive educational leaders. Participants knew the right words to say, but evidence of true self-reflection on their changing role was missing. They had not engaged in courageous conversations of this nature before, and no one had encouraged them to examine their privilege and power and how this might impact their students, who in many cases were culturally different. They had not been challenged to adjust their pedagogy to ensure all students were being included in the curriculum and classroom practices. In spite of this, Dr. Campbell is hopeful because he has seen people engaging in intentional self-reflection, which has impacted their practices. The growth he has seen is evident in the work of teacher candidates he has taught on topics such as anti-discrimination, equity, inclusive leadership, and social justice over the last two years.

Throughout our experiences as educational leaders, we have noticed the deficit thinking, attitudes, and practices that impact students' identity and sense of belonging, and how such practices have influenced how educational leaders engage students in schools. It affects what they are offered and the opportunities they are afforded. This chapter challenges educational leaders to engage in authentic reflection that allows them to examine who they are and articulate how they should use their power and privilege to disrupt and dismantle the increase in deficit thinking seen in so many of our schools.

## The Dangers of Deficit Thinking in Schools

Deficit thinking is rooted in our daily practices as educational leaders (Portelli, 2010). Unfortunately, many educational leaders are not aware of the deficit thinking that subtly and unconsciously distracts us from recognizing the cultural richness that diverse students bring to the education system (Gerstein, 2016). Most educational leaders and educational bureaucrats view public schools in deficit terms and seldom focus on the individual assets of students and school-wide strengths. All students enter the educational system with their own gifts and abilities, and it is the responsibility of educational leaders to focus on students' abilities (rather than their inabilities) and help them discover those talents (Gerstein, 2016).

So what, then, is deficit thinking? And how does it impact our ability to engage in inclusive practices? Over the years, many theories have been developed and revamped to explain school failure among marginalized students from economically disadvantaged backgrounds. Among all the theories that have been introduced, deficit thinking theory has best managed to maintain its potency and longevity, with roots lodged in early racist discourses from as far back as the early 1600s through to the late 1800s (Valencia, 1997). Deficit thinking, at its very core, maintains that marginalized students fail in school as a result of their internal deficit or deficiencies (Valencia, 1997). Sharma (2018), drawing on the earlier work of Portelli (2010, 2013), explains the term as follows:

> Deficit thinking is a very common way of thinking which affects our general way of being in and constructing the world. Differences from the "norm" are immediately seen as being deprived, negative, and disadvantaged. It never questions the legitimacy of what is deemed to be normal nor does it consider that differences may actually go beyond expected norms. It discourages teachers and administrators from recognizing the positive values of certain abilities, dispositions and actions. Deficit thinking leads to stereotyping and prejudging. It marginalizes certain people on the basis of misinformation and misconstructions. (p. 137)

Portelli and Koneeny (2018) argue that educational leaders with deficit thinking privilege the norms of white, middle-class values while neglecting the importance of diverse perspectives. Gorski (2011) and Valencia (2010) also added that anything that is not in accordance with the dominant norm is categorized as being less valuable and unworthy. This deficit thinking ideology is a danger to diverse students' opportunity to achieve at their fullest potential and also counteracts the notion of schools being a democratic environment for all students regardless of their cultural differences. In fact, history has shown us that schools have marginalized students on racial and ethnic grounds, sexual orientation, social class, and ability (Portelli & Koneeny, 2018). The ideology of deficit thinking places the blame on marginalized students who are often the victims; blaming the students, their families, culture, and social context whenever they fail academically rather than the education system, with its institutional oppressive/suppressive practices that often view marginalized students who are culturally different as a direct failure in comparison to privileged students. The danger in all of this is that students and their families buy into the ideology and internalize these deficits (Valencia, 2010).

Similarly, Weiner (2006) articulates that a bureaucratic school culture undercuts many of the pedagogical practices that draw on students' strengths. Rather than draw on these strengths, the bureaucratic culture of schools sees a need to "fix" students because they are the problem and are the ones to be blamed for their own failures (Shields, Bishop, & Mazawi, 2005). For example, a study on pre-service teachers found that white teachers believe that their students of colour are deficient and they blame their educational failures on the students' communities rather than on the institutions that are inequitably serving them (Picower, 2009). Additionally, educational leaders who hold a deficit thinking ideology towards marginalized students

> see their students only as a laundry-list of problems [and] are unable to look past students' more challenging behavior, [thus] making meaningful and reciprocal relationships impossible. Unable to connect to their students, their efforts at classroom management and instruction fail, and they in turn blame their students for what has ultimately stemmed from their negative and stereotyped views for their students. (Katsarou, Picower, & Stovall, 2010, as cited in Sharma & Portelli, 2014, p. 254)

As educational leaders, we have to be more aware of the students we cater to and avoid falling into the trap of engaging in stereotypes about students who are different and those we cannot identify (Katsarou et al., 2010) because they do not fit the dominant mould. Perhaps educational leaders who subscribe to deficit thinking need to engage in more reflection on their roles concerning the fostering of a diverse and inclusive learning environment for all students. According to Portelli and Koneeny (2018), deficit thinking is really the double-edged sword of inclusivity, and educators who practise deficit thinking often ignore inclusive practices and, believing that students must change to meet the needs of the curriculum/program rather than changing the curriculum/program to meet the needs of students. There is no doubt that deficit thinking is alive in our educational systems and is breathing through our school culture and climate, curricula, support programs, classroom practices, school–community relationships, and English as a Second Language (ESL) and English Language Learning (ELL) programs, affecting how accommodations and modifications are offered.

In Ontario, for example, we continue to see deficit thinking being exercised in how we stream students in schools. In a study conducted on the Toronto District School Board (TDSB), Galabuzi (2014) highlights that Black students are significantly overrepresented in Applied, Essential, and Undefined programs. While Black students only make up 12.6 per cent of the student population, they make up 23 per cent of students in Applied courses and close to 30 per cent of those in the Essential program. The study also shows that they are overrepresented in Undefined classes, with the result being that they have much lower post-secondary education application rates compared to their counterparts in the Academic stream; the application rate for students in the Academic stream is 81.6 per cent, whereas it is only 39.2 per cent for students in the Applied stream, 20.3 per cent for students in the Essential stream, and 41.4 per cent for those in the Undefined stream.

Deficit thinking cultivates educational leaders' biases and assumptions about students from diverse backgrounds and causes them to have low expectations of many of their students and their ability to succeed. It has been our experience that colleagues often form assumptions about particular students and their abilities, which become an issue in how they view and interact with students who are different. This approach is damaging in itself, but the major issue with these biases, assumptions, and stereotypes is that they are transferred into labels and identifiers and work their way into classroom policies and practices. Because of this, diverse students who do not fit the norm of the dominant group are often taught less, offered less attention, and challenged less by their teachers, who see them as different. We have seen practices like this from educational teachers who are said to be well-intentioned. For example, a student enters the Canadian education system from one of the countries in Africa and, unconsciously, our biases, assumptions, and stereotypes come to the forefront. We hear the word "Africa," and some of us start to think of hunger, starvation, bare-feet, walking long distances to school, poverty, and so on. The negative depictions of Africa we see and read about in the news and on social media often fuel these stereotypes. But surely as educational leaders these deficit views cannot be the only knowledge we have of Africa or of the students who come from any of the countries on the continent. Educational leaders unintentionally allow their deficit thinking to take control without pausing to self-reflect on what students can bring to the learning process, and how their differences can add value to the curriculum and pedagogy. It is deficit behaviours like this that cause educational leaders to ignore the strengths of these students (Portelli, 2010) and that cause well-intentioned educational leaders to harm and further disenfranchise marginalized students (Sharma, 2018).

Educational leaders who function through a deficit thinking lens fail to acknowledge the diverse life experiences of marginalized students (Heinbach, Fiedler, Mitola, & Pattni, 2019). Instead of nurturing and engaging students to inform the nature of their learning, educational leaders try to reshape them so that they can fit the mould defined by society, which is pervade by inequities such as racism, ableism, sexism, and classism (Heinbach et al., 2019). Because deficit thinking rejects all that is outside the norm of society, educational leaders must refrain from putting the onus of social inequities on marginalized students and redirect it on the systems that often disadvantage them (Martin, Smith, & Williams, 2018; Portelli, 2013). The only way educational leaders can work towards disrupting and dismantling deficit thinking is to change their mindset on how they view marginalized students from diverse backgrounds. We believe that educational leaders who understand and apply culturally relevant and responsive pedagogy in their practices are crucial to disrupting and dismantling deficit thinking in their respective educational institutions.

## The Value of Culturally Relevant and Responsive Pedagogy

Deficit thinking will continue to negatively affect how we view, engage with, and respond to diverse students in our classrooms and educational institutions if we do not act to eradicate it. If, as educational leaders, our wish is to teach students from diverse backgrounds effectively, we need to equip ourselves with tools that promote students' success (Brown, Boda, Lemmi, & Monroe, 2019) through culturally relevant and responsive pedagogy. Nearly three decades ago, Gloria Ladson-Billings (1992) first coined the term "culturally relevant pedagogy," which calls on educational leaders to incorporate the cultures and experiences of marginalized students into the mainstream classrooms. Milner (2011) adds that culturally relevant and responsive pedagogy is an approach that

> serves to empower students to the point where they will be able to examine critically educational content and process and ask what its role is in creating a truly democratic and multicultural society. It uses the students' culture to help them create meaning and understand the world. Thus, not only academic success, but also social and cultural success is emphasized. (p. 110)

Students do not come to our classrooms as blank slates. They enter learning environments with cultural capital that is rich in diversity and differs from mainstream norms and perspectives (Howard, 2003). As a result, the application of culturally relevant and responsive pedagogy becomes the centrepiece for educational leaders to model if they hope to make teaching and learning relevant for the diverse students to whom they cater (Jackson & Boutte, 2018). Lim, Tan, and Saito (2019) suggest that culturally relevant and responsive pedagogy uses the "cultural knowledge, prior experiences, frames of reference, and performance styles of ethnically diverse students to make learning more relevant and effective ... It teaches to and through the strengths of these students [and] is culturally validating and affirming" (p. 44).

Educational leaders can harness the cultural and social capital that students bring to their classrooms and learning spaces and make students' learning and engagement experiences more meaningful (Lim et al., 2019). Breaking down deficit thinking has a lot to do with educational leaders who see student diversity as an asset rather than as a detriment to their success (Milner, 2011). These educational leaders make it their duty to create culturally relevant learning environments by incorporating students' cultures into curriculum planning and implementation. They equip students with the skills they need to question how power structures are created and perpetuated throughout society (Milner, 2011). Through culturally relevant and responsive pedagogy, students can learn to identify the contradictions and inequities that exist inside and outside the classroom and be better able to question and fight against the numerous -isms and phobias that plague them and stifle their opportunities for success. These are examples of student outcomes that are rooted in culturally relevant and responsive pedagogical practices.

## Examining the Outcomes of Culturally Relevant and Responsive Pedagogy

Educational leaders should seek to create an inclusive learning environment that considers students' diverse cultures and experiences to help drive student outcomes (Johnson, 2019). Student outcomes go far beyond standardized test scores and are cemented in the learning environments that educational leaders create with culturally relevant and responsive pedagogy (Milner, 2011). Table 5.1 shows a comparison of the student outcomes of the culturally relevant and responsive pedagogies advanced by Ladson-Billings (1992, 1995, 2001, 2006), Gay (2010), and Milner (2011).

Educational leaders who can model culturally relevant and responsive pedagogy in their learning environments create a more inclusive culture for all their learners (Johnson, 2019). As outlined in table 5.1, Milner (2011) suggests that when students are empowered about what they are learning they begin to challenge inequities. Through the experience of culturally relevant and responsive pedagogy, students see themselves reflected in the curriculum, which helps them to understand how their culture impacts the wider society. As Milner (2011) and Ladson-Billings (2001) demonstrate (see table 5.1), the instructional experience of culturally relevant and responsive pedagogy provides learning opportunities that enable students to be innovative and to comprehend fully the socio-political nature of society. Ladson-Billings's (2001) framework for culturally relevant and responsive pedagogy sees the development of a socio-political consciousness as a broader outcome that "allows [students] to critique the cultural norms, values, and institutions that produce and maintain social inequities" (Johnson, 2019, p. 130004-3).

A culturally relevant and responsive pedagogy also allows educational leaders to take a step back in their pedagogical practices and refrain from comparing and measuring their students against the norms of society, instead seeing students for who they are. These educational leaders know that each student, irrespective of his or her cultural background, will come to the classroom with various identities and cultural capital to be valued in the learning process. As a result, leaders create a learning experience that leverages students' strengths to drive their pedagogy and curriculum design (Milner, 2011). Rather than allow deficit thinking to strip students of who they are, educational leaders use culturally relevant and responsive pedagogy to build on students' value and transform them into who they should be by providing them with formal opportunities that will enable them to evolve and grow.

Table 5.1. A comparison of the culturally relevant and responsive pedagogies of Ladson-Billings, Gay, and Milner

| Gloria Ladson-Billings (1992, 1995, 2001, 2006) | Geneva Gay (2010) | H. Richard Milner (2011) |
|---|---|---|
| *Academic achievement* is evident in classrooms where:<br>• the teacher presumes that all students are capable of being educated.<br>• the teacher clearly delineates what achievement means in the context of his or her classroom.<br>• the teacher knows the content, the learner, and how to teach content to the learner.<br>• the teacher supports a critical consciousness towards the curriculum.<br>• the teacher encourages academic achievement as a complex conception not amenable to a single, static measurement.<br><br>*Cultural competence* occurs in classrooms where:<br>• the teacher understands culture and its role in education.<br>• the teacher takes responsibility for learning about students' cultures and communities.<br>• the teacher uses the cultures of his or her students as a basis for learning.<br>• the teacher promotes a flexible use of students' local and global cultures.<br><br>*Socio-political consciousness* includes:<br>• the teacher knowing the larger socio-political context of the school-community-nation-world.<br>• the teacher having an investment in the public good.<br>• the teacher planning and implementing academic experiences that connect students to their larger social context.<br>• the teacher believing that students' success has consequences for his or her own quality of life. | • Culturally responsive teachers are *socially and academically empowering* by setting high expectations for students with a commitment to every student's success.<br>• Culturally responsive teachers are *multidimensional* because they engage cultural knowledge, experiences, contributions, and perspectives.<br>• Culturally responsive teachers *validate every student's culture*, bridging gaps between school and home through diversified instructional strategies and multicultural curricula.<br>• Culturally responsive teachers are *socially, emotionally, and politically comprehensive* as they seek to educate the whole child.<br>• Culturally responsive teachers are *transformative of schools and societies* by using students' existing strengths to drive instruction, assessment, and curriculum design.<br>• Culturally responsive teachers are *emancipatory and liberating from oppressive educational practices and ideologies* as they lift "the veil of presumed absolute authority from conceptions of scholarly truth typically taught in schools" (p. 38). | *Empowers* students to:<br>• examine educational content and processes.<br>• create, construct, and deconstruct meaning.<br>• succeed academically and socially.<br>• see contradictions and inequities in local and larger communities.<br><br>*Incorporates* student culture in:<br>• curriculum and teaching.<br>• maintaining identity.<br>• transcending negative effects of the dominant culture.<br><br>*Creates* classroom contexts that:<br>• are challenging and innovative.<br>• focus on student learning (and consequently academic achievement).<br>• build cultural competence.<br>• link curriculum and instruction to socio-political realities. |

Culturally relevant and responsive pedagogy teaches marginalized students to develop critical consciousness, which not only enables them to challenge pervasive injustices but also increases their engagement, learning, and academic achievement (El-Amin et al., 2017; Mitchell, 2010; Nykiel-Herbert, 2010; Thomas & Williams, 2008). Ginwright (2010) and Diemer, Rapa, Park, and Perry (2014) also contend that, in a broader communal struggle to attain social justice for all students, critical consciousness of repressive social forces can supplant feelings of isolation and self-blame for one's challenges with a sense of engagement. Marginalized students can also be motivated to resist oppressive forces by persisting in school and achieving academic success when they have a critical consciousness about racism (El-Amin et al., 2017). These marginalized students are further motivated to wrong the deficit thinking engrained in racist structures and institutions (Carter, 2008).

We believe that it is time for educational leaders who engage in deficit thinking to first see their diverse learners by holding high expectations for all students. As Portelli (2010) firmly noted, we need to be more aware of the nature of deficit thinking, its pervasiveness, and its dangers. Similarly, Pearson (2014) warns educational leaders and those working in the field of education to be cautious of the pervasive and destructive effect of having low expectations of students from diverse backgrounds. When we have low expectations of our students, especially those who are already marginalized, we only foster deficit thinking and reinforce the use of terms and phrases such as "underachievement" and "closing the gap" (Buxton, 2017). In the case of Indigenous students, for example, Galabuzi (2014) noted that in 2011, only 45 per cent of Indigenous students in Ontario's Grade 10 classes were on track to graduate based on credit accumulation compared to an overall average of 74 per cent for the Grade 10 population as a whole. The data further showed that as Indigenous students continue to make their way through the school system, this gap continues to increase, and they are further subjected to streaming due to deficit thinking and how they are perceived by their teachers (Galabuzi, 2014). As educational leaders, we can begin the work of disrupting and dismantling deficit thinking by modelling culturally relevant and responsive pedagogy which

> focuses on good teaching-strong pedagogy, collaborative classroom climates, and rapport between students and [educators]. It involves getting to know students well enough to learn their "social rules and conventions," taking an interest in their backgrounds and their lives … This approach involves teaching in ways that are likely very different from the ways we as [educational leaders] were taught; it involves personal transformation. (Johnson, 2019, p. 130004-3)

Taking a deficit thinking approach towards students who are different prevents educational leaders from valuing diversity and inclusion in schools.

According to Milner and Smithey (2003), "teachers need to recognize the differences inherent in the many cultures and races represented in their classroom" (p. 298). This requires a genuine desire and commitment from educational leaders to devote time and energy into self-reflection and educating themselves on their students' cultures, which is a great way to bridge the chasm that separates the worldviews of students from different backgrounds (Milner & Smithey, 2003). This is a sizeable task, but not an impossible one to achieve.

## The Impact of Authentic Self-Reflection on Deficit Thinking

As educational leaders, sometimes we work overtime trying to get students from marginalized groups to adhere to the dominant culture. Getting marginalized students to transform themselves and blend into the norms and culture of the dominant group makes our pedagogy less challenging, but are we being authentic to ourselves? How can we work extensively to change students to meet the needs of the standardized curriculum when we are not working overtime to improve our pedagogy to better cater to the diverse needs of our students? If educational leaders are going to commit to the process of eradicating deficit thinking in schools, they need to first engage in authentic self-reflection, where they can examine their power, privilege, biases, stereotypes, and assumptions about diverse marginalized students. Only after this self-reflection can they genuinely tackle the best practice approach to culturally relevant and responsive pedagogy, which stems from their dispositions as educators.

As authors of this chapter who are also educational leaders, we are challenging our colleagues to critically self-reflect on who they are and the philosophy of their pedagogical practices. If we are seeking change from our students, then the change has to start with us (Briscoe, 2017). In our experiences, we have found that many educational leaders are quick to say that they are engaging in culturally relevant and responsive pedagogy before realizing that it is not, in fact, the philosophy behind their pedagogical practice. Educational leaders cannot successfully administer the work of culturally relevant and responsive pedagogy if they refuse to examine their dispositions and pedagogical practices when working with students from diverse backgrounds.

Briscoe (2017) argues that educational leaders ought to engage in critical self-reflection and transformative practices to disrupt and dismantle deficit thinking in schools. Merely having good intentions is not enough; educational leaders need to stop blaming students and take ownership of their own role in the teaching and learning process. Educational leaders who participate in self-reflection can tap into their dimensions (institutional, personal, and instructional), which allow them to change their mindsets and practices and propel them to fully support all students (Student Achievement Division, 2013). Educational leaders need to examine their contributions to the classroom because their beliefs guide their practices and inform their pedagogical choices and interactions with students (Gosselin, 2009). We are all familiar with the common saying that asks us "to first pick the beam from our own eyes before pull it from the eyes of our students." Doing this can be very challenging because the process of self-reflection can make us vulnerable and bring to the forefront our power, privilege, biases, and assumptions that only serve to reinforce our deficit thinking towards students who are culturally different. However, we can consider asking ourselves the following self-reflection questions:

• What questions might we reflect upon to examine our biases towards diversity and cultural responsiveness?
• How might we integrate specific life experiences of our students into daily instruction and learning processes?
• How would we start a staff discussion on moving towards culturally relevant and responsive pedagogy?
• How might we support students in making decisions about their learning that integrate who they are and what they already know base on their home and community experiences?
• How can we lessen dominant perspectives in our curriculum so that contributions from different backgrounds can be better understood and integrated into learning? (Student Achievement Division, 2013, pp. 3, 6)

These reflective questions are meant to challenge those of us who are willing to engage in culturally relevant and responsive pedagogy, but they are by no means the definitive answer to how we can dismantle deficit thinking in our schools. Reflecting on these questions can help educational leaders who want to make a difference in their students' lives to think critically and to interrogate their own pedagogies. Examining their beliefs about marginalized students will allow them to create a welcoming learning space where every student has the best possible chance to perform at his or her maximum potential.

Educational leaders who have a great awareness of students' diversity are better able to challenge deficit thinking. They know that to maximize students' learning opportunities, but they must develop the skills they need to translate their knowledge of students' diversity into equitable instructional practices. Not recognizing the cultural differences that students possess can lead to miscommunication about their cultural backgrounds and lead to discriminatory institutional practices towards students who are different (Milner & Smithey, 2003). Social and political changes constantly alter our educational systems, which is why we, as educational leaders, should continuously engage in self-reflection that challenges and scrutinizes our assumptions about students who are often marginalized. Self-reflection can help us make changes that can influence deficit thinking when we recognize the strengths of students who are diverse (Weiner, 2006).

We believe that when educational leaders are constantly engaged in self-reflection, they are better positioned to identify, understand, and unpack their own power, privileges, biases, and assumptions that often cloud their pedagogy towards students who do not fit the dominant culture. Having a clear view of how their power, privileges, biases, and assumptions are linked and how they work together to impact students academically and socially can be a driving force for how they exercise culturally relevant and responsive pedagogy. Self-reflection nurtures changing mindsets, and changing mindsets, in turn, nurture culturally relevant and responsive pedagogy, which generates inclusive practices (Ryan, 2015). We acknowledge that not all educational leaders are ready to give up their power and privileges by recognizing their biases and being ethically accountable for them, as doing so entails a continuous struggle that is arduous and challenging (Sharma, 2018). It is crucial, however, that all educational leaders are aware of the impact they have on diverse students and think about how they can recognize exclusive practices and work together to change them by implementing inclusive practices (Ryan, 2015). If we do not engage in critical self-reflection and examine our deficit thinking towards students who are culturally different, we are only nurturing our assumptions and pathologizing them (Sharma, 2018).[2]

As educational leaders, we know that colonial and imperial history are the roots from which the pathologizing of the lived experiences of racially marginalized students emerges (Shields et al., 2005). We cannot allow deficit thinking behaviours to impact how we engage and teach our marginalized students. If we do, this deficit thinking and deficit pedagogy can lead to students' underachievement, which reinforces the stereotypes about the capabilities of racially marginalized students in our education system (McMahon & Portelli, 2012). For us to challenge deficit thinking, educational leaders should model transformative leadership (Shields et al., 2005) juxtaposed with inclusive leadership practices (Ryan, 2015) that promote social justice by intervening in educational processes to address wrongs and ensuring that "equitable outcomes are accompanied by more equitable use of power and widespread empowerment" for all students (Shields et al., 2005, p. 21).

Through authentic self-reflection, educational leaders become critically conscious of the symbolic power of their curriculum and can use this to teach students valuable information and values about their cultural backgrounds. Such leaders practise culturally relevant and responsive pedagogy to change how they perceive students who are marginalized in the education system due to deficit thinking (Gay, 2002). As a result, students become agents of change (Brown et al., 2019) and respond to the use of culturally relevant and responsive pedagogy to empower themselves socially, intellectually, and politically. Culturally relevant and responsive pedagogy takes a transformative approach that shows students the value of their culture and allows educational leaders to understand the pedagogical steps they need to take to improve students' learning in relation to their culture (Brown et al., 2019). Educational leaders who engage in culturally relevant and responsive pedagogy do not see their students as empty vessels to be filled. Rather, they construct classrooms that enable students to question their social context through conversations about the inequities impacting their lives. Conversely, educational leaders who do not practise culturally relevant and responsive pedagogy will be unaware of the cultural influences impacting their students' learning and may find it challenging to understand students who are culturally different from them (Lopez, 2013).

## Conclusion

With the continuous diversification of Ontario's classrooms, educational leaders are tasked with providing an equitable learning environment for all students regardless of their ethnic, racial, or cultural diversity (Shields et al., 2005). Educational leaders are thus faced with the challenge of engaging in self-reflection and applying culturally relevant and responsive pedagogy to disrupt and dismantle deficit thinking in our educational systems. Throughout this chapter, we have outlined the dangers of deficit thinking and its negative impact on marginalized students' educational outcomes (Gay, 2010; Ladson-Billings, 2001, 2006; Milner, 2011). Using the standardized curriculum in a "one-size-fits-all" approach (Sharma, 2018) does not work, and educational leaders must recognize this if they want to see a change in how marginalized students are viewed in comparison to the dominant group and engage in best practices that fully cater to the learning needs of all students. We all have to recognize the damage that deficit thinking has done to our marginalized students and the education system as a whole (Portelli, 2010). We must change our pedagogical practices to ensure that we are supporting the achievement and success of all our students (Ministry of Education, 2017).

We believe it is time for educational leaders to abandon deficit perspectives and take a step back and immerse themselves in authentic self-reflection where they can critically examine their power, privileges, biases, and assumptions and truly welcome the cultural richness, assets, and cultural capital that racially marginalized students bring to the classrooms. Rather than pathologizing the lived experiences of diverse students and focusing on the students, their homes, their parents, and their communities as the main cause of their failure at school (Sharma, 2018), educational leaders should instead focus on students' individual and school-wide strengths (Gerstein, 2016) and the abundant abilities they possess that enrich the learning experience of all students.

We strongly believe that the effectiveness of students' educational development and academic outcomes is rooted in the ability of education leaders to engage in culturally relevant and responsive pedagogy. If educational leaders who practise deficit thinking can change their mindsets through self-reflection and incorporate inclusive practices through culturally relevant and responsive pedagogy, then diverse students will be able to succeed academically on par with their non-marginalized counterparts and no longer be viewed from a deficit thinking model.

## NOTES

1  The Cultural Competence Receptivity Scale is a non-scientific instrument designed to guide individuals through a process of self-reflection. It contains fifteen items on a Likert scale with responses ranging from 1 (strongly disagree) to 7 (strongly agree) (Lindsey, Roberts, & CampbellJones, 2013). According to Juniel and Williams (2017), scoring between 6 and 7 demonstrates that participants value differences and see diversity as a benefit.
2  According to Shields et al. (2005), pathologizing is "a process where perceived structural-functional, cultural, or epistemological deviation from an assumed normal state is ascribed to another group as a product of power relationships, whereby the less powerful group is deemed to be abnormal in some ways. Pathologizing is a mode of colonization used to govern, regulate, manage, marginalize, or minoritize, primarily through hegemonic discourses" (p. x).

## REFERENCES

Briscoe, P. (2017). Using a critical reflection framework and collaborative inquiry to improve teaching practice: An action research project. *Canadian Journal of Action Research, 18*(2), 43–61. https://journals.nipissingu.ca/index.php/cjar/article/view/334/159

Brown, B.A., Boda, P., Lemmi, C., & Monroe, X. (2019). Moving culturally relevant pedagogy from theory to practice: Exploring teachers' application of culturally relevant education in science and mathematics. *Urban Education, 54*(6), 775–803. doi: 10.1177/0042085918794802

Buxton, L. (2017). Ditching deficit thinking: Changing to a culture of high expectations. *Issues in Educational Research, 27*(2), 198–214. http://www.iier.org.au/iier27/buxton.pdf

Campbell, C. (2020). Educational equity in Canada: The case of Ontario's strategies and actions to advance excellence and equity for students. *School Leadership & Management, 41*(4–5), 409–28. doi: 10.1080/13632434.2019.1709165

Carter, D.J. (2008). Cultivating a critical race consciousness for African-American school success. *Educational Foundations, 22*(1–2), 11–28. https://files.eric.ed.gov/fulltext/EJ839495.pdf

Diemer, M., Rapa, L., Park, C., & Perry, J. (2014). Development and validation of a critical consciousness scale. *Youth & Society, 49*(4), 461–83. doi: 10.1177/0044118 X14538289

El-Amin, A., Seider, S., Graves, D., Tamerat, J., Clark, S., Soutter, M., Johannsen, J., & Malhotra, S. (2017). Critical consciousness: A key to student achievement. *Phi Delta Kappan, 98*(5), 18–23. https://www.kappanonline.org/critical-consciousness -key-student-achievement/

Galabuzi, G. (2014). Race and the streaming of Ontario's children and youth. In D. Clandfield, B. Curtis, G. Galabuzi, A.G. San Vincente, D.W. Livingstone, & H. Smaller (Eds.), *Restacking the deck: Streaming by class, race and gender in Ontario schools* (pp. 185–225). Ottawa, ON: Canadian Centre for Policy Alternatives.

Gay, G. (2002). Preparing for culturally responsive teaching. *Journal of Teacher Education, 53*(2), 106–16. doi: 10.1177/0022487102053002003

Gay, G. (2010). *Culturally responsive teaching: Theory, research, and practice* (2nd ed.). New York, NY: Teachers College Press.

Gerstein. J. (2016, May 8). Approaching marginalized populations from an asset rather than a deficit model of education. *User Generated Education.* https:// usergeneratededucation.wordpress.com/2016/05/08/approaching-marginalized -populations-from-an-asset-rather-than-a-deficit-model/

Ginwright, S. (2010). *Black youth rising: Activism and racial healing in urban America.* New York, NY: Teachers College Press.

Gorski, P.C. (2011). Unlearning deficit ideology and the scornful gaze: Thoughts on authenticating the class discourse in education. *Counterpoints, 402*, 152–73. http:// www.jstor.org/stable/42981081

Gosselin, C. (2009, October). *Emerging awareness: Pre-service teachers' reflections.* Paper presented at the National Association for Multicultural Education, Denver, CO.

Heinbach, C., Fiedler, B.P., Mitola, R., & Pattni, E. (2019, February 6). Dismantling deficit thinking: A strengths-based inquiry into the experiences of transfer students in and out of academic libraries. *In the Library with the Lead Pipe.* http:// www.inthelibrarywiththeleadpipe.org/2019/dismantling-deficit-thinking/

Henry, F., Dua, E., James, C.E., Kobayashi, A., Li, P., Ramos, H., & Smith, M.S. (2017). *The equity myth: Racialization and Indigeneity at Canadian universities.* Vancouver, BC: UBC Press.

Howard, T. (2003). Culturally relevant pedagogy: Ingredients for critical teacher reflection. *Theory into Practice, 42*(3), 195–202. doi: 10.1207/s15430421tip4203_5

Jackson, T.O., & Boutte, G.S. (2018). Exploring culturally relevant/responsive pedagogy as praxis in teacher education. *The New Educator, 14*(2), 87–90. doi: 10.1080/1547688X.2018.1426320

Johnson, A. (2019). A model of culturally relevant pedagogy on physics. *AIP Conference Proceedings, 2019*(1), 130004-1–4. doi: 10.1063/1.5110152

Juniel, P.M., & Williams, H.S. (2017). Cultural proficiency receptivity scale: A critical analysis of prospective school leaders. *National Forum of Educational Administration and Supervision Journal, 35*(4), 1–9.

Katsarou, E., Picower, B., & Stovall, D. (2010). Acts of solidarity: Developing urban social justice educators in the struggle for quality public education. *Teacher Education Quarterly, 37*(3), 137–51. https://files.eric.ed.gov/fulltext/EJ902713.pdf

Krasnoff, B. (2016). *Culturally responsive teaching: A guide to evidence-based practices for teaching all students equitably.* Region X Equity Assistance Center at Education Northwest. https://educationnorthwest.org/sites/default/files/resources/culturally -responsive-teaching-508.pdf

Ladson-Billings, G. (1992). Liberatory consequences of literacy: A case of culturally relevant instruction for African American students. *Journal of Negro Education, 61*(3), 378–91. doi: 10.2307/2295255

Ladson-Billings, G. (1995). But that's just good teaching! The case for culturally relevant pedagogy. *Theory into Practice, 34*(3), 159–65. doi: 10.1080/0040584950 9543675

Ladson-Billings, G. (2001). *Crossing over to Canaan: The journey of new teachers in diverse classrooms.* San Francisco, CA: Jossey-Bass.

Ladson-Billings, G. (2006). Yes, but how do we do it? Practicing culturally relevant pedagogy. In J. Landsman & C.W. Lewis (Eds.), *White teachers/diverse classrooms: A guide to building inclusive schools, promoting high expectations and eliminating racism* (pp. 29–42). Sterling, VA: Stylus Publishers.

Lim, L., Tan, M., & Saito, E. (2019). Culturally relevant pedagogy: Developing principles of description and analysis. *Teaching and Teacher Education, 77,* 43–52. doi: 10.1016/j.tate.2018.09.011

Lindsey, R.B., Roberts, L.M., & CampbellJones, F. (2013). *The culturally proficient school: An implementation guide for school leaders.* Thousand Oaks, CA: Corwin Press.

Lopez, A.E. (2013). Embedding and sustaining equitable practices in teachers' everyday work: A framework for critical action. *Teaching & Learning, 7*(3), 1–15. doi: 10.26522/tl.v7i3.421

Martin, G.L., Smith, M.J., & Williams, B.M. (2018). Reframing deficit thinking on social class. *New Directions for Student Services, 162,* 87–93. doi: 10.1002 /ss.20264

McMahon, B., & Portelli, J.P. (2012). *Student engagement in urban schools: Beyond neoliberal discourses.* Charlotte, NC: Information Age Publishing.

Milner, H.R. (2011). Culturally relevant pedagogy in a diverse urban classroom. *Urban Review, 43,* 66–89. doi: 10.1007/s11256-009-0143-0

Milner, H.R., & Smithey, M. (2003). How teacher educators created a course curriculum to challenge and enhance preservice teachers' thinking and experience with diversity. *Teaching Education, 14*(3), 293–305. doi: 10.1080/1047621032000 135195

Ministry of Education. (2017). *Ontario's education equity action plan*. Queen's Printer for Ontario. http://www.edu.gov.on.ca/eng/about/education_equity_plan_en.pdf

Mitchell, R. (2010). Cultural aesthetics and teacher improvisation: An epistemology of providing culturally responsive service by African American professors. *Urban Education, 45*(5), 604–29. doi: 10.1177/0042085909347839

Nykiel-Herbert, B. (2010). Iraqi refugee students: From a collection of aliens to a community of learners. *Multicultural Education, 17*(30), 2–14. https://files.eric.ed.gov/fulltext/EJ902693.pdf

Pearson, N. (2014). A rightful place: Race, recognition and a more complete commonwealth. *Quarterly Essay, 55*, 1–72. https://www.quarterlyessay.com.au/essay/2014/09/a-rightful-place

Picower, B. (2009). The unexamined whiteness of teaching: How white teachers maintain and enact dominant racial ideologies. *Race Ethnicity and Education, 12*(2), 197–215. doi: 10.1080/13613320902995475

Portelli, J.P. (2010, January 19). Leadership for equity in education: Deficit thinking is a major challenge [Blog post]. https://www.federationhss.ca/en/node/163

Portelli, J.P. (2013). Deficit thinking and the need for subversion: Reflections on Milani. In C. Borg, M. Cardona, & S. Caruana (Eds.), *Don Lorenzo Milani and education* (pp. 213–18). Basingstoke, UK: Palgrave Macmillan.

Portelli, J.P., & Koneeny, P. (2018). Inclusive education: Beyond popular discourses. *L-Universita, 10*(1), 133–44. https://files.eric.ed.gov/fulltext/EJ1177635.pdf

Ryan, J. (2003). *Leading diverse schools*. Boston, MA: Kluwer Academic Publishers.

Ryan, J. (2015). What is inclusive leadership? In D. Griffiths & J.P. Portelli (Eds.), *Key questions for educational leaders* (pp. 111–15). Burlington, ON: Word & Deed Publishing.

Sharma, M. (2018). Seeping deficit thinking assumptions maintain the neoliberal education agenda: Exploring three conceptual frameworks of deficit thinking in inner-city schools. *Education and Urban Society, 50*(2), 136–54. doi: 10.1177/0013124516682301

Sharma, M., & Portelli, J.P. (2014). Uprooting and settling in: The invisible strength of deficit thinking. *LEARNing Landscapes, 8*(1), 251–67. doi: 10.36510/learnland.v8i1.684

Shields, C., Bishop. R., & Mazawi, A. (2005). *Pathologizing practices: The impact of deficit thinking on education*. New York, NY: Peter Lang.

Statistics Canada. (2021). *Table 17-10-0009-01: Population estimates, quarterly.* doi: 10.25318/1710000901-eng

Student Achievement Division. (2013). Culturally responsive pedagogy: Towards equity and inclusivity in Ontario schools. *Capacity Building Series: Secretariat Special Edition, 35*, 1–8. https://thelearningexchange.ca/wp-content/uploads/2017/02/CBS_ResponsivePedagogy.pdf

Thomas, C.D., & Williams, D.L. (2008). An analysis of teacher defined mathematical tasks: Engaging urban learners in performance-based instruction. *Journal of*

*Urban Teaching and Research, 4*, 109–21. https://files.eric.ed.gov/fulltext/EJ837809.pdf

Valencia, R.R. (Ed.). (1997). *The evolution of deficit thinking: Educational thought and practice.* London, UK: Falmer Press.

Valencia, R.R. (2010). *Dismantling contemporary deficit thinking: Educational thought and practice.* New York, NY: Routledge.

Weiner, L. (2006). Challenging deficit thinking. *Educational Leadership, 64*(1), 42–5. https://files.ascd.org/staticfiles/ascd/pdf/journals/ed_lead/el200609_weiner.pdf

# 6 Perspectives of Social Justice Leadership: A Duo-Ethnographic Study

JACQUELINE KIRK AND AYODEJI OSINAME

School leaders who have a responsibility to create a safe and welcoming culture need to consider how leadership can create an environment where demographic diversity becomes a strength and marginalized voices are heard and valued. To develop their personal capacity to address social inequities, leaders need to become more self-aware and prepare to appreciate and accept the diversity of perspectives within their schools. Scholars (e.g., DeMatthews & Mawhinney, 2014; Guerra & Pazey, 2016; Ryan, 2006, 2014; Shields, 2010, 2015; Theoharis, 2007; Theoharis & Scanlan, 2015) have argued that it is important for leaders to examine their own values and beliefs that dictate, to a large degree, their day-to-day leadership practice and decision-making. As a result of this self-reflection, leaders are in better positions to build relationships and facilitate connections between the diverse individuals and groups that make up the school community. Shields, Dollarhide, and Young (2018) explain that social justice leaders need to "know themselves, identify their non-negotiables, and know what guides and grounds them" (p. 3). They go on to say that this necessary self-reflection is a "pre-requisite" for leaders who are focused on social justice.

In this study, we utilized a duo-ethnographic methodology (Norris & Sawyer, 2012) to engage in critical self-reflection and growth in our personal and professional work as social justice leaders. Through duo-ethnography, we endeavoured to investigate and interrogate our own metanarratives about social justice leadership as a way to deepen our understandings, to articulate our specific roles, and to focus on how social justice leadership has become part of our personal identities. We have diverse backgrounds and approach the work from very different perspectives. We are:

- Ayodeji, a Black male from Nigeria who has been living and attending university in Canada for more than seven years. Ayodeji is a PhD candidate

in Educational Administration and Diversity Education at the University of Manitoba in Winnipeg.
- Jackie, a white female who was born and raised in Saskatchewan, Canada, and is currently working as an associate professor in the Department of Leadership and Educational Administration at Brandon University in Brandon, Manitoba. She has held this position for more than ten years and has served as a department chair, a program chair, and an associate dean.

Our diverse backgrounds, yet complementary interests, expose our unique experiences with power, privilege, marginalization, and misunderstanding. As we share and interrogate these personal narratives of our own life experiences, we invite readers to utilize our stories and reflections to consider and to disrupt their own metanarratives about social justice leadership. In an effort to examine our own values and beliefs about social justice leadership, to create a space for readers to engage in self-reflection, and to bring deeper understanding to what it means to be a social justice leader, this chapter will detail the results of the duo-ethnographic study we undertook to become more aware of our values and beliefs about social justice leadership.

In the following section, we define the framework of social justice leadership as it is used in this chapter and explore how the literature describes the act of self-reflection within that framework. Next, we describe the methods that we used and then share our examination of the development of our own understandings and viewpoints through the narratives that are part of the research data. We conclude with our findings, our personal and professional growth, and the implications for social justice leaders in education.

## Understanding Social Justice Leadership in Education

Social justice leadership involves recognizing the unequal circumstances of marginalized groups with actions directed towards eliminating inequalities (Armstrong, Tuters, & Carrier, 2013; Dantley & Tillman, 2006; Goldfarb & Grinberg, 2002; Ottmann, 2009; Ryan, 2006, 2014; Shields, 2010, 2015; Shields et al., 2018; Theoharis, 2007). Dantley and Tillman (2006) and Ryan (2006, 2014) explain that social justice leaders investigate, make sense of, and generate solutions to social inequality and marginalization owing to race, class, gender, disability, sexual orientation, and other forms of diversity. These leaders interrogate the policies and procedures that shape schools and at the same time perpetuate social inequalities along the lines of race, class, gender, disability, and sexual orientation, as well as the intersections of those inequalities (Armstrong et al., 2013). Goldfarb and Grinberg (2002) describe social justice leadership as "the exercise of altering these inequitable arrangements by engaging actively in reclaiming, appropriating, sustaining, and advancing inherent human rights of equity, and fairness in social, economic, educational, and personal dimensions" (p. 162). Ottmann (2009) and Theoharis (2007) expand upon these ideas to suggest that leadership for social justice is action-oriented and involves identifying and undoing oppressive and unjust practices and replacing them with more equitable, culturally appropriate ones. Social justice leaders need to recognize inequalities within the school system in Canada and have the necessary competence to act in ways that replace pre-existing structures of inequality with more equitable structures.

Leading for social justice incorporates a heightened commitment and a sense of awareness to issues related to oppression, exclusion, and marginalization (Armstrong et al., 2013; DeMatthews & Mawhinney, 2014; Ryan & Tuters, 2017; Theoharis & Scanlan, 2015). Both Ryan and Tuters (2017) and Theoharis and Scanlan (2015) describe persistence and commitment as key characteristics or traits of social justice leadership because these leaders confront tremendous resistance and pressure as they work to transform schools. DeMatthews and Mawhinney (2014) expound that for schools to serve the common good and promote social justice, school leaders need the knowledge, skills, and disposition to create school environments that eliminate marginalization. Jansen (2006) affirms that social justice leaders demonstrate moral courage to take personal and professional risks and to actively engage in the struggle of creating schools that are more equitable, inclusive, and socially just (see also, Armstrong et al., 2013; Shields, 2010, 2015). Social justice leadership acknowledges and recognizes power inequalities in the school and society and challenges conditions that create inequity and injustice (DeMatthews & Mawhinney, 2014; Ryan & Tuters, 2017; Shields, 2010). Social justice leadership is also committed to affecting deep and equitable changes (Armstrong et al., 2013; Ryan & Tuters, 2017; Shields, 2010, 2015).

School leaders who are committed to social justice have pre-existing values and conceptions of justice that enable them to maintain their commitment to actively work for change (Armstrong et al., 2013; DeMatthews & Mawhinney, 2014; Ryan, 2006; Shields, 2010; Shields et al., 2018; Theoharis, 2007). Social justice leaders approach leadership as a collective process that involves people working together for inclusive schools and communities (Ryan, 2006, 2014; Ryan & Tuters, 2017; Shields, 2010, 2014). Furman (2012) adds to this understanding and describes that social justice leaders connect groups of people while fostering collaboration, democratic dialogue, and shared decision-making. For example, Theoharis (2007) explains that "social justice leaders resist the historic disconnect between marginalized families and schools to create welcoming school climates and reach out to the community and in particular to disenfranchised families" (p. 237). Social justice leaders foster community relationships and take responsibility for engaging families and the external school community in building an inclusive school culture (Furman, 2012;

Ottmann, 2009; Ryan, 2006, 2014; Ryan & Tuters, 2017; Shields, 2010, 2014; Theoharis, 2007). Social justice leadership understands that the school alone cannot do the job of education, nor can parents or members of the community, and that they must work collaboratively with everyone (i.e., the "stakeholders" in a child's education) to make the achievement of socially just and democratic schooling realizable (Ottmann, 2009; Ryan, 2006, 2014; Ryan & Tuters, 2017; Shields, 2015; Shields et al., 2018).

## The Importance of Self-Reflection for Social Justice Leaders

Self-reflection is one of the foundations for the professional implementation of social justice leadership. Jean-Marie (2008) highlights the importance of ongoing reflection in maintaining a commitment to social justice despite challenges and resistance, and Shields (2010, 2015) recognizes that social justice leaders need to begin their tasks with critical reflection and analysis and to work through responsibilities with enlightened understanding and actions that ensure that every member of the school is provided, as much as possible, with a level playing field. Furman (2012) and Armstrong et al. (2013) explain that self-reflection is aimed at personal awareness and growth. In describing the significance of self-reflection, Furman (2012) expounds that it allows leaders to identify and recognize that prejudices and assumptions are products of their own cultural backgrounds. Brown (2004) adds to this understanding by affirming that critical self-reflection involves a deep examination of personal assumptions, values, and beliefs. Similarly, self-reflection involves social justice leaders intentionally and strategically asking questions about (in)equity, fostering dialogue about injustices, and establishing common ground for everyone to participate in the school, as well as to engage the larger school community in deeper forms of equity work (Armstrong et al., 2013; Furman, 2012). The practice of self-reflection allows social justice educational leaders to be completely honest with their own prejudices and imperfections within the context of their own cultural backgrounds, which in many ways serve as the foundation for their professional practice (Brown, 2004; Furman, 2012).

These descriptions of the characteristics and actions of social justice leaders help us establish an understanding of social justice leadership that will provide a framework for the remainder of the chapter. Schools reflect the values and beliefs of individuals and groups within the community (Furman, 2012). As such, schools are subject to the same issues of power and privilege, marginalization, and misunderstanding that are present within the community at large (Furman, 2012; Ottmann, 2009; Ryan, 2006, 2014; Ryan & Tuters, 2017; Shields, 2010, 2015; Shields et al., 2018). Issues that arise from unequal circumstances and power imbalances are perpetuated through policy statements and continuous discourses rooted in the grand narratives of the majority group

(Armstrong et al., 2013; Normore & McMahon, 2007). The literature describes social justice leaders through their

- **knowledge and skills** (including change, justice, and collaborative process);
- **mindsets** (including the ability to be reflective, courageous, tenacious, and open to diverse perspectives); and
- **actions** (including building relationships, confronting marginalizing practices, and developing equitable policies, practices, and structures).

School leaders who address social justice issues have an opportunity to develop schools that embrace deep and equitable change and are characterized by community connection, safe and welcoming environments, and shared decisions that support the needs of all individuals and groups (Furman, 2012; Ottmann, 2009; Ryan, 2006, 2014; Ryan & Tuters, 2017; Shields, 2010; Shields et al., 2018).

## Duo-Ethnographic Methodology

Duo-ethnography (Norris & Sawyer, 2012) is a new research method in which two or more individuals interrogate the cultural contexts of their personal past experiences to develop understanding of their present perspectives on, and experience of, issues related to personal or professional identities. According to Norris, Sawyer, and Lund (2012), duo-ethnography draws on two narrative research traditions: storytelling and the concept of "currere" – a notion that theorizes individuals' histories and lived learning experiences as informal curriculum (Pinar, 1994). Originating from the work of William Pinar (1994), duo-ethnography views a person's life as a curriculum. Currere, as enacted in duo-ethnography, is an act of self-interrogation that is extended to the "other" in the quest for mutual reclamation of the self (Pinar, 1994). With this understanding, duo-ethnography suggests that one can only understand oneself when one is present in the reality of the other (Norris & Sawyer, 2012). Unlike auto-ethnography, where individuals who are the subject of the study are expected to understand their lives and world by themselves (Creswell & Poth, 2018), the journey of discovery in duo-ethnography is shared and reciprocal (Norris et al., 2012). To that end, duo-ethnography is a "collaborative methodology in which two or more researchers of difference juxtapose their life histories to provide multiple understandings of the world" (Norris & Sawyer, 2012, p. 9). As a research methodology, duo-ethnography is collaborative, participatory, dialogic, and non-prescriptive (Norris & Sawyer, 2012; Norris et al., 2012).

Duo-ethnography creates a space for researchers to critically examine their own values and beliefs towards social justice work when they see their own perspectives juxtaposed with those of another (Breault, 2016; Norris et al., 2012). As such, through the examination of the individual's unique lived experiences and mutual dialogic stories, duo-ethnography holds that meaning can be and often is transformed as a result of the research act (Norris et al., 2012). A duo-ethnographic methodology eschews the creation of metanarratives through the counter narratives of the researchers and gives deeper meaning to their beliefs and actions (Norris & Sawyer, 2012; Norris et al., 2012). Breault (2016) affirms that the poly-vocal dialogic quality in duo-ethnography is designed to deliberately disrupt the metanarrative of the self and question long-held personal and cultural beliefs. Through this act of juxtaposition, researchers unsettle the metanarratives that can appear in single-author papers (Breault, 2016; Norris et al., 2012). Duo-ethnographies encourage and promote subjugated knowledge – that is, local or situated knowledge – and can act as counter narratives to the norm (Norris et al., 2012).

Norris and Sawyer (2012) describe three interconnected intentions of duo-ethnographers: to learn about oneself from the "other," to explore and articulate personal and collective narratives of resistance, and to use one's self as a site for inquiry (p. 10). Duo-ethnography is focused on critical thought, manifested within the researchers upon their own insights, that leads to the process of personal or professional transformation (Norris & Sawyer, 2012). Change and transformation are key in duo-ethnographic research (Norris et al., 2012). Breault (2016) and Norris et al. (2012) explain that changes in both the stories and the duo-ethnographers are expected to occur throughout the research process and be evident in the text. Norris and Sawyer (2012) assert that a duo-ethnographic methodology is "not about telling one's stories to reify self, it is about telling one's stories to assist both the self and the other in an act of conscientization" (p. 18). To this end, change and transformation articulated within conversations of inter–self-reflexivity are fundamental to a duo-ethnographic methodology (Breault, 2016; Norris & Sawyer, 2012).

## Data Collection and Analysis

With the intent to conduct a duo-ethnographic investigation into our own development and understanding of social justice leadership, we agreed that we would design our study to include several cycles of duo-ethnographic data gathering and dialogue. The first round was initiated with the question, "What is social justice leadership?" On a shared online document that had been divided into three columns, one column with the question, and one for each person's remarks, we endeavoured to respond to that question using Pinar's (1994) concept of currere to guide us. The task was to consider how our individual past experiences had led us to our current understanding of the concept of social justice leadership. When both of us had completed this initial reflection, we took time to read what the other had written and then write our own response in a different colour in the other's column. Because we found that responding to our partner's ideas elicited both intriguing questions and interesting discoveries about our similarities and differences, we moved on to a third step of recording dialogue that could be transcribed and analysed as additional data.

In the second cycle, we agreed to develop an understanding of our individual identities as social justice leaders using the same process described above. Following this, we decided to meet at the Canadian Museum for Human Rights in Winnipeg, Manitoba for the remaining four cycles. Over the course of the 2018–19 school year, we visited the museum on three separate occasions and selected four different exhibits (Nelson Mandela, Viola Desmond, Residential Schools, and the Indigenous Perspectives exhibit that screens the film *Circle of Knowledge: A Good Life for Us All*) to help us reflect on social justice leadership. After experiencing each exhibit, we completed the three-step procedure of journaling, responding to our partner's journal, and recording a final dialogue.

At this point, we engaged in a thematic analysis (Vaismoradi, Jones, Turunen, & Snelgrove, 2016) of our original journals, the resulting comments, and the transcripts of our face-to-face dialogue by highlighting and working back and forth on shared documents until we had distilled several themes and corresponding quotations. Then, we transferred the passages that we had identified as belonging to selected themes to separate documents so we could engage in a process of using interpretive comments (Creswell & Poth, 2018) for further development and sense-making. To do this, we employed an interpretive two-column journal approach with the data in the left-hand column and our dialogue about the data in the right-hand column. This process allowed us to document key reflections and to come to agreements about the findings that were emerging from the data.

## Dialogues about Social Justice Leaders and Social Justice Leadership

We identified thirteen themes through our initial thematic sorting. We have since condensed those themes into six sections: (1) understanding the issues, (2) developing a mindset for social justice, (3) learning as students and teachers, (4) developing an understanding of self as a social justice leader, (5) contentious points in our dialogue, and (6) a knowledge that we are all connected. These six sections outline both the affirming and disrupting experiences that we shared throughout this journey. Using duo-ethnography to explore the development of our personal perspectives about social justice and diversity led to a deeper and more complex understanding of the issues and allowed us to gain new insight into how diverse perspectives develop and how that diversity can be understood, accepted, and utilized to promote individual and organizational growth.

The following sections are framed around our personal narratives. These stories were told as part of our duo-ethnographic undertaking to allow each other an opportunity to see oneself in relation to the other and thereby know oneself better. In the process of sharing these stories with the readers of this chapter, we offer our own journeys towards becoming social justice leaders not to illustrate how or what social justice leadership is, but to create a space and a medium for readers to consider their own stories and their own identities as social justice leaders. In doing so, we recognize that our stories are imperfect, and we accept the vulnerability inherent in describing our emergent understandings.

*Understanding the Issues*

When encouraged by our chosen methodology to reflect on our current knowledge of social justice and how that knowledge had developed through our lived experiences, we both identified times when we had experienced marginalization and times when we had been aware of our own privilege. We grew up in different socio-economic circumstances, in different decades, and in different countries, so it was not surprising that many of our childhood stories were starkly different. We became fascinated, however, by the recognition that we also had some common points of intersection. This recognition opened the space for deeper sharing and greater acknowledgment of the value of taking time to explore the lived experiences of another.

Ayodeji noted that although he did not experience racism before coming to Canada, he understood poverty and powerlessness, implicitly as a result of his experiences living within his community in Nigeria's depressed economy. For example, Ayodeji shared stories about a time when he was teaching in Nigeria. The cost to ride the bus back and forth to work was greater than his teaching salary, but he believed that the experience of working and teaching would be worth it. So, he continued to do petty sales on the side and to pick up odd jobs when he could, but he remembers that there were times when he went hungry because he could not afford food.

Although Jackie grew up in a white, middle-class family in rural Canada, she was able to reflect on her personal understanding of what it feels like to be marginalized:

> [I thought] about how I understand marginalization from my experiences as an overweight woman in a world that idealizes a size-5, hourglass figure. The marginalization that occurs as a result of being overweight is rarely discussed ... Yet, this experience helps me to understand what it means to be judged as unworthy.

In addition to sharing his experiences with poverty and racism, Ayodeji shared a story about being bullied in school: "In Grade 3, all I can remember was how I was bullied by my classmates for being quiet in class. I experienced verbal and physical teasing almost every day in school." Jackie's response to Ayodeji's reflection about being bullied illustrates how Jackie's status within her community provided her with the resilience that she needed to maintain a positive perspective despite being bullied:

> I was bullied a bit in high school, too, because I was the fat girl and because I had acne, but I didn't value the people who treated me like that. Your story of how you were bullied in elementary school helps me to see how my personal power helped me be resilient in the face of a bully.

This recognition of the differences in how bullying is understood by the victim acknowledges that marginalization is experienced differently depending on an individual's perspective and context.

Although our life experiences have been very different from each other, we both recognized within our stories our own relative experiences with privilege and with marginalization. For social justice leaders, acknowledging and negotiating personal privilege is an important part of developing a more authentic knowledge of self (see Brown 2004; Furman 2012). The data provided a variety of examples of both privilege and marginalization from each of the partner's experiences. The knowledge that both an individual who would be considered by society to be privileged and an individual who would be considered to be marginalized could pinpoint their own privilege and marginalization suggests that the two concepts are neither binary nor static in nature. Levine-Rasky (2011) explains that "who one 'is' is not static; it is wholly relational to others, to culture, and to organizations in which one moves" (p. 242). In this sense, both marginalization and privilege are human experiences that are complex and contingent upon the social, political, and ideological contexts that produce and sustain them (see Levine-Rasky, 2011). The acknowledgment of this complex connection between privilege and marginalization allows for a deeper understanding among members of a community and suggests hopefulness for leaders' capacity to change the experiences of those within their communities who are marginalized.

## Developing a Mindset for Social Justice

Duo-ethnography asks researchers to access past experiences as a medium through which they can develop a deeper understanding about current beliefs. Within our journal entries, we each identified examples of how, through modelling and mentorship, our parents' acts of compassion formed a foundation for our respective beliefs. The shared dialogue that emerged from reading each other's journals led to a realization that our parents were purposeful in guiding the development of our values and in helping us to understand the importance of justice. The foundational beliefs that we learned in our childhood homes prepared us to be more aware of inequity and to take action when we identified unjust circumstances. Ayodeji wrote about his mom's influence:

> I remember growing up, my mom was a school teacher at a public school in the city. She is a strong woman that has had a strong and lasting influence on my family. My mom would encourage us to treat each other with respect. She would tell us that charity begins at home and that we needed to provide support for each other at all times. She always pushed us to see our privileges and understand our positions within our community. She would often talk to us about the importance of lifting up people who might need our help.

As evidence that Ayodeji absorbed his mom's values, he also wrote about his own acts of compassion when he shared a small one-room residence at university with several of his friends:

> I remember supporting my friends who were from even more impoverished backgrounds and could not afford to get accommodations on campus. Even though I was staying in a one-room suite, I invited two of my friends to join me ... In retrospect, I realize that my mother's motivation and encouragement about the need to support each other has provided a foundation for me helping others.

Our childhood stories continue to inform our knowledge of social justice even though those experiences took place at points in our lives when we were unaware of the roles that power and privilege play within our social contexts. The values our parents taught us and their determination to take action heightened our awareness of injustice and our beliefs that we could make a difference. Jackie referred to a story that her dad often told about his mom and her compassion for those in the community that struggled to survive during the Great Depression:

> My grandma came to Canada in 1919 and just ten years later her husband died, leaving her with a farm and five children at the beginning of the most destructive drought that has ever been experienced on the Canadian prairies. My dad talked about how she would tell them to load the wagon with food to take to town because the people in town didn't have the resources to produce their own food nor the funds to purchase food. My grandma's family was also poor, and they struggled to make it through that time, but they had meat because they had the ability to raise cattle, poultry, and pork. They also planted a garden and preserved vegetables that lasted through the winter. By working together and supporting each other, they found that they had excess and my grandma taught them about the importance of sharing with those who were in need.

Through journals and discussions, we shared many examples of how our parents shaped our values and beliefs. They taught us to look for those in need, to take action, and to understand the responsibility of individuals within interdependent communities. When we reflected on our initial learning experiences, we both wrote about the values that were established within our childhood homes and how those values led our personal beliefs that social justice leadership is crucial.

Sifting through and sharing our earliest memories of the acknowledgment of social inequity helped us to identify personal similarities and to create a shared space that was characterized by understanding, kindness, and trust – a space that welcomed deep and vulnerable reflections and ultimately led to an ability to self-reflect, change, and grow. We were surprised that despite our diverse backgrounds we could identify similarities in how we had developed the values that motivate us to want to contribute to a more socially just society. We were intrigued by the thought that these values that formed the foundations for our separate interests in social justice leadership had been passed down through the generations of our families. At the outset of the study, it was easy to identify our differences and we did not expect to learn that our families had guided us in similar ways despite the differences in the environments in which we each grew up. These dialogues about our childhood experiences led to an authentic understanding of our personal perspectives and to a discussion about how social justice leaders could use the principles of duo-ethnography. Creating space for community members to share stories about the lived experiences that have led to their personal understandings and perspectives could foster relationship-building and authentic self-reflection within the community.

## Learning as Students and Teachers

Similar to how we both identified that adopting our parents' values led us to discover the study of social justice, both of us recognized how teachers had acted as social justice leaders within our lives. In our individual reflections, we considered how we had been shaped by interactions with educators who modelled a commitment to making a difference for marginalized groups. In Ayodeji's reflections, he described how his Grade 5 teacher addressed the bullying issues that figured prominently in his memories from Grades 3 and 4:

> The teacher asked every student who had experienced bullying in school to come in and talk to him. I took the courage to speak to him about my challenges and from that point on he supported me to speak up for myself.

One of Jackie's recollections was about her high school principal who also taught Canadian History at the senior level:

I remember when I learned about residential schools in high school. Our teacher was so genuine, and he cared so much about people. He moved me to think deeply about how relationships between the European settlers and the Indigenous communities had affected the development of Canada as a country ... When I am confronted with this issue in my life, I always remember the compassion and the emotion that he conveyed when he described this history.

The mentoring and modelling that we received from our teachers helped us to understand the important roles that teachers, as social justice leaders, play in communities.

Predictably, then, each of us also identified times that we had, as teachers ourselves, enacted our own roles as leaders of social justice. We both reflected on times when we had accepted the challenge of trying to make a difference for students that were marginalized in some way. Ayodeji reminisced about his work at a community school in Nigeria:

[My students] lived in poverty. Their parents could not afford to provide nutritious meals that would prepare them for learning in school. Before the start of my class I made sure the kids had something to eat and I explained to them the importance of having regular meals. I could see a difference in the way the children interacted and engaged in class.

Ayodeji utilized the knowledge that his mom, as a teacher, had taught him about creating conditions for academic success and, as a community leader, had taught him about using what he had to address the needs in his community. Although at the time Ayodeji was unable to articulate the deeper value of his actions, he had positioned himself to provide his students with shelter from the injustices within their social world. To change the circumstances for students in his class, social justice leadership theory would direct Ayodeji to critically examine the school system's structures, policies, and practices for injustices and barriers to students' academic success and to make meaningful change despite the resistance that he might encounter (Furman, 2012; Ryan, 2006, 2014; Ryan & Tuters, 2017; Shields, 2010; Shields et al., 2018). Once he had examined the specific context, he would need to plan a way forward that might include policy and practice changes that would address the issue of child hunger beyond the scope of the teacher providing meals for the student and extend the benefits to students in other classes and in other schools.

Jackie's first recollection of thinking purposefully about making a difference for those who were marginalized within society came in her third teaching position when she was working with students who had been formally identified with a learning disability:

I was amazed to meet highly intelligent students, who had been in many schools but achieved only dismal results. I became impassioned about making a difference for them. Students with diagnosed learning disabilities are misunderstood and often mistreated in the school system. I learned so much from my students at [this school] about how the school system has been constructed in a way that privileges students that fit into the average mould. They helped me to see something that had been invisible to me before, and it changed the way that I thought about teaching and the way that I thought about myself as a teacher … I learned how "able" they were and how the label of "disabled" left them marginalized.

These initial memories illustrate how knowledge of social justice leadership progresses from childhood learning and educator modelling to individuals having the knowledge and skills to take up the issues of social justice as teachers and as school leaders. Furthermore, these examples help us to understand the importance of parents and teachers in the development of a future that includes more individuals who are prepared to become social justice leaders within their own communities of influence.

## Understanding Self as Social Justice Leader

Because the notion of social justice leadership is relatively new to each of us, and because the methodology demands that participants critique their own metanarratives, we found numerous examples of our struggles to understand ourselves as social justice leaders. Ayodeji explained that he started to see the thread of continuity after his move to Canada:

> My passion for supporting people who cannot face their challenges alone conti-
> nued to be my driver, even when I moved to Canada. These beliefs and values have
> helped me to provide support for youth in foster care, seniors in care homes, and
> children with learning and physical disabilities. Through my engagement in this
> important work, I can see myself as a social justice leader. For example, although
> I work in respite care with many other immigrants, I have sought an appointment
> to the board of the non-profit that employs me and I have endeavoured to become a
> voice both for my colleagues and for the disabled clients for whom we provide care.

This passage from Ayodeji's journal illustrates how he has shifted his work from helping individuals to becoming an advocate for change within the organization that employs him.

Jackie's reluctance to engage in research through a critical lens made it difficult for her to see herself as a social justice leader. She explained that during her PhD while her classmates were choosing critical methodologies for their dissertations, she was determined to choose a more "concrete" methodology that would produce answers rather than questions. She also shared a moment of realization years later when a conversation with her dean helped her to understand that her ongoing advocacy for students was a form of social justice leadership.

Jackie shared that this exchange inspired her to reflect on her practice. She began to see how knowledge of student experiences had often helped her to understand how marginalized students were further marginalized by the system. This critical reflection about the systemic barriers often spurred her to try to make changes to policies and practices at her university. Although she was aware that her colleagues knew her as a person who supported the plight of students and suggested changes to policy and practice that would be more supportive to student needs, she had not made the connection to how this was social justice leadership. For Jackie, this transition required an awareness of the external world and the social dynamics therein.

For Ayodeji, on the other hand, the transition was internal and happened when he developed a deeper understanding of his own marginalization. He described the emancipatory experience of being encouraged to critique the power and privilege that he had experienced within his known contexts. He described how his confidence shifted when one of his professors asked him to interpret articles by making personal connections and writing stories about those connections to share with others in his class:

> The assignment empowered me to reflect critically on how I had been assimilated to accept Western cultural beliefs and about how my life might have been different if I had understood the implications of the process. My stories that were written as letters to my nephew in Nigeria gave me the opportunity to speak the truth and to share it with my family. The experience of sharing these stories with my classmates and understanding how they valued my opinions made me feel confident, free to be myself, connected to my family, and proud of my Nigerian heritage.

The confidence that Ayodeji found by critiquing his experiences and through understanding the injustices that he had experienced unleashed his willingness to accept the responsibility of sharing his stories to help others understand marginalization in Canadian society. As such, his recent understanding of the dangers of assimilating Western perspectives through school curriculum has allowed him to reflect on his past experiences as a student in Nigeria. The curriculum used in his primary and high school education was developed outside of Nigeria, taught in a foreign tongue, and designed to acculturate the Nigerian people into a monoculture of the mind. Until he was able to look back with understanding, he found himself caught up in the movement of trying to achieve academic success from a Western perspective and denying the importance of his Nigerian identity.

### Contentious Points in Our Dialogue

Within the data, we identified several issues that provoked discussion, pushed us to think more deeply, and helped us to clearly identify some very difficult hurdles that are encountered within the work of social justice in education. This section outlines and describes some of our reflections about whether or not it is appropriate for members of the majority group to lead social justice initiatives, the responsibility that educators have to ensure that education is not used as a tool for marginalizing others, and the knowledge that Canada and Canadians are not free from racial prejudice.

WHO CAN LEAD SOCIAL JUSTICE? WHAT IF I AM TOO WHITE?

Is it possible for someone from the dominant culture to succeed as a leader of social justice? Although Jackie wrote about some occasions when she felt unwelcome within a space for social justice, she recognized during our face-to-face dialogues how it is important to identify the right circumstances for taking a leadership role. She described a teaching experience where she was able to lead a group of students to understand the significance of Canada's Truth and Reconciliation Commission report:

> Despite being very nervous, I chose to teach two sections of a course about Truth and Reconciliation [and] I learned the most important lesson of all: I can be a social justice leader. Not unlike what I had known about leadership all along, I learned again that you can only lead in a place where you have established an ability to have influence through shared trust ... My role as a social justice leader needs to take place within my own circles of influence ... That's how I can make a difference.

After rereading this passage, Jackie reflected that she thought her success with leading students to confront difficult topics in class seemed to be rooted both in the depth of her care and concern for her students, and in her ability to be vulnerable and admit her mistakes.

As we worked through this topic, we identified our conflicting views within our dialogue regarding the role of allies. Ayodeji wrote:

> I believe the white majority can make a difference to the experiences of those who are living on the margins in our community; they can become advocates and allies. But understanding racism, issues around diversity, inequity for example, can only be understood deeply by those who experience injustice ... If one has not walked in those shoes, one's commitment to these issues might be superficial.

Jackie's reflection came from a slightly different perspective when she shared her viewpoint that it was critical for the white majority to be part of the change:

> I understand the [need for the marginalized to find voice and take a stand against oppression] but I believe even more strongly that if we need change within white

Western culture, then white Western culture *also* needs to be involved in making the change.

These reflections led to a deeper face-to-face dialogue about the role of allies within the work of social justice. The authentic sharing of personal experiences in our journals had created a spirit of greater understanding and care within our relationship and facilitated a more honest dialogue about our values and beliefs. Our diverse perspectives increased both the intensity and the importance of this discussion, and we emerged with a deeper understanding of each other and of self. Through this experience we were able to recognize that our discussion was an example of how authentic dialogue enables the development of trusting space where legitimate connection between community members can build.

Social justice school leaders seek to facilitate the development of a community where all voices are important within organizational dialogue and decision-making. Freire (2002) explains that the paternalistic conditions and struggles of the marginalized will be transformed when the marginalized become involved in the resolution. Overcoming the issues of power that are at the heart of social justice and positioning both marginalized and privileged to work together to build a more harmonious community is possibly the greatest challenge of social justice work.

WHAT DOES RACISM LOOK LIKE IN CANADA?
Viewing the Viola Desmond video at the Canadian Museum for Human Rights necessitated consideration of the issue of racism within the Canadian context. Ayodeji, who had previously written about issues of racism in Canada, drew a personal connection between himself and Viola Desmond:

> I really enjoyed watching and learning about how she challenged racial discrimination at the theatre in Nova Scotia. I believe racism is still very much alive in Canadian society and I believe one of the ways to approach the reality of racism is to challenge it and be courageous enough to speak up whenever it is experienced. As a Black African living in Canada, I experience implicit and explicit racism. Uninformed white Canadians treat me differently because of my skin colour and because of my accent.

Ayodeji went on to write about his experience when a Canadian family told him that they thought the government should not have accepted their Black neighbours into the country:

> I was able to find a way to diffuse their assumptions about people of colour and to challenge them to embrace diversity without being rude. I think as a social justice

leader it is important to be courageous and reject any forms of discrimination and/ or exclusionary practices that we perceive.

Ayodeji also reflected on how he had only been made aware of racial discrimination since he came to Canada:

> Before I moved to Canada, I had never experienced racial discrimination because we are all of the same skin colour in Nigeria. [W]hen I moved to Canada, I started experiencing prejudicial treatment on different levels, particularly based on my race … I have never imagined that you could be hated for being you … I have always been Black; I did not choose that. I was born Black.

For Jackie, the Viola Desmond story pushed her to articulate her own misunderstandings about racism in Canada:

> One of the most significant parts … was a quotation by Mayann Francis about how Canadians were polite about their racism. So polite, in fact, that I grew up thinking that we were not racist. I comforted myself and neglected to engage … because I believed that it wasn't part of my story. I feel both annoyed that I wasn't better informed and ashamed that I was unable to think more critically.

Our narratives placed side by side illustrate very diverse experiences of life in Canada. Jackie's admission that she believed that Canadians, herself included, were kinder and politer juxtaposed against Ayodeji's experiences of being marginalized based on his skin colour or accent show the gap between the reality and the myth that many believe. The pervasive narrative that Canadians are more polite belies the reality that social justice issues like racism, for example, are persistent within Canadian society. As a result, this narrative, intended to commend the good manners of Canadians, becomes an obstacle to progress for the social justice movement.

EDUCATION AS A TOOL FOR GENOCIDE

The final part of this section emerges from the reflections that we wrote following our experience of the residential schools exhibit at the Canadian Museum for Human Rights. Ayodeji wrote about how he felt when he learned about Canada's history with residential schools, about how it affected him, and about the frustration he feels that the effects are still evident in Canada:

> [The residential school history] was similar to the colonization we experienced in Nigeria but different in the sense that we gained independence, but the Canadian Aboriginal people are still living or co-existing with their oppressors … After I learned about the history of residential schools, my biased perspectives,

assumptions, and opinions about Aboriginal people changed. I was able to see the need for healing … [T]he oppression of the Aboriginal people is still obvious in Canadian society. They still live in extreme poverty, and their kids are still not meeting the benchmarks in our schools, for example.

In Jackie's response to Ayodeji's reflection, she recognized how the colonization of Nigeria gave Ayodeji a personal point of view from which to understand the atrocity of residential schools. She also expressed her disappointment that she has only a surface-level knowledge of the history of Canada:

As I see my story next to yours, I understand that so much of what I know about residential schools is generalized *and* misinformed because the government chose not to share the truth about our history. So much of what you know about residential schools is implicit. It is a deeper and richer knowledge.

Again, our narrative passages and the process of duo-ethnography helped us to see things differently when we allowed our individual reflections to stand next to each other.

This section has considered three difficult issues that emerged from the data. The first issue dealt with our dialogue about whether or not those who are privileged can be social justice leaders. The second issue acknowledged that racism exists in Canada, and the third issue recognized that historically, education has been used as a tool against marginalized populations. Each of these issues adds a layer of complexity to the work of social justice leaders in education.

## We Are All Connected

In our final duo-ethnographic cycle, we chose to view the film *Circle of Knowledge: A Good Life for Us All*. This short film is shown several times a day in a round theatre within the Indigenous Perspectives and Canadian Journeys exhibit at the Canadian Museum for Human Rights. As a guest, you sit facing other viewers in a circle, and the film, projected on a screen that goes all around the top of the walls, places you within a natural outdoor setting. Many diverse characters, who come onto to the screen from different directions, offer words of wisdom to the audience. The film was an effective culminating piece to our work and led us into deeper thinking about our hopes for the future and about the potential that exists within schools and communities to make a difference. Both of us reflected on the uplifting messages in the film. A excerpt from Ayodeji's journal summarizes the value of this experience for our study:

I was able to reflect on the saying "an injustice to one is an injustice to all." It shows the importance of social harmony and the need to treat one another with sympathy, empathy, care, and love. This world will be a better place when we, as a people, can see how we are connected and able to treat ourselves, and others, with love and care.

The saying "injustice to one is an injustice to all" illuminates the need for communities to become conscious of the "interdependence, inter-connectedness, and global awareness" that informs the work of social justice and advocacy for equity and inclusion (Shields, 2015). Awareness of the connectedness in our world provides a strong foundation from which to think about social justice leadership. Rather than considering how we can make changes that will address the needs of the marginalized, it is much more powerful and effective to think about how we are all connected and how changing marginalizing ways benefits everyone. It beckons us away from the concept that change needs to be made by the privileged to serve the powerless and away from debating about whether or not the more powerful members of our society will allow change to take place because they do not benefit.

## Personal and Professional Growth: The Culmination of Duo-Ethnography

The final step in the completion of the duo-ethnographic process is to describe the personal or professional growth that the researchers actualized through their participation. Our complementary interests, unique experiences, and diverse backgrounds inspired narratives that clearly illustrated how we developed different perspectives based on our life experiences. The foundational goal of duo-ethnography is one of personal and professional growth; researchers have an opportunity to observe how their personal history has prepared them to perceive a common event in a way that is unique compared to their partner. This knowledge helps participants to challenge and critique their own perspectives and to evolve through the process. The following passages written into the shared online document following the final sequence of face-to-face dialogue sum up our transformative experiences.

*Ayodeji*

The juxtaposition of my stories with Jackie's showed both the differences and similarities in our lived experiences and backgrounds. Our families instilled strong beliefs in us that have shaped our understanding of social justice leadership work. Jackie's stories allowed me to understand that there are individuals within the majority group who care genuinely about social justice leadership and who are committed to effecting deep and equitable change.

Transformative dialogue cannot occur in an environment that does not foster trust (Breault, 2016). Without the level of trust that we cultivated through our ongoing discussions about social justice leadership, this research would not have been possible. Sharing and critiquing each other's stories, asking tough questions, and responding in an uncensored manner led to the development of the trust that we needed to succeed in this act of critical self-reflection. I believe that the safe environment we created through trust allowed me to continue and to be courageous enough to share my experiences, stories, vulnerabilities, and emotions. As such, I have learned so much about social justice leadership through the lens of someone whose perspective is so different from my own.

*Jackie*

Our study pushed me to think deeply about who I am and about how I am connected to some of the atrocities of social injustice. I realize that when I am threatened by the friction of adversity within the social justice movement, I step back. When the environment seems safe, I lean in. This is yet another example of my privilege. I have the luxury to choose to get involved or not. I have become more aware of the choices that I make.

I will never truly understand the experience of racial prejudice. Yet, the trusting and authentic narratives that we shared with each other in this study brought me much closer to understanding how our unique experiences position us to see the world in different ways. I learned how significant it could be to share experiences so honestly with another person.

Ayodeji and I grew up in families that were distanced by time, space, language, economics, and culture. Yet, we discovered that it was a similarity within our families' values and beliefs that created the foundation for each of us to feel like we needed to take up the work of social justice. The creation of a safe space for sharing our truths created a place for us to stand side by side. This experience was one that broke down barriers, shifted our power differences, and left us understanding each other more fully. In doing so, it helped me to understand implicitly how important it is for social justice leaders to create spaces where community members can share their truths and learn to stand side by side despite their diverse perspectives.

## Conclusion

This chapter outlined a duo-ethnographic study that utilized the stories of a Black male graduate student and a white female university professor to explore and disrupt their metanarratives about social justice leadership, including their knowledge of themselves as social justice leaders, their capacity to make change, and their strategies for engagement. The authors used earlier studies to establish a common definition of social justice leadership (e.g., Ryan, 2006, 2014; Shields, 2010, 2015; Shields et al., 2018; Theoharis, 2007), which includes the belief that self-reflection is one of the foundational acts of social justice leaders (Brown, 2004; Furman, 2012; Jean-Marie, 2008; Shields, 2010, 2015); shared a theoretical understanding of duo-ethnographic methodology (Norris & Sawyer, 2012); explained the process that they designed to engage in this study; and presented a condensed version of their narratives. The common understandings developed through their dialogue included (1) the importance they ascribed to the creation of a safe space where they were able to openly share lived experiences and diverse perspectives, (2) the importance of having an opportunity to identify similarities when on the surface only differences were visible, and (3) the importance of self-reflection to confront one's assumptions and to critically evaluate one's future praxis as a social justice leader.

These findings have implications for social justice leaders, both for their own practice and for the outcomes they strive to achieve within their communities. We found that when we reflected on our past experiences, wrote about them, shared them with each other, and engaged in open and frank dialogue about them, we had an opportunity to see ourselves, our experiences, our values, and our beliefs more clearly as they existed in juxtaposition. Furthermore, we were able to see how someone else's experiences led to different perspectives. Knowledge of the other's past built empathy and authentic understanding about their present. Rather than wanting to argue against each other's points, we found ourselves leaning in and listening with curiosity and interest to stories that made our diverse perspectives feel normal. This experience of listening to understand someone else's perspective as it has developed through their unique life curriculum is one that leaders need to facilitate within their schools and school communities (Guerra & Pazey, 2016). This experience of knowing oneself in the presence of another has led us to feel like we have had the opportunity to access knowledge of self that would not have been possible within the practice of independent self-reflection (Norris & Sawyer, 2012). Leaders of social justice, for whom self-reflection is critical, should adopt the practice of duo-ethnography as a vehicle for cultivating a deeper and more authentic knowledge of self. Participation in planned duo-ethnographic exercises could be transformative for both leaders and community members and could lead to ongoing dialogue that included deeper acceptance and appreciation for diverse perspectives within a more connected community (Breault, 2016; Guerra & Pazey, 2016; Norris & Sawyer, 2012).

As we got deeper into our discussions, we realized that in addition to understanding how we had developed our diverse perspectives, we were beginning to recognize that we were sharing some stories that had remarkable similarities. Those stories served to establish connection and feelings of familiarity. Within a school or community, connection is also important. For us, the connection happened as a result of persistent focus on trying to understand ourselves and each other. Within a school, that persistence and focus needs to be held within the leader's vision for building a more connected community (Ryan, 2014; Ryan & Tuters, 2017; Shields, 2010).

Reflecting together on our pasts, sharing our present, and grappling with the future helped us to be more aware of our own positionality, to remain humble, and to see both our strengths and weaknesses. Social justice leaders need to ensure that they listen with the intention of understanding and make time for the important task of self-reflection (Brown, 2004; Furman, 2012; Jean-Marie, 2008; Shields, 2010, 2015). Furthermore, leaders have the responsibility to create school communities that invite students, teachers, and other community members to engage within connected communities that are characterized by authentic dialogue and shared decision-making (Ryan, 2006, 2014; Ryan & Tuters, 2017; Shields, 2010, 2015; Shields et al., 2018). Based on our experience, we know that sharing our personal histories helped us to create an open, trusting space within our relationship where it felt safe to be vulnerable and where we could stand together, in the midst of our diversity, side by side. If honest communication could transform our understanding of ourselves and each other, surely, it can also lead to similar transformation within a school or community.

## REFERENCES

Armstrong, D., Tuters, S., & Carrier, N. (2013). Micropolitics and social justice leadership: Bridging beliefs and behaviours. *Journal of Educational Administration and Foundations, 23*(2), 119–37.

Breault, R.A. (2016). Emerging issues in duo-ethnography. *International Journal of Qualitative Studies in Education, 29*(6), 777–94. doi: 10.1080/09518398.2016.1162866

Brown, K.M. (2004). Leadership for social justice and equity: Weaving a transformative framework and pedagogy. *Educational Administration Quarterly, 40*(1), 77–108. doi: 10.1177/0013161X03259147

Creswell, J.W., & Poth, C.N. (2018). *Qualitative inquiry and research design: Choosing among five approaches* (4th ed.). Thousand Oaks, CA: SAGE Publications.

Dantley, M.E., & Tillman, L.C. (2006). Social justice and moral transformative leadership. In C. Marshall & M. Oliva (Eds.), *Leadership for social justice: Making revolutions in education* (2nd ed., pp. 19–34). Boston, MA: Allyn & Bacon.

DeMatthews, D., & Mawhinney, H. (2014). Social justice leadership and inclusion: Exploring challenges in an urban district struggling to address inequities. *Educational Administration Quarterly, 50*(5), 844–81. doi: 10.1177/0013161X13514440

Freire, P. (2002). *Pedagogy of the oppressed* (30th anniversary ed.) (M.B. Ramos, Trans.). New York, NY: Continuum.

Furman, G. (2012). Social justice leadership as praxis: Developing capacities through preparation programs. *Educational Administration Quarterly, 48*(2), 191–229. doi: 10.1177/0013161X11427394

Goldfarb, K.P., & Grinberg, J. (2002). Leadership for social justice: Authentic participation in the case of a community center in Caracas, Venezuela. *Journal of School Leadership, 12*(2), 157–73. doi: 10.1177/105268460201200204

Guerra, P.L., & Pazey, B.L. (2016). Transforming educational leadership preparation: Starting with ourselves. *The Qualitative Report, 21*(10), 1751–84. doi: 10.46743/2160-3715/2016.2440

Jansen, J.D. (2006). Leading against the grain: The politics and emotions of leading for social justice in South Africa. *Leadership and Policy in Schools, 5*(1), 37–51. doi: 10.1080/15700760500484027

Jean-Marie, G. (2008). Leadership for social justice: An agenda for 21st century schools. *The Educational Forum, 72*(4), 340–54. doi: 10.1080/00131720802362058

Levine-Rasky, C. (2011). Intersectionality theory applied to whiteness and middle-classness. *Social Identities, 17*(2), 239–53. doi: 10.1080/13504630.2011.558377

Normore, A.H., & McMahon, B. (2007). Educational administrators' conceptions of whiteness, anti-racism and social justice. *Journal of Educational Administration, 45*(6), 684–96. doi: 10.1108/09578230710829874

Norris, J., & Sawyer, R.D. (2012). Toward a dialogic methodology. In J. Norris, R.D. Sawyer, & D. Lund (Eds.), *Duo-ethnography: Dialogic methods for social, health, and educational research* (pp. 9–39). Walnut Creek, CA: Left Coast Press.

Norris, J., Sawyer, R.D., & Lund, D. (Eds.). (2012). *Duo-ethnography: Dialogic methods for social, health, and educational research.* Walnut Creek, CA: Left Coast Press.

Ottmann, J. (2009). Leadership for social justice: A Canadian perspective. *Journal of Research on Leadership Education, 4*(1), 1–9. doi: 10.1177/194277510900400105

Pinar, W.F. (1994). The method of "currere" (1975). *Counterpoints, 2*, 19–27. https://www.jstor.org/stable/42975620

Ryan, J. (2006). Inclusive leadership and social justice for schools. *Leadership and Policy in Schools, 5*(1), 3–17. doi: 10.1080/15700760500483995

Ryan, J. (2014). Promoting inclusive leadership in diverse schools. In *International handbook of educational leadership and social (in)justice* (pp. 359–80). Dordrecht, Netherlands: Springer.

Ryan, J., & Tuters, S. (2017). Picking a hill to die on: Discreet activism, leadership and social justice in education. *Journal of Educational Administration, 55*(5), 569–88. doi: 10.1108/JEA-07-2016-0075

Shields, C.M. (2010). Transformative leadership: Working for equity in diverse contexts. *Educational Administration Quarterly, 46*(4), 558–89. doi:10.1177/0013161X10375609

Shields, C.M. (2014). The war on poverty must be won: Transformative leaders can make a difference. *International Journal of Educational Leadership and Management, 2*(2), 124–46. doi: 10.4471/ijelm.2014.14

Shields, C.M. (2015, October 1). *Transformative leadership for social justice* [Video]. YouTube. https://www.youtube.com/watch?v=7YEsZNbfg-c

Shields, C.M., Dollarhide, C.T., & Young, A.A. (2018). Transformative leadership in school counseling: An emerging paradigm for equity and excellence. *Professional School Counseling, 21*(1b), 1–11. doi: 10.1177/2156759X18773581

Theoharis, G. (2007). Social justice educational leaders and resistance: Toward a theory of social justice leadership. *Educational Administration Quarterly, 43*(2), 221–58. doi: 10.1177/0013161X06293717

Theoharis, G., & Scanlan, M. (2015). *Leadership for increasingly diverse schools.* New York, NY: Routledge.

Vaismoradi, M., Jones, J., Turunen, H., & Snelgrove, S. (2016). Theme development in qualitative content analysis and thematic analysis. *Journal of Nursing Education and Practice, 6*(5), 100–10. doi: 10.5430/jnep.v6n5p100

# 7 Anti-racist Teaching and Leadership in Higher Education: Decentring Whiteness and Addressing Alt-right Resistance

VIDYA SHAH AND STEPHANIE TUTERS

This chapter reports on an investigation into the challenges of leading and teaching for social justice in faculties of education in Ontario universities in the context of a resurgence of conservative performance of white power and privilege. Informed by critical race theory (Ladson-Billings & Tate, 2006) and critical whiteness studies (Nayak, 2007), we engaged in a critical co-constructed auto-ethnographic research study (Cann & DeMeulenaere, 2012). Our aim was to process and unpack our experiences and share them with readers in the hopes of informing more racially just practices and policies in higher education in Canada and elsewhere. Our work is done in response to the racism that operated at the structural and individual levels that we have witnessed in our practice. Evidence is clear that racism is unfortunately on the rise in Canada, including on university campuses (Armstrong, 2019; Barth, 2018), and we hope our work can be helpful in mitigating this trend.

We interviewed one another about our perceptions and experiences to inform the writing of this chapter. Both of us work in faculties of education in Ontario – Vidya as a South Asian assistant professor and Stephanie (Steph) as a white, part-time contract lecturer and researcher. Our universities are part of an increasing trend wherein faculties of education in Ontario and elsewhere advertise and include a focus on social justice and equity in their program descriptions. Programs are praised for this focus, and students enrol in said programs with the aim of becoming better equipped to teach and lead for social justice upon graduation. Along with program components such as courses and practicum experience focused on equity and social justice, many faculties also advertise a focus on helping teacher candidates to develop social justice dispositions through their programs.

We find ourselves continually questioning the extent to which these faculty programs are actually working towards those aims and how, as educators, we are and are not leading students towards these advertised goals. The purpose of this chapter is to critically reflect on our experiences leading, teaching, and working for racial justice in our faculties of education and how we have been helped and challenged in those aims. Throughout this chapter we question how race and racism have been institutionalized and how they are maintained in the context of our work and in our practices. Our work is informed by critical race theories, similar to the work of Sleeter (2016). While the focus of Sleeter's 2016 study is the US, we see many parallels between the context she describes and our contexts of work. She describes how many of the students enrolled in faculties of education are white, yet they are often being prepared to teach in schools that serve higher proportions of racialized students (Sleeter, 2016; see also Holden & Kitchen, 2018). We are also concerned with the focus and content of teacher education. Sleeter (2016) describes how teacher education programs in her context attempt to teach students critical race theory and culturally responsive pedagogies. Yet, this is often done largely in one or two courses and is not necessarily infused throughout the entire program – and unfortunately much of the work is done in white contexts, inevitably perpetuating white power and privilege. Some teacher education programs in our context include courses that focus on anti-racism and anti-oppressive education, yet these subjects are not necessarily taught consistently throughout the programs.

Concurring with the focus we see in our faculties of education on social justice and equity at the institutional level is an escalation of white, conservative sentiment and power in social and political circles in North America. There has been a marked change in social sentiment in Canada and the US since the US election in 2016 when Donald Trump was elected President of the United States; conservatism and violent expressions of white power and privilege are on the rise on and off higher education campuses. Research recently conducted by the National Association for the Advancement of Colored People (NCAAP) demonstrates an increase in hate crimes on higher education campuses in the US and Canada since the Trump election (Levin & Reitzel, 2018). In the US, white supremacist literature is proliferating at colleges and universities, and racial slurs are being written in public places and dormitories (Bauer-Wolf, 2019).

The initial response of many liberal white Canadians in 2016 was to declare their displeasure with the situation in the US and simultaneously express their relief that Canadians were not nearly as racist as their southern neighbours. Prior to the 2016 election results, many Americans even joked about fleeing the US and moving to Canada should Trump be elected (Mock, 2016). Yet, this sense that Canada is somehow "better" and less racist than the US is misinformed. In recent years there has been a marked increase in discrimination and oppression in Canada, including more police reported hate-crimes and unprovoked police brutality perpetuated against Black Canadians (Barth, 2018). Statistics Canada reported a 47 per cent increase in hate crimes between 2014 and 2017, with total numbers of reported incidents being the highest they have ever been since tracking of incidents began in 2009 (Armstrong, 2019). Moreover, there were 130 far-right extremist groups identified in Canada in 2019, a 30 per cent increase from 2015 (Habib, 2019), and these groups have been active on higher education campuses, distributing flyers and posting banners advertising their organizations, recruiting members, and perpetuating their propaganda (Zhou, 2017).

Tension exists for us regarding our role in this process of attempting to address racism while simultaneously contributing to the work of universities as systems through our roles as professors and teacher educators. As critical scholarly practitioners, we know how members of faculty and students inevitably come under attack by individuals with inequitable alt-right agendas, and how students and faculty experience discrimination from systemic forces of whiteness. We hope that through sharing reflections on our experiences, readers will be able to reflect on their own experiences and find ways to inform racial justice policies and practices in their places of work. We recognize that as a body of work, this field of social justice and anti-racism in higher education research and instruction is growing. There are researchers talking about and collecting data on access to higher education (James & Taylor, 2008; Villegas & Aberman, 2019; Yosso, Parker, Solorzano, & Lynn, 2004) and experiences of racialized students and faculty in higher education (Chesler, Lewis, & Crowfoot, 2005; Henry & Tator, 2012; Henry et al., 2017, James, 2012b). Evidence exists about how whiteness is being weaponized in higher education by white students (Cabrera, 2014). Some research discusses the emotional labour of doing this work (Zembylas, 2012). However, much less data exists about the experiences of higher education faculty in leading and teaching for social justice, especially in Canada (Shultz & Viczko, 2016). Our study helps to fill this gap in the existing research.

## Theoretical and Methodological Framework

Through co-constructed auto-ethnographic interviews, we questioned one another and dialogued about our experiences and interactions with conservative white power and privilege within the contexts of our respective positionalities. We explored our understandings of ourselves, our leadership practice, white power, conservativism, and the alt-right, critically questioning our beliefs and experiences. We hope that through this explorative dialogue we can help to articulate our way forward as educators, leaders, and researchers working to achieve social justice in higher education. We begin by explaining the theoretical and methodological frameworks informing our investigation, articulating our positionalities as they pertain to this study and defining the context of our work, our understanding of whiteness, and the alt-right. Our discussion of the findings of our investigation focuses on our practices as leaders in higher education. We conceive of and explore our leadership as intrapersonal, interpersonal, institutional, and ideological. Finally, we discuss the implications of our investigation for higher education and the changes that can be made in faculties of education, and in higher education in general, to decentre whiteness and better support students and faculty in their pursuits of racial justice and in their experiences of discrimination and oppression.

Like Smith-Maddox and Solórzano (2002), we reflect on our pedagogical approaches to addressing inequities in our work in teacher and educational leader preparation programs. Our work is informed by critical race theory (Ladson-Billings & Tate, 2006; Lynn, Yosso, Solórzano, & Parker, 2002; Sleeter, 2016) and critical whiteness theory (Nayak, 2007). In alignment with critical race theory, we see racism as an intentional and permanent fixture in institutions, expressed and maintained at the ideological, interpersonal, and internalized levels, to perpetuate white supremacy and whiteness. We see whiteness as "a set of assumptions, beliefs and practices that place the interests and perspectives of white people at the center of what is considered normal and everyday" (Gillborn, 2015, p. 278), resulting in the othering of racialized persons that is embodied by both people and institutions. While focusing on the expression of racism at the ideological, intrapersonal, and interpersonal levels may never lead to the sort of institutional changes required for racial justice, failing to focus on these levels of expression allows whiteness to re-emerge and reformulate in seemingly anti-racist policies and practices.

In Canada, our public school systems and universities have a long history of perpetuating whiteness at the cost of racialized people and members of other under-represented groups through both individual acts against and by means of racist policies and programs (Ontario Ministry of Education, 2008). We recognize that policies and programs exist to support the creation of more equitable and inclusive schools and education systems, and that many faculty and support staff are working to create more racially just universities. However, white power and privilege remains at both the individual and system levels in higher education in Canada. This paper centres critical whiteness studies as a lens in relation to critical race theory; they are in dialogue with one another. We were conscious to not centre critical whiteness studies alone, as this would inevitably recentre and give more power to whiteness. Therefore, we act and investigate with the awareness of whiteness as a systemic force that is present and performed by both white bodies and bodies of colour, and we centre the work of critical race scholars to inform our work. We also centre the experiences of marginalized students and faculty by engaging with critical whiteness in a form of critique of white supremacy, refusing to centre the comfort and needs of white students and faculty above students and faculty of colour. Our approach is to problem-pose our experiences in the manner of Freire (2000, 2003) to bring about greater equity and inclusion in our institutions and beyond, with radical love leading our work.

Employing a critical co-constructed auto-ethnographic methodology (Boy-lorn & Orbe, 2016; Cann & DeMeulenaere, 2012), we are both researchers and the researched, undergoing a process of change and aiming to become more socially just by engaging in narrative inquiry (Connelly & Clandinin, 1990), and by reflecting internally upon our identities – our experiences in our practice as researchers, teachers, and leaders – and externally on the political, social, and economic structures influencing this experience (Jones, Adams, & Ellis, 2013). Our data sources include transcripts of interviews and conversational-style dialogue between the researchers, narrative journal entries constructed using guided questions, and a discussion thread from a direct message Twitter chat we started at the beginning of the study. Our data collection and analysis process and our conversational-style dialogue evolved through the course of our investigation; it was ongoing and adapted based on our needs and interests. Over the course of six months, from May to late October of 2019, we interviewed one another for the project. We began with some shorter phone conversations during which we discussed the aims and purposes of the project and made plans for the interview protocol. We had three longer in-person meetings where we interviewed one another according to our established interview protocol.

We engaged in multiple rounds of data analysis after each interview, and we revised and added to our interview protocol prior to each subsequent meeting. Once our longer interview sessions were over and we felt we had answered our big questions, we each analysed the data on our own, and then came together to discuss our findings. We used our interview questions as a preliminary framework for analysis and used grounded theory to inform our study and engage in qualitative content analysis in the analysis process (Cho & Lee, 2014), allowing the data to demonstrate main themes through constant comparison. Our interview questions centred around how we conceive of the nature of our identities, how we consider ourselves to be defined, how we are different from and similar to one another, how we feel we have worked to lead and teach for racial justice in our places of work, and what we have experienced through those processes.

As we analysed our data, we found that acts of racial injustice may be happening at ideological, intrapersonal, interpersonal, or institutional levels, and that racial justice that decentres whiteness needs to occur at all four levels simultaneously to be truly effective. Focusing too much attention on institutionally racist practices, for example, dismisses the racial trauma and violence experienced by individuals in those systems based on ideological, intrapersonal, or interpersonal acts of racial injustice. Conversely, focusing too much on ideological acts of racism prevents socially just policies from being created at the institutional level. The data we share below from our conversations and reflections is intended to help readers to critically reflect on the ways they are and are not leading and teaching for racial justice. While we want to share as much as possible, there are times when we have not been able to share the exact details of our experiences and/or conversations because whiteness and white power render the information dangerous and would make our positions fragile.

## Positionalities

Vidya identifies as a second-generation South Asian, cisgender, heterosexual and able-bodied female. She also negotiates being a colonial settler and treaty person in Tkaronto,[1] Canada, with her family and ancestors having previously been subjugated to colonialism and indentured labour in different parts of the world. She also comes to her work as someone who is deeply committed to a spiritual practice with roots in Eastern spirituality (Hinduism, Jainism, and, more intentionally, Buddhism). Vidya is an assistant professor at York University in the Faculty of Education, pre-tenure, with a research focus on anti-racist approaches to leadership, community engagement, and school district reform. Vidya is also a former practitioner in K–12 schooling contexts and engages in community activism.

Steph identifies as a white, cisgender, able-bodied female. She is a second-generation colonial settler and treaty person living with her family on the Brant Tract, the land of the Mississaugas of the Credit First Nation, in Burlington, Canada. Steph considers herself a researcher by trade and nature, with an interest in how quantitative and qualitative data can be used in concert to address complex inequities and help achieve greater social justice through the creation of more equitable and inclusive policies and practices. Steph is an assistant professor, teaching stream with the Ontario Institute for Studies in Education of the University of Toronto in the Department of Leadership, Higher and Adult Education.

## Context and Focus of Our Work

Both researchers work in Southern Ontario in faculties of education that have undergraduate and graduate education programs. Student populations in Ontario vary in their diversity. Many who are enrolled in education programs in Southern Ontario hope to one day teach in schools in the Greater Toronto and Hamilton Area or the Niagara Region, which have more diverse student populations than many of the other school boards in Ontario. Students come to our respective universities to become teachers who should be prepared to teach and lead in their contexts in a way that honours and respects their diverse students and community members. In this project, we reflect on the parts we play in their preparation for this important work.

Our engagement in this critical reflection of our practice is not done from the perspective of asserting that our faculties are either "bad" or "good." In our conversations, we were both able to identify times when we have felt supported and unsupported by our institutions when attempting to support students and other faculty experiencing discrimination. Though we might be able to identify institutions as being "better" or "worse" than one another on a theoretical scale of equitability, that is not the purpose of this investigation. Nor do we see that as a particularly useful exercise. Instead, we encourage our readers to consider the ways in which their own institutions are both supportive and unsupportive of students and faculty experiencing discrimination. Importantly, we feel that no institution, department, or individual faculty member should ever be identified as an "equity empire" (Shah, 2019) that is above critique. All institutions, departments, and faculty members should continually engage in critical reflection, considering the ways that whiteness operates and is operated by individuals and systems.

## Findings

In this section we begin with an overview of our conceptualization of whiteness and the alt-right. We go on to discuss how we believe that leadership in faculties of education both disrupts and recentres whiteness and operates at the following overlapping and mutually reinforcing levels: ideological, intrapersonal, interpersonal, and institutional. At times, we use narrative excerpts from our interviews to illustrate our thought processes. One of the findings we uncovered as we analysed the data was the unfinished and ongoing nature of our conversations and our learning on this topic; our use of narrative helps to illustrate this state of being.

### Conceptions of Whiteness and the Alt-right

When we initially conceived of this study, we used "alt-right" to describe the experiences that were troubling us in our practices. As we progressed through our discussions with one another we continually found ourselves questioning what we meant by alt-right, and how the alt-right might be different from and similar to white power and privilege in general. This line of questioning is common, as members of the alt-right strategically position themselves in juxtaposition to white supremacy to carve out a more appealing persona – one that is more covert in its racism (Hartzell, 2018). This allows members of the alt-right to recentre their whiteness in ways that are harder to identify as overt. While "alt-right" may very well be little more than a new term for conservative white supremacists, we were able to articulate ways we feel the alt-right has changed its course of action in relation to more recent historical approaches of conservative white supremacists. Covert recentring of whiteness, the use of social media to advertise and mobilize, censorship of anti-racist efforts (particularly when those efforts have been enacted by people of colour), and refusing the title of "white" in relation to one's experiences of immigration are the main ways we have seen this alt-rightness enacted in our faculties of education. In the dialogue transcribed below, we explore these ideological tricks in comparing and contrasting alt-right perspectives and whiteness:

> V: How is alt-rightness similar to or different from white supremacy and whiteness? There are arguments that say that alt-rightness, a more intense version of white supremacy, is more prevalent in academia now, although whiteness has always been cemented in academia. Science has been used to justify racial hierarchies of intelligence and capability for a long time, so how is this really different?
>
> S: My initial instinct was to say it is different because of social media, but then I was reading this article on propaganda and how it has always been a tool of white conservatives. And I thought, that's true! So, I think there are subtle differences there – like there are ways that people can be anonymous that they couldn't before because of social media, [and] it's a lot faster and more easily accessible and many more people can be in charge of controlling the message than there were before. But it's still the propagandization of an agenda. It's easier for people to mobilize now.
>
> V: Which is true in the opposite sense as well. People committed to racial justice movements can more easily mobilize. I feel like that's a function of social media in general, in that things are happening in a more decentralized way – there are fewer "experts" and many more perspectives. And that can be a good thing.
>
> S: I wonder if it is easier or harder to censor messages now. I've been using Instagram to engage with activists and learn. One of the things that keeps happening is that activists of colour are highly censored and Instagram will just remove their posts, whereas white activists who are promoting whiteness and conservatism don't have their posts removed. But is that different from historical distributions of power when large media outlets like the newspaper and historical ways of perpetuating propaganda were largely controlled by white people? I feel like it's a bit different, but it's a similar process.
>
> V: While alt-rightness has particular manifestations in faculties of education today, which are important to name in order to disrupt them, how does focusing on alt-rightness, independent of a history of white supremacy, serve to reinforce white supremacy? If we're not connecting the dots historically and politically, we get distracted in thinking about alt-rightness as a new, disconnected form of racial oppression.

As we progressed in our conversation from the ways we define whiteness in opposition to alt-rightness, we struggled in our attempts to identify whiteness as a system, as opposed to only thinking about it in relation to individual bodies. Vidya struggled with this in relation to South Asian students and Steph

154 Vidya Shah and Stephanie Tuters

struggled with this in relation to her teaching of white students. We discussed our attempts to non-essentialize whiteness in our processes of helping students to understand the intersectionality of their identities – looking at the plurality of whiteness without spending too much time there, so as not to give power back to whiteness. We discussed how whiteness can be harmful and dangerous for white people as well as people of colour, while being careful not to minimize the material, political, cultural, and psychic impacts of whiteness on Indigenous, Black, and racialized people. We continued to return to our fear of spending too much time unpacking whiteness with one another and our students, identifying how easily focusing on whiteness bolsters whiteness instead of decentring it.

## Ideological, Intrapersonal, Interpersonal, and Institutional Disruption and Decentring of Whiteness

Ahmed (2004) warns that in making whiteness visible, we run the risk of recentring it. As instructors and researchers committed to anti-racist education and critical whiteness studies, we conceptualize our brand of leadership as one that disrupts whiteness by continuously holding it in tension with leadership approaches that recentre it. While whiteness studies focus on institutional and ideological dimensions of racism and white supremacy, our analysis also explores the intrapersonal and interpersonal realms, which are deeply connected to the institutional and ideological dimensions. Therefore, leadership in faculties of education that both disrupts and recentres whiteness operates at all four of these overlapping and mutually reinforcing levels: ideological, intrapersonal, interpersonal (i.e., faculty relationships with students and faculty relationships with other colleagues), and institutional. While these categories are all influenced by one another, we treat each in a more distinguished and categorical way for greater clarity.

### IDEOLOGICAL

In the ideological realm, leadership manifests as ideas and relationships between people, power, and knowledge (Foucault, 1980). Leadership that recentres whiteness at an ideological level perpetuates fragmentation and binary thinking (e.g., either/or, good/bad, us/them); protects white innocence and maintains white people as "ideal" subjects (Ahmed, 2004); prioritizes rationality, objectivity, facts, and "truth" over multiple ways of knowing and being; and maintains closed, non-relational, non-transparent, and hierarchical forms of leadership in faculties of education, where power is held among a few (almost always white) leaders. While faculties of education might express a commitment to equity and social justice in name, there are both intentional and unintentional gaps between the outer presentation and the inner manoeuvrings of policies, structures, and pedagogy. For example, many faculty members (often white faculty members) circumvent anti-racist and whiteness discourses from their course syllabi and classroom discussions. This increases the burden on those faculty members (often racialized and/or contract faculty) teaching courses focused specifically on anti-racism and equity to address these knowledges and experiences. This latter group must then engage in a "self-othering" process in which they must name their theoretical framings, positioning themselves and their frameworks as different, subpar, and abnormal while maintaining white objectivity and centrality. This is especially evident in subject-specific content courses in Initial Teacher Education such as mathematics, science, language, the arts, technology, and physical education, which are often taught in the absence of these "abnormal" frameworks, and which inadequately challenge the canon in these subject areas.

Leadership that disrupts whiteness not only challenges these ideologies but also questions whose knowledge is being centred and for what purpose; for example, course syllabi and class discussions that centre the knowledge and experiences of racialized and Indigenous scholars and activists who have been speaking against whiteness long before white scholars (who continue to profit off of white supremacy in book sales, speaking engagements, etc.) – and who do so often in the face of personal and professional risk. For Steph and Vidya, these scholars include Audre Lorde (1984), bell hooks (1997), Gloria Anzaldúa (2015), Sandy Grande (2004), Patricia Hill Collins (1990), James Baldwin (1993), Gloria Ladson-Billings (2005), Ann Lopez (2005), Carl James (2012a), and Denise Armstrong (2010), among others. White scholars who speak against whiteness and white supremacy are used strategically by those disrupting whiteness to elevate and sustain the discomfort and unlearning for white students, and to take risks that buffer the harm directed at Black, Indigenous, and racialized colleagues, students, and staff.

In our conversations with one another, we spoke of the ways in which exploring critical whiteness studies risks recentring white students in our classes and does little to advance the learning of many racialized students for whom whiteness studies provide minimal new learning. At the same time, whiteness that manifests as greater credibility assigned to white scholars by both white students and (at times) racialized students can be a useful initial tool to disrupt whiteness. As problematic as it is, white, anti-racist and whiteness scholars help create the conditions for white students to reckon with whiteness, which increases safety for racialized students to express their experiences in school and society and allows them to be heard and/or believed in ways that may not have previously existed for them.

Ideologically, leaders in faculties of education who disrupt whiteness are also acutely aware of the ways in which whiteness is repurposed, repackaged, recycled, or positioned ahistorically and apolitically to distract from the intentional and systematic nature of its oppression. Vidya and Steph explore these ideological tricks in comparing and contrasting alt-right perspectives and whiteness. In addition to contextualizing and historicizing ideas, leaders with ideological manifestations of leadership who disrupt whiteness are also dissatisfied with easy, well-packaged frames of reference that fail to capture the complexity and nuance of multiple, and at times contested, racialized and Indigenized experiences. Finally, this form of leadership invites us to resist the temptation to camp out in our well-defined theories, and instead to be in continuous dialogue with theories that have been crucial to anti-racist education, and yet are inevitably partial (Shah, 2019). As such, this chapter, and all writing and knowledge, are necessarily incomplete.

INTRAPERSONAL

Intrapersonal leadership explores a leader's relationship to self. Leadership that disrupts whiteness at the intrapersonal level continuously questions one's complicity in whiteness, even as it aims to disrupt it. For example, Ahmed (2004) urges those committed to whiteness studies to continue focusing on manifestations of white racism and white privilege that are heightened through seemingly anti-racist assertions of "seeing whiteness" and outright declarations of "being a racist" and "feeling ashamed about being racist." These assertions and declarations reposition the white subject as the social ideal and allow self-declared informed white people to distance themselves from white people and ideas they deem racist. This "fantasy of transcendence" of whiteness serves to absolve self-declared white anti-racists of their ongoing responsibility and complicity in disrupting whiteness through critical, institutional action (Ahmed, 2004).

In faculties of education, the fantasy of transcendence operates when individual faculty members engage in theoretical acrobatics of anti-racism in their research and teaching, with minimal commitments to challenging the institutional and ideological manifestations of whiteness within the faculty. This further entrenches white power and dominance because white faculty can benefit from addressing racism as a performative mode of career advancement without having to take any personal risks in support of racial justice. For example, both Vidya and Steph note that while metrics of success for contract, tenure-stream, and tenured faculty are deeply informed by features of neoliberalism and whiteness (i.e., meritocracy, neutrality, competition, individualism, narrow conceptions of knowledge production and objectivity), many faculty continue to uphold these same metrics for research and teaching awards or for tenure and promotion processes, further inscribing whiteness into their work and their faculties of education.

Leadership that disrupts whiteness at the intrapersonal level means that all faculty, especially white faculty, continuously question their complicity in whiteness. For example, in reflecting on how their "success" is intimately connected to their white skin, and how their "success" is often predicated on the "failure" of racialized faculty, especially Black and Indigenous faculty, white leaders might question if they need to step down, turn away an opportunity, not apply for a particular position, or leave the institution altogether to redress racial injustice and to make space for greater representation and diversity in thinking and lived experience. For example, in discussing first and second author attributions for this chapter, Steph grappled with whether her name should even appear on this publication as she does not want to profit from anti-racism work, nor perpetuate the system of meritocracy that praises researchers for productivity thereby perpetuating whiteness. We shared examples of how we actively resist metrics of success based on whiteness in prioritizing student mentorship and public scholarship over traditional metrics of success such as publications in top-tier, peer-reviewed journals. Vidya named the importance of using her positionality as a tenure-stream faculty member to provide a platform for racialized and other marginalized educators and community members to share knowledge and expertise, even if it meant that the insights shared could not be used towards her *personal* publications. She also spoke of the balance between healing her own internal wounds and trauma connected to experiences of violence, harm, and oppression, and the trauma simultaneously being informative in recentring the importance and purpose of this work.

INTERPERSONAL

In faculties of education, leadership at the interpersonal level that disrupts whiteness manifests with students, colleagues, and the broader public. We believe that whiteness should be distinguished from individual white students. Failing to distinguish the system of whiteness from white students perpetuates white supremacy by denying its embedded persistence in systems and structures. Furthermore, focusing on white students and not whiteness and white supremacy may result in the dehumanization of white students and a disregard for how whiteness operates in racialized bodies.

*Relationships with Students.* In exploring our relationships with students, we noticed differences in how we conceived of our role as leaders in relation to both racialized and white students, influencing whose voices were centred in the process and how. Leadership that recentres whiteness protects white racial solidarity and racial comfort and promotes racial dominance, even under the guise of protecting racialized students. Steph and Vidya have both seen examples of faculty leaders ending potentially difficult conversations about race in classrooms or faculty gatherings and attempting to buffer racialized students from expressions of white victimhood and white injury (Bloch, Taylor, & Martinez, 2020) that manifest in white tears (Accapadi, 2007), white fragility (DiAngelo, 2018), or white rage (Anderson, 2016). This attempt to protect racialized students from these experiences is then addressed by meeting individually with white students to support them in their expressions of racial discomfort without it having to be witnessed by racialized students in the class, who often experience these displays of white fragility as violent (DiAngelo, 2018). However, these individual and private approaches assume a white racial innocence and protect the racial comfort of white students at the expense of racialized students. This denies opportunities for racial justice and denies racialized students opportunities for dignity.

In the dialogue shared below, we discuss the importance and challenges of responding to and teaching about racial injustice in our classes in ways that are educational for our students but do not recenter whiteness.

> V: One of the distinctions we have to make is in our attempts to think about how we address this in our classes. There were many moves to recentre whiteness even as we attempted to challenge whiteness in our last interview. How are we thinking about this? Is it about the immediate students in front of us? Or is it about a larger movement, discourse, or transformative experience? If we take the immediate view of the students in our care, it changes our perspective of who might feel accepted or included in that space. If we take a longer-term view, it's like yes, you're experiencing discomfort right now, you'll get through it, but we're aiming for a larger racial justice movement and this is a necessary step. So, in Teacher Education, how do we have that dual view? How do we respond to the students in front of us now – and, in that view, not recenter individual white people? And then, how do we have that longer-term vision in mind without recentring whiteness? … Steph, you mentioned that you see it as your role as a white faculty member to support white students in unpacking their whiteness so that the burden does not fall on racialized faculty. But if you choose to spend time one-on-one with white students, or in small groups, that means there is less time for racialized students and developing anti-racist initiatives, curriculum, etc. So, first, there's the question of priorities given limited time and resources. Then there's the question of … even if we had all the time and resources in the world, would that be the right approach to sit one-on-one with a white student who is in their fragility to work through stuff that's happening for them? Or, is intervening actually perpetuating the very thing that we're trying to dismantle (fragility, aversion to discomfort, etc.)? How do you negotiate that? If what we're trying to do is name that discomfort and allow people to be in that discomfort because it's an important part of their growth, how do we do that in ways that don't recenter whiteness and support white supremacy? I love that you talk about asking them, "Now what?" in your one-on-one conversations with them.
>
> S: I'd like to see more of a recognition that students are at different places as they come into the program rather than treating them as though they're all starting at the same place. I don't exactly know how I'd do that practically speaking, but

treating students as equals creates a lot more problems in terms of how time is spent and what it is spent on. There seems to be an assumption that all students understand their identities in the same ways coming into the program, but in reality, that's not actually the case. So we're stuck in a position of teaching people about identity and systems of oppression, and because students are at such different places in their learning, it's almost like at times I need to come back to the beginning. And then that does things like centring whiteness and conservative power and privilege at the expense of not centring students that are already far beyond that work, towards whatever they want to work towards in their practice. I think about times when I'm having entry-level conversations about whiteness and identity and I feel like I'm wasting time … it's a harmful conversation to have for students in my class who are not white. There's got to be a way to mitigate that and to have them learning.

V: So, the benefit that I see of having students that are early or late in their learning journey together in class is that we are supporting students for whom this is not new (mostly non-white students) to hone their skills in naming and challenging racist perspectives, behaviours, and dispositions. I have had students say to me that to watch me model how to not demonize someone but still call out the ideologies that are problematic in their thinking is helpful to their growth as an anti-racist educator. Over the years, I have become increasingly skilled at unpacking and challenging the myths of neutrality and meritocracy and unpacking ahistorical and decontextual narratives. I have also become better at encouraging students to see their perspective as one of many partial perspectives operating in the classroom, and allowing conversations to be unfinished as a way of increasing cognitive and emotional dissonance and discomfort.

S: At most universities I work at, we ignore the fact that white students don't understand their whiteness and we end up spending a lot of time in class to help white people unpack themselves. If that's going to happen anyway, not to say it should, why not have opportunities for a white faculty member to address it instead of a faculty [member] of colour? It shouldn't be an expectation as a faculty [member] of colour, but it should be an expectation for me. Not necessarily paid, but mentorship, so that we can decentre the focus at the class level so that we're taking less time away from all students at the class level … but that's just centring whiteness again. I just feel like there's so much time spent at the classroom level dealing with whiteness and I don't know how to mitigate that without centring whiteness in a different way.

V: It's tricky because this can easily be taken up as systemically recentring whiteness.

S: It is! I don't know how to address whiteness without centring it. I almost want to come back to the idea of a test or gatekeeping in some way. Even a bootcamp … any idea I come up with is just recentring whiteness. Why can't it be like the police where it's just like we're not hiring white people? I don't necessarily think that we need more white teachers. But then white teachers would just go to private universities.

Leadership that aims to disrupt whiteness at the interpersonal level also recognizes the ways in which whiteness operates between racialized faculty and white students, and between racialized students and white students. Steph noticed that white students will often want to speak to her privately to work through their white fragility in an attempt to become "better" white people. Steph feels a responsibility to engage with white students about their whiteness and not have students graduate from faculties of education where she works without learning about and unlearning their identity. Yet, Steph is troubled by how this promotes aims at white exceptionalism and takes time and resources away from racialized students in the program who have experienced discrimination. White students tend not to approach Vidya to work through their fragility; instead, she noticed that they will often try to declare their understandings of whiteness and how whiteness operated through them as another manifestation of white exceptionalism, engaging in self-credentialing and distancing themselves from their white peers who were resistant to conversations on whiteness and white supremacy. The incentive to break racial solidarity is greater when white students believe personal benefits might be gained in the form of perceived respect from the professor or better grades, so Vidya is continuously negotiating potential student performativity with the accountability structures necessary to engage difficult knowledges.

We both noticed the ways in which white fragility was used as a defence to shut down conversations in class, with white students claiming that they felt "unsafe" during these conversations; visibly emoting in the class (i.e., crying, laughing, rolling their eyes); questioning the validity of the research and "facts" about collective identities; making claims to common or similar experiences of sadness and trauma and thereby reducing the extent of trauma caused by intergenerational, persistent, and intentional forms of anti-Black racism, anti-Indigenous racism, Islamophobia, or other forms or racism; and claiming that they want to "prefect" their anti-whiteness to protect their innocence and purity.

We both also noted that students who are white or white-passing and who also identify as either first- or second-generation Canadians or as having grown up in poverty find it more difficult to name their white privilege than other white students, even though they have experienced other forms of marginalization. This is particularly true for white students who do not identify as Caucasian or Western European. Steph also noted that some white students use their knowledge of their rights as students and the language of social justice to claim that they are being discriminated against in class. In Vidya's case, there was one incident in which students spread a rumour that she was "racist against white people" and assumed that she must have had white teachers who were mean to her growing up after engaging in an activity that explicitly named white privilege. Ironically, the students did not consider her white graduate assistant racist, despite the fact that he spoke about white privilege quite regularly in class. This is one of many examples of the additional burdens placed upon racialized faculty who address anti-racism and whiteness.

*Relationships with Colleagues and the Broader Public.* Both Vidya and Steph noted that while there is some discussion about whiteness and anti-racism in their faculties of education, there is limited understanding and conversation about the ways that the logics of whiteness operate at all levels. Relationally, leadership aimed at disrupting whiteness prioritizes justice over a fear of conflict that often manifests in silence and aversion. From this perspective, white faculty are aware of, and willing to name and disrupt, racial microaggressions towards racialized faculty despite the risk of a loss of connection or belonging and the potential for conflict. White faculty are also willing to honestly reflect on the racial dynamics of who they "feel more comfortable with," – that is, with whom they have a better "fit" or stronger connection, with whom there is "greater trust," and with whom they have more in common. These "personal" relationships have political ramifications. They maintain whiteness as normalized and further white privilege through the creation of "unintentional" networks and connections that inevitably impact collaborations, favours, perks, nepotism, special projects, and access to information. Leaders aiming to disrupt whiteness also actively and intentionally build relationships with the broader public to blur the lines between universities and communities; to centre community knowledge as legitimate knowledge in the university; to engage in research that is based more in relationality, justice, and access than in extraction, ownership and careerism; and to connect community organizations to funding opportunities and structures in the university that might support their work.

INSTITUTIONAL

Leadership that disrupts whiteness at the institutional level challenges institutional silences and erasures in the distribution of power as a result of practices, policies, and structures. There is a recognition that whiteness, anti-racism, white privilege, and white supremacy are rarely spoken of and even less often addressed in policies, practices, and structures that continue to marginalize racialized students, staff, and faculty. There is a sense of urgency that informs the need to address manifestations of white supremacy in admissions practices, hiring, tenure and promotion structures, institutional foci, resource allocation, and student programming and supports. There is an intentional focus on going deeper with anti-racist initiatives instead of bigger and broader through surface-level initiatives that become showpieces for strategic and multi-year plans.

162 Vidya Shah and Stephanie Tuters

Leadership that recentres whiteness at the institutional level is slow, performative, and safe. It delays the important work that creates the conditions for racial justice through manoeuvres of distraction.

Leadership that disrupts institutional whiteness recognizes patterns of racism reflected in practices such as teacher evaluations, unaccounted labour (such as higher levels of service and student supervision), and narrow notions of research and service that inadequately account for community service and that perpetuate elitist barriers between scholars, practitioners, and communities. This form of leadership actively supports racialized faculty by providing additional resources and opportunities and changing metrics to redress racial injustice. For example, mentorship and networking opportunities are available to support new faculty members of colour in navigating the social and political landscapes of the faculty/university. Furthermore, there are additional resources to support faculty of colour in coming together to dialogue and inform faculty- and university-wide practices and structures are important starting places. Simultaneously, institutions must guard against "expert" or "celebrity-status" anti-racist educators being held above the standards of justice and human rights because they bring with them recognition, celebrity, and funding. For racialized "experts" or "celebrity-status" anti-racist educators, this constitutes a form of interest convergence, wherein the interests of racialized people are accommodated when they converge with the interests of white people (Bell, 1980).

This form of leadership is also strong and courageous in its desire to centre justice over the fear of human rights allegations; it is rooted in a strong understanding of human rights that does not mistake white students' claims of "reverse racism" or of "feeling unsafe" in a class on whiteness and white privilege with actual human rights abuses. Simultaneously, there are checks and balances in place through strong governance models and strong relationality that ensure that social justice language is also not being used by administration and staff to camouflage whiteness and distract from anti-racist action. Therefore, institutional leadership that disrupts whiteness is distributed among many partners; is clear, open, and transparent; values slower and more democratic processes over flashy final products that claim to do more/better/bigger (even in the name of equity or anti-racism); has regular checks and balances in governance, policies, and practices; and uses mechanisms and structures that welcome conflict and contradiction as opportunities for learning, creativity, and justice.

## Approaches for Consideration

While we are careful not to provide a decontextualized "list of best practices" for leaders in faculties of education to use to disrupt whiteness, we will share some of the strategies we ourselves use and orientations we find useful in our specific contexts and classrooms. We will also share stronger considerations for faculties of education more broadly that are interested in the ongoing project of disrupting institutional whiteness.

IN THE CLASSROOM

Both Vidya and Steph spoke of the importance of balancing the interpersonal aspects of this work with the systemic aspects. Vidya named the importance of needing to "expert it up" to counteract students' initial (and sometimes enduring) perceptions of her capacity and capability as an instructor and scholar by drawing on the tremendous scholarship in this area and being over prepared with examples and data on white supremacy in schooling and society. She also named the importance of using a strong, unapologetic tone in her teaching and "dropping truth" or "real talk," which she defines as naming what students may be thinking, whether or not they are conscious of it or comfortable with it. For racialized students, this approach tends to build trust because it exposes and affirms truths that they were taught to stifle to protect the racial comfort of white people. For white students, this unapologetic approach results in both moments of fragility and moments in which Vidya gains the students' respect by naming their thoughts or reactions as they are happening and situating them within the literature.

Vidya will also use humour to call out common reactions to difficult knowledge; reactions that range from using social media during class time, to the weaponized use of the emotionalities of whiteness (Matias, 2016) and the ensuing aggressive or defensive body language that ensues (e.g., eye rolling, crossing arms, laughter), to waiting to share "real" feelings about the professor in anonymous evaluations that are rooted in racist or sexist ideas. She openly questions the "unconscious" in unconscious bias, the "implicit" in implicit bias, and the "micro" in microaggressions, disrupting white racial innocence that focuses on intention over impact. She also asks white students to reflect on the ways in which their responses are socialized and coded in whiteness (i.e., racial comfort, racial innocence, racial purity and objectivity) and to be conscious of the ways in which their response to these topics might be received by peers whose lived realities both in and out of faculties of education are often erased, silenced, and dismissed.

Steph identified the first three years after moving from the role of researcher to teacher as having a steep learning curve. This shift was harder than she initially anticipated. Her strategies for engaging in challenging conversations have become more robust and intentional in the last few years, but she is still learning a great deal. As she engages with students, Steph is conscious of the conversations she has had with white friends and family members about how white people often feel they are "losing" something while working towards equity. Steph has even had white people admit to her that they have "done the math" and realized that if equity is ever achieved, they will have less – and that that is not a price they are willing to incur. While it has become popular for white people to use the language of social justice, in practice, there is a big difference between those who are and those who are not willing to "give something up" to contribute to greater equity and social justice. Steph reflected, "I honestly do find that when I use the language of white people with white people to talk about or to help them to understand oppression, it seems to work the best." This leads Steph to include both quantitative and qualitative data in her lectures to inform conversations on social justice, as she finds students (particularly white students) are quick to dismiss conversations on discrimination if they are informed only by qualitative studies. Similarly, Steph focuses on the broader social, political, and economic contexts of schooling and society, outlining the ways that more equitable societies are more beneficial for all citizens. Students seem to respond well to these approaches, and arguments against equity are fewer and less intense when the conversations begin with this context-setting data. While Steph initially began each course with discussions on how she and the students could work together to create a safe classroom, she is now more cautious about claims of achieving safety.

We both find class norms helpful in explicitly stating that there is no such thing as a "safe" environment for all people, that there is a distinction between safety and discomfort, and that, together, the class can work to develop multiple, critical lenses through which we can identify who might not feel safe in a particular context and why. We also challenge the criteria by which "success is measured." Vidya tells her students that the class is unsuccessful unless there are regular experiences of discomfort and disruption or moments when she has to put her slide deck aside because the class is leading her in a different direction. She expects that in any class there will be students who feel affirmed (some for the first time in their learning journey) and students who feel angry and, at times, vengeful. Steph, on the other hand, has shifted away from the standard lecture format to a greater focus on collaborative group work where the research and theories explored in class are put to test in practical ways. Students are informed they will be testing their skills in the class in ways that will challenge them. We both use readings about the emotional responses of white students to difficult knowledge to draw parallels between the politics of white emotions and white supremacy. Finally, we both also attend to systemic injustices built into schooling through the use of identity-based data that demonstrates racial achievement and opportunity gaps and makes fluid and intentional movements between the individual and the system, such as personalizing the effects of systemic practices like access initiatives on admission practices in faculties of education.

IN THE FACULTY OF EDUCATION

At the student level, faculties of education need a robust access initiative that actively recruits teacher candidates from underrepresented parts of cities/

suburbs; supports racialized and other marginalized students in understanding their rights navigating the system and addressing the racism they will inevitably face in their courses, practicum, and beyond; and provides networking and mentorship opportunities for racialized and other marginalized teacher candidates to support their transition and next steps. However, access initiatives can also address the limits of whiteness (and other forms of privilege) in being able to relate to and teach students with different social identities. One suggestion is that the application process to Initial Teacher Education programs have an explicit statement about commitments to challenging privilege and oppression and centring difficult and marginalized knowledges. *All* students can then be required to reflect on the ways in which experiences of privilege and marginalization have influenced their experiences of teaching and learning. This means that settler, white, male, Christian, able-bodied, middle-upper class, cisgender students would be asked to reflect on how settler identities, whiteness, maleness, and other forms of power and privilege influence how they learn and how they teach. This process will necessarily be imperfect, as are all processes, but would indicate to students a serious commitment to redressing injustice in schooling and society through education. It is especially important that student supports such as an access coordinator and greater access to mental health, spiritual, and community-based services be available and easily accessible to racialized and other marginalized students. Individuals and institutions should be willing to commit to centring the concerns and experiences of racialized students, acknowledging that more and different supports will be required to meet their needs. Moreover, racialized students should never pay a price in having to prove they have experienced discrimination and oppression; the burden should be on the faculty and the cost should always be greater for faculty and staff.

Faculties of education can be more vigilant in ensuring that commitments to social justice and equity are not simply marketing tools but are meaningfully incorporated into all courses, committee work, systemic decisions and policies, governance models, funding decisions, research allocation, programming, special initiatives, community partnerships, and leadership training. Within this umbrella of equity and justice, race needs to be explicitly stated, and racism, whiteness, and white supremacy need to be explicitly attended to. For example, white colleagues could share the labour of creating the conditions in which to confront whiteness and support efforts to provide additional time, resources, and support for Indigenous and racialized instructors who face additional burdens. Moreover, all faculty should be subject to equity audits, with each faculty member being open to critical reflection and continually working towards becoming less oppressive.

Finally, we might consider changing the criteria for what counts as successful teaching, research, and service that intentionally disrupts white comfort, innocence, and objectivity. What if, for example, the absence on a teacher's evaluation of student comments demonstrating white fragility or white rage is positioned as an area of growth for that instructor because it indicates that class discussions and readings are not disruptive enough? Or, what if student comments displaying white fragility or rage were viewed as collective challenges that the university must address? Moreover, in challenging notions of individualism and meritocracy, tenure and promotion processes should devalue "productivity" in terms of number of publications and grants won and place greater value on professors' support of their students and the collaborative productivity of professors and the students who they are mentoring.

## Conclusion

Our exploration of leadership has been dialogical, particularly when discussing our leadership practices and understandings with one another. Our conceptions of whiteness and leadership evolved over the course of our conversations, which genuinely contributed to our co-construction of knowledge. This process of engaging in a critical co-constructed auto-ethnographic study is mutually influential and informative, iterative, constantly in question, and incomplete. From this vantage point, we theorized our leadership as aiming to disrupt and decentre whiteness at the ideological, intrapersonal, interpersonal, and institutional levels.

Ideological leadership that disrupts whiteness questions whose knowledge is being centred and for what purposes. Intrapersonal leadership, on the other hand, explores a leader's relationship to self; leadership that disrupts whiteness at the intrapersonal level means that all faculty members, regardless of the bodies they inhabit, are continuously questioning their complicity in whiteness. Conversely, interpersonal leadership explores relationships between faculty, students, and the broader community; interpersonal leadership that disrupts whiteness manifests with students, colleagues, and the broader public and recognizes the ways in which whiteness operates between and among racialized and white faculty and students. Finally, institutional leadership focuses on the practices, policies, and structures that influence how power is distributed across people, time, and space; at the institutional level, leadership that disrupts whiteness challenges institutional silences and erasures.

In alignment with this theoretical framework of leadership, we offered a series of guiding recommendations and points of consideration. At all four levels of leadership, critical reflective processes should focus on whiteness as a system (and the ideas or incidents in question), not on the individual. This is important since whiteness can operate in different contexts and in different bodies. Critiques of processes such as these are quick to cite concerns relating to workplace norms, union agreements, and resource allocation. This is a challenge that can be overcome through imagining new approaches and different negotiations of reciprocal workplace agreements if faculty members and staff are willing to make the commitment to decentre whiteness in higher education and do the necessary work together.

NOTE

1  The word "Toronto" originates from the Mohawk word *Tkaronto*, meaning "the place in the water where the trees are standing," which is said to refer to the wooden stakes that were used as fishing weirs in the narrows of local river systems by the Haudenosaunee and Huron-Wendat peoples (Mills & Roque, 2019).

REFERENCES

Accapadi, M.M. (2007). When white women cry: How white women's tears oppress women of color. *College Student Affairs Journal, 26*(2), 208–15. https://files.eric.ed.gov/fulltext/EJ899418.pdf
Ahmed, S. (2004). Declarations of whiteness: The non-performativity of anti-racism. *Borderlands E-journal*, 3(2). https://webarchive.nla.gov.au/awa/20050616083826/http://www.borderlandsejournal.adelaide.edu.au/vol3no2_2004/ahmed_declarations.htm
Anderson, C. (2016). *White rage: The unspoken truth of our racial divide*. New York, NY: Bloomsbury Publishing.
Anzaldúa, G.E. (2015). *Light in the dark/Luz en lo oscuro: Rewriting identity, spirituality, reality*. Durham, NC: Duke University Press.
Armstrong, A. (2019). *Police-reported hate crime in Canada, 2017*. Statistics Canada. https://www150.statcan.gc.ca/n1/en/pub/85-002-x/2019001/article/00008-eng.pdf?st=BrGXlOC
Armstrong, D.E. (2010). Rites of passage: Coercion, compliance, and complicity in the socialization of new vice-principals. *Teachers College Record, 112*(3), 685–722.
Baldwin, J. (1993). *The fire next time*. New York, NY: Vintage International.
Barth, B. (2018, October 15). Canada's most prominent Black activist is fighting Doug Ford. He also has a message for white liberals. *Pacific Standard*. https://psmag.com/social-justice/desmond-cole-has-a-message-for-white-liberals
Bauer-Wolf, J. (2019, February 25). Hate incidents on campus still rising. *Inside Higher Education*. https://www.insidehighered.com/news/2019/02/25/hate-incidents-still-rise-college-campuses
Bell, D. (1980). *Brown v. Board of Education* and the interest-convergence dilemma. *Harvard Law Review*, 93(3), 518–33. doi: 10.2307/1340546
Bloch, K.B., Taylor, T., & Martinez, K. (2020). Playing the race card: White injury, white victimhood and the paradox of colour-blind ideology in anti-immigrant discourse. *Ethnic and Racial Studies, 43*(7), 1130–48. doi: 10.1080/01419870.2019.1648844

Boylorn, R.M., & Orbe, M.P. (2016). Negating the inevitable: An autoethnographic analysis of first-generation college student status. In R.M. Boylorn and M.P. Orbe (Eds.), *Critical Autoethnography: Intersecting cultural identities in everyday life* (pp. 47–61). London, UK: Routledge.

Cabrera, N.L. (2014). Exposing whiteness in higher education: White male college students minimizing racism, claiming victimization, and recreating white supremacy. *Race Ethnicity and Education, 17*(1), 30–55. doi: 10.1080/13613324 .2012.725040

Cann, C.N., & DeMeulenaere, E.J. (2012). Critical co-constructed autoethnography. *Cultural Studies – Critical Methodologies, 12*(2), 146–58. doi: 10.1177/1532708 611435214

Chesler, M., Lewis, A.E., & Crowfoot, J.E. (2005). *Challenging racism in higher education: Promoting justice.* Lanham, MD: Rowman & Littlefield.

Cho, J.Y., & Lee, E.H. (2014). Reducing confusion about grounded theory and qualitative content analysis: Similarities and differences. *The Qualitative Report, 19*(32), 1–20. doi: 10.46743/2160-3715/2014.1028

Collins, P.H. (1990). *Black feminist thought: Knowledge, consciousness, and the politics of empowerment.* Boston, MA: Unwin Hyman.

Connelly, F.M., & Clandinin, D.J. (1990). Stories of experience and narrative inquiry. *Educational Researcher, 19*(5), 2–14. doi: 10.3102/0013189X019005002

DiAngelo, R. (2018). *White fragility.* Boston, MA: Beacon Press.

Foucault, M. (1980). *Power/knowledge: Selected interviews and other writings, 1972–1977* (C. Gordon, Ed.). New York, NY: Pantheon Books.

Freire, P. (2000). *Pedagogy of freedom: Ethics, democracy, and civic courage.* Lanham, MD: Rowman & Littlefield.

Freire, P. (2003). *Pedagogy of the oppressed.* New York, NY: Continuum.

Gillborn, D. (2015). Intersectionality, critical race theory, and the primacy of racism: Race, class, gender, and disability in education. *Qualitative Inquiry,* 21(3), 277–87. doi: 10.1177/1077800414557827

Grande, S. (2004). *Red pedagogy: Native American social and political thought.* Lanham, MD:    Rowman & Littlefield.

Habib, J. (2019, July 13). Far-right extremist groups and hate crime rates are growing in Canada. *The Passionate Eye.* https://www.cbc.ca/passionateeye/features /right-wing-extremist-groups-and-hate-crimes-are-growing-in-canada

Hartzell, S.L. (2018). Alt-white: Conceptualizing the "alt-right" as a rhetorical bridge between white nationalism and mainstream public discourse. *Journal of Contemporary Rhetoric, 8*(1–2), 6–25.

Henry, F., Dua. E., James, C.E., Kobayashi, A., Li, P., Ramos, H., & Smith, M. (2017). *The equity myth: Racialization and Indigeneity at Canadian universities.* Vancouver, BC: UBC Press.

Henry, F., & Tator, C. (2012). Interviews with racialized faculty members in Canadian universities. *Canadian Ethnic Studies, 44*(1), 75–99. doi: 10.1353 /ces.2012.0003

Holden, M., & Kitchen, J. (2018). Where are we now? Changing admission rates for underrepresented groups in Ontario teacher education. *Canadian Journal of Educational Administration and Policy, 185,* 45–60. https://journalhosting .ucalgary.ca/index.php/cjeap/article/view/42930

Hooks, B. (1997). Representing whiteness in the Black imagination. In R. Frankenberg (Ed.), *Displacing whiteness: Essays in social and cultural criticism* (pp. 165–79). Durham, NC: Duke University Press.

James, C.E. (2012a). *Life at the intersection: Community, class and schooling.* Halifax, NS: Fernwood Publishing.

James, C.E. (2012b). Strategies of engagement: how racialized faculty negotiate the university system. *Canadian Ethnic Studies, 44*(1), 133–52. doi: 10.1353/ces .2012.0007

James, C.E., & Taylor, L. (2008). "Education will get you to the Station": Marginalized students' experiences and perceptions of merit in accessing university. *Canadian Journal of Education/Revue Canadienne de l'Éducation, 31*(3), 567–90. https:// www.jstor.org/stable/20466716

Jones, S.H., Adams, T.E., & Ellis, C. (2013). *Handbook of autoethnography.* New York, NY: Routledge.

Ladson-Billings, G. (2005). The evolving role of critical race theory in educational scholarship. *Race Ethnicity and Education, 8*(1), 115–19. doi: 10.1080/13613320 52000341024

Ladson-Billings, G., & Tate, W.F. (2006). Toward a critical race theory of education. In A.D Dixson and C.K. Rousseau (Eds.), *Critical race theory in education: All God's children got a song* (pp. 11–30). New York, NY: Routledge.

Levin, B., & Reitzel, J.D. (2018). *Report to the nation: Hate crimes rise in US cities and counties in time of division and foreign interference.* Center for the Study of Hate and Extremism. https://csbs.csusb.edu/sites/csusb_csbs/files/2018%20Hate%20 Final%20Report%205-14.pdf

Lopez, A.E.I. (2005). *Implementing integrative anti-racist education: Negotiating conflicts and tensions utilizing experiential collaborative mentorship* (Doctoral dissertation, University of Toronto, ON). https://www.bac-lac.gc.ca/eng/services /theses/Pages/item.aspx?idNumber=75810136

Lorde, A. (1984). *Sister outsider: Essays and speeches.* Trumansburg, NY: Crossing Press.

Lynn, M., Yosso, T.J., Solórzano, D.G., & Parker, L. (2002). Critical race theory and education: Qualitative research in the new millennium. *Qualitative Inquiry, 8*(1), 3–6. doi: 10.1177/1077800402008001001

Mills, S., & Roque, S. (2019, September 18). Land acknowledgements: Uncovering an oral history of Tkaronto. *Local Love.* https://locallove.ca/issues/land -acknowledgements-uncovering-an-oral-history-of-tkaronto/#.Xt7kPkVKg2x

Mock, B. (2016, March 4). The long history of African Americans escaping to Canada. *Bloomburg CityLab.* https://www.citylab.com/transportation/2016/03 /the-long-history-of-african-americans-escaping-to-canada/472362/

Nayak, A. (2007). Critical whiteness studies. *Sociology Compass, 1*(2), 737–55. doi: 10.1111/j.1751-9020.2007.00045.x

Ontario Ministry of Education. (2008). *Realizing the promise of diversity: Ontario's equity and inclusive education policy.* Queens Printer for Ontario. http://www.edu.gov.on.ca/eng/policyfunding/equity.pdf

Shah, V. (2019). Calling in the self: Centering socially engaged Buddhism in critical pedagogy through personal narrative. *The International Journal of Critical Pedagogy, 10*(2), 19–43. http://libjournal.uncg.edu/ijcp/article/view/1898

Shultz, L., & Viczko, M. (Eds.). (2016). *Assembling and governing the higher education institution: Democracy, social justice and leadership in global higher education.* London, UK: Palgrave Macmillan.

Sleeter, C. (2016). Wrestling with problematics of whiteness in teacher education. *International Journal of Qualitative Studies in Education, 29*(8), 1065–8. doi: 10.1080/09518398.2016.1174904

Smith-Maddox, R., & Solórzano, D.G. (2002). Using critical race theory, Paulo Freire's problem-posing method, and case study research to confront race and racism in education. *Qualitative Inquiry, 8*(1), 66–84. doi: 10.1177/107780040200800105

Villegas, P.E., & Aberman, T. (2019). A double punishment: The context of postsecondary access for racialized precarious status migrant students in Toronto, Canada. *Refuge, 35*(1), 72–82. doi: 10.7202/1060676ar

Yosso, T.J., Parker, L., Solorzano, D.G., & Lynn, M. (2004). Chapter 1: From Jim Crow to affirmative action and back again: A critical race discussion of racialized rationales and access to higher education. *Review of Research in Education, 28*(1), 1–25. doi: 10.3102/0091732X028001001

Zembylas, M. (2012). Pedagogies of strategic empathy: Navigating through the emotional complexities of anti-racism in higher education. *Teaching in Higher Education, 17*(2), 113–25. doi: 10.1080/13562517.2011.611869

Zhou, S. (2017, May 23). Canada's university administrators must pay attention to right-wing activism on campus. *Academic Matters.* https://academicmatters.ca/canadas-university-administrators-must-pay-attention-to-right-wing-activism-on-campuses/

# PART III

# Decentring Discrimination

# 8 Canadian Indigenous Leadership for Social Justice in the Face of Social Group Apraxia: Renovating the State Colonization Built

MARLENE R. ATLEO, ?EH ?EH NAA TUU KᵂISS, AHOUSAHT FIRST NATION

Getting stuck in the dualities, in the oppositionalities that the colonial state has wrought, is the worldwide lot of Indigenous peoples. Over hundreds of years, the Western technology of education has reproduced these oppositions/dualities/polarities that deny *hisuk-ish-tsawalk*, or the "oneness/connectedness," of all things (E.R. Atleo, 2012), humanity and its surrounds. This has been accomplished through epistemic, institutional, and linguistic violence and genocide via the process of education (Adams, 1995). In this telling, I will begin by providing a case study of transformative leadership from the oral tradition of the people of the central west coast of Vancouver Island, a story of a territory materialized in the face of changing resource configurations. In an earlier examination of the storywork of the narrative (M.R. Atleo, 2001), an analytic framework was identified in which the structural and dynamic dimensions of the story could be viewed in light of more recent changing resource contexts to identify potential factors that reveal opportunities or create barriers for Indigenous transformative leadership. The whole is framed by the colonial evolution and elaboration of the Indian Act, which orchestrates the lives of Indigenous Canadians by means of a policy that is continuously altered as the conductors in Ottawa see fit to manage Indigenous Canadians in an evolving genocidal process (Woolford, 2021). By constantly revising its Indigenous policy, the Canadian state could be seen as operating in a condition termed "group apraxia" (Neal, 1990), a type of double consciousness (Du Bois, 1996) or two-eyed seeing (Archibald, 1997, 2008) wherein one way of seeing is based in "my interests/my systems" and the other in "their interest/their systems." The early Black American author W.E.B. Du Bois identified the nature of this sort of double consciousness as being constructed through the structural racism of American society. Du Bois identified the reification of this double consciousness of the Black person in 1904 before leaving for Ghana to free himself of that burden that was projected by but invisible to White people. Indigenous people, too, are shackled by centuries of "otherness."

As such, Indigenous people may be seen by the mainstream of Canadian society as not legitimately participating in Canadian society due to the dualities that operate at the core of the Canadian psyche, as argued by Neal (1990).

This chapter is a reflection on the existing barriers for Indigenous leaders that have curtailed their ability to liberate and create equities through the educational development of Indigenous people (M.R. Atleo, 2009). I offer this chapter as a witness in this examination of transformative leadership in Indigenous communities in an era of public calls for socio-economic reconciliation and Indigenization of education. I write as a participant and witness (Brant, 1994) to attempt to bring competing interpretations to light to get at the truth that is forever in the present and for Indigenous people forever in the past since time immemorial. It is part of the deep history with which Indigenous identity is culturally developed through storywork of territory, ancestors, song, dance, and language. For Indigenous people, the past and the present are one, simultaneously the past and the present: the embodied now or *Dasein* (Heidigger, 1962; Trimble, 1988, 2019). In this work, I am interested in illuminating the competing interpretations to build bridges of what works for the now of community, my children, grandchildren, and all my relations in the ambivalence of Canadian colonial mindsets. This dualism is evidenced by what is laterally called "structural racism" in, for example, policy (Daschuk, 2019) and education (Adams, 1995; Huff, 1997) resident in colonial institutions that have evolved with the founding impulse to keep Indigenous people subordinated through cultural institutions, language, law, and so forth. The current mechanism of this structural racism can be seen to be a lack of conscious acceptance of the historical facts of colonial social biases that have been enshrined in Canadian society, creating the group apraxia (Neal, 1990). Education is the mediating social and moral technology that can make a difference in providing social justice and equities.

This witness/reflection begins with a traditional story about an Indigenous transformative leader to better understand what it takes and "how he does it" to identify attributes of leadership and the heart of the means for success that includes the cultural socialization of the man (Keitlah, 1995). The story includes the context in which this leader achieves his goal and the ensuing social disruptions that arise in the face of structural upheaval. A series of contextualized examples follow to illustrate the barriers to transformative leadership across social domains in Canadian Indigenous lifeways.

## A *Nuu-chuh-nulth* Transformative Leader: How Does He Do It?

This 4,500-year-old story – according to the archaeological record (Marshall, 1993) – provides a rich glimpse into the social, economic, physical, and spiritual situation in which a young *hawith* (chief) finds himself, wherein he must lay everything aside and seek a completely new way of being, seeing, and doing through the trusted ritual practice of *oosumsh*. *Oosumsh* is the ritual practice of fasting and praying in a natural, sacred site (M.R. Atleo, 1998) that is understood to be part of the ecology of where the *hawith* expects the appearance of a new resource, in this case, the ocean, to reveal itself.

The young chief, Tsatsotalthmeek (he who may hunt [seal] in the margins), was discouraged by the lack of seals available for his household in his allocated hunting grounds on the outer shores of the large island in the Northwest Pacific Rim where his family had lived for millennia. He was surprised that the seals seemed to be disappearing. The *hahoothee* (lineage territory and resources) of his relative, Tséitlas (the feast giver), seemed to provide access to a much more favourable, seal-rich environment. But Tsatsotalthmeek was respectful of his elder brother's right to his territory, and so he turned to the ceremony of *oosumsh* (Wilson, 2009). First, he bathed in his *hahoothee* area to find a remedy in a new vision. Tsatsotalthmeek ritually scoured himself with hemlock to expunge his human smell that was repugnant to non-humans and immersed himself in the waters of his *hahoothee*. During his ceremonial bathing, a "Friendly Stranger" spoke to his heart, suggesting that he focus in a new direction to seek the answer to his household's needs and look to the waters that carried the dissolved traces of the surrounding environment, the silent messages of the plants and animals, the fish and the birds, the trees, the moss, and the ferns. Day after day, Tsatso-talthmeek opened his body in the water to their voices. Finally, after some time, he began to see wonders he had never seen before with new eyes, mentored, as he was, by the Friendly Stranger, who transformed his heart and sight by guiding his pursuit of knowledge. The young chief's reward was insight into the "High-way of Whales" through which *iihtuup* (whales) passed on their annual migrations from California to Alaska and back. He studied them, and with his wife by his side, he learned to call to them – to sing their songs, woo them, and bring them close. Communicating with the whales, thusly, he struck a social contract with them (Cullon, 2017), persuading them to submit themselves to him in exchange for recognition and respect in the form of adoration by the people and welcome into the territory. He shared his knowledge with his relatives so they could participate with him in the large canoe slicing through the offshore rollers. Tsatsotalthmeek was the first harpooner, the first Nuu-chah-nulth whaler.

Through this quest and the insight gained, Tsatsotalthmeek was transformed into a new man who culturally needed to mark the change with a new name. He became Umeek (a person who learns how to materialize his visions to serve his people), because he fervently embraced his responsibilities and rights, trusted the Creator, and engaged completely with his environment, following the Friendly Stranger to discover novel resources and solutions to help his people live. He was disoriented, but then by engaging with the dilemma he was transformed, not only by his recognition of this new resource, but through learning of its ways and means that allowed him to convey the practice to his relatives so that they might participate with him. He gained followers because one whale was worth the equivalent in meat and fat of about 3,000 seals (M.R. Atleo, 2001). It seemed miraculous. His personal transformation transformed the leadership dynamic that in turn transformed the community.

The chief's reorientation provided a new narrative for the community (M.R. Atleo, 2012b). His transformation led to its transformation. Then, when he and his crew started landing whales, additional relatives were astounded and sought to follow his lead. Umeek instituted a new social order that allowed many to participate on equitable footing in a new resource economy with the knowledge of whales, their habitat, and the necessary technology to hunt them. He was humble. He participated with his people. He was a transformative leader. He could now provide for his household and community with this whaling knowledge, and with this innovative technology, which meant a new social order reflecting the roles of the participants in the seats of the canoe. New songs came forth that celebrated this whaling knowledge with a new language. New dances came forth that commemorated his great deed so that it could be shared with others (M.R. Atleo, 2001).

## Oral Tradition, Archaeology, Survivance

Indigenous leadership stands for economic and social justice for the people, and the 4,500-year-old story of Umeek suggests that this has been a long-standing attribute of Indigenous leadership (Marshall, 1993). So how is it that for more than 500 years such leadership has been stymied continuously? In the face of the unknown and often unknowable forces from afar, it was impossible to gain a strategic upper hand in the colonial process. Traditional stories make it clear that the principles of socio-economic justice of equity, access, and participation, as well as inherent and achieved rights, were not foreign to Indigenous communities. Communities built on dialogue and consensus, even if leadership was hereditary, and were finely tuned to social and economic equities. Nuu-chah-nulth oral tradition (M.R. Atleo, 2001) features the story wherein a leader submitted himself to classic challenges to provide for his people, guided by cultural ceremonies and protocols (E.R. Atleo, 2004, 2012; M.R. Atleo, 2006). Leaders submitted themselves to the problem at hand in the environment (M.R. Atleo, 2008d) and gained insight (ʔeh ʔeh naa tuu kʷiss, 2020), developing cultural strategies (M.R. Atleo, 2012a, 2016a) by which they and their societies were transformed to provide survivance. *Survivance*, a word coined by Vizenor (2008), combining "survival" and "resistance," provides a unique articulation of Indigenous cultural strategies that create an Indigenous presence as a form of resistance rather than merely as an accommodation to or assimilation into a colonial strategy that results in self-erasure in the dualism of the colonial system (Du Bois, 1996). Survivance, as evoked here, requires unique strategies by which Indigenous leaders, embodying their socialization and learnings, submit themselves from infancy to this work of becoming a vehicle of provision for those who depend on them. This is not technology but a person in relationship to the people and the environmental context that they together occupy (Keitlah, 1995).

In the story of Umeek, for example, the original Umeek was later slain by his elder brother. The elder brother first suppressed his younger brother's success and later also slew his younger brother's son to suppress the knowledge that his younger brother brought to the community. But the new-found knowledge could not be denied. The braggart elder brother, who named himself "Getter with one spear-thrust," died of shame when he wavered in his whale hunt. The whaling continued as the knowledge became available to community members. The innovative whaling technology (large ten-man canoe, toggled spearhead and lanyard [*atlieu*], hunt models development in *oosumch*, etc.) and the whaling knowledge spread throughout the territory, orienting Nuu-chah-nulth people for millennia (M.R. Atleo, 2001).

Societal transformation in a changing resource environment required the deep engagement of one man who drew the whole community into changes at all levels of society. Without a deep engagement of community members in the resource environment that provides for their livelihood, acceptance of new ways and means arrived at through mere talk, even over prolonged periods of time, is no equivalent. Consequently, it is not surprising that after thirteen years of arduous and expensive treaty negotiations, contemporary Nuuchahn-ulth Nations leaders, participating with the provincial government of British Columbia and the Canadian federal governments in tri-partite treaty negotiations, cited "process issues, mandated issues, government actions or inactions, and lack of mandated dispute resolution as barriers within the process that limit their ability to accept treaties as they are currently presented" (Corfield, 2007, p. 109). Dialogue and negotiation were merely an opening gambit.

## Transformative Leadership

Transformative leadership is not merely mythological. In particular, the work of Shields (2011) has interrogated the nature of leadership that creates far-reaching liberating change that is transformative for communities and people. She has distinguished between institutionally bound transactional and transformational and transformative leadership with a nuanced institutional approach in education. Both transactional and transformational leadership elaborate upon existing institutions and make them more complex, thereby developing people and structures for reproduction, effectiveness, and improvement therein. Transformative leadership reaches beyond the institution for the ideals of an elusive social democracy, with the plain sight of pragmatism that is tuned to equity and social justice. The work of that reach is deep and wide, dealing with the inter-sectorial issues in moral and ethical ways that create emancipation from oppressive structures. That reach beyond is to embrace the dynamics of culture through new diachronic synergies and synchronicities to maintain wholeness that is at the same time liberatory in the context of an ever-evolving social justice. The means of such holistic change is facilitated through dialogue in social co-creation that is more than just talk (Shields & Edwards, 2004).

## Exposing Dualism

To achieve this end, in this chapter I attempt to call out the ambivalence that is created by dualistic mindsets/two-eyed seeing (M.R. Atleo, 2001), terrorizing dualities (Shields, Bishop, & Mazawi, 2004), de-legitimating curricula (Goddard, 1997), and dominance in health care (M.R. Atleo, 1997) to carve out a space for holistic thinking in which all is one, *hisuk-ish-tsawalk* (E.R. Atleo, 2004), and in which there can be justice of multiplicities (Tully, 1995) because we are all in the same canoe. To begin to achieve such an outcome, the revelations of the Nuu-chah-nulth ancestor, Umeek, have been presented through the lens of a storywork methodology. This framework is based on the insight gained from an analysis of this 4,500-year-old story in a finite territory. By using a structural and dynamic analysis through storywork (M.R. Atleo, 2001), the "barbaric civilization" (Powell, 2011) of the colonial evolution of Canada in the context of ensuing group apraxia (Neal, 1990) can potentially freeze-frame the ambivalence caused by dualism. There is potential to expose how Indigenous Canadian transformative leadership is prevented from materializing by exposing the dualisms.

## A Colonial Legacy

The legacy of colonization (Miller, 1996; Powell, 2011) effectively has and continues to create barriers between the Indigenous cultural understanding of traditional environments and those based on Western worldviews and increasingly in a context of globalized systems of governance and environmental degradation. In the face of such structural constraints, Indigenous Canadians have attempted to transform through both assimilation and accommodation, finding little to no fit. In the face of pressures of democratization and the interests of equities and social justice, dialogue is increasingly the route to develop relationships; break barriers; build understanding, community, and trust; and have fun, thereby creating a common discourse in which to live and educate future generations (Shields & Edwards, 2004).

In 1966, Harry Hawthorn, a New Zealander by birth, an educator of Māori children, and then an anthropologist working in Canada, exposed the fault line with his *Survey of the Contemporary Indians of Canada: Economic, Political, Educational Needs and Policies*. Hawthorn provided empirical evidence of the marginalization and poverty of Status Indians across Canada, calling them "citizens minus." The Government of Canada (1969) responded with a White Paper that was the policy response of the P.E. Trudeau government

(1968–70) that proposed to (1) eliminate Indian Status, (2) abolish the Indian Act, (3) convert reserve land to fee simple ownership, (4) decentralized and devolve responsibility for Indians to the provinces to harmonize service systems, (5) support economic development with funding, (6) negotiate outstanding land and treaty claims, and (7) dissolve the Indian Affairs department since the problem would be solved. The policy development that intended to "free" Status Indians and make them self-sufficient is well documented by Weaver (1993). The Indian Chiefs of Alberta (1970) responded with a statement, countering with the treaty chiefs' position that rights-based treaties trumped the power of the Canadian state.

Fifty years later, Indian Status has been more highly differentiated and elaborated in ways that increase the "citizens minus" through initiatives that "repatriated" children and grandchildren of those who "lost" or had to relinquish their status by "voluntary" enfranchisement and through marriage to non-Indian males. And while Métis are not under the Indian Act, they have also been recognized with Inuit peoples as "Aboriginal" under the 1982 Constitution Act. Instead of disappearing, the Indian population under the Indian Act has increased!

In the counterproposal by the Indian Chiefs of Alberta (1970) – also known as the Red Paper – treaties were identified as the source of sufficiency in home territories that supported people in community relations with each other and with the environment, and opened the floodgates of Indian active public discontent. This discontent had been growing throughout the 1960s in the US and Canada. By 1970, the American Indian Movement (AIM) had already been actively organizing to raise awareness about the termination policy that had emptied reserves in the US starting in the mid-1940s into the 1960s and had sent people to urban centres to work in industry as part of an ongoing assimilation and civilization program. AIM members were now travelling across Canada warning of the termination policy that the Americans had pursued and the displacement it had caused. Through the "moccasin telegraph," Canadian Indians organizing as Red Power (Lannon, 2013) were increasingly aware of the effects of termination on communities, language, culture, families, and children, and they targeted the K–12 education system, which could be the key to conserving culture (Davis, 2013; Huff, 1997). These policies were proposed in Canada in direct response to the termination policy in the US, which even President Nixon would come to ask Congress to repeal because he saw the negative fallout (Nixon, 1970). Termination was a failure in the US, even as Canada proposed the same agenda.

The group apraxia (Neal, 1990) of such policymaking demonstrates an unconscious mental break in mainstream society and its social institutions that preclude the very "bootstrapping" expected from the "lazy Indian." Group apraxia could then be used by non-Indigenous society to hypothesize a failure of

Indigenous people to "evolve" based on the commonly held notion of Darwinian evolutionary theory. However, the power of law, the police, and the military compelled Indigenous people to comply with a colonial system that evolved in the grip of bureaucrats with little relief in the suppression of Indigenous agency.

In the face of such a system, Canadian society had only begun to question a break from the historical reality through the Royal Commission on Aboriginal Peoples (RCAP) that arose from the 1990 Oka Crisis. The Oka Crisis was a land dispute that shone the spotlight on the divide of values between the Quebec government and the Mohawk peoples with a seventy-eight-day standoff between Mohawks and the Sûreté du Québec resulting in a fatality that shook Canadians out of their complacency (CBC Archives, 2000). The subsequent five volume *Report of the Royal Commission on Aboriginal Peoples* (1996) outlined an ambitious process of reconciliation that would span twenty years. While the document might have represented a federal government commitment, twenty years later, Paul Chartrand, one of the original commissioners, suggested that RCAP provided a template for change that should be used by the new Liberal government to create positive change since the previous Conservative governments had done little to advance the agenda (Carleton University, 2016). The document may have been aspirational, but the recommendations were and still are well out of reach. Another RCAP commissioner, Viola Robinson, a Mi'kmaq from Nova Scotia, remarked that the most heart-wrenching aspect of the process was collecting the stories of residential schools.

This brought us to next government research project, the Indian Residential School Truth and Reconciliation Commission (2009–15) led by commissioners Justice Murray Sinclair, Dr. Marie Wilson, and Chief Wilton Littlechild, who spent their mandate travelling to public gatherings across Canada from sea to sea to sea, listening to and documenting the stories of those who as children had attended residential schools. Lest we forget, schooling was highly desired by Indigenous peoples of the land, but it was not available to them until recently (Miller, 1996). The Truth and Reconciliation Commission (TRC) provided Canada an education through its action research project; commissioners elicited Survivor memories that came alive in the media, education system, and research programming that raised awareness of the facts of the government treatment of generations of Indigenous children. Consequently, ceremonial and community healing activities were writ large in the process of Indigenous work towards reconciliation. Unfortunately, engagement was by Indigenous communities with little buy in from non-Indigenous Canadians. The repository of the data and materials gathered, the activities engaged in by the commissioners, all the Survivor testaments, and all donated materials are in a searchable archive at the University of Manitoba's National Centre for Truth and Reconciliation (nctr.ca).

## Suffer the Little Children

But we were not yet finished. The First Nations Child and Family Caring Society (FNCFCS) was established by Indigenous social workers to advocate between governments and First Nations families and children. The FNCFCS spokesperson, Cindy Blackstone, a Gitxsan social worker and child and youth advocate, exposed the inequities that the "citizens minus" are yoked with from the day they are born, pointing out the high potential of such children being seized from their mothers before they even leave the hospital – mothers who, because of their racialization, are deemed "at-risk" (FNCFCS, n.d.). Which leads us to the devaluation of Indigenous mothers, the backbone of Indigenous communities (M.R. Atleo, 2016a) since it is Indigenous women who beget Indigenous children. The fallacy continues that if Indigenous children are taken away from their mothers at birth they will somehow be "saved." It seems only logical, then, that reducing the number of children in care is possible by reducing the number of reproducing Indigenous women.

## Missing and Murdered Indigenous Women and Girls

What followed was the 2015–19 National Inquiry into Missing and Murdered Indigenous Women and Girls (MMIWG) led by commissioners Marian Buller, Michèle Audette, Brian Euolfson, and Qajaq Robinson who, in the engagement style of the TRC, met with the families of the murdered and missing women (CBC Archives, 2000). The meetings were both traumatizing and cathartic for Indigenous people, but the stark facts of the commissioners' investigation was a system of racism so blatant they could only label it as genocidal in their supplementary report (National Inquiry into Missing and Murdered Indigenous Women and Girls, 2019). They suggest that there exists a genocidal system in Canada in which there is ancient inertia and a resistance that still precludes the real valuing of inclusive and supportive environments as it affects Indigenous Canadians. This long-lived inertia raises the spectre of group apraxia (Neal, 1990) in which the government and its institutions, as well as the Canadian public, are fundamentally deaf and ignorant to the true needs for the well-being of Indigenous people.

Group apraxia fits with the way Lyotard (2004) speaks to the issue of what Canadians do with their basic desires and impulses when there is such conflict in society that denies what is happening to Indigenous people for such a long time. How can the plight of Indigenous people be hidden for centuries under different circumstances and conditions? Lyotard (2004) would suggest that there is shadow-work to be done by Canadians that deals with deep epistemic angst around economies that include reproduction, sexuality, and property. These are areas to which MMIWG's final and supplementary reports speak loudly. Canadian public discourse has not found the words or social ways of organizing the unconscious desire to deal with the dissonance in which Canadians find themselves in the face of undefined Indigenous inherent rights under the 1982 Constitution Act. The education system has historically not dealt with this level of learning or even disclosed it. It forms part of the "shadow-work" of the Canadian psyche, the hidden work of the unconscious. It is not enough to promise Indigenous Canadians welfare-to-work programs in which they are expected to shed their identities that are tied to territories and histories. Mezirow (2000) had glimpsed Black women transforming when they went to college to engage in welfare-to-work programs in which they shed old identities with the promise of new ones that allowed them into the socio-economic structures of the era. As with these Black women, there are adult programs without end to reduce socio-economic ills by training Indigenous people to integrate into the Canadian system. However, the outcomes do not deliver access to social justice and resource equities. If the programming goal is transformation and the transformation does not move people towards social justice but merely towards institutional goals, then the learning is not necessarily transformative but merely transactional (Shields, 2010). There is still little in the Canadian system to reduce the barriers to truly transformative change, especially for Indigenous leadership, in large part because of the lack of structural change to provide the affordances that would allow Indigenous articulation in the duality of the Canadian mind and institutional structures. The group apraxia could recognize such issues at the public/social level, but at the private/intimate level the desires are still unorganized affective territories. There is a lack of knowledge, understanding, experience – a lack of sharing of being, of *Dasein* – by both parties. The reconciliatory aims of the TRC, for instance, are still at a great distance.

## Superficial Indigenous Trappings: Material Culture = YES, Indigenous People = NO

Canadian society has shifted from hiding Indigenous people on reserves and residential schools to releasing the ephemera of the vanishing race like fireflies onto the air everywhere for the world to see as, for example, in British Columbia. The state has developed a strategy of spectacle and public showcases objectivizing, exoticizing, and eroticizing Indigenous cultures, including their ceremonial objects and traditional stories (e.g., Bill Reid's "The Spirit of Haida Gwaii: The Jade Canoe" sculpture installed in the heart of the Vancouver International Airport [Bringhurst, 1991]), languages (e.g., signage along the Olympic route from the Vancouver International Airport to Whistler), and territorial acknowledgments by institutions and politicians and formal activities of all sorts (see Howell, 2017) that are merely aspiration belying the legal, economic, and social realities of the relationships between Indigenous communities and non-Indigenous Canada at all levels, education systems, the economy, research, and innovation. Achievement awards are given to Indigenous people who excel in their articulation of the values of Canadian institutions, and millions of dollars in scholarships and bursaries for Indigenous post-secondary students are provided by governments, corporations, and individuals through the charity Indspire for the future of Indigenous participation in Canadian society (indspire.ca). The National Indian Brotherhood gave up its spirit with the repatriation of the 1982 Constitution Act in exchange for the recognition of Aboriginal rights to emerge as the Assembly of First Nations (AFN). The transformation was in name only. The AFN became an official national and provincial advocacy organization of Indian Act band chiefs to play an intermediary role between federal and provincial governments and band governments. The Canadian Museum for Human Rights (CMHR) in Winnipeg, the self-proclaimed centre of the North American continent (CMHR, n.d.) and champion of human rights, could not bring itself to acknowledge the ongoing Indigenous genocide in Canada, even with genocidal studies elaborated to include colonization of groups as pre-genocide activity (Woolford, 2021). Even when genocide was affirmed by the MMIWG report (2019), the CMHR could not stand for the social injustice. In the face of such dissonance between Indigenous staff and the administration, the CEO resigned under allegations of racism, sexism, and discrimination in administrative practice (Canadian Press, 2020).

Using phenomenological orienteering across worldviews as an analytic tool (M.R. Atleo, 2012b), structural oppressions and power issues as they relate to the potential of Indigenous leaders to become transformative leaders (Shields, 2013, p. 22) in the face of dominant institutional social systems maintaining the status quo are readily recognizable. With a public theme of reconciliation heralded by the educational systems of Canadian society and government, based on the recommendations of the TRC, it will be interesting to see if there are indeed changes that constitute the reconciliation of settlers and Indigenous people in what constitutes equities and social justice to elaborate a democracy in which there is room for inclusive living.

## Tools of Oppression

Law, education, health care, fisheries, and social programs can all be used to illustrate relational tools for oppression and development. In my daily life, as well as in my research and practice, I run into the invisible walls these programs create. I use some of these examples to illustrate barriers to transformative leadership. In the late 1980s, my master's research was inspired by my outrage about a land claim ruling against the Dunna Za (Treaty 8) made by Justice Addy, who maintained that the First Nation people did not plan, but only thought about their daily needs as they arose (M.R. Atleo, 1993). In my formal and personal life, as a member of the Ahousaht House of *Klaaqishpeethl* and as a member of a potlatching family, I have participated in planning over lifespan and community cycles that were decades-long, referencing stories and experiences that moved into ceremony and diachronic time in which long historical and future time frames were referenced.

In the Dunna Za instance, it was a case of the rule of law being administered by Justice Addy, a powerful professional ignorant of the people on whom he was passing judgment. Planning is a human competency that looks different in the face of power, a lack of resources, or contextualization (Fauconnier, 1997; Forester, 1974; Friedman, Scholnick, & Cocking, 1987; Randall, 1987). Not only did Addy's lack of education about the culture and lifestyle of Dunna Za lead to a lack of moral imagination (Gaztambide-Fernandez & Sears, 2005; Lakoff & Johnson, 1999), but that lack made him blind to their ancient means of planning for the future (Turner & Fauconnier, 1999), creating a legal injustice over which they had no control. Even Justice McEachern, who ruled against the Gitxsan in 1991 in *Delgamuukw vs British Columbia*, a ruling that was overturned twice in the higher courts, acknowledged that it was the only way Addy *could* have ruled because he had no training or knowledge about Indigenous worldviews, lifeways, history, and inherent Indigenous rights (E.R. Atleo, personal communication, 1992).

## Day Schools: The Legacy on Reserves in the Face of Bureaucratic Power

As a young mother, my husband and I played host to a gathering of superintendents of education from the Department of Indian and Northern Affairs in our home. They suggested that a new Indigenous teacher might do well going to his home community to teach in the day school there. These superintendents had the power to make such decisions because they hired and fired school staff across the province. The communities had no say about who came to instruct their children. Assimilative forces were hard at work here. The newly minted Indigenous teacher was keen to go home to infiltrate the school system to provide cultural connections in the community school. The tensions inherent in such a position, however, were challenging in their contradictions. Those tensions and contradictions continue even now.

Recently, the Day Schools (McLean) Class Action and the Day Scholars (Gottfriedson) Class Action suits are seeing ex-students seeking compensation for the assimilationist processes experienced during their schooling (see justicefordayscholars.com). Community professionals and paraprofessionals have administered the local K–12 school in a "self-government" agreement. However, on-reserve schools are still required to teach the provincial curriculum. The local traditional language is now just beginning to be legitimately integrated across the curriculum fifty years later. While the young Indigenous teacher/principal managed the school, he was still subject to the provincial curriculum and the Indian Affairs regime that sent in teachers who often did not fit into the community very well. Teachers who were citizens of the British Commonwealth could teach without local certification because they worked for the federal schools through Indian and Northern Affairs based on their membership in the Commonwealth. In our community, there were teachers from Hong Kong, India, South Africa, and Bermuda, to mention just a few. Some of the teachers had strong accents that the children could not understand. Some of them had mental health problems that were exacerbated by the remoteness and isolation of the community, as well as the strain of the cross-cultural communication demands of the classroom. As such, some teachers became a liability to the school and the community, in part because there was little medical support except by "fly-in" doctors and nurses from Health Canada who service reserves across Canada. In these circumstances, there was little opportunity or inclination to provide leadership to make progressive change because it was hard enough to maintain basic order and legitimately infuse a limited amount of local culture. During my frequent stints of "supply teaching" in that situation, for which I had no training or certification, the superintendent explained that it was more important to essentially socialize children into the "hidden curriculum" of schooling, such as regular attendance, respect for authority, sitting quietly, being orderly, developing listening skills, and behaving in the classroom. Managing children, rather than educating them, was the agenda. At one point, this superintendent even said that we should be happy that 4 per cent of our students were at that time graduating from Grade 12.

## Indigenous Bodies Are to Be Colonized: Immunizations, Nutrition, Pre-natal Health

Mission hospitals were sprinkled over the country and supported by governments, especially if they served the interests of both the local Indigenous and non-Indigenous communities. Those communities were fortunate because most small communities had little to no medical services (M.R. Atleo, 2012a). My younger son was born in such a facility that served the Central Region Coast in British Columbia in the early 1970s. The hospital furnishings were austere, the food was plain, and the medical staff was competent. Local people did the housekeeping, cooking, maintenance, and volunteering while the nurses and doctors were hired from away. Maternal and child health, as well as community immunization, was an important focus (Culhane Speck, 1987; Kelm, 1999). When things went wrong in these small hospitals, they could go very wrong, especially with the added possibility of cross-cultural miscommunication. Such was the case when a child died of a burst appendix while in the care of an alcoholic doctor and a team of Filipina nurses in Alert Bay in 1979, resulting in a provincial inquest that documented the case as an "error in judgement" (Culhane Speck, 1987). That racialization as a barrier to effective health care was recognized as a major fault line in the medical services that led to that death. The medicalization of Indigenous bodies was still about keeping the non-Indigenous community healthy.

In the mid-1980s, there was a shift to tribal councils that were organizing politically to take on self-governance in administering services devolving from the federal and provincial governments (M.R. Atleo, 2012a). As these administrative entities developed capacity, some tribes hired nurses and socialized them culturally through workshops and community experience to meet community needs. The

Indigenous Community Health Representatives (CHRs) were no longer funded because they were no longer relevant in those professionally evolving contexts. The bureaucratic shifts required continuous adaptation by communities that were used to adapting to environments that were visible, but not ones that were socially constructed at a distance and without their ability to engage with the changes first-hand, even as their lives depended on learning in context. The adaptive energies that are needed to keep up with the bi- and tri-polar nature of Canadian political governance (Liberal–Conservative–NDP) that is enacted as policy keep Indigenous leadership fully engaged in a transformative leadership modality that is designed to adapt Indigenous communities to Canadian settler mindsets, right down to the cul-de-sac town sites required in community plans to meet eligibility requirements for funding. As in post–Second World War colonial states, social and mental domination continues, as does socio-economic underdevelopment and poverty.

## Needed: A New Orientation

We started with the Nuu-chah-nulth traditional story of the transformation of Umeek and his subsequent transformative leadership that changed the economic orientation and social structure of his community. Orientation to the resources changed the community that over millennia became an elaborated potlatching society. It took mere decades of global over-exploitation of whales to drive the whales and the Indigenous people of the coast close to extinction. And while salmon has always been a backup and staple on the West Coast of Canada, the global industrial whaling economy was eclipsed by an industrial salmon economy. Indigenous peoples of the coast had always relied on an annual cycle of salmon as their staple. They had a relationship with salmon that was intimate and mythologically embedded in their territories (Cullon, 2017), as had been the whales. As the salmon economy seemed to be going the way of the whaling economy, and seeing the writing on the wall, the Ahousaht First Nation was one of the few Indigenous groups that demanded access to the fish on which the communities are dependent for survival (see Canadian Press, 2013). By winning this court case, Ahousaht hereditary chiefs now manage their local fisheries for home-use salmon, halibut, and cod. These fish are distributed to community members and paid for by own-source income from taxation of open pen fish farm operations. It also allows fishers to sell their catch on the open market. The catch, timing, and quotas are still being negotiated with Fisheries and Oceans Canada, which has oversight of the whole fishing industry.

Increasingly, knowledge about and by Indigenous peoples has become part of the provincially managed K–12 public school curriculum (Gaztambide-Fernandez & Sears, 2005; Goddard, 1997). Now, too, provincial governments are supporting the integration of traditional Indigenous knowledges and practices into their professional curricula at the post-secondary level because students graduating into their membership will be working with Indigenous populations in all walks of life. Indigenous knowledges are becoming increasingly desirable, as the diversity they produce is deemed especially valuable for environmental sustainability in the face of climate change (M.R. Atleo 1998, 2006, 2008a; 2008b; 2008c; 2008d; 2012c; 2020). Supportive research to legitimize Indigenous practices has been at the forefront more recently with revitalization and health practices (M.R. Atleo, 2012a; M.R. Atleo & Fitznor, 2010; Battiste, 1986; Norris, 2004; Shaw, 2004), as well as legal approaches becoming top-funded university agendas for Indigenization. However, most of the work being done is still dominated by non-Indigenous professionals.

Until both Indigenous leaders and Canadian non-Indigenous leaders, as well as their constituents, can understand the collective Canadian interdictions against Indigenous peoples, there is, as Neal (1990) maintained, no basis for reconciliation. Reconciliation is impossible without structural de-racialization. That state requires an awakening of people from all walks of life in Canadian society. Last week, the granddaughter of my first cousin by marriage was shot five times by the RCMP during a wellness check in New Brunswick (Shakeri, 2020). The calculated superiority of Canada was shattered afresh! The Canadian Senate Subcommittee on Diversity has called for major structural change. Prime Minister Trudeau has acknowledged the racialized nature of Canada's institutions in press briefings on national television. The wellspring of protest has erupted into a groundswell! Negotiation seems to be required posthaste!

But to live with each other together in one society requires a dialogical path that needs the negotiation of the group apraxia (M.R. Atleo, 2016b) and the "shadow." Such dialogue must allow empathy for everyone involved – an understanding of the respective roots of professional and policy thinking so that a mutuality can develop to create new spaces in which to dwell, exposing the grand historical narratives that are foundational to each and through which the dualities arise. There are increasing numbers of articulate Indigenous people who return to school as adults (M.R. Atleo, 2012a), who are persistent in the face of racism (Garcia, 1999), and who, if nurtured culturally, are protected from suicide (Chandler & Lalonde, 2000); from their many walks of life, these individuals can meaningfully participate in articulating the ways of change. The institutions that have been the guardians of change need to be able to dismantle barriers and work with those Indigenous people who can negotiate a common ground so that all can live.

Indigenous people must have their own institutions that honour their languages, histories, and all aspects of their cultures, and they must have access to territories to reclaim and revive worldviews that hold the keys to success. Cultures and languages that have developed and survived over millennia have infinite value in the face of the future. Health, nutrition, childrearing, and community-making were all geared to survivance of Indigenous people until the disruption came – a disruption that stripped away what was of value, leaving death and destruction in its wake. However, Indigenous peoples have always remembered their histories. My Ahousaht *tyee* (head chief) Earl George (2005) always said, "We have very long memories. Memories that are longer than any Canadian settler." It is time for partnerships with Indigenous lives to deconstruct the oppression. Communities can legitimately say how it should be done because they embody what keeps them stuck. Non-Indigenous people need to learn to listen to the complex traumas that have been inscribed on Indigenous bodies and psyches.

Indigenous people are dying to transform while mainstream settler society continues to envision Indigenous people as ghosts of the past – as stereotypes perpetuated by the status quo. The examples provided in this chapter demonstrate a few of the barriers that exist in every aspect of Indigenous life. Education across disciplines and professions, from early years throughout the lifespan, is key, as it is the social technology that mediates the curriculum of the nation-state, its policies, professions, laws, practices, and accreditations. Non-Indigenous citizens of Canada must participate in the decolonization of Canadian education before true reconciliation can occur. Until we can together deconstruct each other culturally in a more complex union that meets everyone's needs so that we may reconstruct ourselves in a process of Canadian citizenship that some might call reconciliation, we are stuck in a ghost dance. Good intentions are not enough. To paraphrase James Tully (1995), we are all in the canoe together.

## REFERENCES

ʔeh ʔeh naa tuu kʷiss (Atleo, M.R.) (2020). Nuučaan̓uł plants and habitats, as reflected in oral traditions: Since Raven and Thunderbird roamed. In N. Turner, (Ed.), *Plants, people and places: The roles of ethnobotany and ethnoecology in Indigenous peoples land rights in Canada and beyond* (pp. 51–64). Montreal, QC: McGill-Queen's University Press.

Adams, D.W. (1995). *Education for extinction: American Indians and the boarding school.* Lawrence, KS: University Press of Kansas.

Archibald, J-A. (1997). *Coyote learns to make a story basket: The place of First Nations stories in education* (Unpublished doctoral dissertation). Simon Fraser University, Burnaby, BC.

Archibald, J-A. (2008). *Indigenous storywork: Educating the heart, mind, body, and spirit.* Vancouver, BC: UBC Press.

Atleo, E.R. (2004). *Tsawalk: A Nuu-chah-nulth worldview.* Vancouver, BC: UBC Press.

Atleo, E.R. (2012). *Principles of tsawalk: An Indigenous approach to global crisis.* Vancouver, BC: UBC Press.

Atleo, M.R. (1993). *The effects of social role attitudes on the planning behaviour of First Nations mothers* (Unpublished master's thesis). University of British Columbia, Vancouver, BC.

Atleo, M.R. (1997). First Nations healing: Dominance or health? *The Canadian Journal for the Study of Adult Education, 11*(2), 63–77.

Atleo, M.R. (1998). Hishuk-ish-ts'awalk: The role of sacred sites in the embodiment of the territories of Nuu-chah-nulth First Nations [Abstract]. In *"Natural" sacred sites: Cultural diversity and biological diversity* (p. 7). Paris, France: UNESCO. https://unesdoc.unesco.org/ark:/48223/pf0000113456

Atleo, M.R. (2001). *Learning models in the Umeek narratives: Identifying an educational framework through storywork with First Nations elders* (Unpublished doctoral dissertation). University of British Columbia, Vancouver, BC.

Atleo, M.R. (2006). The ancient Nuu-chah-nulth strategy of hahuulthi: Education for Indigenous cultural survivance. *The International Journal of Environmental, Cultural, Economic, and Social Sustainability, 2*(1), 153–62. doi: 10.18848/1832-2077/CGP/v02i01/54158

Atleo, M.R. (2008a). Decolonizing Canadian Aboriginal health and social services from the inside out: A case study – The Ahousaht Holistic Society. In K. Knopf (Ed.), *Aboriginal Canada revisited* (pp. 42–61). Ottawa, ON: University of Ottawa Press.

Atleo, M.R. (2008b). Indigenous learning models in the context of socio-economic change: A storywork approach. In W. Heber (Ed.), *Indigenous education: Asia/Pacific* (pp. 21–32). Regina, SK: Indigenous Studies Research Centre, First Nations University.

Atleo, M.R. (2008c). Strategies for equities in Indigenous education: A Canadian First Nations case study. In A. de Oliveira, (Ed.), *Routledge studies in anthropology: Decolonizing Indigenous rights* (pp. 132–64). London, UK: Routledge.

Atleo, M.R. (2008d). Watching to see until it becomes clear to you: Metaphorical mapping – A method for emergence. *International Journal of Qualitative Studies in Education, 21*(3), 221–33. https://doi.org/10.1080/09518390801998338

Atleo, M.R. (2009). Understanding Aboriginal learning ideology through storywork with elders. *Alberta Journal of Educational Research, 55*(4), 452–67.

Atleo, M.R. (2012a). Adult health education and practice: Working with Aboriginal people. In L. English (Ed.), *Adult education and health* (pp. 90–106). Toronto, ON: University of Toronto Press.

Atleo, M.R. (2012b, April). *Phenomenological orienteering, metaphoric mapping, Indigenous knowing: Across worldviews.* Paper presented at the meeting of the American Educational Research Association, Vancouver, BC.

Atleo, M.R. (2012c). Storywork of place: Ecotourism and literacies for Indigenous adults. In G. Williams (Ed.), *Talking back, talking forward: Journeys in transforming Indigenous educational practice* (pp. 92–106). Darwin, Australia: Charles Darwin University Press.

Atleo, M.R. (2013). The zone of Canadian Aboriginal adult education: A social movement approach. In T. Nesbit, S.M. Brigham, N. Taber, & T. Gibb, (Eds.) *Building on critical traditions: Adult education and learning in Canada* (pp. 39–50). Toronto, ON: Thompson Publishers.

Atleo, M.R. (2016a). All my relations: Networks of First Nations/Métis/Inuit women sharing the learnings. In D.E. Clover, S. Butterwick, & L. Collins (Eds.), *Women, adult education, and leadership in Canada: Inspiration, passion, and commitment* (pp. 33–44). Mississauga, ON: Thompson Publishing.

Atleo, M.R. (2016b). Committing apraxia: Understanding our own praxis in contexts of diversity and Indigenization in particular. In L. Lane & R. McGray (Eds.), *Proceedings of the 35th CASAE/ACEEA Annual Conference* (pp. 337–9). Calgary, AB: University of Calgary.

Atleo, M.R., & Fitznor, L. (2010). Aboriginal educators discuss recognizing, reclaiming, and revitalizing their multi competences in heritage/English language usage. *Canadian Journal of Native Education, 32*, 13–34, 154.

Battiste, M.A. (1986). Micmac literacy and cognitive assimilation. In J. Barman, Y. Hebert, & D. McCaskill (Eds.), *Indian education in Canada, Vol. 1: The legacy* (pp. 23–44). Vancouver, BC: UBC Press.

Brant, B. (1994). *Writing as witness: Essay and talk*. Toronto, ON: Women's Press Literary.

Bringhurst, R. (1991). *The Black Canoe: Bill Reid and the Spirit of Haida Gwaii*. Vancouver, BC: Douglas & McIntyre.

Canadian Museum for Human Rights (CMHR). (n.d.). *About us*. https://humanrights.ca/about-us

Canadian Press. (2013, July 4). B.C. First Nation awarded right to commercial fishery after court fight. *CTV News*. https://www.ctvnews.ca/canada/b-c-first-nation-awarded-right-to-commercial-fishery-after-court-fight-1.1352846

Canadian Press. (2020, June 25). Museum of Human Rights CEO resigns after allegations of systemic racism. *canoe.com*. https://canoe.com/news/national/museum-of-human-rights-ceo-resigns-after-allegations-of-systemic-racism

Carleton University. (2016, June 10). *Paul Chartrand reflects on the continuing struggle for Indigenous rights* [Press release]. https://carleton.ca/fpa/2016/paul-chartrand-reflects-continuing-struggle-indigenous-rights/

CBC Archives. (2000). *Revisiting the Oka Crisis of 1990*. CBC-TV. https://www.cbc.ca/player/play/1558491458

Chandler, M.J., & Lalonde, C. (2000). Cultural continuity as a protective factor against suicide in First Nations youth. *Lifenotes: A Suicide Prevention and Community Health Newsletter, 5*(1), 10–11.

Corfield, M.M. (2007). *A First Nations leadership perspective on the British Columbia treaty process* (Unpublished doctoral dissertation). University of Phoenix, AZ.

Culhane Speck, D. (1987). *An error in judgement: The politics of medical care in an Indian/White community.* Vancouver, BC: Talonbooks.

Cullon, D.A. (2017). *Dancing salmon: Human-fish relationships on the Northwest Coast* (Unpublished doctoral dissertation). University of Victoria, BC.

Daschuk, J. (2019). *Clearing the plains: Disease, politics of starvation, and the loss of Indigenous life* (2nd ed.). Regina, SK: University of Regina Press.

Davis, J. (2013). *Survival schools: The American Indian movement and community education in the Twin Cities.* Minneapolis, MN: University of Minnesota Press.

Du Bois, W.E.B. (1996). *The souls of Black folks.* New York, NY: Penguin Books. (Original work published in 1903)

Fauconnier, G. (1997). *Mappings in thought and language.* London, UK: Cambridge University Press.

First Nations Child and Family Caring Society (FNCFCS). (n.d.). *About us.* https://fncaringsociety.com/about-us

Forester, J. (1974). *Planning in the face of power.* Berkley, CA: University of California Press.

Friedman, S.L, Scholnick, E.K., & Cocking, R.R. (1987). Reflections on reflections: What planning is and how it develops. In S.L. Friedman, E.K. Scholnick, & R.R. Cocking (Eds.), *Blueprints for thinking: The role of planning in cognitive development* (pp. 515–34). London, UK: Cambridge University Press.

Garcia, F.M. (1999). *Native American warriors in education: Journeys of persistence, stories from the heart* (Unpublished doctoral dissertation). Montana State University, Bozeman, MT.

Gaztambide-Fernandez, R.A., & Sears, J.T. (Eds.) (2005). *Curriculum work as a public moral enterprise.* Landham, MD: Roman & Littlefield.

George, E. (2005). *Living on the edge: Nuu-Chah-Nulth history from an Ahousaht Chief's perspective.* Victoria, BC: Sono Nis Press.

Goddard, T.J. (1997). Reversing the spirit of delegitimation. *Canadian Journal of Native Studies, 17*(2), 215–25.

Government of Canada. (1969). *Statement of the Government of Canada on Indian Policy, 1969.* Indian and Northern Affairs Canada. https://publications.gc.ca/collections/collection_2014/aadnc-aandc/R32-2469-eng.pdf

Hawthorn, H.B. (Ed.) (1966). *A survey of the contemporary Indians of Canada: Economic, political, educational needs and policies* (Vol. 1). Ottawa, ON: Indian and Northern Affairs. http://caid.ca/HawRep1a1966.pdf

Heidigger, M. (1962). *Being and time.* New York, NY: Harper & Row.

Howell, M. (2017, February 6). Activists target "Welcome to Vancouver" signs with First Nations message. *Vancouver Is Awesome.* https://www.vancouveris awesome.com/courier-archive/opinion/activists-target-welcome-to-vancouver -signs-with-first-nations-message-3046415

Huff, D.J. (1997). *To live heroically: Institutional racism and American Indian education*. New York, NY: University of New York Press.

Indian Chiefs of Alberta. (1970). *Citizens plus*. Edmonton, AB: Indian Association of Alberta.

Keitlah, W. (1995). *Wawaaciakuk yaqwiiʔitquuʔas: The sayings of our first people*. Penticton, BC: Theytus Books.

Kelm, M.E. (1999). *Colonizing bodies: Aboriginal health and healing in British Columbia, 1900–50*. Vancouver, BC: UBC Press.

Lakoff, G., & Johnson, M. (1999). *Philosophy in the flesh: The embodied mind and its challenge to Western thought*. New York, NY: Basic Books.

Lannon, V. (2013, August 23). From the Red Power movement to Idle No More. *Socialist.ca*. http://socialist.ca/node/1872

Lyotard, J-F. (2004). *Libidinal economy*. New York, NY: Continuum.

Marshall, Y.M. (1993). *A political history of the Nuu-chah-nulth people: A study of the Mowachaht and Muchalaht tribes* (Unpublished doctoral dissertation). Simon Fraser University, Burnaby, BC.

Mezirow, J. (2000). *Learning as transformation: Critical perspectives on a theory in progress*. Hoboken, NJ: Jossey-Bass.

Miller, J.M. (1996). *Shingwaulk's vision: A history of Native residential schools*. Toronto, ON: University of Toronto Press.

National Inquiry into Missing and Murdered Indigenous Women and Girls. (2019). *A legal analysis of genocide: Supplementary report of the National Inquiry into Missing and Murdered Indigenous Women and Girls*. https://www.mmiwg-ffada.ca/wp-content/uploads/2019/06/Supplementary-Report_Genocide.pdf

Neal, A. (1990). Group apraxia: The phenomenology of acculturalism. *Canadian Journal of Native Studies, 10*(2), 219–42. http://www3.brandonu.ca/cjns/10.2/neal.pdf

Nixon, R. N. (1970, July 8). Special message on Indian affairs [Speech transcript]. In *Public papers of the Presidents of the United States: Richard Nixon, 1970* (pp. 564–7, 576). Washington, DC: Office of the Federal Register.

Norris, M.J. (2004). From generation to generation: Survival and maintenance of Canada's aboriginal languages, within families, communities, and cities. *TESL Canada Journal, 22*(1), 1–16. doi: 10.18806/tesl.v21i2.171

Powell, C. (2011). *Barbaric civilization: A critical sociology of genocide*. Montreal, QC: McGill-Queen's University Press.

Randall, R.A. (1987). Planning in cross-cultural settings. In S.L. Friedman, E.K. Scholnick, & R.R. Cocking (Eds.), *Blueprints for thinking: The role of planning in cognitive development* (pp. 39–75). London, UK: Cambridge University Press.

Royal Commission on Aboriginal Peoples (RCAP). (1996). *The report of the Royal Commission on Aboriginal Peoples* (Vols. 1–5). Government of Canada. https://www.bac-lac.gc.ca/eng/discover/aboriginal-heritage/royal-commission-aboriginal-peoples/Pages/final-report.aspx

Shakeri, S. (2020, June 4). Indigenous mom Chantel Moore killed by New Brunswick police. *Huffington Post*. https://www.huffpost.com/archive/ca/entry/chantel

-moore-police-shooting_ca_5ed99019c5b6aaebfd2b32f0?ncid=other_trending _qeesnbnu0l8&utm_campaign=trending

Shaw, P.A. (2004). Negotiating against loss: Responsibility, reciprocity, and respect in endangered language research. In S. Osamu (Ed.), *Lectures on endangered languages 4: From Kyoto Conference 2001* (pp. 181–94). Osaka, Japan: Osaka Gakuin University.

Shields, C.M. (2010). Transformative leadership: Working for equity in diverse contexts. *Educational Administration Quarterly, 46*(4), 558–89. doi: 10.1177 /0013161X10375609

Shields, C.M. (2011). *Transformative leadership: A reader.* New York, NY: Peter Lang.

Shields, C.M. (2013). *Transformative leadership in education: Equitable change in an uncertain and complex world.* New York, NY: Routledge.

Shields, C.M., Bishop, R., & Mazawi, A.E. (2004). *Pathologizing practices: The impact of deficit thinking on education.* New York, NY: Peter Lang.

Shields, C.M., & Edwards, M.M. (2004). *Dialogue is not just talk: A new ground for educational leadership.* New York, NY: Peter Lang.

Trimble, J.E. (1988). Putting the etic to work: Applying social psychological principles in cross-cultural settings. In M.H. Bond (Ed.), *The cross-cultural challenge to social psychology* (pp. 109–21). Newbury Park, CA: SAGE Publications.

Trimble, J.E. (2019). "Being grounded in the ancestors and looking forward..." Blending culturally competent research with Indigenous leadership styles. *Prevention Science, 21*, 98–104. doi: 10.1007/s11121-019-01063-9

Truth and Reconciliation Commission of Canada. (2015). *Honouring the truth, reconciling for the future: Summary of the final report of the Truth and Reconciliation Commission of Canada.* Ottawa, ON: Truth and Reconciliation Commission of Canada. https://publications.gc.ca/collections/collection_2015 /trc/IR4-7-2015-eng.pdf

Tully, J. (1995). *Strange multiplicity: Constitutionalism in an age of diversity.* London, UK: Cambridge University Press.

Turner, M., & Fauconnier, G. (1999). A mechanism of creativity. *Poetics Today, 20*(3), 397–418.

Vizenor, G. (2008). *Survivance: Narratives of native presence.* Lincoln, NE: University of Nebraska Press.

Weaver, S.M. (1993). The Hawthorn Report: Its use in the making of Canadian Indian Policy. In N. Dyck & J.B. Waldram, (Eds.), *Anthropology, public policy, and Native peoples in Canada* (pp. 75–97). Montreal, QB: McGill-Queen's University Press.

Wilson, S. (2009). *Research as ceremony: Indigenous research methods.* Winnipeg, MB: Fernwood Publishing.

Woolford, A. (2021, December 1). *With intent to destroy a group: Genocide's past and present in Canada.* [Video]. YouTube. https://www.youtube.com/ watch?v=5mDNvBDuv3E

# 9 Washroom Dramas and Transgender Politics: A Transformative Approach to Gendered Spaces in Canadian Public Schools

THOMAS ZOOK

It is widely understood that in order to be successful in school, children need to feel welcome, included, and safe (Hatchel, Espelage, & Huang, 2018; Herriot, Burns, & Yeung, 2018; Saewyc, Konishi, Rose, & Homma, 2014; Shields, 2018). Yet, numerous studies have demonstrated that sexual minority youth experience significantly more exclusion, bullying, and harassment at school due to their sexual orientation than their heterosexual peers, and transgender students are even more likely to be the targets of school-wide hostility than lesbian, gay, and bisexual youth. As a result, LGBTQ2+ students experience higher rates of depression, anxiety, and suicidal ideation; report feeling less safe at school; skip classes and miss school all together more frequently; have lower feelings of self-esteem; and are more likely to drop out before completing high school (Hatchel et al., 2018; Kosciw, Greytak, Zongrone, Clark, & Truong, 2018; Russell, Kosciw, Horn, & Saewyc, 2010; Saewyc et al., 2014; Taylor & Peter, 2011).

For some children, everyday life involves navigating a rigidly binary-gendered world in which their authentic self is repeatedly called into question. From official requirements that insist on labelling each child as either a boy or girl based solely on their birth-assigned gender, to the unreasonable demands for compliance with socially regulated gender norms, transgender and gender diverse students face a range of uniquely oppressive social and institutional barriers that make the educational experience particularly inequitable and untenable.

Across Canada, transgender and gender diverse students are now protected from discrimination by provincial and territorial human rights acts and codes through explicit citation, and in 2017 the Canadian Human Rights Act was amended to enumerate both sexual orientation and gender identity or expression as classes protected from discrimination (Cossman, 2018; Trans Equality Society of Alberta, 2016; Walker, 2016). In spite of these human rights laws, the unsupervised spaces of gender-segregated washrooms and change rooms continue to be contested areas of gender politics where hostility towards transgender and gender diverse students plays out through the enactment of cultural stereotypes, myths, and dramas, adding to an educational experience already fraught with consternation and the real possibility of harm (Davies, Vipond, & King, 2019; Herriot et al., 2018; Ingrey, 2018; Jonah, 2016; Ng, Haines-Saah, Knight, Shoveller, & Johnson, 2019). Equity in education is a matter designated to provincial and territorial regulation, and in light of human rights laws that specifically prohibit discrimination based on gender identity or gender expression in all Canadian provinces and territories, educational leaders across the country who have not already will need to come to terms with this fundamental social justice issue.

The purpose of this chapter is to focus attention on these contested spaces while providing school leaders with useful insight into the origin, evolution, and deconstruction of the tensions signified by washroom dramas. Transformative leadership theory (Shields, 2016, 2018) offers educators a framework to guide and ground their efforts towards eliminating the gender politics that make the essential use of washrooms and change rooms perilous spaces for transgender and gender diverse students.

## Being Gendered Beings

There seems to be much confusion and quite a bit of drama over the production of gender that falls outside the socially constructed norms of a gender binary paradigm that assumes all individuals must be either male or female based on anatomical characteristics present or absent at birth. Contingent upon this dichotomous classification, individuals are expected to adhere to strict guidelines of gendered expression and behaviour. In reality, however, gender is a complex relationship between biology, the social expectations of heterosexism[1] and cisnormativity,[2] and one's personal understanding of who they are in relation to gender.

During foetal development, most biological males begin to develop external genitalia that distinguishes them from biological females; though, approximately one in 2,000 infants are born intersex, with indeterminate external genitalia muddling the gender binary even further.[3] From the moment of birth – and, increasingly, even before – most people begin to apply socially constructed gender guidelines onto infants and expect children, as they grow, to adhere to the progressively complex rules of gender compliance assigned to either the male gender or the female gender. For the majority of children, these social expectations are adopted without question, but for some, the performative standards that apply to their birth-assigned gender do not make sense.

## Gender Identity and Gender Expression

Over time, societal notions of gender roles and stereotypes have evolved, but they still remain steadfastly binary and firmly anchored to one's birth-assigned sex (Davies et al., 2019). The pervasive nature of heterosexism throughout society necessitates genders that are diametrically opposed based on biological characteristics in order to reify itself and to ensure the intelligibility of socially sanctioned relationships. In order to maintain the binary separation of genders, normative structures have evolved around the concepts of what it means to be male/masculine or female/feminine. These rules regulate the presentation of gender and social interactions aligning rigidly with one's birth-assigned sex as either male or female. For roughly 1 per cent of the population, however, the body into which they are born does not match their deeply personal understanding of gender (Abramowitz, 2018).

When contemplating matters related to gender, it is important to understand the meaning of several specific terms. *Gender* is typically considered a dichotomous marker for one's biological sex, either male or female. *Gender identity*, on the other hand, refers to an individual's sincere and deeply personal understanding of who they are in relation to the social concept of gender. *Cisgender* refers to an individual whose gender identity and birth-assigned sex are in alignment, and *transgender* is a term used to signify an individual whose gender identity does not match their birth-assigned sex. While most people (including transgender individuals) understand their gender as either male or female, some are uncomfortable with the limits implied by the gender binary and identify as genderqueer, nonbinary, or simply refuse to accept the need to be defined by gender at all. An individual's gender identity does not automatically correspond to their biological or anatomical sex characteristics, nor does it predictably relate to their sexual orientation. Research suggests that children begin to comprehend gender at a very early age and that already by kindergarten many have a consistent understanding of their own gender identity (Abramowitz, 2018; Conard, 2017; Olson & Gülgöz, 2018). Not all children fully appreciate their gender identity during their preadolescent years, however. While there is no "right age" at which a person should fully understand their gender identity, there is some evidence to suggest that the age at which children begin to comprehend their gender identity is bimodal, with a peak around the age of five and another in mid to late adolescence (Kennedy & Hellen, 2010).

*Gender expression* refers to the ways in which individuals communicate their gender identity in the public sphere – through clothing, hairstyle, accessories, speech, elocution, mannerisms, interests, and the like. The relationship between one's gender identity and gender expression is predicated upon one's desire and ability to publicly represent their gender authentically as they understand it. Some transgender and gender diverse individuals may be supported and feel comfortable expressing their authentically understood gender identity through acts that push against the traditional expectations of masculinity and femininity, while others may feel compelled by social pressure to hide their transgender identity and conform to gender standards that do not authenticate the true sense of who they are. Regardless, for many transgender and gender diverse youth, the struggle between an internal desire to perform the social rituals of the gender with which they identify and the external pressure to conform to the socially acceptable rules of the gender assigned to them at birth can be a source of significant distress (Olson, Durwood, DeMeules, & McLaughlin, 2016; Sherer, 2016; Turban, 2017).

## Transgender Hostilities and Schooling

Numerous studies have documented the inherently hostile nature of public schools vis-à-vis transgender and gender diverse students (Porta et al., 2017; Veale, Watson, Peter, & Saewyc, 2017; Weinhart et al., 2017; Wernick, Kulick, & Chin, 2017). More specifically, the results of a 2008 national survey of Canadian high schoolers investigating the experience of sexual and gender minority students found that nearly all transgender students (90 per cent) reported hearing transphobic comments on a regular basis and almost a quarter reported hearing teachers and other school staff using transphobic language regularly (Taylor & Peter, 2011). Worse still, nearly three in four transgender students reported being verbally harassed about their gender expression, while 25 per cent reported that they had been physically harassed or had property damaged or stolen as a result of their gender identity or expression. Moreover, transgender students were nearly four times as likely to be the victims of physical harassment or assault because of their gender expression as compared to their hetero/cisgender peers. Most trans and gender diverse students (78 per cent) reported that they often felt unsafe at school as a result of the hostile and unwelcoming atmosphere and nearly half said that they had missed school because they felt unsafe (Taylor & Peter, 2011).

## Transgendered Beings in Gendered Spaces

Although the monitored hallways and classrooms of many Canadian schools may still be unwelcoming venues for trans and gender diverse students, two essential spaces in particular can be foreboding and the source of significant consternation. Gender-segregated washrooms and change rooms are often the unsupervised stage where gender dramas are acted out between and among peers in what can be hostile and sometimes even dangerous encounters for transgender youth. About half of all trans and gender diverse students report feeling unsafe when using these facilities, and many go to great lengths to avoid them all together (Jonah, 2016; Kosciw et al., 2018; Taylor & Peter, 2011). There can be no question that all students need to tend to personal hygiene and the elimination of bodily waste during the extended periods they are at school, and therefore must be able to safely and comfortably access washrooms and change rooms. Nevertheless, some trans and gender diverse students are required to either use facilities that do not match the gender they live every day, single-occupant staff facilities, or some other inequitable option resulting in a discriminatory educational experience.

Requiring transgender and gender binary children who are supported in some measure of social transition[4] to use the washroom and change room facilities that match their birth-assigned gender is entirely inappropriate. Prepubescent children who are living as their transgender identity are quite likely to be identified by their peers in these spaces and become targets of gender policing. The act of calling into question someone's personal understanding of their gender identity is oppressive – as when a boy, for instance, calls out a trans-identified girl in the boys' washroom, saying, "Hey, you are in the wrong bathroom! What kind of boy are you?" This scenario only escalates in higher grades. Because adolescents often conflate gender and sexuality, a transgender student who is required to use the washroom and change room consistent with their birth-gender might be confronted with the same indictment that is then followed with verbal abuse – "You faggot!" – and potentially physical abuse, such as being dragged out of the room by force.

Another common, yet completely inappropriate and humiliating policy is requiring trans-identified students to use single-occupancy facilities, often designated for staff and located in the nurses' station or some other conspicuously out of the way place. This option merely shines a spotlight on the transgender student, singling them out as different, and because these spaces are often locked, transgender students have to negotiate access each time they need to use the facilities. Moreover, these amenities are often located a considerable distance from the school's classrooms. Sometimes the manner in which schools have handled washroom and change room access for transgender youth is simply hard to believe. In 2012, an Ontario transgender male student was restricted from access to the boys' washroom and told that he could use the facilities at the nearby Harvey's restaurant (Bowers & Lopez, 2012).

## Gender Politics: The Regulation of Gender Segregated Spaces

When it comes to washrooms and change rooms, even the most non-discriminatory policies often fall short of providing equitable and safe experiences for trans-identified students. These unsupervised and gender-segregated spaces cultivate microcosms of communal gender politics, where binary gender-compliance is not only normative but also privileged (Davies et al., 2019). Within what can be very biased spaces, cisgender students work through a multitude of myths and stereotypes about transgender people and enforce their own understanding of gender rules in ways that can pose real and significant danger to trans-identified students.

Judith Butler (1988) describes gender as a performative act that is only rei-fied through the expression of cultural expectations ascribed to traditional masculinity and femininity:

> Gender reality is performative which means, quite simply, that it is real only to the extent that it is performed. It seems fair to say that certain kinds of acts are usually interpreted as expressive of a gender core or identity, and that these acts either conform to an expected gender identity or contest that expectation in some way. (pp. 527–8)

From this perspective, gender is a concept used to subjectify and categorize others based upon certain performative expectations and upon whom socially constructed rules and standards are applied to regulate those expectations and behaviours. Nowhere is this more accurate than within the segregated spaces of washrooms and change rooms. In the absence of adults, students employ the rules of binary gender compliance as they understand them and regulate who is and who is not allowed access. Even the customary signage outside these spaces ("boys' room" or "girls' room") signifies that trans-identified youth are not rec-ognized and do not belong.

In reality, the washroom becomes a "courtroom of public opinion" where bodies are analysed and gender presentations are judged for "worthiness to enter." As Rasmussen (2009) explains, washrooms "don't just tell us where to go; they also tell us who we are, where we belong, and where we don't belong" (p. 440). For most cisgender youth, entering these spaces is a gender-affirming experience, while transgender youth are subject to intense scrutiny and judge-ment as to their worthiness to enter based on their ability to "pass" as acceptable specimens of a specific gender (Davies et al., 2019). Transgender students who are able to "pass" nevertheless must constantly work to "perform" a near perfect representation of their gender identity. The anxiety created by the possibility of exposure and resultant hostility merely adds to the inequity of their educational experience.

On the other hand, trans and gender diverse students who are unable or unwilling to "pass" as the gender opposite their birth sex are relegated to an "othered" status and subsequently become hyper-visible to their cisgender peers who rigorously police these areas. These trans and gender diverse students are caught in an impossible double-bind – banned from washrooms and change rooms that match their lived gender and equally not fitting the gender specif-ics of their birth-assigned sex means they are unable to safely care for their essential personal needs while at school. In an effort to minimize the need to use these gendered spaces, many trans-identified students will limit their intake of food and water before and during school, leading to increased incidences of bladder and kidney infections, urinary stones, chronic dehydration and hunger, and the inability to concentrate, among other serious consequences (Abramowitz, 2018; Conard, 2017; Gower et al., 2018; Hatchel et al., 2018; Wernick et al., 2017). Other transgender students will forego lunch and free periods to dash off campus and use the facilities at neighbouring businesses or stash empty bottles in which to relieve themselves in their cars.

## Stereotypes, Myths, and Trans Tropes: Fuelling Gender Politics

Although the actors in these washroom dramas are often children, the gender politics of segregated spaces frequently reach beyond the school and are influenced by parents and other "concerned" adults. A spate of negative transgender tropes, myths, and stereotypes circulate and are circulated through the school community, fuelling distrust and hatred towards individuals who do not strictly conform to the traditional socially accepted norms of the binary paradigm and instigating the inflexible regulation of gender-segregated spaces. One of the most fundamental misconceptions undergirding nearly all other negative transgender tropes involves the complete nullification of a transgender identity.

### Being Invisible

Many cisgender people are unwilling or unable to fathom the concept that one's birth-gender and gender identity are truly separate entities. The idea that a person can experience an authentic gender identity that does not match their birth sex is simply dismissed as mere confusion or perhaps mental illness – although this misconception has been thoroughly discredited by medical and mental health professionals for some time. In 2012, the American Psychiatric Association removed from its Diagnostic and Statistical Manual (DSM-V) the diagnosis of "gender identity disorder," which had historically been used by mental health professionals to diagnose transgender individuals with a mental disorder (Heffernan, 2012). In its place, the term *gender dysphoria* is now used by medical and mental health professionals to describe "discomfort or distress related to an incongruence between an individual's gender identity and the gender assigned at birth" (American Psychological Association, 2018). In the spring of 2019, the World Health Organization followed suit, replacing the diagnosis of "gender identity disorder" with the term *gender incongruence* in its latest revised version (ICD-11) of the International Classification of Diseases (Lewis, 2019).

### Being Incapable

Moreover, the notion that young children could possibly possess the necessary agency to make such a personal decision about their own authentic gender identity is highly suspect for many people. The fallacy of this argument, of course, is that while (incorrectly) assuming that a child is incapable of comprehending their trans-identified gender, it simultaneously (correctly) assumes that young children are capable of understanding a cisgender identity. As previously noted, children are aware of gender at a very early age, and by the age of five, most children have a consistent understanding of their own (cis or trans) gender identity (Abramowitz, 2018; Conard, 2017; Olson & Gülgöz, 2018). Trans-identified children who encounter opposition when attempting to express their gender identity learn to suppress and conceal those feelings, potentially at considerable emotional expense. Numerous studies have documented the increased rates of anxiety, depression, and suicidal ideation in transgender children who are not supported in performing their understood gender identity (Conard, 2017; Gower et al., 2018; Olson et al., 2016; Russell, Pollitt, Li, & Grossman, 2018; Sherer, 2016; Turban, 2017). On the other hand, there is now a growing body of evidence documenting that trans-identified children who are supported and allowed to socially transition even before entering school are more socially adjusted, less likely to suffer from anxiety or depression, and have increased feelings of self-worth than those who are forced to conform to birth-gender norms (Abramowitz, 2018; Olson et al., 2016; Sherer, 2016; Turban, 2017). Still, some people refuse to acknowledge, let alone respect, the notion of a transgender identity.

*Being Deceptive*

Refusing to recognize the existence of a transgender identity leads to the misconception that trans-identified individuals must have some other motivation for pressing against the binary distinctions of one's birth-assigned gender. In the context of gender segregated spaces such as washrooms and change rooms, that reason is most commonly assumed to be some perverted assault on cisgender females by birth-assigned males (Herriot et al., 2018). The notion that a child would have the forethought and persistence to contravene gender norms consistently for any length of time merely for the opportunity to gain access to the opposite gender's washroom for some nefarious reason is simply laughable. As previously outlined, trans and gender diverse students (and presumably any cisgender student feigning a transgender identity) experience such significant humiliation and hostility on a constant basis that the payoff would be altogether unworthy of the price. This myth is particularly difficult to justify when one considers the ease with which any determined student could, in any instant, walk through the unlocked door of a washroom for the same purpose. Moreover, the idea that a cisgender child could deceive gullible teachers simply for the opportunity to gain access to the opposite gender's washroom is equally laughable. Insincere requests to use the opposite gender's washrooms and change rooms by mischievous students for disreputable reasons should be easily discernible to any trained educator. Moreover, merely having trans-inclusive washroom and change room policies in place does not eliminate a school's legal obligation to ensure the safety and privacy of all students and to take action if any student engages in inappropriate behaviour. Regardless, the trope of the "deceptive transsexual" (Serano, 2007, p. 36) is particularly enduring and has been forwarded as the basis for vehement opposition to transgender-affirming washroom and change room policies in schools and public places throughout Canada (Cossman, 2018).

*Being Deviant*

Denying the existence of a transgender identity coupled with a deep scepticism and mistrust towards anyone who identifies as such are also the basis from which trans and gender diverse individuals are pathologized as deviant sexual predators. Transgender females in particular are assumed to be a threat to cisgender females in the confines of gender segregated spaces (Davies et al., 2019; Schilt & Westbrook, 2015). In an analysis of the public comments offered in the spring of 2014 at five community meetings to discuss and debate a Vancouver School Board policy change that would allow trans students access to the washrooms and change rooms corresponding to their gender identity, researchers discovered a dominant theme shared by parents in opposition to the change. Consistent with the belief that transgender females are really just boys masquerading as girls, several outspoken parents were concerned that their daughters' physical safety and privacy would be in jeopardy (Herriot et al., 2018). Again, the notion that a sexual predator would go to the trouble to pose as a transgender female child just to gain access to this (unlocked) space is absurd. In terms of actual crime statistics, sexual assaults rarely take place in public washrooms (Davies et al., 2019); moreover, a determined perpetrator would not need to carry out such a rouse to gain access to these (unguarded) spaces. In reality, research has shown that trans-identified youth are far more likely to be harassed or attacked in these unsupervised, gender-segregated spaces by cisgender individuals than the other way around (Human Rights Watch, 2016; Philips, 2017; Porta et al., 2017; Taylor & Peter, 2011; Watkins & Moreno, 2017). Also, by focusing only on the defence of cisgender women and girls, this myth also implies that transgender students are unworthy of protection.

*Being Exposed*

Another common myth used in the objection to trans-affirming washroom and change room policies is the idea that children, and in particular cisgender female children, will be negatively affected by being exposed to individuals whose birth-assigned gender does not match the sign on the outside of the space (Herriot et al., 2018). The notion here is that in the presence of transgender individuals these spaces become sites of all-out nudity and debauchery rather than facilities used for the purpose of personal hygiene and bodily functions. First of all, it is not at all uncommon for small children to be exposed to people of the opposite gender in public washrooms without any lasting harm. A mother out shopping will routinely take her young son into the women's washroom. Similarly, a father out with his young daughter will take her to the men's washroom when nature calls, and no one seems to be enduringly disturbed. In the context of public-school washrooms, most, if not all, are equipped with privacy stalls and dividers that limit one's exposure to the gendered bodies of others, and if not already configured thusly, change rooms can be retrofitted with privacy curtains and other accommodations for any individual requesting additional concealment.

## Being Converted

Often the objections to transgender-inclusive washroom and change room policies come down to myths of a deep-state effort to indoctrinate children into a "gay/trans" agenda or the belief that exposing cisgender children to transgender bodies in these confined spaces may somehow cause gender confusion in otherwise gender-compliant children. According to their analysis of Vancouver parents' concerns, Herriot et al. (2018) discovered that some parents believed gender-inclusive washroom policies were an attempt by the school to circumvent a family's right to control the moral education of their children. In their analysis of what often comes down to objections based on religious beliefs, the researchers explain that parents must understand that mere exposure to alternative conceptions of gender identity are not substantively different than, for instance, a vegan child's exposure to another student eating foods they are not permitted to eat or a Christian student observing a Muslim child engaging in morning prayers (Herriot et al., 2018). Transgender and gender diverse students are merely a facet of the normal human diversity that is revered and protected by Canadian law and philosophy.

## A Transformative Approach to Gendered Spaces

Clearly, trans-identified students experience discrimination when they are not afforded safe and affirming access to the same multi-user washrooms and change rooms as their cisgender peers. Likewise, cisgender privilege and gender politics can make these necessary facilities hostile and even unsafe for transgender youth. The eight tenets of transformative leadership theory (Shields, 2018) offer committed educators a promising pathway towards providing equitable access to essential facilities, thereby helping to ensure that transgender and gender diverse students have a safer, more welcoming, and equitable educational experience.

Transformative leadership theory begins with the goal of equity and justice for all and focuses on the process of liberating the oppressed through democratic principles. Unlike many process-oriented or prescriptive theories of educational administration, transformative leadership "is as much a way of life and a way of (re)thinking as it is a leadership theory" (Shields, 2016, p. 22). Understood as anchors and touchstones guiding and grounding a leader's practice, the following tenets when engaged simultaneously represent transformative leadership (Shields, 2018):

1. A mandate to effect deep and equitable change.
2. A need to deconstruct knowledge frameworks that perpetuate inequity and injustice and to reconstruct them in more equitable ways.
3. A need to address the inequitable distribution of power.
4. An emphasis on both private and public (individual and collective) good.
5. A focus on emancipation, democracy, equity, and justice.
6. An emphasis on interdependence, interconnectedness, and global awareness.
7. The necessity of balancing critique with promise.
8. A call to exhibit moral courage.

Applied specifically to the context of equitable washroom and change room access for transgender and gender diverse students, transformative leadership theory calls for a critical evaluation of the material realities and lived experiences of transgender and gender diverse students as they endeavour to participate in the totality of the school experience. The transformative leader will first engage in a deeply personal analysis of their own beliefs and attitudes towards transgender and gender diverse students. It is essential that the trans-identified perspective is respected and foregrounded throughout this exploration. The transformative leader will consider questions such as the following:

- What do I not know about gender identity and gender expression?
- How do I understand the development and permanence of gender identity?
- What are my beliefs and attitudes regarding transgender children?
- How do my religious/philosophical views influence those beliefs and attitudes?

Reaction to these and other inquiries guide the transformative leader towards a more enlightened appreciation of their own biases with regard to transgender and gender diverse people.

## Critical Awareness

Next, the transformative leader will turn the spotlight outward and engage in critical analysis of the official policies, unofficial practices, and school climate that impact the lives of trans and gender diverse individuals within the school community. The transformative leader will consider questions such as the following:

- How might this policy affect students who do not identify with their birth-gender?
- If I were a transgender person, how would I perceive this practice?
- As a transgender person, would I feel safe in this space? Would I feel welcome and included here?
- How are trans-identified individuals disenfranchised in this situation?
- What steps can we take to make sure the agency of gender diverse people is not limited?

Engaging the voices of trans-identified individuals and their allies in this exploration is the only way of ensuring an accurate representation of the current reality in which they live.

## A Mandate to Effect Change

Once armed with what Shields (2009) describes as a "critical awareness" of an inequitable situation, the transformative leader understands they have a personal "mandate to effect deep and equitable change" (Shields, 2018, p. 20). This obligation represents promise, both in the confidence that a more equitable outcome for those who are disenfranchised is possible and in the assurance that democratic change will occur. Any useful theory of leadership must not only endeavour to imagine a more equitable school but also be committed to critical action. Transformative leadership theory calls for leaders to take definitive steps to ensure that trans-identified and gender diverse youth can participate equitably in the entirety of the educational experience, and this certainly includes their right to safe and equitable access to washrooms and change rooms that affirm the gender they live every day.

## Focusing on Equity

Requiring transgender students to use alternative washrooms and change rooms, such as single-occupancy facilities designated for staff, almost never represents an equitable option. This practice identifies transgender students as different and is humiliating and discriminatory. A more equitable option would be to make some or all multi-user facilities inclusive of all genders and allow students to decide what makes sense to them. Some relatively simple modifications may be necessary to convert single-gender facilities into universal-gender spaces. For instance, adding floor-to-ceiling dividers and locking doors on individual stalls helps to increase privacy, while the addition of features for the provision and disposal of feminine hygiene products in all-gender facilities supports both cisgender females and transgender males. Meanwhile, one common fixture may need to be removed: The urinal, while efficient for cisgender males, does not work well in universal-gender washrooms for several reasons, not the least of which is its inherent lack of privacy and its ability to sort users by anatomical gender. Schwartz (2018) discovered that in all-gender washrooms, the presence of urinals makes everyone uncomfortable. Change rooms can also be modified to accommodate students who desire additional privacy by adding curtains and single-user shower stalls or staggering dressing and shower schedules, while modifications should be designed into all new construction.

At the same time, not all trans-identified or cisgender youth feel comfortable or safe in multi-user facilities. Making single-user, all-gender facilities readily available and accessible to any student who desires more privacy removes the stigma associated with this option. These modifications must also be accompanied by practices that work towards changing the attitudes and beliefs undergirding the discriminatory gender politics that occur in these spaces.

## Deconstructing and Reconstructing Faulty Logic

Though a necessary starting point, policy changes, especially those that attempt to alter behaviours instigated by deeply held oppressive beliefs, must be accompanied by diplomatic and democratic communication. The second tenet of transformative leadership theory calls on educators to dismantle illogical and discriminatory knowledge frameworks while engaging in constructive dialogue designed to stimulate inclusive and equitable patterns of thought and behaviour. Much of the impetus behind the attitudes undergirding the gender politics playing out within the gender-segregated facilities results from misconceptions, stereotypes, and myths about trans and gender diverse individuals that have no basis in reality. Educating students, teachers, and families about trans and gender diverse individuals and their realities is a critical step in combating the hostility that may accompany the implementation of gender-affirming washroom and change room policies. This involves engaging in what some might believe are uncomfortable or controversial conversations with students, parents, and staff. When these dialogues become commonplace, the stigma and controversy disappear. The transformative leader will help hesitant cisgender people to appreciate how their hostile reactions towards gender-inclusive facilities are based upon faulty logic and are hurtful to trans and gender diverse individuals.

For instance, helping people to understand the complex relationship between gender and identity can assist in reducing hostile gender politics. It is important to dispel the myth that trans identification is not merely confusion or some form of mental disorder. Trans and gender diverse individuals, like cisgender individuals, have a deep understanding of who they are – or more accurately, who they are not – in relation to gender. Just as an individual who is cisgender simply understands their gender as either male or female in alignment with their birth sex without any conscious thought, transgender individuals understand that who they are in relation to gender does not match their biological sex. Furthermore, not all transgender individuals identify with the opposite sex. Some people understand their gender as fluid, changing periodically between masculine and feminine or finding some middle ground that fits best. Some children appreciate their gender identity at a very early age, while others take a more circuitous route, preferring to experiment with gender identities well into their adolescence or even adulthood, and others do not see the need to be defined by a gender binary paradigm at all. Additionally, remembering Butler's (1988) notion that gender is essentially performative, trans-identified individuals may choose to express their gender identity in any number of ways, or not at all. Indeed, many children, and especially adolescents, will press against the socially constructed normative rules of gender irrespective of their gender identity.

### Summoning the Moral Courage to Redistribute Power and Privilege

Transformative leaders who are dedicated to the goal of ensuring transgender students have safe and affirming access to gender-segregated facilities are prepared to take the courageous steps necessary to deconstruct faulty logic and thought patterns throughout the school community and to reconstruct them in more equitable ways. Furthermore, they are prepared to commit to the equitable redistribution of power necessary to interrupt the gender politics and dramas that play out within these segregated spaces. Taking the simple step of replacing gender-specific signs outside washroom and change room doors with signs that indicate universal-gender access demonstrates a commitment to the elimination of gender politics and sends a clear message that washroom dramas will no longer be tolerated. Lastly, transformative leaders must understand that whenever the structures of privilege and access to power are challenged, "those in the dominant position will resist and retaliate to the extent they are able" (Quantz, Rogers, & Dantley, 1991, p. 103).

In terms of creating safe and affirming policies for transgender access to gender-segregated facilities, troubling the nearly ubiquitous nature of cisgender power and privilege is perhaps the most challenging aspect of transformative leadership. Quantz et al. (1991) note that "if schools are understood to be arenas of cultural politics characterized by asymmetrical power relations, then any attempt to use power to transform social relations will be met with hostility" (p. 103). Regardless of provincial human rights laws intended to protect transgender individuals from discrimination, educational leaders and school boards will almost certainly face resistance from some students, teachers, parents, and other "concerned" adults against policies that threaten the "sanctity" of gender-segregated spaces.

Generating safer and more equitable educational environments for trans and gender diverse students may require calling into question the deeply held religious beliefs or philosophical views of those who might seek to block such efforts. Interrupting and reversing the gender politics and dramas surrounding transgender access to washroom and change room facilities requires transformative leaders to demonstrate true moral courage in the face of potentially vehement opposition from within the school and the greater community. However, as Shields (2016) explains, "If we do not have moral courage, we will be reluctant to act. We will retreat into our fears and insecurities, our discomfort with conflict, and our need to be liked and remain secure" (p. 154). Ultimately, it is the responsibility of educators to ensure the rights of every student to a safe and equitable educational experience free from discrimination, and since 2017, in every province and territory across Canada, that includes protection from discrimination based on sexual orientation, gender identity, and gender expression.

## Conclusion

For several years now, many school boards in almost all major cities throughout Canada have been successfully implementing various washroom and change room policies that allow transgender students to use the facilities in which they feel comfortable and supported, provide universal-gender options for all students, or provide some combination of single and all-gender supportive alternatives with no reported issues or concerns (Davies et al., 2019). Washroom dramas and gender politics create an unsafe and discriminatory school experience for the roughly 1 per cent of Canadian public-school children who are transgender or gender diverse and have no place in the educational realm.

Educational leaders have, at a minimum, an ethical and legal responsibility to ensure that all students are protected from discriminatory policies and procedures, as well as from hostile school environments. Transformative leaders also understand that standing up for the rights of trans and gender diverse people signals to all Canadians and the world that diversity strengthens our society. On the surface, it may seem the debate is only about equitable washroom access, but on a profound level, it is about the recognition and respect of transgender individuals as well as their right and freedom to be the most authentic version of themselves. Transformative leadership calls for action that seeks to democratize gender politics and eliminate washroom dramas not only because it is the right thing to do, but also because it sends a clear message that transgender and gender diverse people are worthy of being included in Canadian society.

## NOTES

1  A systematic process of privileging heterosexuality relative to homosexuality based on the assumption that heterosexuality and heterosexual power and privilege are normal and ideal (Chester-Teran, 2003).
2  The ubiquitous assumption that all people identify as either male or female based on their birth-assigned gender and express themselves according to the socially sanctioned rules and customs attributed to either gender (Kosciw et al., 2018).
3  For a more complete discussion on intersex individuals, visit http://interact advocates.org/faq/.
4  Social transition involves non-medical gender-affirming support in all aspects of a child's life from the use of chosen names and pronouns to hairstyle and clothing choices and access to gender-affirming washrooms and change rooms. Social transition is an effective, affirming, and completely reversible means of reducing a transgender child's distress while offering an immersive experience into the world of their authentic gender identity (Conard, 2017).

## REFERENCES

Abramowitz, J. (2018). Transgender medicine – transitioning transgender children to adulthood. *Reviews in Endocrine and Metabolic Disorders, 19*, 227–30. doi: 10.1007/s11154-018-9458-z

American Psychological Association. (2018). A glossary: Defining transgender terms. *Monitor on Psychology, 49*(8), 32. https://www.apa.org/monitor/2018/09 /ce-corner-glossary

Bowers, G., & Lopez, W. (2012). Which way to the restroom? Respecting the rights of transgender youth in the school system: A North American perspective. *Education and Law Journal, 22*(3), 243–66. https://youthrex.com/wp-content /uploads/2019/01/Trans-Youth.pdf

Butler, J. (1988). Performative acts and gender constitution: An essay in phenomenology and feminist theory. *Theatre Journal, 40*(4), 519–31. doi: 10.2307/3207893

Chester-Teran, D. (2003). Conceptualizing and assessing heterosexism in high schools: A setting-level approach. *American Journal of Community Psychology, 31*(3–4), 267–79. doi: 10.1023/A:1023910820994

Conard, L.E. (2017). Supporting and caring for transgender and gender nonconforming youth in the urology practice. *Journal of Pediatric Urology, 13*(3), 300–4. doi: 10.1016/j.jpurol.2017.02.019

Cossman, B. (2018). Gender identity, gender pronouns, and freedom of expression: Bill C-16 and the traction of specious legal claims. *University of Toronto Law Journal, 68*(1), 37–79. https://www.muse.jhu.edu/article/684530

Davies, A.W.J., Vipond, E., & King, A. (2019). Gender binary washrooms as a means of gender policing in schools: A Canadian perspective. *Gender and Education, 31*(7), 866–85. doi: 10.1080/09540253.2017.1354124

Gower, A.L., Rider, N.G., Brown, C., McMorris, B.J., Coleman, E., Taliaferro, L.A., & Eisenberg, M.E. (2018). Supporting transgender and gender diverse youth: Protection against emotional distress and substance use. *American Journal of Preventive Medicine, 55*(6), 787–94. doi: 10.1016/j.amepre.2018.06.030

Hatchel, T., Espelage, D.L., & Huang, Y. (2018). Sexual harassment victimization, school belonging, and depressive symptoms among LGBTQ adolescents: Temporal insights. *American Journal of Orthopsychiatry, 88*(4), 422–30. doi: 10.1037/ort0000279

Heffernan, D. (2012, December 3). The APA removes "gender identity disorder" from updated mental health guide. *GLADD.* https://www.glaad.org/blog/apa-removes-gender-identity-disorder-updated-mental-health-guide

Herriot, L., Burns, D.P., & Yeung, B. (2018). Contested spaces: Trans-inclusive school policies and parental sovereignty in Canada. *Gender and Education, 30*(6), 695–714. doi: 10.1080/09540253.2017.1396291

Human Rights Watch. (2016, September 14). Shut out: Restrictions on bathroom and locker room access for transgender youth in US schools. https://www.hrw.org/report/2016/09/14/shut-out/restrictions-bathroom-and-locker-room-access-transgender-youth-us-schools

Ingrey, J. (2018). Problematizing the cisgendering of school washroom space: Interrogating the politics of recognition of transgender and gender non-conforming youth. *Gender and Education, 30*(6), 774–89. doi: 10.1080/09540253.2018.1483492

Jonah, J.J. (2016). *Trans youth and the right to access public washrooms: A critical perspective on a social policy.* Toronto, ON: Youth Research and Evaluation eXchange (YouthREX). doi: 10.15868/socialsector.33746

Kennedy, N., & Hellen, M. (2010). Transgender children: More than a theoretical challenge. *Graduate Journal of Social Science, 7*(2), 25–43. http://gjss.org/sites/default/files/issues/chapters/papers/Journal-07-02--02-Kennedy-Hellen.pdf

Kosciw, J.G., Greytak, E.A., Zongrone, A.D., Clark, C.M., & Truong, N.L. (2018). *The 2017 National School Climate Survey: The experiences of lesbian, gay, bisexual, transgender, and queer youth in our nation's schools.* GLSEN. https://www.glsen.org/sites/default/files/2019-10/GLSEN-2017-National-School-Climate-Survey-NSCS-Full-Report.pdf

Lewis, S. (2019, May 29). World Health Organization removes "gender identity disorder" from list of mental illnesses. *CBS News.* https://www.cbsnews.com/news/world-health-organization-removes-gender-dysphoria-from-list-of-mental-illnesses/

Ng, C.K., Haines-Saah, R.J., Knight, R.E., Shoveller, J.A., & Johnson, J.L. (2019). "It's not my business": Exploring heteronormativity in young people's discourses about lesbian, gay, bisexual, transgender, and queer issues and their implications for youth health and wellbeing. *Health, 23*(1), 39–57. doi: 10.1177/1363459317715776

Olson, K.R., Durwood, L., DeMeules, M., & McLaughlin, K.A. (2016). Mental health of transgender children who are supported in their identities. *Pediatrics, 137*(3), 1–8. doi: 10.1542/peds.2015-3223

Olson, K.R., & Gülgöz, S. (2018). Early findings from the TransYouth Project: Gender development in transgender children. *Child Development Perspectives, 12*(2), 93–7. doi: 10.1111/cdep.12268

Philips, R.R. (2017). The battle over bathrooms: Schools, courts, and transgender rights. *Theory in Action, 10*(4), 100–17. doi: 10.3798/tia.1937-0237.1729

Porta, C.M., Gower, A.L., Mehus, C.J., Yu, X., Saewyc, E.M., & Eisenberg, M.E. (2017). "Kicked out": LGBTQ youths' bathroom experiences and preferences. *Journal of Adolescence, 56*, 107–12. doi: 10.1016/j.adolescence.2017.02.005

Quantz, R.A., Rogers, J., & Dantley, M. (1991). Rethinking transformative leadership: Toward democratic reform of schools. *Journal of Education, 173*(3), 96–118. doi: 10.1177/002205749117300307

Rasmussen, M.L. (2009). Beyond gender identity? *Gender and Education, 21*(4), 431–47. doi: 10.1080/09540250802473958

Russell, S.T., Kosciw, J., Horn, S., & Saewyc, E. (2010). Safe schools policy for LGBTQ students and commentaries. *Social Policy Report, 24*(4), 1–25. doi: 10.1002/j.2379 -3988.2010.tb00065.x

Russell, S.T., Pollitt, A.M., Li, G., & Grossman, A.H. (2018). Chosen name use is linked to reduced depressive symptoms, suicidal ideation, and suicidal behavior among transgender youth. *Journal of Adolescent Health, 63*(4), 503–5. doi: 10.1016/j.jadohealth.2018.02.003

Saewyc, E.M., Konishi, C., Rose, H.A., & Homma, Y. (2014). School based strategies to reduce suicidal ideation, suicide attempts, and discrimination among sexual minority and heterosexual adolescents in Western Canada. *International Journal of Child, Youth and Family Studies, 5*(1), 89–112. doi: 10.18357/ijcyfs .saewyce.512014

Schilt, K., & Westbrook, L. (2015). Bathroom battlegrounds and penis panics. *Contexts, 14*(3), 26–31. doi: 10.1177/1536504215596943

Schwartz, M. (2018). Inclusive restroom design. *Library Journal, 143*(8), 1–5.

Serano, J. (2007). *Whipping girl: A transsexual woman on sexism and the scapegoating of femininity.* Emeryville, CA: Seal Press.

Sherer, I. (2016). Social transition: Supporting our youngest transgender children. *Pediatrics, 137*(3), 1–2. doi: 10.1542/peds.2015-4358

Shields, C.M. (2009). *Courageous leadership for transforming schools: Democratizing practice.* Norwood, MA: Christopher-Gordon Publishers.

Shields, C.M. (2016). *Transformative leadership: Primer.* New York, NY: Peter Lang.

Shields, C.M. (2018). *Transformative leadership in education: Equitable and socially just change in an uncertain and complex world.* New York, NY: Routledge.

Taylor, C., & Peter, T. (2011). *Every class in every school: The first national climate survey on homophobia, biphobia, and transphobia in Canadian schools.* Toronto, ON: Egale Canada Human Rights Trust.

Trans Equality Society of Alberta. (2016). *Fact page: Human rights across Canada.* http://www.tesaonline.org/human-rights-across-canada.html

Turban, J.L. (2017). Transgender youth: The building evidence base for early social transition. *Journal of the American Academy of Child & Adolescent Psychiatry,* 56(2), 101–2. doi: 10.1016/j.jaac.2016.11.008

Veale, J.F., Watson, R.J., Peter, T., & Saewyc, E.M. (2017). Mental health disparities among Canadian transgender youth. *Journal of Adolescent Health,* 60(1), 44–9. doi: 10.1016/j.jadohealth.2016.09.014

Walker, J. (2016). *Legislative summary of Bill C-16: An Act to amend the Canadian Human Rights Act and the Criminal Code.* Ottawa, ON: Library of Parliament.

Watkins, P.J., & Moreno, E. (2017). Bathrooms without borders: Transgender students argue separate is not equal. *The Clearing House: A Journal of Educational Strategies, Issues and Ideas,* 90(5–6), 166–71. doi: 10.1080/00098655.2017.1361285

Weinhart, L.S., Stevens, P., Xie, H., Wesp, L.M., John, S.A., Apchemengich, I., Kioko, D., Chavez-Korell, S., Cochran, K.M., Watjen, J.M., & Lambrou, N. (2017). Transgender and gender nonconforming youths' public facilities use and psychological wellbeing: A mixed-methods study. *Transgender Health,* 2(1), 140–50. doi: 10.1089/trgh.2017.0020

Wernick, L.J., Kulick, A., & Chin, M. (2017). Gender identity disparities in bathroom safety and wellbeing among high school students. *Journal of Youth and Adolescence,* 46, 917–30. doi: 10.1007/s10964-017-0652-1

# 10 Supporting Newcomer Refugee Students' Adaptation in Schools: Challenges, Practices, and Recommendations through the Lens of a Compassion-Based Framework

RAGHAD EBIED

According to the United Nations High Commissioner for Refugees (UNHCR), the number of forcibly displaced persons worldwide at the end of 2020 who are fleeing conflict, human rights infringements, and violence has surpassed 82.4 million (UNHCR, 2020). Forcibly displaced persons are "those who are forced to move, within or across borders, due to armed conflict, persecution, terrorism, human rights violations and abuses, violence, the adverse effects of climate change, natural disasters, development projects or a combination of these factors" (Office of the High Commissioner for Human Rights, 2018, para. 4). Of the 82.4 million forcibly displaced persons, approximately 26.4 million are refugees, nearly half of whom are children and youth under eighteen years of age (UNHCR, 2020). Over half of these refugees have fled from conflict in South Sudan, Afghanistan, and Syria, with Syria having the highest number of refugees worldwide, recently estimated at 6.7 million people (UNHCR, 2020).

For this chapter, I will be looking specifically at refugees as a subset of forcibly displaced persons. I define "refugee" in accordance with the 1951 Geneva Refugee Convention relating to the Status of Refugees, which is the definition likewise used in Canadian law and generally agreed upon internationally (Canadian Council for Refugees, n.d.). According to the 1951 Refugee Convention, a refugee is "someone who is unable or unwilling to return to their country of origin owing to a well-founded fear of being persecuted for reasons of race, religion, nationality, membership of a particular social group, or political opinion" (as cited in UNHCR, 2010, p. 3). Therefore, the main difference between forcibly displaced persons and refugees is that while the former may be temporarily displaced within or across their country's borders, refugees are indefinitely unable to return to their country of origin due to safety reasons.

Also, the term "newcomer" in the literature and in Canadian policy and practice may refer to both refugees and immigrants who have recently arrived to

Canada (Mulholland & Biles, 2004), usually within the last five years (Canadian Commission for UNESCO, 2019). However, immigrants and refugees are two distinct groups, since immigrants usually chose to emigrate to a different country and are technically defined as "those who are landed in Canada according to the rules or regulations governing immigration to Canada" (Mulholland & Biles, 2004, p. 5). On the other hand, as already cited, refugees are forced to flee for reasons of safety and are technically defined as "those individuals acknowledged as Geneva Convention refugees" (Mulholland & Biles, 2004, p. 5). As such, for the purposes of this chapter, I will mainly use the term "newcomer refugee students" when referring to supporting K–12 refugee students who have resettled in Canada with their parents within the last five years.

Between 2015 and 2017, some 84,000 refugees, 43 per cent of whom were school-age (seventeen years old and under) children and youth, resettled in Canada (Immigration, Refugees and Citizenship Canada, 2017), meaning that since 2015, there are approximately 36,000 newcomer refugee students in Canadian schools. With such a substantial number of culturally, linguistically, and religiously diverse refugee students in schools across the country, nearly half of whom are coming from Syria (Immigration, Refugees and Citizenship Canada, 2017), Pieloch, McCullough, and Marks (2016) have rightly noted that there is currently a global interest in understanding how to support the "positive adaptation of refugee children … [who] can experience numerous stressors and traumatic events because of their migration, resettlement, and acculturation experiences" (p. 330). Researchers advocate that promoting environments that encourage refugee students to succeed is instrumental for social cohesion as well as economic competitiveness (Volante, Klinger, Bilgili, & Siegel, 2017). Moreover, Tuters and Portelli (2017) contend that cultivating equity in schools is essential to the success of all students, including refugee students: "Equity and social justice are always central to genuine and meaningful education and hence not a frill" (p. 602).

In this chapter, I begin by defining equity as it pertains to supporting newcomer refugee students in schools. Following that, I discuss the role of schools in supporting newcomer refugee students' positive adaptation; the needs and challenges of newcomer refugee students; challenges for school staff; international and local practices and recommendations; and school leadership. Acknowledgment of the impact of trauma and adverse childhood experiences on children's well-being has led to emerging frameworks of support, including a compassion-based framework that offers important considerations for supporting student well-being through an emphasis on equity and system-level shifts (Lavelle, Flook, & Ghahremani, 2017). As such, the final section of this chapter will explore the ability of this compassion-based framework to better support newcomer refugee students' positive adaptation more holistically.

## Defining Equity

At a time when diversity and the gap between the privileged and the less privileged is increasing, Ryan (2006) rightly argues that school leadership approaches need to evolve to serve moral goals, such as social justice, which are important for fostering more equity. For the purposes of this chapter, educational equity is defined as "raising the achievement of all students while narrowing the gaps between the highest and lowest-performing students; and eliminating the racial predictability and disproportionality of which student groups occupy the highest and lowest achievement categories" (Singleton & Linton, 2006, p. 46). With refugee students coming largely from racialized groups (UNHCR, 2020), the goal of addressing any disadvantages due to race are especially important.

Furthermore, the Center for Mental Health in Schools at UCLA (2014) describes the importance of an "integrated student support and equity" strategy that "connects school, home, and community resources as essential to the well-being of children and youth and to enhancing equity of opportunity for them to succeed at school and beyond" (pp. 1–2). Therefore, both academic achievement and well-being are important components of equity, and this approach has increasingly become an interest in educational policy. For example, in 2017, the Ontario Ministry of Education released *Ontario's Education Equity Action Plan*, which is "the province's roadmap to identifying and eliminating discriminatory practices, systemic barriers and bias from schools and classrooms to support the potential for all students to succeed" (p. 4). This document compliments the Ontario Ministry of Education's 2009 strategy, *Realizing the Promise of Diversity: Ontario's Equity and Inclusive Education Strategy*. As part of the 2009 strategy, "all 72 school boards developed equity and inclusive education policies ... [and] seven regional equity networks have been established to support schools and boards in the effective implementation of the strategy" (Ontario Ministry of Education, 2017, p. 5).

## The Role of Schools in Supporting Newcomer Refugee Students' Positive Adaptation

In her work on refugee education and its impact on a global scale, Dryden-Peterson (2016) explains, "Education is important to the life chances of individual refugees; to the present stability of the nation-states in which they find exile; to the future reconstruction of the conflict-affected societies from which they fled; and to the economic and political security of an interconnected world polity" (p. 474). Researchers support this claim by arguing that "schools have a critical role to play in the settlement of refugee young people and in facilitating transitions to citizenship and belonging" (Taylor & Sidhu, 2012, p. 1). Also, Tavares (2012) states that education can be a type of healing process for refugee children coming from war-torn backgrounds, and other researchers suggest that promoting social integration and well-being for refugee students can contribute to fewer emotional challenges and less aggression (Beiser, Puente-Duran, & Hou, 2015), as well as improved academic achievement (Ratkovic et al., 2017).

However, some researchers report that schools in Canada lack sufficient preparedness to manage the socio-psychological needs of refugee students as they enter the school system (Gagné, Shapka, & Law, 2012; Kovačević, 2016). Furthermore, research has indicated that refugee students may be even more likely than immigrant students to experience academic challenges, in part due to "untreated psychological trauma and educators' lack of understanding of refugee children's pre-migration experiences and current needs ... [which include] the complex integration process" (Ayoub & Zhou, 2016, pp. 2–3). As such, Taylor and Sidhu (2012) emphasize the necessity for educators to understand the difficult experiences many refugees have faced and recognize any potential barriers to "social inclusion."

## Understanding the Needs and Challenges of Refugee Students

Researchers claim that until recently, the literature on migration did not pay sufficient attention to forced migration, therefore undermining the distinct experiences of refugee students (Pinson & Arnot, 2007). Consequently, researchers argue that the particular needs of refugee students have not been sufficiently recognized by research and education policy-makers (Taylor & Sidhu, 2012). As such, in agreement with Ratkovic et al. (2017), Taylor and Sidhu (2012) claim that policies and organizational approaches lack guidance to address the "significant educational disadvantages confronting refugee youth ... and that the discursive invisibility of refugees in policy and research has worked against their cultural, social and economic integration" (p. 4). This "discursive invisibility" also presents itself in viewing refugees as a "homogeneous group [which] prevented detailed examination of pre-migration and post-migration factors which are relevant to understanding their particular needs and developing appropriate educational support" (Taylor & Sidhu, 2012, p. 6). Furthermore, refugee students in some cases are grouped under the umbrella of English as a Second Language (ESL) students without targeted policies to support their specific social and emotional well-being needs (Taylor & Sidhu, 2012).

Some of the other disadvantages confronting refugee students may include experiencing trauma in the form of separation from family, the death of loved ones, and exposure to violence including torture and sexual abuse (Vongkhamphra, Davis, & Adem, 2011). Research tells us that traumatic experiences can result in several academic challenges including slow language development, poor scores on standardized tests, failing a grade, and being diagnosed with special needs (Wolpow, Hertel, Johnson, & Kincaid, 2016). Additionally, trauma can impact students' relationships and behaviours, which often subjects them to more disciplinary measures and keeps them from reaching their greatest potential (Delaney-Black et al., 2002). As such, researchers argue that refugee students may become more vulnerable to not only school disengagement but also unsafe sexual practices, drug use, suicidal thoughts (Allard & Santoro, 2008), and criminal behaviour (Rossiter & Rossiter, 2009).

Furthermore, in addition to potentially including physical and emotional trauma, refugee students' pre-migration experiences may also have included residing in conflict zones or refugee camps where securing basic needs may have been very challenging (Ayoub & Zhou, 2106). For example, it may be common for refugees to have spent five to ten years in a refugee camp, where children may have had no or interrupted access to education. These circumstances can consequently have detrimental implications for the educational and academic success of refugee students (Van der Stouwe & Oh, 2008).

Once refugee students arrive in Canada, there also needs to be consideration of challenges associated with resettlement and adaptation, which may be broadly characterized by language learning, social integration or a sense of belonging, and well-being (Ratkovic et al., 2017; Taylor & Sidhu, 2012). With the current wave of refugees to Canada coming largely from culturally and linguistically diverse countries where English is not a first language, including Syria, Afghanistan, and South Sudan (UNHCR, 20202), research reveals that recent student newcomers who are ESL learners will encounter more academic challenges than other students (Dei, James, Karumanchery, James-Wilson, & Zine, 2000). Moreover, they may experience additional challenges such as racism, Islamophobia, and other types of discrimination (Banks, 2008; Zine, 2001).

As a result, it is reported that "psychological isolation at school and discriminatory attitudes from some teachers place refugee students' self-esteem, social competence, and academic achievements at risk, hindering the student's social, economic, and political integration in the receiving society" (Ratkovic et al., 2017, p. 3). Instead of offering protective factors, which support students in the face of challenges, researchers argue that school experiences can contribute to worse mental health challenges for some newcomer refugee students (Rossiter & Rossiter, 2009).

## Challenges for School Staff Supporting Refugee Students

A pan-Canadian research report examining the literature and policy over the past twenty years on support for refugee students states that schools and policymakers "continue to lack cross-cultural competence, a social justice focus, transformative leadership skills, and policy guidance" (Ratkovic et al., 2017, p. 3).

Additionally, some Canadian researchers have revealed that educational leaders who attempt to engage with equity, which is arguably related to social justice and cross-cultural competence, may experience challenges such as a lack of support from their colleagues, supervisors, and policymakers (Armstrong, Tuters, & Carrier, 2013). These challenges may stem from the difficulties that lie in contesting systemic discrimination and the oppression of students based on their ethnicity, social class, gender, academic ability, and so on (Theoharis, 2008).

Also, with greater pressures on principals related to "work intensification" due to factors such as "school pedagogical, social, and demographic changes," researchers have started to increasingly consider principals' well-being (Wang, Pollock, & Hauseman, 2018, p. 73). It has been reported that principals often experience feelings of helplessness and self-doubt, which demonstrates the need for principals to model self-care (McAdams & Foster, 2008). Furthermore, while educators may genuinely wish to support refugee students, studies have suggested that some did not feel prepared to help refugee students in managing emotional distress (Szente, Hoot, & Taylor, 2006). Specifically, some educators feared the impact on their own personal well-being in the form of becoming over-invested emotionally and suffering vicarious trauma due to the lack of training and support they themselves receive (Alisic, Bus, Dulack, Pennings, & Splinter, 2012). Other researchers support the claim that there is a general lack of training for Canadian teachers on how to adapt their teaching strategies to meet the unique needs of diverse refugee students (Rossiter & Rossiter, 2009; Ratkovic et al., 2017).

## Support for Newcomer Refugee Students: Positive Practices and Recommendations

Internationally, researchers refer to the three areas identified by Rutter (2006) as characterizing "good practice" for the support of refugee students: "the importance of a welcoming environment, free of racism; the need to meet psychosocial needs, particularly if there are prior experiences of trauma; and [the need to meet] linguistic needs" (Taylor & Sidhu, 2012, p. 45). Pinson and Arnot's (2007) research on school values, policies, and practices for the education of refugee and asylum-seeking children also recognized "an ethos of inclusion," the "celebration of diversity," and "a caring ethos and the giving of hope" (p. 51) as important characteristics of good practice. Building upon this, Taylor and Sidhu (2012) add the following factors:

> [1] targeted policies and system support [including funding] ... [2] a commitment to social justice [visible in] school ethos ... [3] a holistic approach to education and welfare which considers the learning, social and emotional needs of refugee

students and those of their families [and draws on] community and inter-agency collaborations, and … [4] leadership. (pp. 46–9)

In particular, a sense of belonging appears to be a recurring and important theme in the literature on supporting refugee students' positive adaptation. For example, researchers reveal that "there appears to be a strong connection between engagement in the school context, feelings of belonging, and positive adaptation across cultures" (Pieloch et al., 2016, p. 337). In support of this, Correa-Valez, Gifford, and Barnett (2010) have indicated that refugee students' well-being is connected to their sense of belonging and level of social cohesion, which is one of the most important elements in building resilience (Edge, Newbold, & McKeary, 2014) and civic participation (Abu El-Haj, 2007).

In Canada, key recommendations from Ratkovic et al.'s (2017) report on support for refugee students at the programs and policy level include enacting cross-cultural transformative leadership and developing "multi-tiered and inter-agency partnerships based on trust, community, and mutuality" (p. 1). In addition, they suggest that the provinces that draw on an asset-based approach, that emphasize refugee students' strengths or assets and empowerment, and that understand the distinct nature between immigrant and refugee student experiences are more prepared to offer appropriate direction and policies for educators. Disseminating relevant policies and resources at the provincial and school district levels is also recommended because, as Ratkovic et al. (2017) note, the existing Canadian literature outlining the experiences of English-language learners and immigrant students does not pay sufficient attention to supporting specifically refugee students in Canada, which impacts the availability of policies designed to support this population of students.

Recent research on leading K–12 refugee integration in Ontario, Canada, further suggests that leaders and researchers need to "critically interrogate educational programming for refugees offered at all levels of the school system; inspire educators of varying perspectives to commit to a particular vision of inclusion for newcomers; and manage resources morally, strategically, sustainably, and flexibly" (Faubert & Tucker, 2019, p. 53).

### School Leadership and Support for Refugee Students

Researchers emphasize the important role of school leaders in creating inclusive environments and school cultures that support refugee students' positive adaptation (Ratkovic et al., 2017; Taylor & Sidhu, 2012). Tuters and Portelli (2017) argue that educational leaders need particular skills and behaviours to enable them to navigate the challenges related to equity. For example, Ross and Berger's (2009) work on equity and leadership included sixteen strategies that principals can draw on to increase equity in their schools. The underlying belief guiding each of these strategies is that "principals' influence equity indirectly, by increasing the technical skills of staff, transforming their beliefs about equity, and strengthening school partnerships with parents and the community" (p. 472). Moreover, Theoharis (2008) states that "the work of these social justice leaders is deeply connected to who they are, their passion, and their inner personalities" (p. 17).

When it comes to leadership with a focus on advocacy for refugee students, Taylor and Sidhu (2012) explain that leadership is not only important at the system level but also at the school level. Specifically, they state the importance of leaders "promoting positive images of refugee students within the school and local community" (p. 53). They also advocate cultivating a whole school approach that includes "a positive and welcoming attitude towards refugee students" (Taylor & Sidhu, 2012, p. 53). Ratkovic et al. (2017) likewise suggest that cross-cultural transformative leadership can be "a powerful approach to refugee students' education, social integration, and well-being" (p. 1). This approach, which developed from Shields's (2010) work on transformative leadership, encourages leaders to critically analyse the existing school culture in which they operate, as well as to consider how to cultivate a culture that prioritizes equity through policy and practice (Nur, 2012). Overall, the emphasis in this leadership approach is on fostering cultural competence in educators and administrators in order to address the needs of refugee students who may feel marginalized (Peček, Čuk, & Lesar, 2008). The cross-cultural transformative leadership approach also discourages a deficit-based perspective towards refugee students wherein educators might engage in "categorizing, separating or stereotyping refugee students" (Kovačević, 2016, p. 17), which could lead to marginalization and discrimination (Shields, 2003).

Nur (2012) builds upon Shields's (2010) work on transformative leadership by discussing three important characteristics that define this leadership approach: "an ethic of care, an ethic of justice and [an ethic of] dialogue and understanding" (p. 47). Nur's (2012) research demonstrated how two of these components, the ethic of care, coined by Noddings (2002), and dialogue and understanding, are instrumental to supporting the social integration and well-being of refugee students. The first component, an ethic of care, emphasizes the need for school leaders to be emotionally invested in their students. This can occur through principals participating in discussions with students to gain a greater awareness of their socio-psychological and academic challenges, as well as through encouraging this ethic of care in teachers. Dialogue and understanding is the second transformative leadership characteristic Nur (2012) discusses as pertinent to supporting the integration and well-being of refugee students, and this characteristic promotes inclusion and the development of strong relationships between educators, administrators, students, and parents. The development of these strong relationships, which is an aspect of transformative leadership, is considered key in cultivating a "strong support system for refugee students [since it] encourages educators to consult with refugee students and ask for their input in the creation of effective strategies that will better support their needs as they integrate into the system" (Kovačević, 2016, p. 13). Arguably, both an ethic of care and dialogue and understanding are connected to a compassion-based framework, which focuses on enhancing student well-being (Lavelle et al., 2017).

Moreover, with the prevalence of trauma, particularly among refugee students in this case (Ayoub & Zhou, 2016; Pieloch et al., 2016), researchers, including Gomez-Lee (2017), have also referred to the importance of leadership practices that consider trauma-informed, compassionate approaches in schools. Such approaches are characterized by "the importance of building relationships, knowing the stories of our students, [and] having compassion and empathy to treat the whole child" (Gomez-Lee, 2017, p. 120). Research has also indicated that early recognition, intervention, and follow through are essential to mitigating or lowering the impact of trauma (Finkelhor, Turner, Ormrod, Hamby, & Kracke, 2009). The main criteria for these approaches is that they strive to address the attitudes and beliefs of educators towards the impact of trauma on students (Gomez-Lee, 2017).

A successful trauma-informed approach in schools requires a change of school culture. It requires the understanding that students who have experienced trauma need specialized supports, including mental health resources and supports *in* schools as opposed to simply referring students to external mental health supports (Gomez-Lee, 2017), which they are less likely to access (Beauregard, Gauthier, & Rousseau, 2014). Furthermore, leadership practices include having a positive, non-intimidating approach to supporting teachers; developing strong relationships with staff, students, and parents through showing care by being visible and approachable; and seeking relevant information and expertise that is shared with staff during professional development (Gomez-Lee, 2017). Arguably, leadership practices in a trauma-informed, compassionate school have important similarities to cross-cultural transformative leadership practices since they include providing a "welcoming, affirming, and safe environment, and recognizing that each member of [the] community has unique learning styles, personal strengths, and cultural backgrounds which they strive to celebrate" (Wolpow et al., 2016, p. 18).

Finally, in light of the more recent need for leadership shifts to support an increasingly vast number of refugee students who may have experienced trauma, it is important to consider the factors related to leadership practices that are required to successfully adopt new approaches in schools. These factors "include policies and financing [and] university/community partnerships, ... mission-policy alignment, resources, school climate and culture, and organizational health ... [as well as] training, ongoing coaching, and implementation tools" (Gomez-Lee, 2017, p. 49). These leadership approaches inform a greater compassion-based framework, which is pertinent to support refugee students' positive adaptation through a holistic lens that considers multiple elements.

## Compassion-Based Framework

Given the magnitude and recency of the latest refugee crisis, I examined several different emerging leadership approaches to assess their appropriateness in supporting refugee students and found particular merit in the compassion-based framework. This framework is part of a "prosocial education" approach linked to social-emotional learning (SEL), which can contribute to greater student well-being by "enhancing the social, emotional, cultural, and ethical aspects of schooling" (Lavelle et al., 2017, p. 1). The literature currently describes the compassion-based framework as a largely holistic approach that considers the importance of student well-being based on a recognition that students may be exposed to trauma and violence (Hammack, Richards, Luo, Edlynn, & Roy, 2004). Thus, after observing a rise in educators' interest, mobilization, and growing movements in addressing students' well-being – which largely happened in silos – this framework developed in an effort to begin to provide a "comprehensive theoretical model of prosocial development" and "an organizing principle" (Lavelle et al., 2017, pp. 1–2) for the prosocial education field. Research suggests that taking this increasingly holistic approach to education improves students' academic success and well-being (Brown, Corrigan, & Higgins-D'Alessandro, 2012; Wentzel, Battle, Russell, & Looney, 2010), which are important considerations for equity (Center for Mental Health in Schools at UCLA, 2014).

Arguably, such a framework, which focuses on well-being (Lavelle et al., 2017, p. 1), can be particularly helpful for refugee students who may have experienced trauma (Pieloch et al., 2016) and who face increased social and emotional challenges as a result (Ayoub & Zhou, 2016; Ratkovic et al., 2017). Peterson (2017) also argues that compassion is an especially necessary individual and collective approach in twenty-first-century education in light of the fact that we are seeing the highest level of global suffering since the Second World War due to the incidence of natural disasters, disease, and conflict, impacting over 65 million people (UNHCR, 2020). Peterson (2017) defines compassion as the ability to "recognize and care about the suffering of others and to take some form of appropriate action in response" (p. 2). He further locates compassion in the field of civic and moral education as an important component of schools' growing emphasis on "character education, positive psychology, well-being, mindfulness, global citizenship … and values education" (Peterson, 2017, p. 10).

It is also important to note that while in some cases the literature may use "compassionate" and "trauma-informed" interchangeably because there are some commonalities between the two terms, there are also some important nuances. One such nuance is research that suggests that viewing refugee students *only* as "traumatized" impedes a real analysis of their backgrounds and experiences and masks "the significance of post-migration experiences such as poverty, isolation, racism and uncertain migration status" (Rutters, 2006, p. 5). Thus, while a trauma-informed approach is an important *part* of supporting refugee students' positive adaptation, I argue for the value of a compassion-based framework that, as recommended by the literature, approaches supporting students' positive adaptation, including their social integration and well-being, from a more holistic and asset-based perspective that focuses on strength and agency rather than a "deficit-based" perspective (Kovačević, 2016; Ratkovic et al., 2017).

The success of a compassion-based framework considers six elements: (1) school leadership, (2) a safe and caring school culture, (3) effective teaching and learning, (4) parental and community involvement, (5) compassion training programs, and (6) professional development for educators (Lavelle et al., 2017, p. 1). As discussed earlier, I propose *school leadership* and *school culture* may be further informed by cross-cultural transformative leadership, which emphasizes the importance of culture and equity (Peček et al., 2008; Shields, 2010). Furthermore, the compassion-based framework considers the importance of *a safe and caring school culture* and *effective teaching and learning*. These elements align with recommendations and best practices for supporting refugee students, which include cultivating an equitable and inclusive environment (Pinson & Arnot, 2007); addressing the social and emotional well-being of refugee students through cultivating strong relationships (Pinson & Arnot, 2007; Taylor & Sidhu, 2012); and meeting language learning needs by considering teaching and learning (Taylor & Sidhu, 2012).

Another important element of the compassion-based framework is *parental and community involvement*, which once again complements researchers' recommendations to build multiple levels of partnerships, including community partnerships, to support newcomer refugee students (Pinson & Arnot, 2007; Ratkovic et al., 2017). Furthermore, Lavelle et al.'s (2017) ongoing development of the compassion-based framework suggests "systematic methods of cultivating compassion" (p. 5) through engaging in different *compassion training programs*, which research has shown may contribute to prosocial behaviour (Condon, Desbordes, Miller, & DeSteno, 2013). While there are varying compassion training programs that have begun piloting in schools, including in the US, and in some cases explicitly focused on equity and system-level shifts, the training programs should to some degree seek to broaden the following natural capacities to extend beyond one's "in-group": "attention, affection, empathy, insight ... and courage" (Lavelle et al., 2017, p. 5).

For example, one compassion training program is the Compassion Integrity Training (CIT) program developed by the Center for Compassion,

Integrity and Secular Ethics. CIT is a "multi-part [resilience-based] training program that cultivates basic human values as skills for the purpose of increasing individual, social and environmental flourishing" (Compassion Integrity Program, n.d., para. 1). The program was developed through the expertise of academics and practitioners in the fields of "neuroscience, psychology, trauma-informed care, peace and conflict studies, and contemplative science" and draws on initiatives related to SEL (Compassion Integrity Program, n.d., para. 3). The program has been adopted by agencies such as the United Nations Educational, Scientific and Cultural Organization to train both staff and students (UNESCO MGIEP, 2018). It includes ten modules divided into three series: Series I on "Self-Cultivation," which includes modules on (1) Calming Body and Mind, (2) Ethical Mindfulness, (3) Emotional Awareness, and (4) Self-Compassion; Series II on "Relating to Others," which includes modules on (5) Impartiality and Common Humanity, (6) Forgiveness and Gratitude, (7) Empathic Concern, and (8) Compassion; and Series III on "Engaging in Systems," which includes modules on (9) Appreciating Interdependence and (10) Engaging with Discernment (Compassion Integrity Program, n.d., para. 4).

Thus, elements of the compassion-based framework once again align with cross-cultural transformative leadership, since both focus on equity and system-level shifts through developing specific policies, system-wide supports, and socially just–oriented leadership and values to meet the needs of refugee students. Finally, a compassion-based framework also supports *professional development* for students and educators on aspects related to SEL and mindfulness to promote the success of school-wide programs such as compassion training (Lavelle et al., 2017). Some researchers argue that school-wide professional development programs that involve student participation outside of school, including at home and after school settings, are the most successful (Bond & Hauf, 2004). Lavelle et al. (2017) also explain that "teacher development is critical, as research has also shown that teachers with weak social and emotional skills may actually hinder their own students' social and emotional development" (p. 10). Therefore, such professional development opportunities can contribute to improved management of instructional time, enhanced relationships between students and teachers, as well as reduced educator stress and burnout (Jennings, Frank, Snowberg, Coccia, & Greenberg, 2013), which can begin to address concerns with well-being for educators (Alisic et al., 2012) and students. Lavelle et al. (2017) suggest that "the potential for synergistic effects of pairing training for educators and students is a promising avenue for further investigation" (p. 10).

One noteworthy example that draws on a compassion-based framework in order to support students who have experienced great levels of stress and trauma (as well as offering support to their educators) is demonstrated in the work of Wolpow et al. (2016) in the US. Their work is a unique example of a compassionate, systems-level collaboration between public schools, Western Washington University, and the Washington State Office of the Superintendent of Public Instruction (OSPI), the results of which reportedly contributed to the increased resilience and academic success of students. The collaboration was led by the Washington OSPI to launch a Compassionate Schools Initiative to cultivate Compassionate Schools into a working practice. The goal was to develop a better understanding of "the implementation, growth, and sustainability of Compassionate Schools and to distill a set of Lessons Learned as a final project outcome" (Wolpow et al., 2016, p. 164). Spokane and Pierce counties were chosen as pilot sites, where training on how trauma affects learning was provided to teachers and school staff. The initiative led to trauma-informed practices being implemented in eleven school buildings, and the development of a process designed to help schools develop a Compassionate School infrastructure. This infrastructure included (1) engaging school leadership, (2) assessment, (3) training for school staff and community partners, (4) review of similar "compassionate" care models in other agencies such as health care facilities and communities of faith, (5) review of school policies and procedures, (6) partnerships, (7) action planning with short- and long-term goals, and (8) reassessment and evaluation (pp. 165–6). As Lavelle et al. (2017) likewise concluded, an emerging, compassion-based framework – though requiring multi-year interdisciplinary collaboration, theoretical development, research, and prototyping – "holds promise" (Lavelle et al., 2017, p. 4) for contributing to student well-being and is valuable for supporting refugee students' positive adaptation.

One of the challenges to consider when drawing on a compassion-based framework is that educational policies focus mainly on academic achievement and standardized testing, which may underemphasize attributes such as care and compassion (Lampert, 2003; Lavelle et al., 2017). Nonetheless, I believe with increasing interest in student well-being and holistic education in both literature and practice, a compassion-based framework that strives "to cultivate a deep-rooted concern for and commitment to the welfare of others, with an appreciation for the interdependent global community" (Lavelle et al., 2017, p. 9) holds real value.

A compassion-based framework also aligns with literature on cultivating an "ethic of care" (Noddings, 2002; Nur, 2012) in schools and a compassionate approach that supports refugee students more holistically (Gomez-Lee, 2017). Therefore, while the importance of qualities such as compassion may be sidelined due to school environments increasingly characterized by stress related to supporting students with trauma and academic performance expectations, researchers argue that it is these very circumstances that call for a more holistic approach that cultivates care and compassion in an effort to contribute to the betterment of our students' well-being, our education systems, and humanity as a whole (Lampert, 2003; Lavelle et al., 2017; Peterson, 2017; Wolpow et al., 2016).

## Conclusion

This chapter explored the issue of leading for equity when supporting refugee students' positive adaptation in Canadian schools. A discussion of the challenges that newcomer refugee students experience demonstrated the lasting influence of the trauma and socio-psychological effects related to their experiences of living amidst or fleeing conflict, and of migration and resettlement. These factors can impact refugee students' academic achievement, social integration, and well-being, and they can pose challenges for school staff and educators, who do not always feel sufficiently prepared to navigate and manage the cultural diversity and emotional distress that newcomer refugee students may bring with them into their schools. Educators also report fearing vicarious or secondary trauma, which poses concerns about educators' well-being as well.

A discussion on leadership approaches to address these challenges in schools included exploring the importance of cross-cultural transformative, compassionate, and trauma-informed leadership, which prioritizes equity, inclusive school communities, and student well-being while simultaneously cultivating parental and community partnerships. These leadership approaches inform a greater compassion-based framework, which is pertinent to support refugee students' positive adaptation through a holistic lens. The compassion-based framework considers school leadership, fostering a safe and caring school culture, effective teaching and learning, parental and community involvement, compassion training programs that focus on equity and system-level shifts, and additional professional development for educators related to social-emotional learning (Lavelle et al., 2017). Despite the great challenges experienced by newcomer refugee students, I believe that with the proper support and resources, school leaders working within a compassion-based framework have the potential to inspire hope and foster a sense of agency in newcomer refugee students such that these students can begin to thrive academically and socially in school and beyond.

REFERENCES

Abu El-Haj, T.R. (2007). "I was born here, but my home, it's not here": Educating for democratic citizenship in an era of transnational migration and global conflict. *Harvard Educational Review, 77*(3), 285–316. doi: 10.17763/haer.77.3.41217m737q114h5m
Alisic, E., Bus, M., Dulack, W., Pennings, L., & Splinter, J. (2012). Teachers' experiences supporting children after traumatic exposure. *Journal of Traumatic Stress, 25*(1), 98–101. doi: 10.1002/jts.20709
Allard, A.C., & Santoro, N. (2008). Experienced teachers' perspectives on cultural and social class diversity: Which differences matter? *Equity & Excellence in Education, 41*(2), 200–14. doi: 10.1080/10665680801957253

Armstrong, D., Tuters, S., & Carrier, N. (2013). Micropolitics and social justice leadership: Bridging beliefs and behaviours. *Journal of Educational Administration and Foundations, 23*(2), 119–37.

Ayoub, M., & Zhou, G. (2016). Somali refugee students in Canadian schools: Premigration experiences and challenges in refugee camps. *Comparative and International Education, 45*(3), 1–18. doi: 10.5206/cie-eci.v45i3.9300

Banks, J.A. (2008). *An introduction to multicultural education* (4th ed). Boston, MA: Pearson Education.

Beauregard, C., Gauthier, M.F., & Rousseau, C. (2014). Fostering solidarity in the classroom: Creative expression workshops for immigrant and refugee students. In C.A. Brewer & M. McCabe (Eds.), *Immigrant and refugee students in Canada* (pp. 202–19). Edmonton, AB: Brush Education.

Beiser, M., Puente-Duran, S., & Hou, F. (2015). Cultural distance and emotional problems among immigrant and refugee youth in Canada: Findings from the New Canadian Child and Youth Study (NCCYS). *International Journal of Intercultural Relations, 49,* 33–45. doi: 10.1016/j.ijintrel.2015.06.005

Bond, L.A., & Hauf, A.M.C. (2004). Taking stock and putting stock in primary prevention: Characteristics of effective programs. *The Journal of Primary Prevention, 24*(3), 199–221.

Brown, P., Corrigan, M.W., & Higgins-D'Alessandro, A. (Eds.). (2012). *Handbook of prosocial education.* Lanham, MD: Rowman & Littlefield.

Canadian Commission for UNESCO. (2019). *Welcoming immigrants and refugees to Canada: The role of municipalities.* https://en.ccunesco.ca/-/media/Files/Unesco/Resources/2019/08/CIMToolkitNewComers.pdf

Canadian Council for Refugees. (n.d.). *Practical information.* https://ccrweb.ca/en/practical-info

Center for Mental Health in Schools at UCLA. (2014). *Integrated student supports and equity: What's not being discussed?* UCLA Center. http://smhp.psych.ucla.edu/pdfdocs/integpolicy.pdf

Compassion Integrity Program. (n.d.). *Compassionate integrity training.* Center for Compassion, Integrity and Secular Ethics. https://www.compassionateintegrity.org/about-the-program/

Condon, P., Desbordes, G., Miller, W.B., & DeSteno, D. (2013). Meditation increases compassionate responses to suffering. *Psychological Science, 24*(10), 2125–7. doi: 10.1177/0956797613485603

Correa-Velez, I., Gifford, S.M., & Barnett, A.G. (2010). Longing to belong: Social inclusion and wellbeing among youth with refugee backgrounds in the first three years in Melbourne, Australia. *Social Science & Medicine, 71*(8), 1399–408. doi: 10.1016/j.socscimed.2010.07.018

Dei, G., James, I., Karumanchery, L., James-Wilson, S., & Zine, J. (2000). *Removing the margins: The challenges and possibilities of inclusive schooling.* Toronto, ON: Canadian Scholars' Press.

Delaney-Black, V., Covington, C., Ondersma, S.J., Nordstrom-Klee, B., Templin, T.,
    Ager, J., & Sokol, R.J. (2002). Violence exposure, trauma, and IQ and/or reading
    deficits among urban children. *Archives of Pediatrics & Adolescent Medicine*,
    *156*(3), 280–5. doi: 10.1001/archpedi.156.3.280
Dryden-Peterson, S. (2016). Refugee education: The crossroads of globalization.
    *Educational Researcher*, *45*(9), 473–82. doi: 10.3102/0013189X16683398
Edge, S., Newbold, K.B., & McKeary, M. (2014). Exploring socio-cultural factors that
    mediate, facilitate & constrain the health and empowerment of refugee youth.
    *Social Science & Medicine*, *117*, 34–41. doi: 10.1016/j.socscimed.2014.07.025
Faubert, B., & Tucker, B. (2019). Leading K–12 refugee integration: A GENTLE
    approach from Ontario, Canada. In K. Arar, J. Brooks, & I. Bogotch (Eds.),
    *Education, immigration and migration: Policy, leadership and praxis for a changing
    world* (pp. 53–71). Bingley, UK: Emerald Publishing Limited.
Finkelhor, D., Turner, H., Ormrod, R., Hamby, S., & Kracke, K. (2009). *Children's
    exposure to violence: A comprehensive national survey*. US Department of Justice.
    https://www.ojp.gov/pdffiles1/ojjdp/227744.pdf
Gagné, M.H., Shapka, J.D., & Law, D.M. (2012). The impact of social contexts in
    schools: Adolescents who are new to Canada and their sense of belonging. In
    C. Garcia Coll (Ed.), *The impact of immigration on children's development* (Vol. 24,
    pp. 17–34). New York, NY: Karger Publishers.
Gomez-Lee, V. (2017). *Leadership practices that foster trauma informed approaches in
    schools* (Unpublished doctoral dissertation). San Diego State University, CA.
Hammack, P.L., Richards, M.H., Luo, Z., Edlynn, E.S., & Roy, K. (2004). Social
    support factors as moderators of community violence exposure among inner-city
    African American young adolescents. *Journal of Clinical Child and Adolescent
    Psychology*, *33*(3), 450–62. doi: 10.1207/s15374424jccp3303_3
Immigration, Refugees and Citizenship Canada. (2017). *#WelcomeRefugees: Canada
    resettled Syrian refugees*. Government of Canada. https://www.canada.ca/en
    /immigration-refugees-citizenship/services/refugees/welcome-syrian
    -refugees.html
Jennings, P.A., Frank, J.L., Snowberg, K.E., Coccia, M.A., & Greenberg, M.T. (2013).
    Improving classroom learning environments by Cultivating Awareness and
    Resilience in Education (CARE): Results of a randomized controlled trial. *School
    Psychology Quarterly*, *28*(4), 374–90. doi: 10.1037/spq0000035
Kovačević, D. (2016). *Yugoslavian refugee children in Canadian schools: The role of
    transformative leadership in overcoming the social, psychological, and academic
    barriers to successful integration* (Master's thesis, Brock University, St. Catherines,
    ON). http://dr.library.brocku.ca/bitstream/handle/10464/10821/Brock_Dragana
    _Kovačević_2016.pdf?sequence=1
Lampert, K. (2003). *Compassionate education: A prolegomena for radical schooling*.
    Lanham, MD: University Press of America.
Lavelle, B., Flook, L., & Ghahremani, D. (2017). A call for compassion and care in
    education: Toward a more comprehensive prosocial framework for the field. In

E.M. Seppälä, E. Simon-Thomas, S.L. Brown, M.C. Worline, C.D. Cameron, & J.R. Doty (Eds.), *The Oxford handbook of compassion science* (pp. 1–19). New York, NY: Oxford University Press.

McAdams, C.R., III, & Foster, V.A. (2008). Voices from "the front": How student violence is changing the experience of school leaders. *Journal of School Violence, 7*(2), 87–103. doi: 10.1300/J202v07n02_06

Mulholland, M-L., & Biles, J. (2004). *Newcomer integration policies in Canada.* York University and Citizen and Immigration Canada. http://p2pcanada.ca/wp-content/blogs.dir/1/files/2015/09/Newcomer-Integration-Policies-in-Canada.pdf

Noddings, N. (2002). *Educating moral people: A caring alternative to character education.* New York, NY: Teachers' College Press.

Nur, S. (2012). *Leadership paradigms informing the way school administrators work with Somali immigrant students: Case studies of two high schools in an urban school district* (Unpublished doctoral dissertation). University of Illinois, Urbana, IL.

Office of the High Commissioner for Human Rights. (2018). *The human rights to water and sanitation of forcibly displaced persons in need of humanitarian assistance: Report.* https://www.ohchr.org/EN/Issues/WaterAndSanitation/SRWater/Pages/ForciblyDisplacedPersons.aspx

Ontario Ministry of Education. (2017). *Ontario's education equity action plan.* http://www.edu.gov.on.ca/eng/about/education_equity_plan_en.pdf

Peček, M., Čuk, I., & Lesar, I. (2008). Teachers' perceptions of the inclusion of marginalised groups. *Educational Studies, 34*(3), 225–39. doi: 10.1080/03055690701811347

Peterson, A. (2017). *Compassion and education: Cultivating compassionate children, schools and communities.* London, UK: Palgrave Macmillan.

Pieloch, K.A., McCullough, M.B., & Marks, A.K. (2016). Resilience of children with refugee statuses: A research review. *Canadian Psychology/Psychologie canadienne, 57*(4), 330–9. doi: 10.1037/cap0000073

Pinson, H., & Arnot, M. (2007). Sociology of education and the wasteland of refugee education research. *British Journal of Sociology of Education, 28*(3), 399–407. doi: 10.1080/01425690701253612

Ratkovic, S., Kovacevic, D., Brewer, C., Ellis, C., Ahmed, N., & Baptiste-Brady, J. (2017). *Supporting refugee students in Canada: Building on what we have learned in the past 20 years.* Social Sciences and Humanities Research Council of Canada. http://citiesofmigration.ca/wp-content/uploads/2018/04/Supporting-Refugee-Students-in-Canada-Full-Research-Report-1.pdf

Ross, J.A., & Berger, M.J. (2009). Equity and leadership: Research-based strategies for school leaders. *School Leadership and Management, 29*(5), 463–76. doi: 10.1080/13632430903152310

Rossiter, M.J., & Rossiter, K.R. (2009). Diamonds in the rough: Bridging gaps in supports for at-risk immigrant and refugee youth. *Journal of International Migration and Integration, 10*(4), 409–29. doi: 10.1007/s12134-009-0110-3

Rutter, M. (2006). Implications of resilience concepts for scientific understanding. *Annals of the New York Academy of Sciences, 1094*(1), 1–12. doi: 10.1196/annals .1376.002

Ryan, J. (2006). Inclusive leadership and social justice for schools. *Leadership and Policy in Schools, 5*(1), 3–17. doi: 10.1080/15700760500483995

Shields, C.M. (2003). *Good intentions are not enough: Transformative leadership for communities of difference.* Lanham, MA: Scarecrow Press.

Shields, C.M. (2010). Transformative leadership: Working for equity in diverse contexts. *Educational Administration Quarterly, 46*(4), 558–89. doi: 10.1177 /0013161X10375609

Singleton, G.E., & Linton, C. (2006). *A field guide for achieving equity in schools: Courageous conversations about race.* Thousand Oaks, CA: Corwin.

Szente, J., Hoot, J., & Taylor, D. (2006). Responding to the special needs of refugee children: Practical ideas for teachers. *Early Childhood Education Journal, 34*(1), 15–20. doi: 10.1007/s10643-006-0082-2

Tavares, T. (2012). *Life after war: Education as a healing process for refugee and war-affected children.* Manitoba Education. https://www.edu.gov.mb.ca/k12/docs /support/law/law_interactive.pdf

Taylor, S., & Sidhu, R.K. (2012). Supporting refugee students in schools: What constitutes inclusive education? *International Journal of Inclusive Education, 16*(1), 39–56. doi: 10.1080/13603110903560085

Theoharis, G. (2008). Woven in deeply identity and leadership of urban social justice principals. *Education and Urban Society, 41*(1), 3–25. doi: 10.1177/001312450 8321372

Tuters, S., & Portelli, J. (2017). Ontario school principals and diversity: Are they prepared to lead for equity? *International Journal of Educational Management, 31*(5), 598–611. doi: 10.1108/IJEM-10-2016-0228

UNESCO MGIEP. (2018, May 18). *UNESCO MGIEP announces CIT training partnership with Life University's CCISE* [Press release]. https://mgiep.unesco.org /article/life-university-s-ccise-announces-cit-training-partnership-with-unesco -mgiep

United Nations High Commissioner for Refugees (UNHCR). (2010). *Convention and protocol relating to the status of refugees.* https://www.unhcr.org/3b66c2aa10.html

United Nations High Commissioner for Refugees (UNHCR). (2020). *UNHCR global trends in forced displacement in 2020.* https://www.unhcr.org/60b638e37 /unhcr-global-trends-2020

Van der Stouwe, M., & Oh, S.A. (2008). Educational change in a protracted refugee context. *Forced Migration Review, 30*(16), 47–9. https://www.fmreview.org/burma /vanderstouwe-oh

Volante, L., Klinger, D., Bilgili, Ö., & Siegel, M. (2017). Making sense of the performance (dis)advantage for immigrant students across Canada. *Canadian Journal of Education, 40*(3), 329–61. https://journals.sfu.ca/cje/index.php/cje-rce /article/view/2557

Vongkhamphra, E.G., Davis, C., & Adem, N. (2011). The resettling process: A case study of a Bantu refugee's journey to the USA. *International Social Work, 54*(2), 246–57. doi: 10.1177/0020872809358397

Wang, F., Pollock, K., & Hauseman, C. (2018). School principals' job satisfaction: The effects of work intensification. *Canadian Journal of Educational Administration and Policy, 185*, 73–90.

Wentzel, K.R., Battle, A., Russell, S.L., & Looney, L.B. (2010). Social supports from teachers and peers as predictors of academic and social motivation. *Contemporary Educational Psychology, 35*(3), 193–202. doi: 10.1016/j.cedpsych.2010.03.002

Wolpow, R., Hertel, R., Johnson, M., & Kincaid, S. (2016). *The heart of learning and teaching: Compassion, resiliency, and academic success.* Washington State Office of Superintendent of Public Instruction (OSPI) Compassionate Schools. https://www.k12.wa.us/sites/default/files/public/compassionateschools/pubdocs/theheartoflearningandteaching.pdf

Zine, J. (2001). Muslim youth in Canadian schools: Education and the politics of religious identity. *Anthropology & Education Quarterly, 32*(4), 399–423. doi: 10.1525/aeq.2001.32.4.399

# 11 New Canadian Student Leadership: "It's More Than Just a Tour"

LYLE HAMM

Student leadership and activism are rising across the world. Recent climate crisis demonstrations are positioning student leader activists as strong political voices for social change (Slaughter & Frisk, 2019; Kaplan, Lumpkin & Dennis, 2019). Throughout my career, I have been challenged to view leadership opportunities for students in multiple ways. I was fortunate to teach and lead in a vibrant rural school district in Alberta that experienced rapid demographic change due to its robust economic conditions. My colleagues and I engaged the global world each day as we searched for new pedagogies of hope that would help us become more culturally responsive and socially just (Lopez, 2016). Most of the new Canadian students we taught were from immigrant, temporary foreign worker, and refugee backgrounds. Most of them did not speak the dominant language and many were marginalized in their educational experiences. Students who did not easily learn the dominant language could not participate democratically in their school culture. They could not navigate the unseen and unwritten rules of social engagement in their school that would bring about more equity and the same opportunities for them as their Canadian peers enjoyed.

Finding Lisa Delpit's work (2006) during my doctoral studies helped me understand that the new Canadian children I was serving in my district did not understand the "culture of power" (p. 25) of which they were now a part. Equipped with a PhD in leadership and social justice when I returned to my leadership service, I found myself locked into the turbulence of school administration, and thus, many of the powerfully important transformative ideas I gained during my graduate work seemed back benched in the leadership I strived to provide. Thank goodness, I was shaken out of my administrative slumber by one of our Grade 6 new Canadian students in our school. The young lad came to my office to describe his perception of an inequitable and unjust action taking place within our community (Stanway, 2011).

### "Mr. Hamm, This Ain't Right!"

While sitting in my office, the student described, in detail, the dilapidated playground equipment in the park behind the housing complex where he lived. He was concerned about the decrepit swings and splintered wooden platforms and believed children in his neighbourhood were at risk playing on them. I realized that the situation he was illuminating was more than simply a teaching moment for me and a leadership opportunity for him. The young student was clearly a socially just and transformative young activist; in my mind, he was doing what equity-minded and socially just scholar-teachers would encourage him to do in the situation (see, for example, Lund, 2003; Sears, Peck, & Herriot, 2014; Shields, 2018). He was raising concern and awareness, he was deciding a plan for action (and practising it on me), and he was preparing to take action to achieve more community equity by respectfully challenging the leadership authority in our community. He was going to work to ensure that the children in his neighbourhood had a safe place to play and grow without injuring themselves. His moral purpose was clear.

I began inquiring more about his cause, as I believed the mayor and council of our community would if we approached them. I learned that as he was walking through several neighbourhoods, he noticed work crews dismantling older playground equipment that resembled the structures behind his home. Through additional inquiry, he learned that the older treated-wood playground structures throughout the community were gradually being replaced with modern playground structures. In his perceptive mindfulness, the playground structures seemed to be getting replaced in the more marketable subdivisions where expensive single-dwelling residences stood. He described the homes in detail as "large, nice, well-kept homes with green lawns." A silence invaded my office. Through his soft and determined voice, he told me straight out, "Mr. Hamm, this isn't right! If the playground equipment should be replaced anywhere, it should be in my neighbourhood where there are lots of children and their parents are not making much money." His story filled me with inspiration and hope, and I said, "Let's go take a look."

### Literature Review

*Encouraging New Canadian Student Leadership*

With immigration increasing in Canada, educators and school leaders must respond to the demographic changes in their communities or suffer professionally (Goldberg, 2000; Merchant, 2000). Years of research on globalization, citizenship education, and diversity in schools has lead James Banks (2017) to claim that "policymakers and educational leaders within nations that are grappling with diversity and citizenship need to realize that individuals and groups that are structurally excluded may not be peacefully apathetic and that structural exclusion produces alienation, resistance, and insurgency" (p. 367). In Canada, Robertson (2005) reported that the dropout rate for English as a Second Language (ESL) students can be as high as 75 per cent, or three times the rate of students who are not part of ESL programming.

The new Canadian students I worked with in my teaching, school leadership, and research program have helped me understand their wisdom, resilience, and leadership capacity. From their narratives, along with a selection of stories from their teachers, I became motivated to learn more about new Canadian student leadership as it might exist or emerge in diverse, intercultural schools in Canada. Dempster and Lizzio (2007) suggest that student leadership is intrinsic to student engagement. I agree, but to engagement and participation I would add that student leadership is also about courage, action, and commitment to a cause. My curiosity about new Canadian student leadership inspired me to construct two related questions for this chapter. First, "How do/can minoritized new immigrant and refugee students (i.e., new Canadian students) provide leadership in their schools?" and second, "What type of leadership support do minoritized students require, and from whom, to help them shape their leadership capacity for more equity in their lives?" I have reviewed a range of studies, articles, and books on student leadership in diverse and intercultural schools to examine how new immigrant and refugee students are providing leadership in their schools and communities. I found the literature limited in scope and depth on this topic, which to my mind is unfortunate given that schools across the world are enrolling increasing numbers of immigrant and refugee students every year.

## Opportunities to Engage and Lead

Magno and Schiff (2010) state that "few studies have examined the extent to which school leaders actively use the assets of immigrant students or adapt a school to its changing population" (p. 87). As Roberts and Nash (2009) note, "students make up around 95 per cent of a school's population … Yet we rarely give them the opportunity to take initiative to improve their school. Instead, they become passive recipients of policy and practice, rather than active agents of change" (p. 174). In my research (Hamm, Massfeller, Scott, & Cormier, 2017; Massfeller & Hamm, 2019), new Canadian students often describe how they feel marginalized in their school. They are not confident in their English language skills, they feel shy approaching their teachers and Canadian peers, and many do not speak in their classes because they do not want to appear foolish during discussions and activities. We have consistently argued that educators who remain passive in their pedagogies and allow new Canadian students to flounder like this in their learning do more harm than service for them (Hamm et al., 2017; Massfeller & Hamm, 2019).

Lizzio, Dempster, and Neumann (2011) report that "peer encouragement and participation has been found to predict adolescents' motivation to engage in community or civic activities" (p. 87). Peer mentoring relationships can help all students build confidence and guide them in their leadership to effect change in their schools and communities. Gagné and Soto Gordon (2015) advocated for "the more equitable distribution of power amongst students in the school by providing opportunities for ELLs [English Language Learners] to take on new roles and interact with an arrangement of people they would not normally meet or interact with including their Canadian-born peers" (p. 543).

As I discovered through my Grade 6 student's experience, the elementary school classroom is ripe with social justice ideas, leadership possibilities for students, and opportunities for engaging social justice activities. When students "create environments where they have opportunities to discover and explore questions rooted in their social experiences, they will inevitably raise issues concerning social inequities and problems. These concerns arise from their daily lives in the classroom, the school, and beyond" (Jennings, Crowell, & Fernlund, 1994, p. 4). One reason that minoritized students do not get to lead is because they are not asked to lead, and they do not know how to get involved. It is up to the educators to make this happen because, as McKibben (2004) observed, "given the opportunity, students quickly demonstrate their potential for leadership by undertaking advocacy in various forms – as ambassadors, action researchers, mentors, academic architects, volunteers, education consultants, advisors, fund-raisers, and translators" (p. 81). Thus, if educators create engaging conditions, leadership will emerge among students. Further, white educators and leaders must "seek means by which the racial identity of students of colour is not sacrificed when students of colour participate in predominantly white groups" (Arminio et al., 2000, p. 506). We have clearly learned in our work that new Canadian students will lead if given the chance, but those chances will be limited unless opportunities are intentionally framed and new Canadian students are encouraged to lead by their teachers and administrators.

### The Role of Educators in Shaping Student Leadership

Franklin (2009) reported how changing classroom pedagogy increased equity and challenged students to engage in inquiry, action, and reflection through participating in a social studies intercultural leadership and peace summit. She argues, "Pedagogically, this participatory approach can serve as a counter to the prevailing climate of social alienation and academic disengagement that has too often characterized the educational experience for our nation's students" (p. 534).

Student leadership can also bridge student cultures, as Brown (2016) described from his teaching experience working with Haitian refugee students. Rather than fight back against the racism and violence that was part of their school experience, the Haitian students engaged the dominant cultures in their new school through music and drumming. "I witnessed this truth as my students built bridges through a shared passion for justice, the universal language of music, and their willingness to share their personal struggles to inspire others" (Brown, 2016, p. 79).

All students need the support and guidance of their teachers, but we have found through our research activities that new Canadian students place greater demand on teachers who serve in diverse intercultural schools and communities. As such, teachers and leaders need to be prepared to serve a diverse society. Lopez (2016) argues for culturally responsive leadership in education systems and communities that are becoming increasingly diverse. Moreover, culturally responsive leaders must possess what Collard (2007) describes as "sophisticated understandings of the concept of culture as a learned and adaptive response to the contextual needs" (p. 750) of school and community stakeholders, with particular nuanced understandings of their new immigrant students and their family backgrounds. Magno and Schiff (2010) identified an "exemplary school leader" (p. 87) who practiced culturally responsive leadership by challenging his new immigrant and refugee students to embrace leadership roles in their school and community. The leader in that inquiry ensured that all new students to his school got involved in the buddy-system – either as a mentor or mentee. In this initiative, new immigrant students were partnered with and mentored by immigrant students who had previously been through the buddy system and had already gained some cultural knowledge and social capital in the school, which they could then lead other new immigrant and refugee students to acquire.

In a more recent study, Kirk et al. (2017) examined how students from marginalized groups gained an authentic sense of empowerment to meet their educational and social needs. The authors interviewed many students who explained that they enjoyed classes and felt empowered when their teachers "created opportunities for students to share in some of the decision making in the classroom" (p. 837). The authors also found an administrative team that worked hard to create and sustain student leadership opportunities in the school. Likewise, Seemiller (2016) suggests that "creating intentional learning environments helps students develop leadership competencies that result in their becoming the leaders aptly referenced in their institution's mission statement" (p. 64). Furthermore, Bradley (2007) insists that student leadership programs that battle and disrupt bias, racism, and discrimination are important for teachers and school leaders to develop and infuse in intercultural schools and communities undergoing rapid demographic change. The author reported on two such programs called the Student Leadership Project and the Controversial Dialogue Unity project. In this joint initiative, student leaders are selected across cultural groups – often from groups in conflict with each other – with the result that students gain "greater understanding of their own power and ability to work together to build a school community of which they can be truly proud" (p. 52).

Finally, Rah (2013) reported on a case study of a school that unexpectedly welcomed in twenty-five refugee students. The leaders and educators in the school worked collaboratively with a community organization inside a distributed leadership framework to adapt an after-school program called Families and Schools Together (FAST). The aim of the program was to build relationships with refugee parents in the community and increase their involvement in the school to support their children alongside educators. "FAST was an integral element that constituted leadership practice since it enabled multiple leaders from inside and outside school to cooperate in various ways" (Rah, 2013, p. 74).

In the next section, I will describe how many of the students and teachers I spoke with created engagement possibilities and leadership opportunities in their schools and communities that created more equity for new Canadian students.

## Understanding New Canadian Student Leadership

For this project, I mined data from previous studies I led in Alberta and New Brunswick (Hamm, 2017; Hamm et al., 2017; Massfeller & Hamm, 2019). I was particularly interested in the new Canadian student narratives in both provinces as well as what their teachers and administrators were describing about student leadership in their schools. By responding to the research questions in this present study, it became apparent that new Canadian students can and must take on significant leadership roles in their schools, but they must have support from their teachers and school administrators to do so. In this section, I will discuss each of the three key ideas that emerged from the data.

### Engagement Stretches Comfort Zones

The new Canadian students spoke highly about the engaging activities and support their teachers provided them that helped them stretch their comfort zones and shape their leadership. In my analysis, I perceived how that support inspired the students to take risks in their own leadership and learning. For instance, one student, who was scared to speak in front of his Canadian peers, described the patience and gentle nudging from his teacher that helped him find his voice: "She gave me the confidence and the belief in myself that I can talk in a class, and by the end of the term, I'm talking … like giving out the answer ... I've done a way better job from not speaking to speaking" (NB New Canadian Student 1).

One educator in the Alberta study described the importance of establishing a mentoring program in the school that brought students together from all linguistic and cultural backgrounds. He described how each teacher in the school was assigned a group of students to mentor, advocate for, and get to know on a more personal level: "It was common to place small numbers of students that emigrated from the same country into groups together. The rationale was to provide similar cultural and language opportunities and reduce marginalization" (AB Educator 9). Teachers highlighted how important safety was for their new Canadian students, as one New Brunswick educator described:

> It has to be safety, but you've got to build [the idea] that they are all here together with me as their teacher. And you are going to help them, protect them, be there for them, advocate for them as best as you can within the [school] framework. (NB Educator 19)

The support that the teacher provided had a trickle-down effect on several students. For instance, one student described in depth how the teacher cared for them and how her care gave him the confidence to step up and support many other new Canadian students as they arrived in his school.

Two teachers in New Brunswick described the importance of getting new Canadian students involved and working with anglophone students in their classes. They got their classes together for outdoor snowshoeing activities – a winter activity the recently arrived Syrian students had never experienced before. The group then worked together to build fires outside in the snow and make hot chocolate. In this situation, the student leadership was reciprocal, giving both newcomer and Canadian-born students opportunities to be in leadership roles while building the fires in the snow.

An Alberta educator described how he had intentionally constructed his Physical Education program to include new Canadian students and provide them with leadership opportunities alongside their Canadian peers. He said, "It was relatively easy for students to follow along with what the other students were doing. Play is a universal language, and students from all cultural and athletic backgrounds quickly enjoyed each other's contributions" (AB Educator 9).

Another New Brunswick educator described in detail how a new Canadian student felt empowered when he was given opportunities to serve in leadership roles in the extracurricular activities of his school. The student, who had been a survivor of two wars, looked for opportunities and worked hard to build his leadership skills under the guidance and mentoring of his teachers. His teachers recognized his leadership potential and created several engaging opportunities for him to develop into a leader.

He'd be sleeping here every night; he just loves being in the gym. We call him the general manager. He is sort of the general manager of basketball and now he's the general manager of the floor hockey [program]. And his big thing is, if there are ever announcements that have to be made, he will go and put them on the announcements. (NB Educator 25)

Another key finding that emerged in our research involved cultural bridging between educators and new Canadian parents and how important these actions were to aid student engagement, their leadership development, and their sense of belonging. Most new Canadian parents have a difficult time being part of the school and their child's education for various reasons (Hamm, 2017). Some of these reasons could be related to parent work schedules, loss of former identity, and lower self-confidence in engaging their children's teachers. One New Brunswick educator said serving as hosts for various events can bring more new Canadian parents to the school, which in turn contributes to new Canadian student engagement in school activities. Clearly, if the engagement opportunities are not present for new Canadian students, it is highly likely that their leadership skills will be overlooked.

### Intentionally Creating Leadership Opportunities for New Canadian Students

There was abundant evidence in the data of many new Canadian students providing leadership in their schools. One new Canadian student in New Brunswick said that after he had adjusted in the school and gained some confidence, he knew his leadership was going to be required when new Syrian students arrived and began their integration process in early 2016. In his case, he did not wait to be asked by school leaders and teachers to help the students with their adjustment process; instead, he took the initiative: "I went to [teacher's name] and said, 'Listen, I know there's more newcomers coming. If you don't mind, I would like to take them and show them around'" (NB New Canadian Student 1). The student explained that when he had arrived at the school, he was simply shown the classrooms where he would have his courses in addition to a few key spaces (i.e., the gymnasium and cafeteria). He explained that after that, he felt like he had to adjust to the large environment on his own, which caused him feelings of loneliness and isolation. He did not want the Syrian students to go through a similar in-take experience. "When I had my walk around, I was just shown the place, but for me, I'm trying to engage in conversation with them [the new Canadian students]. It's more than just a tour" (NB New Canadian Student 1).

One educator described in detail the importance of new Canadian students taking on leadership roles in the welcoming and integration process. "I think that one of the main steps forward is using the peers who have been there and who have figured it out … getting them into those leadership positions, and also just doing more in the school" (NB Educator 20). An Alberta educator agreed and built upon these ideas of integrating new Canadian students through peer leadership, suggesting the following: "Organize activities and classes that allow interactions between groups. Encourage students to join groups and clubs that will help them blend into the school community. Celebrate the differences yet concentrate on the similarities between students" (AB Educator 10). This worked well for many new Canadian students in the schools in both the Alberta and New Brunswick studies. For instance, Syrian students who arrived in 2016 in New Brunswick soon began volunteering in many school activities and even in their community. In both the Alberta and New Brunswick studies, educators and new Canadian students started school social justice–based student action teams that intentionally invited and brought together new Canadian students and their Canadian peers to work on and deliver social action projects. Both programs were deemed huge successes, as outlined by new Canadian students in both provinces in the narratives below:

> In Grade 10, I was in the School Action team. It was a good experience. We used to go around … go to [name of elementary school], work with the kids, to show them, in front of them, we have to represent a drama to show them the good things, like don't do the bad things … educational dramas. (AB New Canadian Student 4)

> We just decided as a group of people … and we're just a bunch of people who have passion towards helping newcomers. So, I was like, this is good … because when I was doing the work, I felt like I needed help, because I knew there was ideas in my mind, and I knew there could be more stuff done. (NB New Canadian Student 3)

One New Brunswick teacher believed that "anytime you give someone the leadership role, it helps build their confidence and maybe they find out they're a leader. They may find out something new about themselves" (NB Educator 30). This was certainly the case with another New Brunswick educator. After listening to and analysing his narrative, I found his educational approach to be in strong alignment with the pedagogical philosophy of Paulo Freire (1970), who wrote, "The teacher is no longer merely the-one-who-teaches, but one who is himself taught in dialogue with the students, who in turn while being taught also teach" (p. 80). The New Brunswick teacher described a situation where he was trying hard to engage a new Canadian student who was originally from India and struggling in his class. He had learned that the student was an excellent athlete in the sport of cricket, and soon the teacher's mind kicked into pedagogical overdrive.

And so I'm thinking … okay, let's see what we can do here. I went online and purchased an indoor cricket set. I said, "You're going to have to teach me to play cricket … I don't understand how to play cricket. I've watched it, I don't understand it. I want you to teach me." So he came down to the gym for a week and he showed me how to do this and that and taught me the rules of the game. And I said, "Good, now we're going to teach other kids how to play." So we started a little cricket club at lunch time, and we'd play inside the gym. We had a lot of students from Nepal, India, and Pakistan come down. They knew how to play the game. And then we also had some of the Canadian students coming down … because they had watched us and they were kind of curious as to what we were doing and they started getting involved. We just started playing like, small mini games … allowed them to practice batting, allowed them to practice pitching … And anyway, the student took control and he started running it and he was doing the teaching and you know, using his language and developing his language skills by teaching. (NB Educator 28)

As these narratives demonstrate, intercultural schools that have students and educators who conceptualize and craft equity and leadership projects allow for new Canadian students to gain traction, momentum, and social and cultural capital quicker. This leads to the last theme in this chapter.

### Help the Students Nourish Their Dreams

Over the years, I have enjoyed learning about the goals and dreams new Canadian students have for their lives in Canada. The students I have worked with in my own K–12 teaching as well as through my research program do not take their opportunities for granted. They clearly understand that these opportunities do not exist in the war-torn countries they left. As one New Brunswick educator stated bluntly during his interview,

I can't imagine being in a refugee camp and wondering, okay what am I going to eat next? Am I going to eat tomorrow? Am I going to eat on the weekend? Am I going to eat on Monday? We are so blessed to live in a free country where we can say what we want; we can do what we want. And our kids, we have to get them to understand that these kids coming over here aren't our enemies. These kids coming here are coming to only get what you've already had. They just want what you've had all of your life. And it's only fair; fairness doesn't mean that everybody gets the same. Fairness means everybody gets what they need and these kids need to have a chance. (NB Educator 25)

Equity-minded teacher leaders like the ones described above go above and beyond to ensure new Canadian students have the chance to grow their potential for leadership. By doing so, they are making their schools a better place to learn.

In 2015, I attended a school event in another city in New Brunswick and watched several new Canadian students tell their Canadian peers what life was like for them in their countries of origin. One student said she had her feelings damaged when she was taunted and called a terrorist by some of her Canadian peers. Instead of turning away, she constructed a professionally crafted Power-Point presentation for over 100 of her Canadian peers complete with pictures of her Syrian home before and after it was destroyed by rockets in the course of civil war. Understanding grew between her and the Canadian students as she described her dreams and told them that she wanted to be a doctor so she could help people. Her resilience was inspiring, and many tears of hope were shed during her presentation.

In that same session, two students from a war-torn country in Africa described to their Canadian peers that when it came down to paying for food or paying for their education in the refugee camp where they lived, they chose education and went hungry for several days. New Canadian students, like these children, are leaders in their schools and have dreams about becoming leaders in their lives and giving back to society, as one new Canadian student explains in the following narrative:

> I'd really like to become a petroleum engineer. Then after that, maybe I can help someone back in my country … someone going to school. Because not everybody's rich, right? It's hard for people there to get into university. Some people want to go to college, but then they have a hard time to get into the university because they have no money and our government is not helping them. (AB New Canadian Student 2)

It is therefore important for Canadian educators and school leaders to listen to and find out what their new Canadian students want to do in their lives and craft programming and opportunities to help them achieve these things. By understanding the hopes and dreams of their students, educators gain a better sense of them as citizens who are seeking to find their rightful place in Canada. The final section will conclude with a brief discussion of these themes and provide suggestions for educators and school leaders in intercultural schools who wish to invite and guide new Canadian students in their own leadership development. But first, what happened with that Grade 6 student in Alberta who wanted to see the playground in his neighbourhood fixed?

## Conclusion: Courage, Commitment, and Cause

The student and I took our school camera and we drove through several neighbourhoods where we saw, first-hand, the new playgrounds he had described and one playground under construction. We then drove over to where he and his family lived, and my heart just sank. It was what he had described, but much worse. He had not described the terrible graffiti, the broken chain link fencing around the park, or the nails piercing through some of the wooden planks on the structure. We took several pictures from multiple angles and went back to our school to conceptualize his response to community officials. It was time to practice democracy (Sears et al., 2014), and I said to him, "I wonder if you can make this a social studies project with your teacher and classmates?" He agreed, and his team quickly grew in numbers. His classroom teacher helped him craft a letter to the mayor and city council expressing his concern and desire to have his neighbourhood's playground structure replaced before several others that were scheduled ahead of it. Shortly after the letter was sent, I received a call from the mayor inviting the student, his teacher, and his large Grade 6 social action team to the city council chambers to present their concerns in public. Dressed professionally, the young student gave a brilliant presentation, complete with selected pictures of the playground and his neighbourhood arranged on PowerPoint slides to provide evidence for his concerns. His courage to talk to me about his community concern motivated him in his leadership action. He demonstrated commitment in his cause and he ultimately transformed his classroom and community. Unanimously, the mayor and council agreed with his claims and proposition for social action and voted to move his playground up the line of redevelopment. The story was captured in the newspaper, the lad was quoted at length, and our community was introduced to a social issue that would otherwise have been overlooked in our city.

As Robinson and Randall (2016) have stressed in their work, "injustices against minorities must be addressed through social action" (p. 237). In the case of our Grade 6 new Canadian student, he argued vehemently for equity in our community. The social action route that he took to deliver his concern publicly and democratically clearly follows the line of critical thought and socially just advocacy outlined in this chapter. Though Sears et al. (2014) found that "students in Alberta feel a pervasive sense of voicelessness in terms of society generally and their schools particularly" (p. 3), this young new Canadian student from Alberta created a new pathway in this moment and was able to find his courage and voice for action through the support and mentoring from his educators and friends in his class. Through his social action, he became "engaged in the democratic process and aware of [his] capacity to effect change in [his] communities, society and world" (Alberta Education, 2005, as cited in Sears et al., 2014, p. 2).

As urban, suburban, and rural communities across Canada continue to welcome new families from all over the world, I encourage and gently remind educators and educational leaders to be aware of the student leadership potential that exists on the fringes in their schools. Leadership clubs, student councils, and social action teams like the ones the student participants in this study described need to be more intentionally inclusive of new Canadian students to provide for equitable opportunities in their learning and future growth.

I encourage educators to become more socially and globally minded and aware of what is happening in the world and how significant events may bring new Canadian students to their schools and classrooms who may have developed their leadership skills in ways that Canadian students have not. Students who have survived war, who have had to travel great distances to find safety, and who have even had to live in foreign countries or refugee camps for long periods of time have developed resilience and leadership skills uncommon for most children in Canada. Several educators in this study noticed this in the new Canadian students they served and created intentional growth opportunities for them that simultaneously increased their enthusiasm in school and their motivation to be important contributors to the life of their learning community.

We agree that empathy for and understanding of refugee student struggles is important during the readjustment phase when students arrive in Canada (Arar, Örücü, & Küçükçayır, 2018), but we have found that once new Canadian students feel a sense of belonging in their new school, they want to be challenged and establish opportunities for personal and academic growth. They are not looking for pity, but they would like their teachers to understand what they have gone through to get to Canada as they work towards establishing their chances for an equitable education that will give them a pathway to a successful future (Hamm, 2017).

I want to make a final recommendation to conclude this chapter. I feel fortunate to have worked in both the K–12 and post-secondary education sectors during the course of my career. I believe we can do more to help our pre-service teachers and our new and experienced teachers across our country become more prepared and confident to teach in diverse and intercultural classrooms in Canada. What I encourage is for university faculty and instructors in education to intentionally, systematically, and theoretically ground, construct, and embed their courses in the principles of equity and social justice (Shields, 2018). This may mean different things to the many different people who are tasked with such academic responsibilities. However, if defining social justice is difficult for educators, I encourage you and your students to think about, recognize, and call out the injustices that are ever-present in our world (Shields, 2017). Follow the lead of my Grade 6 student. Both university and public sector educators can design institution, school, and community projects that will challenge their students to think beyond the grades they achieve and to think instead about how they can make a contribution to their social environments and what that might mean to their own human development. We can all work together in ways that we are comfortable and uncomfortable with to prepare our students for social action (Burrell Storms, 2012). I challenge educators in Canada to consider their own methods for bringing more equity, equality, and meaning to the lives of their students as they make their schools better places to learn and their communities better places to live.

## REFERENCES

Arar, K., Örücü, D., & Küçükçayır, G.A. (2018). Culturally relevant school leadership for Syrian refugee students in challenging circumstances. *Educational Management, Administration & Leadership, 47*(6), 960–79. doi: 0.1177/1741143218775430

Arminio, J.L., Carter, S., Jones, S.E., Kruger, K., Lucas, N., Washington, J., Young, N., & Angela, S. (2000). Leadership experiences of students of color. *NASPA Journal, 37*(3), 496–510. doi: 10.2202/1949-6605.1112

Banks, J.A. (2017). Failed citizenship and transformative civic education. *Educational Researcher, 46*(7), 366–77. doi: 10.3102/0013189X17726741

Bradley, E. (2007). Pursuing peace: Enlisting students in the battle against bias. *Principal Leadership, 73*(4), 49–52.

Brown, S. (2016). What my refugee students taught me. *Educational Leadership, 74*(1), 76–9.

Burrell Storms, S. (2012). Preparing students for social action in a social justice education course. What works? *Equity & Excellence in Education, 45*(4), 547–60. doi: 10.1080/10665684.2012.719424

Collard, J. (2007). Constructing theory for leadership in intercultural contexts. *Journal of Educational Administration, 45*(6), 740–55. doi: 10.1108/09578230710829919

Delpit, L. (2006). *Other people's children: Cultural conflict in the classroom.* New York, NY: New Press.

Dempster, N., & Lizzio, A. (2007). Student leadership: Necessary research. *Australian Journal of Education, 51*(3), 276–85. doi: 10.1177/000494410705100305

Franklin, C. (2009). The promise of hope: Creating a classroom peace summit. *Peace & Change, 34*(4), 533–47. doi: 10.1111/j.1468-0130.2009.00599.x

Freire, P. (1970). *Pedagogy of the oppressed.* New York, NY: Continuum.

Gagné, A., & Soto Gordon, S. (2015). Leadership education for English language learners as transformative pedagogy. *Intercultural Education, 26*(6), 530–46. doi: 10.1080/14675986.2015.1109772

Goldberg, M. (2000). Demographics – Ignore them at your peril: An interview with Harold Hodgkinson. *Phi Delta Kappan, 82*(4), 304–6. doi: 10.1177/0031721 70008200413

Hamm, L. (2017). Becoming a transformative vice-principal in culturally and linguistically rich diverse schools: "Pace yourself. It's a marathon, not a sprint." *International Journal of Mentoring & Coaching in Education, 6*(2), 82–98. doi: 10.1108/IJMCE-11-2016-0072

Hamm, L., Massfeller, H., Scott, A., & Cormier, K. (2017). "They wanted to study us; they didn't want to help us": Socially just and participatory research methodologies for demographically changing schools. *Journal of Contemporary Issues in Education, 12*(1), 53–70. doi: 10.20355/C5S01T

Jennings, T., Crowell, S., & Fernlund, P. (1994). Social justice in the elementary classroom. *Social Studies and the Young Learner, 7*(1), 4–6.

Kaplan, S., Lumpkin, L., & Dennis, B. (2019, September 20). "We will make them hear us": Millions of youths around the world strike for action. *Washington Post.* https://www.washingtonpost.com/climate-environment/2019/09/20 /millions-youth-around-world-are-striking-friday-climate-action/

Kirk, C., Lewis, R.K., Brown, K., Karibo, B., Scott, A., & Park, E. (2017). The empowering schools project: Identifying the classroom and school characteristics that lead to student empowerment. *Youth & Society, 49*(6), 827–47. doi: 10.1177/0044118X14566118

Lizzio, A., Dempster, N., & Neumann, R. (2011). Pathways to formal and informal student leadership: The influence of peer and teacher-student relationships and level of school identification on students' motivations. *International Journal of Leadership in Education, 14*(1), 85–102. doi: 10.1080/13603124.2010.482674

Lopez, A. (2016). *Culturally responsive and socially just leadership in diverse contexts: From theory to action.* New York, NY: Palgrave Macmillan.

Lund, D. (2003). Educating for social justice: Making sense of multicultural and antiracist theory and practice with Canadian teacher activists. *Intercultural Education, 14*(1), 3–16. doi: 10.1080/1467598032000044610

Magno, C., & Schiff, M. (2010). Culturally responsive leadership: Best practice in integrating immigrant students. *Intercultural Education, 21*(1), 87–91. doi: 10.1080/14675981003666274

Massfeller, H., & Hamm, L. (2019). "I'm thinking I want to live a better life": Syrian refugee and new immigrant student adjustment in New Brunswick. *Journal of Contemporary Issues in Education, 14*(1), 33–54. doi: 10.20355/jcie29354

McKibben, S. (2004). The power of student voice. *Educational Leadership, 61*(7), 79–81.

Merchant, B. (2000). Education and changing demographics. In B.A. Jones (Ed.), *Educational leadership: Policy dimensions in the 21st century* (pp. 83–90). Stamford, CT: Ablex Publishing.

Rah, Y. (2013). Leadership stretched over school and community for refugee newcomers. *Journal of Case in Educational Leadership, 16*(3), 62–76. doi: 10.1177/1555458913498479

Roberts, A., & Nash, J. (2009). Enabling students to participate in school improvement through a students as researchers programme. *Improving Schools, 12*(2), 174–87. doi: 10.1177/1365480209106590

Robertson, H-J. (2005). Lost in translation. *Phi Delta Kappan, 86*(5), 410–11. doi: 10.1177/003172170508600516

Robinson, D., & Randall, L. (2016). (Un)Holy spaces: A consideration of religious minorities in health and physical education. In D. Robinson & L. Randall (Eds.), *Social justice in physical education: Critical reflections and pedagogies for change* (pp. 206–47). Toronto, ON: Canadian Scholars' Press.

Sears, A., Peck, C.L., & Herriot, L. (2014). We're here to teach about democracy not practice it: The missed potential of schools as democratic spaces. *One World in Dialogue, 3*(1), 1–9.

Seemiller, C. (2016). Assessing student leadership competency development. *New Directions for Student Leadership, 2016*(151), 51–66. doi: 10.1002/yd.20200

Shields, C.M. (2017, November 20). *Transformative leadership in education: An equitable, inclusive, excellent, and socially just approach to leading change in a VUCA world.* Invited presentation for Dr. Lyle Hamm's Responsive Leadership in Diverse Schools and Communities (Education 6009), University of New Brunswick, Fredericton, NB.

Shields, C.M. (2018). *Transformative leadership in education: Equitable changes in an uncertain and complex world* (2nd ed.). New York, NY: Routledge.

Slaughter, G., & Frisk, A. (2019, September 27). "We are the change": Greta Thunberg tells Canadians to demand action. *CTV News.* https://www.ctvnews.ca /canada/we-are-the-change-greta-thunberg-tells-canadians-to-demand-action -1.4613185?cache=yes

Stanway, S. (2011, May 31). Legitimate concern presented to junior council on Municipal Involvement Day. *The Brooks Bulletin*, p. A9

# 12 School Leadership in the Era of Bill 21: A Call for Commitment and Courage

PHILIP S.S. HOWARD

This chapter is a decolonial reading and race analysis of educational leadership in the contexts in which it occurs in the Canadian settler-colonial nation state. Using the case of Quebec's Bill 21, an Act respecting the laicity of the State, by which public employees "are prohibited from wearing religious symbols in the exercise of their functions" (Assemblée nationale du Québec, 2019, sec. 6), the chapter takes a cautious look at the ways in which those traditionally referred to as school leaders – that is, school administrators such as principals and vice-principals – are positioned, and the (im)possibility of their leadership. Unlike some education scholars, I am unconvinced that the most transformative change in education systems comes from within. Further, I am always conscious of the ways in which educational institutions and their leaders mobilize liberal conceptions of social justice that often do not lead to any substantive commitment to transformation on the ground, and that perpetuate that which they claim to oppose. This chapter therefore serves as a reflection on what might be at stake when one takes up an identity as a school leader for social justice from within educational institutions in a settler state. It is a call for a particular kind of courage.

In part 1 of this chapter, I present the theoretical foundations upon which my arguments in the rest of the chapter are based. I describe the ongoing settler-colonial relations of the Canadian nation state, and the ways in which the discourse and practice of multiculturalism – an ostensibly egalitarian project – perpetuates the foundational injustices of the settler-colonial formation. I locate the practices of schooling within this context to argue that any meaningful social justice leadership that would happen in schools is always already against the grain.

In part 2, I turn to the specific case of Bill 21 in Quebec. I describe the Bill and its effects on education, and I give a genealogy of the dominant logics that have led Quebec to this moment. I then discuss the ways in which high-profile education leaders have opposed the Bill, but been thwarted in their resistance, to highlight the ways in which the possibilities of meaningful social justice out-comes from these leadership positions and through official channels are much narrower than they might at first seem. I end by speculating about other ways of working – against Bill 21, but also more generally towards social justice – that might be more promising. With specific reference to Bill 21, I note that at the time of writing the struggle to oppose this piece of legislation is ongoing and calls for courage, as do all forms of social justice work.

## Part 1

*Foundations*

Canada is a settler-colonial nation state. This is my non-negotiable point of departure. This fact is seldom understood, never mind acknowledged, in a Can-ada that has convinced itself that it is egalitarian and non-racist. Canada as a nation has been made possible through the violence of colonialism and its inter-twined project of racial capitalism. This violence includes the genocidal dispos-session and in some cases the enslavement of Indigenous peoples. This violence includes the enslavement and dehumanization of Black[1] people over centuries of Canada's involvement in the slave trade and the capitalist slave economies of the "West" (Cooper, 2006; Walcott & Abdillahi, 2019). This violence includes the continued exploitation of Black and racialized migrants whose labour is used to build the nation, including disproportionately the provision of its essential and caregiving services, while perpetually constituting migrants as properly belong-ing outside of the nation in order to present Canada as white, both materially and ideologically (Calliste, 1994; Langevin, 2007; Lawson, 2013; Li, 1982).

I have deliberately not drawn lines between historical and contemporary forms of this colonial violence as there are no such clear lines. The essence of each of these forms of violence persists in one manner or another today to sustain the nation state. It persists in such direct forms as the wanton surveil-lance, profiling, violent attacks against, and deaths of Indigenous, Black, Mus-lim, and other racialized persons at the hands of law enforcement and members of civil society in the name of law and order or to preserve national or provin-cial hegemonies. It persists in the ongoing wanton theft and commodification of Indigenous land and the extraction of resources in flagrant defiance of the Indigenous people who protect it. It persists in the intense neoliberal conditions that render life increasingly precarious for those who are considered the state's excess – disproportionately those who are racialized, Black, and Indigenous – resulting in the racialization of poverty, or what Galabuzi has referred to as "Canada's economic apartheid" (Galabuzi, 2006). It also persists in the embed-ded white supremacy, antiblackness, anti-Indigenousness, and racism that undergird "normal" relations in Canadian institutional life and civil society.

In short, the Canadian nation state continues to be a perpetrator of state violence in its direct, institutional, structural, and symbolic forms at federal, provincial, and municipal levels, and this continuance is enabled through the normalized attitudes held by everyday Canadians who act as witting or unwitting agents in carrying it out. Of course, the racist state and interpersonal violence that I am describing have always functioned in and through ethnic, gender, class, religious, sexual, and ableist oppressions.

## Postracialism, Multiculturalism, Liberalism

These foundations serve to identify racist state violence and racist interpersonal relations as mundane – the everyday terms under which we live in Canada. Consequently, these injustices – sometimes called inequities (in the co-opted and therefore now anaemic institutional language of equity and diversity) – are not what happens at ostensibly exceptional moments when things go wrong in Canada and its institutions. Rather, they are the terms of everyday existence when the state is working as it must.

Yet any discussion of the racial colonial nature of Canada must also attend to the postracialism that accompanies it. While Canada is constituted through an unfolding colonial history, it also has a well-developed claim to egalitarianism that denies these relations. Not simply a claim to have transcended racism, postracialism, as defined by David Theo Goldberg (2015), "is a neo-raciality, racisms' extension if not resurrection" (p. 24). In other words, in a postracialist setting, racism is perpetrated through the very mechanisms that deny its existence. Indeed, postracialism involves the "denial of denial" – that is, the reframing of the terms by which one might recognize racism such that the question of denial becomes irrelevant because the racism, past and present, that it would deny has been defined away (Goldberg, 2015, pp. 74–5). The postracialist denial of the denial at various levels of Canadian government has been evident when prominent politicians have denied Canada's history of colonialism (Fontaine, 2016; Razack, 2002, p. 2; Vancouver Sun, 2009), when they denied that the terrorist murder of six Muslims in a Quebec City mosque in 2017 had anything to do with Islamophobia (Shingler, 2018), and most recently in the wake of George Floyd's murder by police in the US in May 2020 and the death of Joyce Echaquan in a Quebec hospital in September 2020, when the Ontario and Quebec premiers denied that systemic racism exists in their provinces (Feith, 2021; Lapierre, 2020; Takeuchi, 2020).

I have argued elsewhere that while postracialist discourse burgeoned in the US around the Obama era, Canada's postracialism long predates the US version (Howard, 2018), going back at least as far as the 1950s with strategic deployment of self-congratulatory historical accounts of the Underground Railroad (Bakan, 2008; Poole, 2012). It has been compounded by Canada's declaration of a state policy of multiculturalism. Black, racialized, and other critical scholars of multiculturalism in Canada and beyond (e.g., Haque, 2012; Simpson, James, & Mack, 2011; Thobani, 2007; Walcott, 2014) have long argued that the discourses, policy, and practices of multiculturalism in Canada mobilize notions of language and culture as proxies for race and eschew rigorous historical and structural analysis. Canadian multiculturalism is deeply invested in the problematic liberal notion of abstract individuals, devoid of race and gender, standing equally before the law (Razack, 1998, p. 24). That multiculturalism is rooted in liberalism is of deep relevance here because, as Kundnani (2017) has noted,

> liberalism is not just a body of ideas; it is also the ideology of a social system – capitalism – that sustains itself through marginalising racial groups, through class exploitation ... The liberal demand to depoliticise culture – to abandon "dangerous ideas," to deradicalise and to integrate to "Western" values – is therefore highly political. (p. 42)

The concept of *inter*culturalism, Quebec's response to multiculturalism, is just as implicated in the same processes – perhaps more so, to the extent that it does not deny a mainstream "culture" with which minority "cultural communities" must learn to interact (Nugent, 2006).

As a consequence, multiculturalist/interculturalist discourses and related institutional equity-diversity-inclusion discourses are not simply well-intentioned, uninformed misunderstanding, but are, in fact, postracialist mechanisms through which radical change is forestalled and injustice is perpetuated (Ahmed, 2012; Kelley, 2018; Walcott, 2014). They become largely performative ways of "simultaneously managing race and making it disappear" (Walcott, 2014, p. 132).

## Schools in the Settler-Colonial Nation State

Institutions of state schooling have not only been influenced by the ongoing settler-colonial project, but they have been crucial arms for perpetrating it. At their inception in the seventeenth century in North America, specifically in New France (now Quebec), schools were designed to indoctrinate, pacify, and Europeanize Indigenous people and the enslaved – both Indigenous and Black (Hampton, 2016, p. 13). This type of schooling persisted for over two centuries, and indeed many of the subjects currently taught in schools were forged through colonial interest and actively served its ends (Coloma, 2013, p. 648).

The progressive education movement that marked mainstream schooling from the mid-nineteenth to mid-twentieth centuries, and which is the source of a number of the taken-for-granted features of education today, also developed within the womb of North American race-based, settler-colonial projects, including the newly formed Canadian federation, and is shot through with injustice (Coloma, 2013, p. 644). It operated in and through racist forms of schooling – not the least of which were segregated schools for Black students, both de jure and de facto, in many provinces, and the genocidal residential school system intended to further the erasure of Indigenous people (Coloma, 2013, p. 645; Hampton, 2016, p. 13). These are not relics of the distant past, particularly when we consider that Canada's last segregated school closed in 1965, and its last residential school in 1996, and that Black and Indigenous experiences with education in Canada continue to be fraught.

Though perhaps less blatant, the features of contemporary public education in Canada are no less colonial. The ideas that justify settler-state projects are perpetuated in schools – explicitly through the official curriculum taught in the classroom, as well as implicitly through school practices in what has been termed the "hidden curriculum." For example, provincial curricula across Canada still sanitize the violence of colonialism and celebrate the rugged heroics of white settlers. They largely elide the stories of Black, Indigenous, and other racialized persons that might disrupt these Canadian mythologies. These curricular trends constitute epistemological violence that confounds what students can come to know about the real conditions of their lives in Canada. At the same time, school policies and practices of discipline result in the disproportionate representation of Indigenous, Black, and certain other racialized students in special education classes, non-university–bound streams, and among those who are excluded from school (see, for example, Bhattacharjee, 2003; James, Turner, George, & Tecle, 2017; Ruck & Wortley, 2002; Wishart, 2009).

These realities considered, schooling remains a site of violence – interpersonal, institutional, structural, and epistemological – for Black people, Indigenous people, and persons of colour. While school has been a place where some Black, Indigenous, and racialized students, to varying degrees, can eke out a critical education with considerable work, or have had access to constrained upward social mobility, this has happened in spite of the colonial desires of schooling.

Within this context, social justice leadership in education can really only be that which struggles *against* colonization, antiblackness, and racism and *for* decolonization, Black freedom, and racial justice (Tuck & Yang, 2018, p. 8). Furthermore, the educational injustice with which we continue to grapple in the contemporary moment cannot accurately be considered aberrant. It is not just the result of benign ignorance on the part of uninformed institutional actors within otherwise just educational institutions. Nor can it be primarily considered that which unenlightened others bring into schools. Rather, injustice in schools must be recognized as the norm, aligned with the colonial desires of the nation state. To be appointed a leader within such a schooling system is to be positioned to advance this dominant agenda of schooling. The expectation is that one carry out one's duties as prescribed by the settler-colonial institution, embedded as these duties are in the colonial agendas that perpetuate injustice. Therefore, social justice work from within the institution via one of these positions is inherently contradictory.

Of course, I do not mean to suggest that no leadership for social justice is possible within schools and education systems, or that no such leadership is possible by superintendents, principals, vice-principals, and so on. However, one who aspires to such a position, but who would lead for social justice, must have a clear understanding of the ways in which the structures of schooling in the racial, settler-colonial state interpellate them. One must ask oneself whether one is willing to align one's work with the normative colonial goals of such a system, and if not, to consider what steps one is prepared to take to challenge them.

Robin D.G. Kelley (2016) discusses this contradictory positioning as it relates to the university in an analysis that has resonance for public schooling. Like universities, schools cannot be considered "an enlightened place ... that would actively seek to disrupt the reproduction of our culture's classed, racialized, nationalized, gendered, moneyed, and militarized stratifications" (para. 18). As such, those who would be a part of struggles for justice must do their work in "a subaltern, subversive way of being in but not of" (para. 18) the school system. Leadership for social justice must be against to the extent that it is within.

Finally, given that one of the ways that the Canadian settler-colonial project takes shape is through a furtive postracialist, liberal multiculturalism, a social justice leader must be wary of educational initiatives and the problematic institutional equity, diversity, and inclusion projects of which they are a part, which operate on this multicultural logic. There is no lack of educational and institutional initiatives of this sort advanced by the various educational jurisdictions within the Canadian state.[2] Recent analyses have shown that Canadian curricula and textbooks take an approach that makes inequity and racial injustice relics of the past and that aligns with the claims of Canadian multiculturalism by making (racial) egalitarianism always already a trait inherent to Canada and Canadians (Bickmore, 2014, p. 262; Thobani, 2007, p. 4). In their most problematic form, these curricula situate racialized groups and migrants as those who bring inequity to Canada, who threaten national or provincial identities and unity, and who therefore need to be taught to become egalitarian Canadians who do things the way "we" do them here (Joshee, 2009, p. 106; Thobani, 2007, p. 4). These groups are then made the primary target of "equity" education. For example, in Quebec (the context under discussion in this chapter), the 1998 document that still governs "educational integration and Intercultural education," and that is still available on the website of Quebec's Ministry of Education, defines its mission as being "to promote the integration of students of diverse origins by fostering democratic values, helping the students master the language of instruction and of public life, and making them aware of our unique historical heritage" and "the common rules of life in our society" (Ministère de l'Éducation et Ministère de l'Enseignement supérieur, 1998, pp. 14, 25). The document advises on how to "instill in all students, *and especially immigrants and the children of immigrants*, the shared values necessary for participation in society" (p. 24, emphasis added). This way of thinking is perhaps the same kind of logic that has seen the name of the Quebec Ministry of Immigration, Diversity, and Inclusion recently changed to the Ministry of Immigration, Francisation, and Integration with the change of government in October 2018. This is the Ministry that authored Bill 21.

In other iterations, these forms of education focus disproportionately on interpersonal interactions between students and decidedly *not* on the normalized colonial, structural, and institutional relations that are much more implicated in creating injustice. Deeply rooted in liberal discourse, these state-sanctioned curricula in Canada (bearing a variety of names such as equity education, multicultural education, diversity education, inclusive education, social studies education, citizenship education, character education, anti-bullying, and so on) do not address Canada's *ongoing* colonization of Indigenous land, and they fail to address in any substantive way the oppression of Indigenous, Black, and other racialized groups (Bickmore, 2014, p. 261). These curricula, along with equity policies where they exist, remain embedded in the logic of liberal multiculturalism, though they have often adopted the terminology of "equity" rather than "multiculturalism," and have moved gradually towards less simplistic understandings of Canada (Bickmore, 2014, p. 261; Segeren & Kutsyuruba, 2012, p. 1). Compounding this problem is the very troubling manner in which policy in Canada related to equity and diversity has been increasingly grounded in the logics of neoconservatism and neoliberal capitalism (Joshee, 2009; Kundnani, 2017).

It is for these types of reasons that Kelley (2016) warns us that in the contemporary postracialist moment, we must be aware that the many current social justice efforts with their key concepts of "cultural-competency training, greater diversity, and demands for multicultural curricula" are not inherently or even at all liberatory projects that envision Black freedom, decolonization, and racial justice. Ultimately, Canadian equity education, under whichever of its various names, built as it is upon liberal multicultural principles, does not promote equity – that is, it does not promote decolonization, Black freedom, and racial justice – and always already frustrates these goals (Walcott & Abdillahi, 2019, p. 81; see also Tuck & Yang, 2018, p. 8).

To summarize part 1, then, if we are to consider what it means to be a school leader for social justice, we must recognize the ways in which state schooling is embedded in the inherently unjust settler-colonial project that is Canada. Social justice leadership must be within but against, understanding the structures of schooling as those that fundamentally need to be contested. Particularly in Canada, such leadership must avoid the logic of liberal multiculturalism that enables the Canadian settler project, exasperates racial justice, and perpetuates educational injustice.

**Part 2**

I now turn to consider some of these matters related to social justice leadership in schools in the context of Bill 21. This Bill was presented in the Quebec legislature on 28 March 2019 by the sitting government headed by the Coalition Avenir Quebec (CAQ) and ultimately passed into law on 16 June 2019 by a 75–35 vote.

For a large swath of public employees, including commissioners, lawyers, law enforcement officers, and educators, Bill 21 makes it illegal to wear religious symbols while at work, ostensibly to underscore that the state is secular. As a concession, Bill 21 allows an exemption for those who wear religious attire who were already in their roles when the law was passed, but it will apply should they change jobs. So, for example, a lawyer who wears a turban and who was already employed at the time the Bill was passed would be allowed to continue wearing the turban in their position as a lawyer but would be disallowed from wearing any religious attire if they were to then seek to become a judge.

Bill 21 also requires that anyone offering a public service must do so with their face uncovered, and that anyone receiving such a service must also have their face uncovered. Interestingly, the clause about religious symbols is a one-liner, while there are four lengthy clauses speaking specifically to the wearing of face coverings.[3]

The effects of the Bill are clearly unjust, and they are devastating. Bill 21 contravenes freedom of religion, forcing those for whom wearing religious symbols is a matter of conscience into the impossible choice between their livelihoods and their convictions. It effectively and deliberately bars certain groups of individuals from several well-paid careers. With respect to education, Bill 21 blocks certain groups from becoming school educators, and in its short tenure has already denied employment to otherwise fully qualified prospective teachers (Leclair, 2019). It also blocks teachers who currently wear religious attire, and who are allowed by the grandfather clause to keep their positions, from pursuing promotion to school administration.

Yet the Bill extends beyond its official reach by creating a poisoned environment for those wearing religious symbols. Teachers whose jobs are protected by the grandfather clause are *not* protected from the chilly climate caused by the Bill. Since the passing of the Bill, some parents have already requested that their children not be taught by a teacher, despite her twenty-seven years of experience, simply because she wears a hijab (Shingler, 2019). Some school boards have also begun to refuse certain pre-service teachers wishing to do their student teaching placements in their schools, even though the Bill does not apply to them (Lajoie, 2019).

It would be a mistake to understand this Bill as only affecting teachers. The significant number of Muslim, Sikh, Jewish, and other students who wear religious symbols now have career options closed to them simply because of their religious convictions. Indeed, it is difficult to imagine how schools required to actively discriminate in terms of who they employ could ever be considered safe spaces for students from targeted backgrounds. Students experience the climate of exclusion and oppression created by Bill 21, knowing members of their family would not be allowed to work there. They are exposed to the possibility of bullying or social exclusion from peers acting on the inspiration of their political leaders and the climate of disregard that they have fomented via Bill 21. And upon what credible authority could school educators intervene to stop this bullying behaviour or suggest that it is not to be tolerated? More broadly, Bill 21 affects students to the extent that they realize that the civil society to which they "belong" has sought, upheld, and defended this assault on who they are. Finally, Bill 21 affects *all* to the extent that it sends a very clear message about the precarity of any and all rights that are afforded by the state if, like religious freedoms in this case, they can be relegated to oblivion at the stroke of a pen and at the whim of whoever might be head of government.

## Historicizing Bill 21

It is impossible to understand Bill 21 divorced from its broader historical context and the specific social and political context(s) of Canada and Quebec. On the broad historical front, Bill 21 must be considered in the context of anti-Muslim modes of thought that have long existed in the "West." Indeed, as Edward Said (1978) pointed out long ago, the constitution of the "West" as an entity is only made possible through an imaginary set of material relations that construct an exotic but simultaneously barbaric, despotic, culturally bound, backward, largely Muslim "Orient" or "East" against which the "West" can know itself as otherwise. This thinking has been at the centre of views across the "West" that Muslims are undesirable others. Its logics lead to the idea that accommodating religion and culture poses a fundamental threat to Canadian and/or Quebec identity.

In the specific context of Quebec, one might trace Bill 21 and the larger accommodation debate of which it is a part to the *Multani v. Commission scolaire Marguerite-Bourgeoys* case concerning whether a Sikh student should be allowed to wear the ceremonial kirpan (a required article for a Khalsa Sikh) to school. This case ended when, in 2006, the Supreme Court of Canada struck down the school board's decision to disallow the kirpan, thereby overturning a judgment by la Cour d'appel du Québec (Multani v. Commission scolaire Marguerite-Bourgeoys, 2006).[4]

However, the decision did not end the debate about accommodation, but rather sparked an intense, long-lasting debate about the extent of accommodation of minority groups that might be considered "reasonable." The debate, which was negotiated at the intersection of notions of accommodation, secularism, Quebec identity, integration, and Quebec interculturalism, took disproportionate aim at Muslims, and specifically Muslim women who wore any kind of veil (Mahrouse, 2010), which explains the otherwise puzzling preoccupation with face coverings in Bill 21. Thus, in 2007, the Liberal Quebec premiere, Jean Charest, launched the Consultation Commission on Accommodation Practices Related to Cultural Differences, which after fifteen months of hearings determined that Quebec identity was not in jeopardy, but recommended that public authority figures should not be allowed to wear religious symbols (Bouchard & Taylor, 2008). This recommended prohibition did not, at the time, include educators.

In the years following, there were several attempts by successive Quebec governments led by three different political parties to craft a legislative response to the "reasonable accommodation" debate and the findings of the Commission. Each of these is a precursor to the current Bill 21.

In 2013, the government led by the Parti Québécois introduced Bill 60, which would prohibit state employees from wearing "conspicuous"[5] religious symbols and require that one's face be uncovered when delivering or receiving services of the state (Assemblée nationale du Québec, 2013). The Parti Québécois government was voted out in a 2014 election before Bill 60 could be passed into law.

The new Liberal-led government, claiming that Bill 60 went too far, passed Bill 62, which required that one's face be uncovered when delivering or receiving services of the state that require person-to-person interaction (Assemblée nationale du Québec, 2017). While not taking broad aim at religious symbols, it would still disproportionately impact Muslim women who wear a face veil. Bill 62 ran into trouble, though. Opposition parties decried its shortened reach, while Quebec courts noted that how it would be implemented remained unclear, and that in any case it would violate both the Quebec and Canadian human rights charters. The courts therefore twice suspended Bill 62 after it became law (Kestler-D'Amours, 2018; Valiante, 2018).

The government changed again in 2018, this time to be led by the Coalition Avenir Quebec (CAQ). Within six months of its election, the CAQ passed Bill 21, fulfilling one of its campaign promises. Having learned from Bill 62's fate, Bill 21 implemented the grandfather clause, pre-empted the religious rights objection by amending the clauses of the Quebec Charter of Human Rights and Freedoms that it contravenes, and invoked Section 33 (the notwithstanding clause) of the Canadian Charter of Rights and Freedoms, which allows a provincial legislature to override rights normally protected by the Canadian Charter.

My intention here is not to suggest that the people of Quebec think as a monolith with regard to the issue of accommodation, or even that the state acts monolithically. Indeed, there is, and has been, much dissent in Quebec on the issue, including the court suspensions of Bill 62. A document produced during this time from Quebec's Ministry of Education, *Violence in Intercultural Relationships*, also appears to have been an effort to make some inroads. To its credit, it mentions "systemic discrimination" and how that might take place in schools, and it recommends anti-racist education for employees – though it otherwise takes an anti-bullying approach and directs students to report instances of discrimination to the school staff, thus failing to take seriously injustice at the level of the institution and the state (for the full document, see Ministère de l'Éducation et Ministère de l'Enseignement supérieur, 2019). My intention is also not to suggest that Quebec's struggle with this issue is unique or that it can be divorced from the Canadian and global climates of Islamophobia (see Mahrouse, 2010, p. 92). Rather, I wish to highlight the very clear ways in which the state, in this case, the government of Quebec, has resolutely pursued the implementation of this inequitable arrangement, and the ways in which, but for legal sleight of hand, it contravenes religious rights recognized nationally and provincially, at least up until Bill 21 was passed.

## Bill 21 as Racism

Some would see Bill 21 as discrimination on the basis of religion only (if they concede that it is discriminatory at all). While this alone makes it heinous, I want to further make the argument that Bill 21 is a clear manifestation of systemic racism. It would certainly be appropriate to draw this conclusion even if we were only to consider the disproportionate impact that the Bill has on persons who are racialized – specifically South Asian Sikhs, many Jewish people, and South Asian and Black Muslims, particularly women. The Bill creates additional barriers to access for these persons to employment and social services, exacerbating the ways in which poverty is racialized in Canada and, as we have seen, exposing them to social exclusion and violence.

But more importantly, arguments that the Bill is not racist because it does not explicitly target people on the basis of skin colour demonstrate a poor understanding of the social construction of race and the complex interplay of nature and culture through which racial injustice comes to be directed at certain people and not others (Haney-Lopez, 1995; Wade, 2010). Such arguments do not grasp the basic principle (so foundational as to be dated) that processes of racialization consist of a confluence of social, ideological, legal, political, and economic interactions through which particular groups of persons are designated as less deserving and worth less, sometimes quite independent of skin colour (see, for instance, Haney-Lopez, 1995; Omi & Winant, 1993). The racialization process serves to justify why the persons targeted by it should not be afforded rights, privilege, access to social goods, and the acknowledgment of their full humanity to which others have access by default, and it works to confirm this subaltern status.

Furthermore, as Massoumi, Mills, and Miller (2017) argue in their analysis of Islamophobia, racism and inequity are not simply free-floating ideas that come from nowhere. Rather, racism, and specifically Islamophobia in this instance, are the result of "concrete social action undertaken ... by particular social actors with particular interests in the particular circumstances in which they find themselves" (pp. 3, 6). Massoumi et al. (2017) argue that there are five pillars through which contemporary Islamophobia, which they recognize as racism, is enacted, and that among these, the state is primary. The history of Bill 21 certainly demonstrates the ways in which the state has been the prime social actor in perpetrating the terms of Islamophobia and racism.

In sum, Bill 21 is perpetrated by the state, discriminates on the basis of religion, and is founded in racist, orientalist logic. The ways in which discourses of race, nation, and language were used together in the production of Bill 21 to manage racialized people is one illustration of the ways in which multiculturalism/interculturalism masks the working of race in the settler-colonial nation state (Walcott, 2014, p. 128). Without any question, Bill 21 is precisely the kind of injustice that anyone committed to social justice would work against.

*Education Leaders' Responses to Bill 21*

There have been a variety of responses to Bill 21 on the part of education leaders. A first, and very unfortunate, set of responses have been those that approve of Bill 21. Those in this category do not see Bill 21 as problematic, and in fact would suggest that it advances equity. One vein of this argument holds that Bill 21 promotes gender equity, providing an "out" for ostensibly oppressed Muslim women who are forced by patriarchy and the men in their lives to wear the veil. A school teacher testified to this effect in support of Bill 21 in legislative hearings (Montpetit, 2019). Arguments such as these invoke white liberal feminism and ignore the insights of women-of-colour feminism – that is, feminisms articulated by women of colour themselves. These arguments negate the agency of Muslim women who declare that they freely choose the veil by suggesting that they are actually dupes of patriarchy. These arguments displace patriarchy onto Islam, even as they, in a patriarchal manner, silence Muslim women's voices and presume to speak in their place, as such displaying their own fundamental racisms (Al-Saji, 2010). After all, if Bill 21 were to protect women who are ostensibly forced by patriarchy to veil themselves, how is it that it does absolutely nothing to protect them by way of providing access to independence, but instead further oppresses them? These liberal "feminists" also conveniently ignore that long-standing legislation already exists to protect women from sexist religious imposition. Therefore, in the context of Bill 21, this brand of feminism, with its liberal desires, is a form of postracialist "equity," which I have argued that those who would be social justice leaders must eschew, for it perpetuates injustice, but does so in the name of equity.

Another kind of response to Bill 21 has been overt, launched by high-profile leaders within the structures of Quebec education. Catherine Harel-Bourdon, the president of the Commission Scolaire de Montréal (CSDM), the largest school board in the province, has been an opponent of the Bill from the outset. Backed by a unanimous vote of the Board, Harel-Bourdon pushed back against the Bill, saying that the CSDM would take a year of consultation with its stakeholders about how best to apply the law before it would implement it (Authier, 2019). More forcefully, Noel Burke, chair of the Lester B. Pearson School Board (LBPSB), called Bill 21 "unnecessary, discriminatory, and divisive … abhorrent to all we believe in" (as cited in Conroy, 2019) and declared that the Board would not comply. Apparently, all its educational leaders – commissioners, and administrators – opposed the Bill (Conroy, 2019). The most protracted battle against Bill 21 is, at this writing, still being waged by the English Montreal School Board (EMSB), the largest English-language school board in Quebec. It also passed a unanimous resolution not to implement Bill 21, led by EMSB Chair Angela Mancini, who has remained outspoken against the Bill (Laframboise, 2019). However, every one of these leaders and their Boards have rescinded and have begun to apply the law. The provincial government simply wielded its power by threatening to put any dissenting board under trusteeship, and to hold the "highest administrative authority in the school board" personally responsible for compliance (Maratta, 2019; Shingler, 2019). While it is currently complying with Bill 21, the EMSB has proceeded with a court challenge. But even here, the Quebec government has exerted pressure by playing on federal–provincial tensions and forcing the Board to renounce federal funding to which it was entitled to help cover legal fees (Authier, 2019). Leaders of other powerful educational organizations such as teachers' unions have spoken against the Bill but have also refrained from challenging its implementation (Maratta, 2019).

The ways that even these powerful leaders and the educational organizations they head have been strong-armed by the government, causing them to abandon, in large part, resistance to implementing Bill 21, speaks to the fraught position of educational leaders whose power is afforded to them by the very institution they seek to oppose. This reality forces us to consider the extent to which leadership for social justice can actually come from these leaders through the exercise of their duties. Certainly, educational leaders of this sort are able to influence equity at the most rudimentary (though necessary) levels of interpersonal relations and bullying. They have much less liberty to work for justice at structural and institutional levels, however, where these are the structures of the state within which they work. Of course, these are precisely the levels at which social justice leadership is most needed. The central issue really is that our social justice work cannot be focussed upon tweaking colonial systems and institutions that are inequitable at the core, but rather needs to be focussed on working towards new and different structures operating on the principles of justice (Kelley, 2016; Walcott & Abdillahi, 2019).

### What Is a Social Justice Leader to Do?

So, what is a social justice leader to do? Clearly, given the pushback from the Quebec government on these multiple attempts at socially just action by powerful persons, we cannot expect that the average school leader or educator could contravene Bill 21 without significant risk.

I have written elsewhere about the lack of leverage one has to stand for racial justice within dominant institutions (Howard, 2019). While in that chapter I specifically addressed the experiences of Black people who do racial equity work in collaboration with white persons, it does have broader application in that it looks at the ways in which equity leaders strategize in light of the precarity and risks inherent in doing equity work within these institutions. Two insights I draw from that research are applicable here. The first is that the choices of specific strategy that one takes to contest injustice within these organizations are complex; one has to negotiate multiple competing concerns, not excluding the risk to one's livelihood. All of us have to reckon with what is at stake, and the risks we are willing to take up to oppose injustice. No prescriptions can be made about how that should be done, but we must also realize that privilege positions some of us in ways that the consequences of choosing not to resist Bill 21 are easier and very different for us than they are for others. Some of us can afford to let this go, and this unfortunately often determines the ways in which decisions to resist or refrain from resisting are made.

Since the risk is increased if we act alone, the second insight is crucial. That is, one cannot underestimate the power inherent in working together. Our social justice work is strengthened when we work in solidarity with groups and leaders outside of the organization, evaluating the consequences for people in the various social locations among the collective, and strategizing about who will do and say what at any given moment in order to mitigate risks. Distributed forms of leadership on multiple fronts are likely to be much more successful than that which invests heavily in individual leaders in ostensibly powerful positions.

Regardless of the strategy taken, there can be no guarantee that this work will be safe. Indeed, it is patently not safe. However, as Dei (2008) writes, "the fundamental question is not really to ask: Who can do anti-racist work? Rather it is to inquire if we are all prepared to take the risks, engage in contestation, and face the consequences that come with doing anti-racist work" (p. 69). The existence of risk cannot be a reason to remain complacent and to do nothing. Social justice work calls for courage!

Furthermore, it is unacceptable for our "equity work" to continue business as usual as we overlook clear and egregious examples of state-sanctioned injustice and fail to call them out. As I consider the broader context of social justice work in the time of Bill 21, I am concerned that there are several who stand in agreement with Bill 21 while imagining themselves to be about justice. I am also concerned about the proliferation of "equity work" through symposiums, research groups, policy documents, white papers, and the like, apparently unfazed by Bill 21, even as such work dutifully reminds teachers to be considerate of their Muslim students during Ramadan and at Eid. The state of "equity" discourse in education has come to the place where many will decry "multiculturalism/ interculturalism" for their tendency to focus on the celebratory and the interpersonal while neglecting the systemic, the historical, and the material. But how is this business-as-usual approach anything other than that? In what ways does such an approach perpetuate the problematic terms of equity and diversity discourse and serve other agendas, such as producing "good" white people, or upholding organizational reputations through performativity but without substantive action?

Indeed, this chapter comes, in part, out of a personal experience of being a member of a group of academics writing an equity competency document and implementation toolkit to guide the training of school leaders in Quebec. We partnered with a group of school administrators for a day of consultation during which the administrators provided scenarios and anecdotes to illustrate principles raised in the toolkit, and offered other feedback through discussions held on the day. Their names are included on an acknowledgment page of the final toolkit, separate and distinct from the page listing the authors of the document.

As chance would have it, the final publication of the toolkit would occur at the height of the debate around Bill 21 after it became law. Seeing the significance of the timing, and understanding the implications of our silence, I proposed that we include a statement in the early pages of the document identifying Bill 21 as openly contravening the principles of equity and justice that we claimed to be pursuing. The statement would be clearly attributed to the academics and not to the administrators. Some colleagues agreed with me, but ultimately my proposal was turned down because some team members felt this was not the place to make such a statement, and because the group of school administrators did not feel comfortable being acknowledged in the document if the proposed statement were to appear, given that they are ultimately employees of the government.

Besides indicating the climate of intimidation and the lack of any real free-dom of expression that Bill 21 and the CAQ government create, I believe that this decision demonstrated a lack of courage on several fronts, and that the team had lost sight of the real goal of producing such a document for two rea-sons. First, the statement was one of dissent and did not constitute a refusal to implement the Bill on the part of the administrators, who in any case would not be signatories to the statement. Second, there were several paths we could have taken to include the statement while protecting the administrators. The worst-case scenario, though we would not likely have had to act this drastically, would have been that we agree together with the administrators to withdraw their names from the document while acknowledging them anonymously, or to move their names to a less conspicuous location, but in all cases ensuring that the document did the work it needed to do. Instead, opting to not include a statement spoke volumes about the team's social justice resolve in the face of risk and fell short of taking a stand against educational injustice. I was frus-trated by the unwillingness to make this admittedly small stand and had to withdraw my participation from the group and remove my own name from the list of authors – not as a show of resentment, but rather in an effort to be con-sistent. I felt I could not remain an author of this document, produced without a statement against Bill 21, without doing violence to my commitment to anti-colonial justice and solidarity with those being oppressed by the Bill.

If we would be about social justice, we can engage this struggle on multiple fronts. What if we sustained a public show of resistance to the Bill? What if we asked affected colleagues, students, and acquaintances what they might need from us in this moment? What might happen if classroom teachers exercised leadership by teaching through the language arts and social studies aspects of their programs about why and how Bill 21 is an injustice, and would be con-sidered so in other parts of Canada, and indeed in Quebec at other times and under other governments? What if administrators organized school-wide cam-paigns to raise awareness, inviting Muslim women and others whose religious/spiritual convictions require that they wear religious attire to speak to their stu-dent bodies? (This might well be a way of supporting the livelihoods of teachers who are excluded from the classroom by the Bill.) What if teacher educators were to ensure that pre-service teachers have a solid, critical analysis of Bill 21, and understood what was at stake for the profession. What if we collaborated with popular educators to hold teach-ins on the Bill?

What would it look like if the research agendas of academics who claim to be committed to equity turned to producing public documents articulating exactly why Bill 21 is a travesty? What might happen if those who are always already considered insiders in Quebec, those in whose name this Bill is ostensi-bly advanced, were to make their voices heard in concert in opposition, dissolv-ing the presumed Quebec consensus that Bill 21 is acceptable? I do not propose to have all the answers or all the ideas, but the possibilities for sustaining resistance to Bill 21 are only limited by the size of our social justice imagination, and the extent of our outrage at the Bill.

To be clear, winning against Bill 21 will not mean that schools have "returned" to being socially just. Bill 21 is just one instance that reminds us of the ways in which education in the nation state is inherently inequitable. It encourages us to fix our eyes on what is really at stake if we want education that is socially just – that is, the building of new ways that will promote decolonization, Black freedom, and racial justice in all their intersectional dimensions.

## Addendum

As this volume makes its way through the publication process, the case I describe above has continued to develop further in the eighteen months since I first penned this chapter.

The English Montreal School Board (EMSB), through its elected commissioners rather than through its administrators/employees, filed a lawsuit against the Quebec government over Bill 21. The Board was able to file this lawsuit not directly contesting the principles of Bill 21, but rather on grounds of a constitutional guarantee in Section 23 of the Canadian Charter of Rights and Freedoms that is not subject to being overridden by the notwithstanding clause (Section 33). Section 23 guarantees access to education for minority language communities (that is, anglophone communities in Quebec and francophone communities in the other Canadian provinces), which through legal precedent, set notably in the case *Mahe v. Alberta* (1990), has come to be interpreted to mean that minority language communities should have exclusive management control over their public school systems – a condition understood to be met through the establishment of school boards governed by elected commissioners. The plaintiffs suggested that by imposing limits on who the EMSB could hire as staff, Bill 21 violated Section 23. In April 2021, the Superior Court of Quebec ruled in favour of the EMSB, thus exempting English-language school boards from Bill 21 (Lowrie, 2021). Nevertheless, the Quebec government is appealing the decision, and, so far, the EMSB is bound by Bill 21 until the appeal is heard, which could take up to a year (Montreal Gazette, 2021).

With regard to this chapter and the constrained agency of individual educational leaders, it is notable that the action in contesting the Quebec government had to be taken by the elected school commissioners on behalf of the Board, notably requiring courageous parent commissioners, one of whom occasionally wears the hijab, to sign on as the main plaintiffs. It was not taken by the Board employees, despite their positions of power in the organization.

## NOTES

1  I capitalize Black in this article, because Black has been claimed by Black people as a political identity.
2  Note that schooling in Canada is mostly provincially regulated.
3  In an ironic turn of events, Quebec now encourages its residents to wear a face covering as a measure against the COVID-19 pandemic. It is telling that there has been no discussion of the need to verify identity or of any ostensible threat to security to accompany this measure (Issa, 2020).
4  Notably, the Cour d'appel du Québec had, in turn, overturned the decision of a lower court declaring the school board's decision null and void.
5  Not surprisingly, the Muslim hijab and niqab and the Jewish kippah were examples of symbols that would be considered conspicuous, while the Christian cross was not.

## REFERENCES

Al-Saji, A. (2010). The racialization of Muslim veils: A philosophical analysis. *Philosophy and Social Criticism, 36*(8), 875–902. doi: 10.1177/0191453710375589

Assemblée nationale du Québec. (2013). *Projet de loi no. 60: Charte affirmant les valeurs de laïcité et de neutralité religieuse de l'État ainsi que d'égalité entre les femmes et les hommes et encadrant les demandes d'accommodement.* http://m.assnat.qc.ca/en/travaux-parlementaires/projets-loi/projet-loi-60-40-1.html

Assemblée nationale du Québec. (2017). *Projet de loi no. 62: Loi favorisant le respect de la neutralité religieuse de l'État et visant notamment à encadrer les demandes d'accommodements religieux dans certains organismes.* http://m.assnat.qc.ca/fr/travaux-parlementaires/projets-loi/projet-loi-62-41-1.html

Assemblée nationale du Québec. (2019). *Projet de loi no 21: Loi sur la laïcité de l'État.* http://m.assnat.qc.ca/fr/travaux-parlementaires/projets-loi/projet-loi-21-42-1.html

Authier, P. (2019, August 22). Fearing trusteeship, CSDM now plans to apply Bill 21. *Montreal Gazette.* https://montrealgazette.com/news/quebec/fearing-trusteeship-csdm-now-plans-to-apply-bill-21

Bakan, A. (2008). Reconsidering the Underground Railroad: Slavery and racialization in the making of the Canadian state. *Socialist Studies/Études Socialistes, 4*(1), 3–29. doi: 10.18740/s4c59d

Bhattacharjee, K. (2003). *The Ontario Safe Schools Act: School discipline and discrimination.* Toronto, ON: Ontario Human Rights Commission.

Bickmore, K. (2014). Citizenship education in Canada: "Democratic" engagement with differences, conflicts and equity issues? *Citizenship Teaching & Learning, 9*(3), 257–78. doi: 10.1386/ctl.9.3.257_1

Bouchard, G., & Taylor, C. (2008). *Building the future: A time for reconciliation.* Quebec City, QC: Commission de consultation sur les pratiques d'accomodement reliées aux différences culturelles.

Calliste, A. (1994). Race, gender and Canadian immigration policy: Blacks from the Caribbean, 1900–1932. *Journal of Canadian Studies, 28*(4), 131–48. doi: 10.3138 /jcs.28.4.131

Coloma, R.S. (2013). Empire: An analytical category for educational research. *Educational Theory, 63*(6), 639–58. doi: 10.1111/edth.12046

Conroy, R. (2019, April 3). LBPSB will not enforce or adhere to Bill 21. *The Suburban.* https://www.thesuburban.com/news/west_island_news/lbpsb-will-not-enforce -or-adhere-to-bill-21/article_512409db-561a-5266-a4ec-0f396e9199ca.html

Cooper, A. (2006). *The hanging of Angelique: The untold story of Canadian slavery and the burning of Old Montreal.* Toronto, ON: Harper-Collins.

Dei, G.J.S. (2008). *Racists beware: Uncovering racial politics in contemporary society.* Rotterdam, Netherlands: Sense Publishers.

Feith, J. (2021, October 5). Systemic racism is "exactly what happened" to Joyce Echaquan, coroner says. *Montreal Gazette.* https://montrealgazette.com/news /local-news/coroner-in-joyce-echaquans-death-to-hold-news-conference-tuesday

Fontaine, T. (2016, April 22). What did Justin Trudeau say about Canada's history of colonialism? *CBC News.* https://www.cbc.ca/news/indigenous/trudeau -colonialism-comments-1.3549405

Galabuzi, G-E. (2006). *Canada's economic apartheid: The social exclusion of racialized groups in the new century.* Toronto, ON: Canadian Scholars' Press.

Goldberg, D.T. (2015). *Are we all postracial yet?* Malden, MA: Polity Press.

Hampton, R. (2016). *Racialized social relations in higher education: Black student and faculty experiences of a Canadian university* (Doctoral dissertation, McGill University, Montreal, QC). https://escholarship.mcgill.ca/concern/theses /q237hv236

Haney-Lopez, I.F. (1995). The social construction of race. In R. Delgado (Ed.), *Critical race theory: The cutting edge* (pp. 191–203). Philadelphia, PA: Temple University Press.

Haque, E. (2012). *Multiculturalism in a bilingual framework: Language, race and belonging in Canada.* Toronto, ON: University of Toronto Press.

Howard, P.S.S. (2018). On the back of Blackness: Contemporary Canadian blackface and the consumptive production of post-racialist, white Canadian subjects. *Social Identities, 24*(1), 87–103. doi: 10.1080/13504630.2017.1281113

Howard, P.S.S. (2019). Forging fortuity, asserting humanity: The emotional labour and resistance of Black racial equity leaders in predominantly white institutions. In T. Kitossa, E. Lawson, & P.S.S. Howard (Eds.), *African Canadian leadership: Continuity, transition and transformation* (pp. 213–40). Toronto, ON: University of Toronto Press.

Issa, I. (2020, May 20). Did coronavirus kill Bill 21? [Blog post]. https://www. idilosophy.com/post/did-coronavirus-kill-bill-21

James, C.E., Turner, T., George, R., & Tecle, S. (2017). *Towards race equity in education: The schooling of Black students in the greater Toronto area.* The Jean

Augustine Chair in Education, Community & Diaspora. https://edu.yorku.ca
/files/2017/04/Towards-Race-Equity-in-Education-April-2017.pdf

Joshee, R. (2009). Multicultural education policy in Canada: Competing ideologies,
interconnected discourses. In J.A. Banks (Ed.), *The Routledge international
companion to multicultural education* (pp. 116–28). New York, NY: Routledge.

Kelley, R.D.G. (2016, March 7). Black study, Black struggle. *Boston Review.* http://
bostonreview.net/forum/robin-d-g-kelley-black-study-black-struggle

Kelley, R.D.G. (2018). Black study, Black struggle. *Ufahamu: A Journal of African
Studies, 40*(2), 153–68. doi: 10.5070/F7402040947

Kestler-D'Amours, J. (2018, June 29). Quebec court extends suspension of law
banning face veils. *Al Jazeera News.* https://www.aljazeera.com/news/2018/06
/quebec-court-extends-suspension-law-banning-face-veils-18062905411
7401.html

Kundnani, A. (2017). Islamophobia as ideology of US empire. In N. Massoumi, T.
Mills, & D. Miller (Eds.), *What is Islamophobia? Racism, social movements and the
state* (pp. 35–48). London, UK: Pluto Press.

Laframboise, K. (2019, March 27). EMSB vows not to comply with Quebec's proposed
religious symbols ban. *Global News.* https://globalnews.ca/news/5103551/emsb
-religious-symbols-ban-quebec/

Lajoie, G. (2019, November 26). Les stagiaires ne sont pas visés par la loi 21, rappelle
Roberge. *Journal de Montréal.* https://www.tvanouvelles.ca/2019/11/26/signes
-religieux-interdits-pour-les-stagiaires-les-etudiants-menacent-de-se-mobiliser-1

Langevin, L. (2007). Trafficking in women in Canada: A critical analysis of
the legal framework governing immigrant live-in caregivers. *International
Journal of Comparative and Applied Criminal Justice, 31*(2), 191–209.
doi: 10.1080/01924036.2007.9678768

Lapierre, M. (2020, June 2). Legault supports protesters, denies there's systemic
racism in Quebec. *Montreal Gazette.* https://montrealgazette.com/news
/premier-legault-stands-in-solidarity-with-anti-racism-protesters

Lawson, E. (2013). The gendered working lives of seven Jamaican women in
Canada: A story about "here" and "there" in a transnational economy. *Feminist
Formations, 25*(1), 138–56. doi: 10.1353/ff.2013.0002

Leclair, A. (2019, September 9). Aspiring teachers denied employment as Montreal
school boards apply religious symbols ban. *Global News.* https://globalnews.ca
/news/5878801/quebec-religious-symbols-ban-teachers-turned-away/

Li, P.S. (1982). Chinese immigrants on the Canadian prairie, 1910–47.
*Canadian Review of Sociology/Revue Canadienne de Sociologie, 19*(4), 527–40.
doi: 10.1111/j.1755-618X.1982.tb00879.x

Lowrie, M. (2021, April 20). Quebec court upholds most of province's secularism law,
exempts English school boards. *Global News.* https://globalnews.ca/news/7772987
/quebec-secularism-law-bill-21/

*Mahe v. Alberta,* 1 S.C.R. 342 (1990).

Mahrouse, G. (2010). "Reasonable accommodation" in Québec: The limits of participation and dialogue. *Race and Class, 52*(1), 85–96. doi: 10.1177/0306396 810371768

Maratta, A.S. (2019, September 1). Montreal school boards to implement Bill 21, Quebec's religious neutrality law. *Global News.* https://globalnews.ca/news /5834010/montreal-school-board-bill-21/

Massoumi, N., Mills, T., & Miller, D. (2017). Islamophobia, social movements and the state: For a movement-centred approach. In N. Massoumi, T. Mills, & D. Miller (Eds.), *What is Islamophobia? Racism, social movements and the state* (pp. 3–32). London, UK: Pluto Press.

Ministère de l'Éducation et Ministère de l'Enseignement supérieur. (1998). *A School for the future: Policy statement on educational integration and intercultural education.* Gouvernement du Québec. http://www.education.gouv.qc.ca /fileadmin/site_web/documents/dpse/adaptation_serv_compl/Politique MatiereIntegrationScolEducInterculturelle_UneEcoleAvenir_a.pdf

Ministère de l'Éducation et Ministère de l'Enseignement supérieur. (2019). *Violence in intercultural relationships: Let's work on it together!* Gouvernement du Québec. http://www.education.gouv.qc.ca/fileadmin/site_web/documents/dpse /adaptation_serv_compl/Feuillet-violence-relations-interculturelles-EN.pdf

Montpetit, J. (2019, May 16). Religious symbols ban pits Quebec feminists against each other. *CBC News.* https://www.cbc.ca/news/canada/montreal/bill-21 -quebec-feminists-on-opposite-sides-of-religious-symbols-ban-1.5139422

Montreal Gazette. (2021, October 19). EMSB seeks exemption from Bill 21 pending appeal decision. *Montreal Gazette.* https://montrealgazette.com/news/local-news /emsb-seeks-exemption-from-bill-21-pending-appeal-decision

*Multani v. Commission scolaire Marguerite-Bourgeoys,* 1 S.C.R. 256, (2006).

Nugent, A. (2006). Demography, national myths, and political origins: Perceiving official multiculturalism in Quebec. *Canadian Ethnic Studies, 38*(3), 21–36.

Omi, M., & Winant, H. (1993). On the theoretical status of the concept of race. In C. McCarthy & W. Crichlow (Eds.), *Race, identity, and representation in education* (pp. 3–10). New York, NY: Routledge.

Poole, C. (2012). "Not of the nation": Canadian history textbooks and the impossibility of an African-Canadian identity. *Southern Journal of Canadian Studies, 5*(1–2), 81–102.

Razack, S. (1998). *Looking White people in the eye: Gender, race, and culture in courtrooms and classrooms.* Toronto, ON: University of Toronto Press.

Razack, S. (2002). When place becomes race. In S. Razack (Ed.), *Race, space, and the law: Unmapping a White settler society* (pp. 1–20). Toronto, ON: Between the Lines.

Ruck, M.D., & Wortley, S. (2002). Racial and ethnic minority high school students' perceptions of school disciplinary practices: A look at some Canadian findings. *Journal of Youth and Adolescence, 31*(3), 185–95. doi: 10.1023/A:1015081102189

Said, E.W. (1978). *Orientalism*. London, UK: Routledge.

Segeren, A., & Kutsyuruba, B. (2012). Twenty years and counting: An examination of the development of equity and inclusive education policy in Ontario (1990–2010). *Canadian Journal of Educational Administration and Policy, 136*, 1–38.

Shingler, B. (2018, January 9). Quebec opposition parties against marking mosque shooting with day against Islamophobia. *CBC News*. https://www.cbc.ca/news/canada/montreal/quebec-mosque-shooting-islamophobia-1.4478861

Shingler, B. (2019, August 29). Quebec school boards fall in line over religious symbols law despite opposition. *CBC News*. https://www.cbc.ca/news/canada/montreal/quebec-bill-21-school-boards-1.5264235

Simpson, J.S., James, C.E., & Mack, J. (2011). Multiculturalism, colonialism, and racialization: Conceptual starting points. *Review of Education, Pedagogy, and Cultural Studies, 33*(4), 285–305. doi: 10.1080/10714413.2011.597637

Takeuchi, C. (2020, June 5). Stockwell Day and Ontario Premier Doug Ford face backlash for denying systemic racism in Canada. *Georgia Straight*. https://www.straight.com/news/stockwell-day-and-ontario-premier-doug-ford-face-backlash-for-denying-systemic-racism-in-canada

Thobani, S. (2007). *Exalted subjects: Studies in the making of race and nation in Canada*. Toronto, ON: University of Toronto Press.

Tuck, E., & Yang, K.W. (2018). Introduction: Born under the rising sign of social justice. In E. Tuck & K.W. Yang (Eds.), *Toward what justice? Describing diverse dreams of justice in education* (pp. 1–17). New York, NY: Routledge.

Valiante, G. (2018, June 28). Quebec's face-covering law suspended for second time, with judge citing rights concerns. *National Post*. https://nationalpost.com/news/politics/quebec-judge-once-again-suspends-application-of-provinces-face-covering-law

Vancouver Sun. (2009, September 28). Really Harper, Canada has no history of colonialism? *Vancouver Sun*. https://vancouversun.com/news/community-blogs/really-harper-canada-has-no-history-of-colonialism

Wade, P. (2010). The presence and absence of race. *Patterns of Prejudice, 44*(1), 43–60. doi: 10.1080/00313220903507628

Walcott, R. (2014). The Book of Others (Book IV): Canadian multiculturalism, the state, and its political legacies. *Canadian Ethnic Studies, 46*(2), 127–32. doi: 10.1353/ces.2014.0018

Walcott, R., & Abdillahi, I. (2019). *BlackLife: Post-BLM and the struggle for freedom*. Winnipeg, MB: ARP Books.

Wishart, D. (2009). Dynamics of education policy and practice for urban Aboriginal early school leavers. *Alberta Journal of Educational Research, 55*(4), 468–81. doi: 10.11575/ajer.v55i4.55340

# Conclusion: The Future of Leading for Systemic Educational Transformation in Canada

ANDRÉANNE GÉLINAS-PROULX AND CAROLYN M. SHIELDS

Systemic transformation is needed because discrimination is rampant in many spheres of society, including education. The chapters in this volume have clearly demonstrated the pervasive nature of systemic discrimination in Canada and have prompted thinking about its impact and ways to overcome it. As Larochelle-Audet et al. (2020) assert, discrimination occurs when a person or a group of persons is treated differently or excluded based on one or more motives like race, skin colour, gender identity or gender expression, pregnancy, sexual orientation, marital status, age, religion, political beliefs, language, ethnic or national origin, social condition, disability, and so on. Discrimination may stem from formal policies or from informal practices and traditions. It may be intentional and deliberate, or it may manifest in unpremeditated or implicit fashion. Regardless of the origin, the result is that individuals and groups are treated unequally and deprived of legitimate rights and freedoms. Systemic discrimination "confers privileges on some groups and has damaging effects on others" (translation by authors, Larochelle-Audet et al., 2020, p. 19).

Given Canada's long history of discrimination, it is ironic that it was the death of George Floyd in the United States in May 2020 that triggered a new consciousness of the prejudice, discrimination, and systemic racism that is also a part of Canadian society. We were again presented with evidence of discrimination when Joyce Echaquan, an Atikamekw woman, died on 28 September 2020 in Quebec after recording hospital staff shouting racist insults at her (Shingler, 2020).

As we have demonstrated clearly in this volume, discrimination and inequity also permeate the education systems in Canada, making leadership for systemic transformation an urgent priority at this time. As frequently stated by the authors of the preceding chapters, a commitment to equity, inclusion, and social justice is necessarily difficult, complex, and demanding for educational leaders. Thus, we recognize that following this path of transformative leadership is a journey – one that requires considerable stamina, commitment, and moral courage. Moreover, for some of the authors of chapters in this book, and likely for many readers, the personal journey has been complicated by marginalization, exclusion, and emotional pain.

The production of this book has also been a journey, starting with the creation in 2018 of the Equity Committee of the Canadian Association for the Study of Educational Administration/Association canadienne pour l'étude de l'administration scolaire (CASEA/ACEAS). Members of this committee were invited to participate in a symposium at the 2019 annual conference of the Canadian Association for the Study of Education/Société canadienne pour l'étude de l'éducation (CSSE/SCÉÉ) in Vancouver. This symposium led to the project of this book, which has allowed seventeen authors of diverse backgrounds, ethnicities, gender identities, and religious beliefs to share their lived experiences of Canadian education as well as their research on the topic of leading for equity and social justice. Senior and junior scholars as well as doctoral students from universities across Canada have been included in this project. Although the voices are unique, the authors all share a common epistemological posture, which is imbedded in critical theory frameworks. In total, twelve chapters have been organized into three distinct sections.

In part I, Transformative Leadership in Practice, Shields; Gélinas-Proulx and Villella; and Roache and Marshall all presented transformative leadership in their respective chapters as an alternative to many of the more technical current leadership theories, recognizing its subversive and oppositional qualities as well as its comprehensive foregrounding of mindsets and beliefs, policies, and practices. Gélinas-Proulx and Villella also explained the minoritized context of French schools in Canada and the discrimination members of these schools often face.

In part II, Equitable and Socially Just Approaches to Leadership, three conceptual chapters by Kowalchuk; Campbell and Watson; and Kirk and Osiname emphasized various aspects of equitable leadership, including the need to critically reflect on our own practice, to include cultural relevance and responsiveness, to eliminate deficit thinking, and occasionally to work subversively. In this same section, Shah and Tuters's chapter on social justice in higher education ensured that we think comprehensively about these concepts from pre-kindergarten all the way through to higher education.

In the final section, Decentring Discrimination, Atleo, using a relevant Indigenous methodology that included the traditional narrative of Umeek, presented the systemic discrimination experienced by First Nations students and their communities; Zook pointed out the exclusion of young gay and transsexual students due, in part, to negative stereotypes; Ebied described the challenges of refugee students and urged compassionate and respectful strategies for inclusion; Hamm showed how immigrant students can be exposed to inequity and suggested the need for more widely distributed leadership opportunities; and, finally, Howard showed, by using the example of Quebec's Bill 21, that teachers also experience discrimination and racism, in this instance if they wish to display religious signs or symbols.

As we reflect on the totality of the ideas presented in this book related to leadership for systemic transformation in Canadian education, we conclude that the twelve chapters deepened our realization that there are still many forms of discrimination, marginalization, injustice, oppression, and exclusion of students, teachers, and other members of the school community in Canadian education systems in the 2020s. It is clear that the problem is not unique to any one province or territory, nor to any one level of the education system. Belief systems, policies, and even laws are problematic throughout the country and at all education levels. That is why, alongside other leading scholars and activists, past and present, we are calling for systemic educational transformation in Canada. We acknowledge that our claims for the rights of minoritized groups are strong, and that some readers may feel uncomfortable as we denounce the privileges and power of majority groups that trigger inequity, discrimination, injustice, and exclusion, sensing, perhaps, a tension between their own positions and the rights of others, particularly those from minoritized groups. This is normal. Yet, if readers are experiencing discomfort, we will have accomplished our purpose. Acknowledging the biases and prejudices that we all hold and reflecting on how and where we might begin to change ourselves and our institutions is an important first step. It is the beginning of a vision of a more socially just education system.

Thus, there is hope for more equity, inclusion, excellence, decolonization, and social justice in education. We would echo here the words and position of Freire (2014):

> I do not understand human existence, and the struggle needed to improve it, apart from hope and dream. Hope is an ontological need ... I am hopeful, not out of mere stubbornness, but out of an existential, concrete imperative. I do not mean that because I am hopeful, I attribute to this hope of mine the power to transform reality all by itself, so that I set out for the fray without taking account of concrete, material data, declaring, "My hope is enough!" No, my hope is necessary, but is not enough. Alone, it does not win. But without it, my struggle will be weak and wobbly. We need critical hope the way a fish needs unpolluted water. (p. 2)

In this book, the hope comes from the authors who have demonstrated how leaders in education, as change agents (Riehl, 2000), can address the challenges they face related to equity and social justice. But hope will also come from the determination of our readers to join us as we strive for equitable change. It will be realized as we implement critical strategies like transformative leadership theory, social justice leadership, or inclusive leadership for diverse educational contexts – approaches to leadership that offer ways of prioritizing the creation of equitable learning environments and working conditions for everyone. As Lewis (2016) found, "evolving leadership roles produced the conditions for the emergence of these equity-oriented leadership styles" (p. 337). It is clear that educational leaders also need to practise culturally relevant and responsive pedagogy as well as critical self-reflection. Leading with critical hope also requires considerable moral courage, subversion, political savvy, and resilience. The authors who have contributed to this volume offer starting points that give us hope that we can do better. But also important are their contributions of conscientization, critique, and promise, because even when we observe progress regarding equity, social justice, and respect for the rights of people from diverse backgrounds, as we saw in the introduction to this book, we are well aware that there is still much to do in this regard.

Furthermore, as we analyse the content of this book, we also recognize that many other topics could have (and perhaps should have) been included in it. These include the topics of homelessness, dis/ability, and religious discrimination, among others. For example, we acknowledge that the need for social justice is very broad and that many environmental concerns, for instance, raise the need for social justice and social responsibility. As Ackley (2009) has suggested, social justice does not only apply to human beings (i.e., to social situations):

> [E]nvironmental concerns must not be forgotten and need to be included in the discussion involving social justice and social responsibility. It should be noted that while few researchers relate environmental issues to social justice theory, as stated, it appears that this theory is directly related to the rights and freedoms of individuals. (pp. 32–3)

Other kinds of justice, including distributive justice, cultural justice, and associational justice (Lewis, 2016), must also be considered as relevant to education. Hence, the social justice–oriented educational leader in Canada should also deploy energy for the protection of the environment and biodiversity. As Ackley (2009) pointed out in her dissertation about the leadership of school principals in "green schools," "we may face obstacles in our day to day lives, but the problems we face as a global community will ultimately motivate us to realize our individual and collective power as change agents capable of responding to the environmental challenges we face" (p. 143).

New crises – for instance, the threat of the H1N1 virus of 2009, the Ebola crisis of 2014–16, or the COVID-19 pandemic of 2020–2 – become new spaces for inequitable situations to appear. Similarly, global crises like drought and famine, political upheaval, and civil war cause displacement of thousands of people. Such crises may give rise to new levels of child abuse and family violence (Slaughter, 2020); they may also shed light on the disparate outcomes of existing inequities, such as a lack of access to resources, more dangerous or precarious employment situations, less desirable housing, or more pre-existing health conditions among those who live in poverty. Thus, we worry about those who can no longer access regular meals, health care (for physical and/or mental health concerns), or even educational services (Breakfast Club of Canada, n.d.; UNICEF Canada, 2020). We are concerned about children with learning difficulties and those with handicaps who are left behind during crises (Phoenix, 2020). We worry about policing strategies that perpetuate violence rather than offer safety and security. And we worry for the health of any society that permits such injustices to continue. What will be the next crisis that will compromise equity, inclusion, social justice, and excellence in education in Canada?

As new challenges compound the vast, historic challenges we already face, we worry that the situation will seem so overwhelming that leaders in education will fail to act. To counter such disempowering emotions, hope and dreams are important to power transformation, as Freire (2014) suggested. But action must follow. Thus, it is our hope and dream that the ideas presented in this book will be catalysts for the leadership necessary to address both present and future challenges related to equity, excellence, inclusion, decolonization, and social justice.

Awareness of the depth and breadth of injustice should lead educational leaders to reflect deeply on their responsibility to transform schools for the benefit of all members of their community and beyond. Why and how are injustices created and perpetuated? How are we complicit? What is our responsibility? Creating equitable, inclusive, excellent, and socially just learning environments is only a starting point. Educational leaders who want to truly transform their schools will also strive to ensure that the policies and practices, pedagogies, and curricula are not only just but also teach students about how to promote societal justice. Summarizing the findings of Elin Kelsey from her study of the feelings of children about the environment, Kretz (2013) reports that "educators and conservation psychologists are finding that despair leads to terror management, where problems are downplayed and hyper-materialism serves as an ineffective panacea. What is needed … is a groundswell of positive stories that inspire ecological hope" (p. 938). Altogether, if we are to find solutions to ongoing global problems and hope for both ecological as well as societal inequities, educational leaders will need to be change agents.

The chapters in this book implicitly raise the question of whether Canadian educational leaders are equipped and prepared to take on this responsibility. Hence, we also challenge all educational leadership training programs in Canada to fully incorporate the concepts of equity, inclusion, social justice, decolonization, and excellence in order to prepare participants to lead for those values and principles. Evidence that this is not the current situation makes our plea even more urgent. For example, in Quebec between 2014 and 2016, only 53.3 per cent of the fifteen university programs in education administration had a minimum of one course in the program that looked at issues of diversity (Borri-Anadon, Potvin, Longpré, Pereira Braga, & Orange, 2018). This is not unique to Quebec. We also challenge anyone providing ongoing professional development to educators in Canada to take seriously the issues of inequity and injustice discussed here, to move beyond technical solutions, and to encourage critical reflection and dialogue that will lead to more hopeful and equitable action.

In 1977, sociologist Pierre Bourdieu asserted that "the primary contribution of social scientists to society is to illuminate the mechanisms of domination and to show how these mechanisms reproduce social inequities" (p. 29). Nearly forty years later, Ryan (2014) suggested that "issues of diversity and leadership are now considered a legitimate area of study" (Ryan, 2014, p. 360). Now is the time, however, to go beyond research, to go beyond illuminating mechanisms of domination and inequity and put what we know into practice. The knowledge, theories, and interventions described in this volume provide a starting point for action. It is our hope that this book will provide the impetus for educational leaders across Canada to become advocates, even activists, for equity and social justice, and that it will inspire them to take action for systemic transformation for more equitable education systems and a more socially just, inclusive, and excellent society.

## REFERENCES

Ackley, C.R. (2009). *Leadership in green schools: School principals as agents of social responsibility* (Unpublished doctoral dissertation). Pennsylvania State University, Pennsylvania, PA.

Borri-Anadon C., Potvin, M., Longpré, T., Pereira Braga, L., & Orange, V. (2018). *La formation du personnel scolaire sur la diversité ethnoculturelle, religieuse et linguistique dans les universités québécoises: Portrait quantitatif de l'offre de cours de deuxième cycle en éducation.* Observatoire sur la formation à la diversité et l'équité. http://ofde.ca/wp-content/uploads/2018/03/Portrait-2e-cycle-VF_v5.pdf

Bourdieu, P. (1977). *Outline of a theory of practice* (R. Nice, Trans.). Cambridge, UK: Cambridge University Press.

Breakfast Club of Canada. (n.d.). *Food insecurity: The impact of COVID-19 on Canadian children.* https://www.breakfastclubcanada.org/covid-emergency-club -funding/

Freire, P. (2014). *Pedagogy of hope: Reliving pedagogy of the oppressed.* New York, NY: Bloomsbury.

Kretz, L. (2013). Hope in environmental philosophy. *Journal of Agricultural and Environmental Ethics, 26,* 925–44. doi: 10.1007/s10806-012-9425-8

Larochelle-Audet, J., Magnan, M.-O., Doré, E., Potvin, M., St-Vincent, L.-A., Gélinas-Proulx, A., & Amboulé-Abath, A. (2020). *Diriger et agir pour l'équité, l'inclusion et la justice sociale: Boîte à outils pour les directions d'établissement d'enseignement.* Observatoire sur la formation à la diversité et l'équité. http://collections.banq.qc.ca/ark:/52327/bs4027379

Lewis, K. (2016). Social justice leadership and inclusion: A genealogy. *Journal of Educational Administration and History, 48*(4), 324–41. doi: 10.1080/002206 20.2016.1210589

Phoenix, M. (2020, May 15). Kids with disabilities face health risks and marginalization under COVID-19: Expert. *CBC News.* https://www.cbc.ca/news/canada/hamilton/children-disabilities-coronavirus-1.5571099

Riehl, C. J. (2000). The principal's role in creating inclusive schools for diverse students: A review of normative, empirical, and critical literature on the practice of educational administration. *Review of Educational Research, 70*(1), 55–81. doi: 10.3102/00346543070001055

Ryan, J. (2014). Promoting inclusive leadership in diverse schools. In I. Bogotch & C.M. Shields (Eds.), *International handbook of educational leadership and social (in)justice* (pp. 359–80). Dordrecht, Netherlands: Springer.

Shingler, B. (2020, October 6). In apology to Joyce Echaquan's family, Quebec premier says public service "failed in its duty." *CBC News.* https://www.cbc.ca/news/canada/montreal/joyce-echaquan-funeral-1.5752176

Slaughter, G. (2020, April 22). How teachers can help students being abused at home during COVID-19. *CTV News.* https://www.ctvnews.ca/health/coronavirus/how-teachers-can-help-students-being-abused-at-home-during-covid-19-1.4906421

UNICEF Canada. (2020, April 17). *The impact of COVID-19 on children in Canada: Short, medium and long-term mitigation strategies.* https://www.unicef.ca/en/press-release/impact-covid-19-children-canada-short-medium-and-long-term-mitigation-strategies

# Author Biographies

**Dr. Marlene R. Atleo**, PhD (UBC), PHEc (MB), is a senior scholar in the Faculty of Education at the University of Manitoba. ʔeh ʔeh naa tuu kʷiss (Ahousaht First Nation, *Nuu-chah-nulth*) identifies as an academic and as a fisher. She coordinated the MEd and PhD Adult and Post-Secondary Education programs at the University of Manitoba and taught inaugural offerings of Aboriginal Education and Cross-Cultural Education in the BEd program. Her first love is doing salmon for "home use." Her research illuminates Indigenous cultural practices through storywork, with a focus on intergenerational transformational change. Now retired in British Columbia, Marlene continues to research, write, and speak on learning, language, and identity development supporting Indigenous and underserved students in post-secondary settings. She can be contacted at marlene.atleo@umanitoba.ca.

**Dr. Andrew B. Campbell** (DR.ABC) is a graduate of the University of Toronto with a PhD in Educational Leadership, Policy, and Diversity. He is presently an adjunct assistant professor at Queens University in the Professional Master of Education (online) program, and at the University of Toronto in the Master of Teaching program in the Department of Curriculum Teaching and Learning. He is an Ontario Certified Teacher and has taught at all levels of the education system for the last twenty-three years in Jamaica, Bahamas, and Canada. His research and teaching focuses on issues of equity and inclusion, educational leadership, LGBTQ+ issues, and teacher performance evaluation. He can be reached at ab.campbell@utoronto.ca.

**Raghad Ebied** is a PhD candidate in the Critical Policy, Equity and Leadership Studies stream at Western University's Faculty of Education, an Ontario Certified Teacher, and an education and training professional supporting schools, government, and organizations in equity, diversity, and inclusion (EDI). She is currently the EDI Education Coordinator at Western University. Her graduate experience includes supporting research and policy development with the Ontario Ministry of Education in 2016 to update the Ontario Leadership Framework for school and district leaders to reflect more equity, inclusion, and well-being. She also has experience working with international scholars studying refugee students' integration in K–12 schools in Canada and Europe. Her current research interests include culturally responsive and compassion-based approaches to teaching in schools and educational institutions that promote equity, inclusion, and well-being, with a particular interest in supporting the positive adaptation of refugee/newcomer students. She can be contacted at rebied@uwo.ca.

**Dr. Andréanne Gélinas-Proulx** is a professor of Educational Administration in the Department of Education Sciences at l'Université du Québec en Outaouais. Her research focuses on the intercultural competence and training of school principals, as well as the leadership of the principals for inclusion, equity, and social justice. She is a member of different research groups like the Laboratoire international sur l'inclusion scolaire (International Laboratory on Inclusive Education) and the Réseau de recherche et de valorisation de la recherche sur le bien-être et la réussite en contexte de diversité (Network for Research on Well-Being and Success in a Context of Diversity). She is also a former elementary school teacher and school principal. She can be reached at andreanne.gelinas-proulx@uqo.ca.

**Dr. Lyle Hamm** is an associate professor of Educational Administration and Leadership in the Faculty of Education at the University of New Brunswick (UNB) in Fredericton. His teaching and research, broadly speaking, focuses on provincial and national immigration trends, demographically changing schools and communities, intercultural education and peace-building, and social justice and transformative leadership. Lyle served as a K–12 educator and administrator in Alberta for twenty-two years prior to joining UNB in 2013. Lyle can be reached at lhamm@unb.ca.

**Dr. Philip S.S. Howard** is an assistant professor in the Department of Integrated Studies in Education at McGill University, Montreal, Quebec. He works in the areas of Black Canadian studies and anti-colonial studies in education, and his interests are in the ways in which relations of race and anti-Blackness mediate the ways we come to know ourselves, create community, and exercise agency in a Canadian settler-colonial context. His work is grounded in his over twenty years of professional experience as a teacher at the secondary and elementary levels in both Quebec and Ontario, and as a consultant for equity, diversity, and race relations at an Ontario school board. He has published in such journals as *Ethnicities*, *Social Identities*, and *Race Ethnicity and Education* and is co-editor of the collections *African Canadian Leadership: Continuity,*

*Transition, and Transformation* and *Crash Politics and Antiracism: Interrogations of Liberal Race Discourse*. He may be contacted at philip.howard@mcgill.ca.

**Dr. Jacqueline Kirk** is a professional teacher, an enthusiastic learner, an associate professor, and the chair of the Department of Leadership and Educational Administration at Brandon University in Manitoba. Her study of educational administration is driven by an intense passion for understanding what brings people together to create positive change within organizations. Her background in the field of education includes experiences in both rural and urban schools, and in both public and private school systems. Her primary and secondary teaching experience includes a variety of positions ranging from kindergarten, to middle school language arts, to senior high school computer science. Before pursuing her PhD in Educational Administration, she worked as a high school principal and as an educational consultant assisting schools with capacity-building and technology integration. Jackie is passionate about helping students to explore their boundaries and to develop a greater understanding of their personal identities using the curriculum as a medium. She may be reached at kirkj@brandonu.ca.

**Dr. Donna Kowalchuk** is an education administrator with twenty years of experience in leading rural and urban elementary and secondary schools in Ontario towards improving student equity, achievement, and well-being. Her research interests include investigating how social and historical constructions of education policy and leadership intersect with critical theory and the practice of social justice. Dr. Kowalchuk continues as a special assignment principal in Canada's largest urban school board, and she is a faculty advisor in the School of Education and Professional Learning and an adjunct professor in the School of Graduate Studies at Trent University. Recently, Dr. Kowalchuk completed a post-doctoral research internship with the University of Toronto's Department of Social Justice Education. She may be contacted at donna.kowalchuk@mail.utoronto.ca.

**Dr. Jason Marshall** holds a PhD in Education with specialization in Educational Psychology. He is an experienced educator, trainer, and research consultant. He is an active researcher with special interests in psychosocial factors that affect teaching and learning; technology infusion in education; autonomy; and self-directed learning within modern-day classroom environments. His email is marshall.jaason@gmail.com.

**Ayodeji Osiname** is a PhD candidate in Education at the University of Manitoba. In 2013, Ayodeji moved from Nigeria, where he taught in the K–12 system, to pursue his post-graduate studies in Canada. His experiences with poverty and injustice within the school system in Nigeria motivated him to advocate for children. His desire for educational change has led him to study educational leadership, diversity and inclusion in education, and leadership for social justice. In Canada, his passion to serve others has led him to advocate for several marginalized groups including recent immigrants to Canada, senior citizens, and individuals with special needs. Ayodeji is dedicated to making a difference for people who have neither the power nor the position to overcome their current challenges. His commitment to this important work continues to inspire him to become a voice for the voiceless within his community. He may be reached at osinamea@myumanitoba.ca.

**Dr. Darcia Roache** worked for private and public sector organizations in Jamaica in the capacity of accountant, director of administration, and chief executive officer. Her previous work experience also included employment as a research assistant for various organization overseers. Her passion for administrative work led to her pursuing both master's and doctoral degrees in Business Administration. She now works as research supervisor, second examiner, and group facilitator for the University of the West Indies Open Campus. Before that, she also had several years of experience working as associate facilitator at the University of the Commonwealth Caribbean, the Management Institute for National Development, and the HEART Trust/NTA Training Institute in Jamaica. Dr. Roache is now pursuing a second PhD in Educational Administration at the University of Saskatchewan. She has published several articles, and her research interests focus on the success of educational leaders and teachers. She is a member of the Resident Magistrates Association in Jamaica and can be reached at dar446@mail.usask.ca.

**Dr. Vidya Shah** is an educator, scholar, and activist committed to equity and racial justice in the service of liberatory education. She is an assistant professor in the Faculty of Education at York University, and her research explores anti-racist and decolonizing approaches to leadership in schools, communities, and school districts. She also explores educational barriers to the success and well-being of Black, Indigenous, and racialized students. Dr. Shah teaches both undergraduate- and graduate-level courses in education, as well as courses in the Master of Leadership and Community Engagement program. She has worked in the Model Schools for Inner Cities program of the Toronto District School Board (TDSB) and was an elementary classroom teacher in the TDSB. Dr. Shah is committed to bridging the gaps between communities, classrooms, school districts, and the academy, and to re-imagining emancipatory possibilities for schooling. She can be reached at vidshah@edu.yorku.ca.

**Dr. Carolyn M. Shields** taught high school across Canada for nineteen years before completing her doctorate at the University of Saskatchewan, Canada.

Since then, at four different universities, she has taught classes and conducted research focused on the creation of inclusive, equitable, excellent, and socially just learning environments. For this work, which has included operationalizing the theory of transformative leadership, authoring twelve books and over 100 articles and chapters, and giving numerous international keynote addresses in Europe, Asia, Australia, New Zealand, and North America, Dr. Shields has received many honours and international recognition, including lifetime achievement awards from UCEA (University Council for Educational Administration) and CASEA (Canadian Association for the Study of Educational Administration), and an honorary doctorate from Université Laval, Quebec, in July 2017. Her email is cshields@wayne.edu.

**Dr. Stephanie Tuters** considers herself a researcher by trade and nature. Engaging in both quantitative and qualitative research in Canada and the US, Stephanie works to address inequities and help achieve greater social justice through the creation of more equitable and inclusive leadership, teaching, policies, and practices. Stephanie has worked for the Ontario Ministry of Education researching and writing education policies and has experience working as a knowledge mobilization manager. Currently, Stephanie is an assistant professor, teaching stream, at the Ontario Institute for Studies in Education at the University of Toronto. Her most recent research is critical and reflective, as she focuses on her identity as a white researcher and educator and questions her role in leading for social justice. Her email is stephanie.tuters@utoronto.ca.

**Mélissa Villella** is originally from the city of Welland, Ontario, and thus comes from a minoritized francophone community in Canada. She is an assistant professor of School Administration at Université du Québec en Abitibi-Témiscamingue. As a researcher, Mélissa is interested in leadership issues and their relationship to inclusive education, such as transformative leadership, students with special education needs, professional intercultural skills, and countering Black systemic anti-racisms. Previously, she was a teacher in Ontario and Quebec, a principal of French-language schools in Ontario, as well as the director of programs and services at one of the largest community centres in a francophone minority setting, and a flight attendant. She may be reached at melissa.villella@uqat.ca.

**Kaschka Watson** is a PhD candidate in the Department of Leadership, Higher and Adult Education in the Educational Leadership and Policy program at the Ontario Institute for Studies in Education at the University of Toronto. He has concurrently earned his MEd from York University in Language, Culture and Teaching, and a DipEd in Community, Culture and Policy. Before that, he earned his BA in Cross-Cultural Studies from the Divine Word College in Iowa.

His research interests include racial and ethnic relations, inclusive leadership and policy, diversity and leadership, social justice and equity, student engagement, and underrepresented faculty in higher education. He has two publications in the *Canadian Journal of Education* and one in *Communiqué Magazine*. His email is kaschka.watson@mail.utoronto.ca.

**Dr. Thomas Zook** received his PhD in Educational Leadership and Policy Studies from Wayne State University in December of 2017. His area of expertise includes transformative leadership theory, LGBTQ+ issues in education, bullying and harassment in primary and secondary education, diversity and equity concerns, and social justice research. He is currently the director of business operations for Hung Duy Nguyen Od, LLC, a multi-office practice serving Central and East Texas' vision care needs. In addition to his scholarly research, he conducts professional development and leadership consultation in and around the Central Texas area. He may be contacted at thomas.zook@wayne.edu.